A Student's Introduction to English Grammar

This groundbreaking undergraduate textbook on modern Standard English grammar is the first to be based on the revolutionary advances of the authors' previous work, *The Cambridge Grammar of the English Language* (2002), winner of the 2004 Leonard Bloomfield Book Award of the Linguistic Society of America. The analyses defended there are outlined here more briefly, in an engagingly accessible and informal style. Errors of the older tradition of English grammar are noted and corrected, and the excesses of prescriptive usage manuals are firmly rebutted in specially highlighted notes that explain what older authorities have called 'incorrect' and show why those authorities are mistaken.

This book is intended for students in colleges or universities who have little or no previous background in grammar, and presupposes no linguistics. It contains exercises and a wealth of other features, and will provide a basis for introductions to grammar and courses on the structure of English not only in linguistics departments but also in English language and literature departments and schools of education. Students will achieve an accurate understanding of grammar that will both enhance their language skills and provide a solid grounding for further linguistic study.

A Student's Introduction to English Grammar

RODNEY HUDDLESTON

University of Queensland

GEOFFREY K. PULLUM

University of California, Santa Cruz

CAMBRIDGE
UNIVERSITY PRESS

PUBLISHED BY THE PRESS SYNDICATE OF THE UNIVERSITY OF CAMBRIDGE
The Pitt Building, Trumpington Street, Cambridge, United Kingdom

CAMBRIDGE UNIVERSITY PRESS
The Edinburgh Building, Cambridge, CB2 2RU, UK
40 West 20th Street, New York, NY 10011–4211, USA
477 Williamstown Road, Port Melbourne, VIC 3207, Australia
Ruiz de Alarcón 13, 28014 Madrid, Spain
Dock House, The Waterfront, Cape Town 8001, South Africa

http://www.cambridge.org

First published 2005

First South Asian edition 2005

Printed in the India by Brijbasi Art Press Ltd.

Typeface Times 10.5/13 pt.   System Quark Express™   [TB]

A catalogue record for this book is available from the British Library

ISBN 0 521 68322X paperback

Contents

Notational conventions

Abbreviations of grammatical terms

Adj	Adjective	O^i	Indirect Object
AdjP	Adjective Phrase	P	Predicator
AdvP	Adverb Phrase	PC	Predicative Complement
C, Comp	Complement	PP	Preposition Phrase
DP	Determinative Phrase	Pred Comp	Predicative Complement
N	Noun	Prep	Preposition
Nom	Nominal	S, Subj	Subject
NP	Noun Phrase	V	Verb
O	Object	VP	Verb Phrase
O^d	Direct Object		

Presentation of examples

Italics are always used for citing examples (and for no other purpose).

Bold italics are used for lexemes (as explained on p. 15).

"Double quotation marks" enclose meanings.

Underlining (single or double) and square brackets serve to highlight part of an example.

The symbol '·' marks a morphological division within a word or a component part of a word, as in 'work·er·s' or 'the suffix ·s'.

The following symbols indicate the status of examples (in the interpretation under consideration):

*ungrammatical	*Know you the answer?
?of questionable acceptability	?The floor began to be swept by Max.
!non-standard	!I done it myself.
%grammatical in some dialects only	%Have you enough money?

Additional conventions

Boldface is used for technical terms when first introduced and sometimes for later occurrences too.

SMALL CAPITALS are used for emphasis and contrast.

Preface

This book is an introductory textbook on modern Standard English grammar, intended mainly for undergraduates, in English departments and schools of education as well as linguistics departments. (See www.cambridge.org/0521612888 for a link to the associated web site, where additional information can be found.) Though it takes note of developments in linguistics over the past few decades, and assumes a thorough knowledge of English, it does not presuppose any previous study of grammar or other aspects of linguistics.

We believe that every educated person in the English-speaking world should know something about the details of the grammar of English. There are a number of reasons.

- There are hardly any professions in which an ability to write and speak crisply and effectively without grammatical mistakes is not a requirement on some occasions.
- Although a knowledge of grammar will not on its own create writing skills, there is good reason to think that understanding the structure of sentences helps to increase sensitivity to some of the important factors that distinguish good writing from bad.
- Anyone who aims to improve their writing on the basis of another person's technical criticism needs to grasp enough of the technical terms of grammatical description to make sure the criticism can be understood and implemented.
- It is widely agreed that the foremost prerequisite for computer programming is the ability to express thoughts clearly and grammatically in one's native language.
- In many professions (the law being a particularly clear example) it is a vital part of the content of the work to be able to say with confidence what meanings a particular sentence or paragraph will or won't support under standard conceptions of English grammar.
- Discussions in a number of academic fields often depend on linguistic analysis of English: not only linguistics, but also philosophy, literature, and cognitive science.
- Industrial research and development areas like information retrieval, search engines, document summary, text databases, lexicography, speech analysis and synthesis, dialogue design, and word processing technology increasingly regard a good knowledge of basic linguistics, especially English grammar, as a prerequisite.

• Knowing the grammar of your native language is an enormous help for anyone embarking on the study of another language, even if it has rather different grammatical principles; the contrasts as well as the parallels aid understanding.

This book isn't the last word on the facts of Standard English, or about grammar more generally, but we believe it will make a very good foundation. It is based on a much bigger one, *The Cambridge Grammar of the English Language* (*CGEL*), written between 1990 and 2002 in collaboration with an international team of other linguists. That book often contains much fuller discussion of the analysis we give here, together with careful argumentation concerning the alternative analyses that have sometimes been advocated, and why they are less successful.

The process of writing this book, and *The Cambridge Grammar* before it, was continually surprising, intriguing, and intellectually exciting for us. Some think the study of English grammar is as dry as dust, probably because they think it is virtually completed, in the sense that nothing important in the field remains to be discovered. But it doesn't seem that way to us. When working in our offices and meeting for lunchtime discussions we usually found that we would have at least one entirely new discovery to talk about over sandwiches. At the level of small but fascinating details, there are thousands of new discoveries to be made about modern English. And even at the level of the broad framework of grammatical principles, we have frequently found that pronouncements unchallenged for 200 years are in fact flagrantly false.

We are pleased that we were again able to work with Kate Brett of Cambridge University Press, the same senior acquisitions editor who saw *CGEL* through to completion, and with Leigh Mueller, our invaluable copy-editor. We have constantly drawn on the expertise that was provided to *CGEL* by the other contributors: Peter Collins, David Lee, Peter Peterson, and Lesley Stirling in Australia; Ted Briscoe, David Denison, Frank Palmer, and John Payne in England; Betty Birner, Geoff Nunberg, and Gregory Ward in the United States; Laurie Bauer in New Zealand; and Anita Mittwoch in Israel. There are many topics covered in *CGEL* that we couldn't have tackled without their help, and this shorter presentation of some of those topics is indebted to them at various points.

The School of English, Media Studies and Art History at the University of Queensland generously continued to provide an academic and electronic home for Rodney Huddleston while he worked full-time on this project. Professor Junko Itô, Chair of the Department of Linguistics at the University of California, Santa Cruz, helped a lot by arranging Geoff Pullum's teaching schedule in ways that facilitated his participation in completing this book. And most importantly, we would like to thank our families, who have been extraordinarily tolerant and supportive despite the neglect of domestic concerns that is inevitable when finishing a book. Vivienne Huddleston and Barbara Scholz, in particular, have seen less of us than (we hope) they would have liked, and taken on more work than was their proper share in all sorts of ways, and we are grateful.

1 Introduction

1   Standard English

English is probably the most widely used language in the world, with around 400 million native speakers and a similar number of bilingual speakers in several dozen partially English-speaking countries, and hundreds of millions more users in other countries where English is widely known and used in business, government, or media. It is used for government communications in India; a daily newspaper in Cairo; and the speeches in the parliament of Papua New Guinea. You may hear it when a hotel receptionist greets an Iranian guest in Helsinki; when a German professor talks to a Japanese graduate student in Amsterdam; or when a Korean scientist lectures to Hungarian and Nigerian colleagues at a conference in Bangkok.

A language so widely distributed naturally has many varieties. These are known as **dialects**.[1] That word doesn't apply just to rural or uneducated forms of speech; the way we use it here, everyone speaks a dialect. And naturally, this book doesn't try to describe all the different dialects of English there are. It concentrates on one central dialect that is particularly important: the one that we call **Standard English**.

We can't give a brief definition of Standard English; in a sense, the point of this whole book is precisely to provide that definition. But we can make a few remarks about its special status.

The many varieties of English spoken around the world differ mainly in **pronunciation** (or 'accent'), and to a lesser extent in **vocabulary**, and those aspects of language (which are mentioned but not covered in detail in this book) do tend to give indications of the speaker's geographical and social links. But things are very different with **grammar**, which deals with the form of sentences and smaller units: clauses, phrases and words. The grammar of Standard English is much more stable and uniform than

---

[1] We use **boldface** for technical terms when they are first introduced. Sometimes later occurrences are also boldfaced to remind you that the expression is a technical term or to highlight it in a context where the discussion contributes to an understanding of the category or function concerned.

its pronunciation or word stock: there is remarkably little dispute about what is **grammatical** (in compliance with the rules of grammar) and what isn't.

Of course, the small number of controversial points that there are – trouble spots like *who* versus *whom* – get all the public discussion in language columns and letters to the editor, so it may seem as if there is much turmoil; but the passions evinced over such problematic points should not obscure the fact that for the vast majority of questions about what's allowed in Standard English, the answers are clear.[2]

Moreover, in its written form, Standard English is regarded worldwide as an uncontroversial choice for something like an editorial on a serious subject in any English-language newspaper, whether in Britain, the USA, Australia, Africa, or India. It is true that a very few minor points of difference can be found between the American English (AmE) and British English (BrE) forms of Standard English; for example, BrE speakers will often use *She may have done* where an AmE speaker would say *She may have*; but for the most part using Standard English doesn't even identify which side of the Atlantic the user comes from, let alone indicate membership in some regional, ethnic, or social group.

Alongside Standard English there are many robust local, regional, and social dialects of English that are clearly and uncontroversially **non-standard**. They are in many cases familiar to Standard English speakers from plays and films and songs and daily conversations in a diverse community. In [1] we contrast two non-standard expressions with Standard English equivalents, using an exclamation mark ($^!$) to indicate that a sentence belongs to a non-standard dialect, not the standard one.

[1]		STANDARD		NON-STANDARD
	i a.	*I did it myself.*	b.	$^!$*I done it myself.*
	ii a.	*I haven't told anybody anything.*	b.	$^!$*I ain't told nobody nothing.*

We should note at this point that elsewhere we use a per cent sign to mark a Standard English form used by some speakers but not all (thus we write $^{\%}$*It mayn't happen* because some Standard English speakers use *mayn't* and some don't). And when our focus is entirely on Standard English, as it is throughout most of the book, we use an asterisk to mark sequences that are not grammatical (e.g., **Ran the away dog*), ignoring the issue of whether that sequence of words might occur in some non-standard dialects. In [1], though, we're specifically talking about the sentences of a non-standard dialect.

- *Done* in [ib] is a widespread non-standard 'past tense' form of the verb ***do***, corresponding to Standard English *did* – in the standard dialect *done* is what is called a 'past participle', used after ***have*** (*I have done it*) or ***be*** (*It was done yesterday*).[3]

2 For example, try writing down the four words *the*, *dog*, *ran*, *away* in all twenty-four possible orders. You will find that just three orders turn out to be grammatical, and there can be no serious disagreement among speakers as to which they are.

3 Throughout this book we use bold italics to represent items from the dictionary independently of the various forms they have when used in sentences: *did* is one of the forms of the item listed in dictionaries as ***do*** (the others are *does*, *done*, and *doing*); and *was* is one of the forms of the item listed as ***be***.

- In [ii] there are two differences between the standard and non-standard versions. First, *ain't* is a well-known non-standard form (here meaning "haven't"); and second, [iib] exhibits multiple marking of negation: the clause is marked three times as negative (in *ain't*, *nobody*, and *nothing*), whereas in [iia] it is marked just once (in *haven't*).

Features of this sort would not be used in something like a TV news bulletin or a newspaper editorial because they are generally agreed to be non-standard. That doesn't mean dialects exhibiting such features are deficient, or illogical, or intrinsically inferior to the standard dialect. Indeed, as we point out in our discussion of negation in Ch. 8, many standard languages (they include French, Italian, Polish, and Russian) show multiple marking of negation similar to that in [1ii]. It's a special grammatical fact about Standard English that it happens to lack multiple negation marking of this kind.

Formal and informal style

The distinction between standard and non-standard dialects of English is quite different from the distinction between **formal** and **informal style**, which we illustrate in [2]:

[2]   FORMAL   INFORMAL
     i a. *He was the one with whom she worked.*   b. *He was the one she worked with.*
     ii a. *She must be taller than I.*   b. *She must be taller than me.*

In these pairs, BOTH versions belong to the standard dialect, so there is no call for the exclamation mark notation. Standard English allows for plenty of variation in style depending on the context in which the language is being used. The [a] versions would generally be used only in quite formal contexts. In casual conversation they would very probably be regarded as pedantic or pompous. In most contexts, therefore, it is the [b] version, the informal one, that would be preferred. The informal Standard English sentences in [b] occur side by side with the formal variants; they aren't non-standard, and they aren't inferior to the formal counterparts in [a].

Informal style is by no means restricted to speech. Informal style is now quite common in newspapers and magazines. They generally use a mixture of styles: a little more informal for some topics, a little more formal for others. And informal style is also becoming more common in printed books on academic subjects. We've chosen to write this book in a fairly informal style. If we hadn't, we wouldn't be using *we've* or *hadn't*, we'd be using *we have* and *had not*.

Perhaps the key difference between style and dialect is that switching between styles within your native dialect is a normal ability that everyone has, while switching between dialects is a special ability that only some people have. Every speaker of a language with style levels knows how to use their native language more formally (and maybe sound more pompous) or talk informally (and sound more friendly and casual). But to snap into a different dialect is not something that everyone can do. If you weren't raised speaking two dialects, you have to be something of an actor to do it, or else something of a linguist. Either way you have to actually become acquainted with the rules of the other dialect. Some people are much better than others at this. It isn't something that is expected of everyone. Many (probably most) Standard English speakers will be entirely unable to do a convincing London working-class, or African American vernacular, or Scottish highlands dialect. Yet all of them know how to recognise the difference in style between the [a] sentences and the [b] sentences in [2], and they know when to use which.

2   Descriptive and prescriptive approaches to grammar

There is an important distinction to be drawn between two kinds of books on English grammar: a book may have either a **descriptive** or a **prescriptive** goal.

Descriptive books try to describe the grammatical system that underlies the way people actually speak and write the language. That's what our book aims to do: we want to describe what Standard English is like.

Prescriptive books aim to tell people how they should speak and write – to give advice on how to use the language. They typically take the form of **usage manuals**, though school textbook treatments of grammar also tend to be prescriptive.

In principle you could imagine descriptive and prescriptive approaches not being in conflict at all: the descriptive grammar books would explain what the language is like, and the prescriptive ones would tell you how to avoid mistakes when using it. Not making mistakes would mean using the language in a way that agreed with the descriptive account. The two kinds of book could agree on the facts. And indeed there are some very good usage books based on thorough descriptive research into how Standard English is spoken and written. But there is also a long tradition of prescriptive works that are deeply flawed: they simply don't represent things correctly or coherently, and some of their advice is bad advice.

Perhaps the most important failing of the bad usage books is that they frequently do not make the distinction we just made between STANDARD VS NON-STANDARD DIALECTS on the one hand and FORMAL VS INFORMAL STYLE on the other. They apply the term 'incorrect' not only to non-standard usage like the [b] forms in [1] but also to informal constructions like the [b] forms in [2]. But it isn't sensible to call a construction grammatically incorrect when people whose status as fully competent speakers of the standard language is unassailable use it nearly all the time. Yet that's what (in effect) many prescriptive manuals do.

Often they acknowledge that what we are calling informal constructions are widely used, but they choose to describe them as incorrect all the same. Here's a fairly typical passage, dealing with another construction where the issue is the choice between *I* and *me* (and corresponding forms of other pronouns):

[3]   Such common expressions as *it's me* and *was it them?* are incorrect, because
           the verb *to be* cannot take the accusative: the correct expressions are *it's I* and
           was it they? But general usage has led to their acceptance, and even to gentle
           ridicule of the correct version.[4]

By 'take the accusative' the author means occur followed by accusative pronoun forms like *me*, *them*, *us*, etc., as opposed to the nominative forms *I*, *they*, *we*, etc. (see Ch. 5, §8.2). The book we quote in [3] is saying that there is a rule of English grammar requiring a nominative form where a pronoun is 'complement' of the verb ***be*** (see Ch. 4, §4.1). But there isn't any such rule. A rule saying that would fail to allow for a construction we all use most of the time: just about everyone says *It's me*. There will be no ridicule of *It is I* in this book; but we will point out the simple fact that it represents an unusually formal style of speech.

What we're saying is that when there is a conflict between a proposed rule of grammar and the stable usage of millions of experienced speakers who say what they mean and mean what they say, it's got to be the proposed rule that's wrong, not the usage. Certainly, people do make mistakes – more in speech than in writing, and more when they're tired, stressed, or drunk. But if I'm outside on your doorstep and I call out *It's me*, that isn't an accidental slip on my part. It's the normal Standard English way to confirm my identity to someone who knows me but can't see me. Calling it a mistake would be quite unwarranted.

Grammar rules must ultimately be based on facts about how people speak and write. If they don't have that basis, they have no basis at all. The rules are supposed to reflect the language the way it is, and the people who know it and use it are the final authority on that. And where the people who speak the language distinguish between formal and informal ways of saying the same thing, the rules must describe that variation too.

This book is descriptive in its approach, and insofar as space permits we cover informal as well as formal style. But we also include a number of boxes headed 'Prescriptive grammar note', containing warnings about parts of the language where prescriptive manuals often get things wrong, using the label 'incorrect' (or 'not strictly correct') for usage that is perfectly grammatical, though perhaps informal in style.

3   Grammatical terms and definitions

Describing complex systems of any kind (car engines, legal codes, symphonies, languages) calls for theoretical concepts and technical terms ('gasket', 'tort', 'crescendo', 'adverb'). We introduce a fair amount of grammatical terminology in this book. To start with, we will often need to employ the standard terms for

---

[4] From B. A. Phythian, *A Concise Dictionary of Correct English* (London: Hodder & Stoughton, 1979).

three different areas within the study of language. Two of them have to do with the grammatical **form** of sentences:

- **syntax** is the study of the principles governing how words can be assembled into sentences (*I found an unopened bottle of wine* is admissible but **I found a bottle unopened of wine* is not); and
- **morphology** deals with the internal form of words (*unopened* has the parts *un·*, *open*, and *·ed*, and those parts cannot be combined in any other order).[5]

But in addition to their form, expressions in natural languages also have **meaning**, and that is the province of the third area of study: **semantics**. This deals with the principles by which sentences are associated with their literal meanings. So the fact that *unopened* is the opposite of *opened*, and the fact that we correctly use the phrase *an unopened bottle of wine* only for a bottle that contains wine and has not been opened, are semantic facts about that expression.

We will need a lot of more specific terms too. You may already know terms like **noun**, **verb**, **pronoun**, **subject**, **object**, **tense**, and so on; but we do not ASSUME any understanding of these terms, and will devote just as much attention to explaining them as to other terms that you are less likely to have encountered before. One reason for this is that the definitions of grammatical terms given in dictionaries and textbooks are often highly unsatisfactory. This is worth illustrating in detail, so let's look at the definitions for two specific examples: the term **past tense** and the term **imperative**.

Past tense

The term 'past tense' refers to a grammatical category associated with verbs: *likes* is a present tense form and *liked* is a past tense form. The usual definition found in grammar books and dictionaries says simply that the past tense expresses or indicates a time that is in the past. But things are nothing like as straightforward as that. The relation between the GRAMMATICAL category of past tense and the SEMANTIC property of making reference to past time is much more subtle. Let's look at the following examples (the verbs we need to compare are underlined):

[4] DEFINITION WORKS   DEFINITION FAILS
   i a. *The course <u>started</u> last week.*   b. *I thought the course <u>started</u> next week.*
  ii a. *If he <u>said</u> that, he was wrong.*   b. *If he <u>said</u> that, she wouldn't believe him.*
 iii a. *I <u>offended</u> the Smiths.*   b. *I regret <u>offending</u> the Smiths.*

The usual definition works for the [a] examples, but it completely fails for the [b] ones.

- In [i] the past tense *started* in the [a] case does locate the starting in past time, but in [b] the same past tense form indicates a (possible) starting time in the future. So not every past tense involves a past time reference.

---

[5] The decimal point of *un·* and *·ed* is used to mark an element smaller than a full word.

- In [ii] we again have a contrast between past time in [a] and future time in [b]. In [a] it's a matter of whether or not he said something in the past. In [b] it's a matter of his possibly saying it in the future: we're supposing or imagining that he says it at some future time; again, past tense, but no past time.
- In [iii] we see a different kind of contrast between the [a] and [b] examples. The event of my offending the Smiths is located in past time in both cases, but whereas in [a] *offended* is a past tense form, in [b] *offending* is not. This shows that not every past time reference involves a past tense.

So if we used the usual definition to decide whether or not the underlined verbs were past tense forms we would get the wrong answers for the [b] examples: we would conclude that *started* in [ib] and *said* in [iib] are NOT past tense forms and that *offending* in [iiib] IS a past tense form. Those are not correct conclusions.

It is important to note that we aren't dredging up strange or anomalous examples here. The examples in the [b] column are perfectly ordinary. You don't have to search for hours to find counterexamples to the traditional definition: they come up all the time. They are so common that you might well wonder how it is that the definition of a past tense as one expressing past time has been passed down from one generation to the next for over a hundred years and repeated in countless books.

Part of the explanation for this strange state of affairs is that 'past tense', like most of the grammatical terms we'll use in this book, is not unique to the grammar of English but is applicable to a good number of languages. It follows that there are two aspects to the definition or explanation of such terms:

- At one level we need to identify what is common to the forms that qualify as past tense in different languages. We call this the **general** level.
- At a second level we need to show, for any particular language, how we decide whether a given form belongs to the past tense category. This is the **language-particular** level (and for our purposes here, the particular language we are concerned with is English).

What we've shown in [4] is that the traditional definition fails badly at the language-particular level: we'll be constantly getting wrong results if we try to use it as a way of identifying past tense forms in English. But it is on the right lines as far as the general level is concerned.

What we need to do is to introduce a qualification to allow for the fact that there is no one-to-one correlation between grammatical form and meaning. At the general level we will define a past tense as one whose PRIMARY or CHARACTERISTIC use is to indicate past time. The examples in the right-hand column of [4] belong to quite normal and everyday constructions, but it is nevertheless possible to say that the ones in the left-hand column represent the primary or characteristic use of this form. That's why it is legitimate to call it a past tense.

But by putting in a qualification like 'primary' or 'characteristic' we're acknowledging that we can't determine whether some arbitrary verb in English is a past tense form simply by asking whether it indicates past time. At the language-particular level we need to investigate the range of constructions, such as [4ib/iib], where the forms used are the same as those indicating past time in the [a] construction – and the conditions under which a different form, such as *offending* in [iiib], can be associated with past time.

◼ Imperative

The typical definition of 'imperative' is that it is a form or construction used to issue a command. To begin with, notice that 'command' is in fact far too narrow a term for the meaning usually associated with imperatives: we use lots of imperatives in talking to friends and family and co-workers, but not (mostly) as commands. The broader term **directive** is more suitable; it covers commands (*Get out!*), offers (*Have a pear*), requests (*Please pass me the salt*), invitations (*Come to dinner*), advice (*Get your doctor to look at it*), instructions (*To see the picture click here*), and so on.

Even with this change from 'command' to 'directive', though, the definition runs into the same kind of problems as the usual definitions of past tense. It works for some examples and fails for others:

[5]   DEFINITION WORKS   DEFINITION FAILS
   i a. *Go to bed.*   b. *Sleep well.*
  ii a. *Please pass me the salt.*   b. *Could you pass me the salt?*

- In [i] both examples are imperatives, but while [a] is a directive, [b] is not. When I say [ib] I'm not directing you to sleep well, I'm just wishing you a peaceful night.
- In [ii] we have the opposite kind of failure. Both examples are directives, but while [a] is imperative, [b] is not. In terms of grammatical structure, [b] is an **interrogative** (as seen in questions like *Are you hungry?*, or *Have you seen Sue?*, or *Could you find any tea?*). But it is not being used to ask a question: if I say [iib], I'm not asking for an answer, I'm asking for the salt. So directives can be issued in other ways than by use of an imperative.

Again the textbook definition is along the right lines for a general definition but, as before, we need to add an essential qualification. An imperative can be defined at the general level as a construction whose PRIMARY or CHARACTERISTIC use is to issue directives.

At the language-particular level, to tie down the imperatives in English, we need to say how the grammatical structure of imperatives differs from that of related constructions. Compare, for example:

[6]   DECLARATIVE   IMPERATIVE
   i a. *You are very tactful.*   b. *Be very tactful.*
  ii a. *They help me prepare lunch.*   b. *Help me prepare lunch.*

The examples on the left are **declaratives**. The characteristic use of a declarative is to make statements. The two most important grammatical differences between imperatives and declaratives are illustrated in [i]:

- The imperative [ib] has a different form of the verb, *be* as opposed to *are* in [ia]. (With other verbs the forms are not overtly distinct, as evident in [ii], but the fact that there is an overt difference in [i] is a clear distinguishing feature.)
- While *you* is overtly present in [ia], it is merely implicit or 'understood' in [ib]. *You* is called the **subject**. It's a major difference between the constructions that subjects are normally obligatory in declaratives but are usually omitted in imperatives.

There's a good deal more to be said about the structure of imperatives (see Ch. 9), but here we just want to make the point that the definition found in textbooks and dictionaries is of very limited value in helping to understand what an imperative is in English. A definition or explanation for English must specify the grammatical properties that enable us to determine whether or not some expression is imperative. And the same applies to all the other grammatical terms we will be making use of in this book.

In dismissing the two meaning-based definitions we just discussed, we don't mean to imply that meaning will be ignored in what follows. We'll be very much concerned with the relation between grammatical form and meaning. But we can only describe that relation if the categories of grammatical form are clearly defined in the first place, and defined separately from the kinds of meaning that they may or may not sometimes express.

Exercises

1. Footnote 1 pointed out that only three orderings of the words *the, dog, ran, away* are grammatical. Which are the three grammatical orders of those words? Discuss any possible grounds for doubt or disagreement that you see.

2. Consider features of the following sentences that mark them as belonging to non-standard dialects of English. Rewrite them in Standard English, keeping the meaning as close as possible to the original.
   i *It ain't what you do, it's the way how you do it.*
   ii *She don't pay the rent regular.*
   iii *Anyone wants this stuff can have it.*
   iv *This criteria is totally useless.*
   v *Me and her brother were late.*

3. Consider what features of the following sentences mark them as belonging to formal style in Standard English. Rewrite them in informal or neutral style, keeping the meaning as close as possible to the original.

   i *To whom am I speaking?*
   ii *It would be a pity if he were to give up now.*
   iii *We hid the documents, lest they be confiscated.*
   iv *That which but twenty years ago was a mystery now seems entirely straightforward.*
   v *One should always try to do one's best.*

4. For each of the following statements, say whether it is a **morphological**, **syntactic**, or **semantic** fact about English.
   i Wherever *I saw a host of yellow daffodils* is true, *I saw some yellow flowers* is also true.
   ii The string of words **He it saw* can be made grammatical by placing the word *it* after the word *saw*.
   iii Nobody could truly say they believe that he saw it if they didn't also believe that it was seen by him.
   iv The verb *hospitalise* is formed from *hospital* by adding *·ise*.

    v A witness who truthfully asserted *I saw a host of yellow daffodils* would have to answer *No* if asked *Was everything blue?*

   vi **Fall** doesn't take the ·*ed* suffix: *fell* occurs, not *falled.

  vii You can't insert *every* in the sentence *A man's got to do what a man's got to do* and get a grammatical result.

 viii When someone says *I was going to walk but I decided not to*, the sense is the same as if they had said *I was going to walk but I decided not to walk*.

   ix *Of* can be the last word of a Standard English sentence.

    x A completed grammatical sentence of Standard English that begins '*I believe that we* . . .' must continue in a way that includes at least one verb.

5. Explain briefly in your own words, in the way you would explain it to someone who had not seen this book, what the difference is between a **descriptive** grammar book and a **prescriptive** one. Choose one or two grammars (of any language) from those accessible to you, and use them as examples, saying whether you think they are descriptive or prescriptive.

6. A significant number of newspapers in English are published in mainly non-English-speaking countries, and many of them have web editions – examples include *The Times of India* (India; timesofindia.indiatimes.com); *Cairo Times* (Egypt; www.cairotimes.com); *Straits Times* (Singapore; straitstimes.asia1.com.sg); *New Straits Times* (Malaysia; www.nst.com.my); *Jamaica Gleaner* (www. jamaica-gleaner.com); etc. Collect some articles from several of these, sticking to subjects that minimise give-away local references, and see if native speakers of English can identify the country of origin purely from the grammar or other aspects of the language.

2 A rapid overview

The primary topic of this book is the way words combine to form sentences in Standard English. Sentences are made up from words in regular ways, and it is possible to describe the regularities involved by giving general statements or rules that hold for all the sentences in the language. To explain the rules for English we will need a number of technical terms. The purpose of this chapter is to introduce most of those (or at least the most important ones). We do it by taking a high-speed reconnaissance flight over the whole terrain covered in the book.

What we mean by calling a word a technical term is simply that you can't guess how to use it on the basis of the way you may have used it so far; it needs an explanation, because its use in the description of a language has a special definition. We may give that explanation just before we first use the term, or immediately following it, or you may need to set the term aside for a few paragraphs until we can get to a full explanation of it. This happens fairly often, because the vocabulary of grammar can't all be explained at once, and the meanings of grammatical terms are very tightly connected to each other; sometimes neither member of a pair of terms can be properly understood unless you also understand the other, which makes it impossible to define every term before it first appears, no matter what order is chosen.

The account we give in this chapter is filled out and made more exact in the chapters that follow. This chapter provides a short overview of the grammar that will enable you to see where the detailed discussions of particular categories and constructions fit into the overall organisation. We'll rely heavily on qualifications like 'usually', 'normally', 'in the most basic cases', and so on, because we're giving an outline, and there are details, refinements, and exceptions to be explained later in the relevant chapter.

Here and there in this chapter we take the opportunity to draw attention to some of the contrasts between our analysis and that of a long tradition of English grammatical description going back to the late sixteenth century. By the eighteenth century this traditional line of work on grammar was quite well developed and began to harden into a body of dogma that then changed very little in the nineteenth and twentieth centuries. Yet many aspects of this widely accepted system are clearly mistaken. We do not want to simply present once again what so many earlier books have uncritically repeated. There are many revisions to the description of English that we think greatly enhance the coherence and accuracy of the description, many of them stemming from research in linguistics since the middle of the twentieth century, and we will offer brief comparative comments on some of them.

1   Two kinds of sentence

The syntactically most straightforward sentences have the form of a single **clause** or else of a sequence of two or more **coordinated** clauses, joined by a **coordinator** (e.g., *and*, *or*, *but*). We illustrate in [1]:

[1]   i   CLAUSAL SENTENCES (having the form of a clause)[1]
         a. *Kim is an actor.*
         b. *Pat is a teacher.*
         c. *Sam is an architect.*
       ii   COMPOUND SENTENCES (having the form of a coordination of clauses)
         a. *Kim is an actor, but Pat is a teacher.*
         b. *Kim is an actor, Pat is a teacher, and Sam is an architect.*

The distinction between the two kinds of sentence is drawn in terms of clauses (one versus more than one), which means we're taking the idea of a clause to be descriptively more basic than the idea of a sentence. Example sentences cited in the rest of this chapter and in the following eleven chapters will almost invariably have the form of a clause; we return to sentences having the form of a coordination of clauses when we discuss coordination more generally, in Ch. 14.

2   Clause, word and phrase

The most basic kind of clause consists of a **subject** followed by a **predicate**. In the simplest case, the subject (Subj) is a **noun** and the predicate (Pred) is a **verb**:

[2]

Subj	Pred	Subj	Pred	Subj	Pred
Things	*change.*	*Kim*	*left.*	*People*	*complained.*

---

[1] In traditional grammar the examples in [i] are called 'simple sentences', but we don't use this term; it covers only a subset of what we call clausal sentences.

More often, the subject and/or the predicate consist of more than one word while still having a noun and verb as their most important component:

[3]

Subj	Pred
All things	*change.*

Subj	Pred
Kim	*left early.*

Subj	Pred
Some people	*complained about it.*

Expressions such as *all things* and *some people* are called **noun phrases** – phrases with a noun as their **head**. The head of a phrase is, roughly, the most important element in the phrase, the one that defines what sort of phrase it is. The other elements are **dependents**.

Similarly, *left early* and *complained about it* are **verb phrases**, phrases with a verb as head. Again, *early* and *about it* are dependents of the verb.

Traditional grammars and dictionaries define a **phrase** as containing more than one word. But it's actually more convenient to drop this requirement, and generalise the category 'noun phrase' so that it covers *things*, *Kim* and *people* in [2], as well as *all things* and *some people* in [3]. There are lots of places besides the subject position where all these expressions can occur: compare *We need* <u>clients</u> and *We need* <u>some clients</u> or *This is good for* <u>clients</u> and *This is good for* <u>some clients</u>, and so on. It would be tedious to have to talk about 'nouns or noun phrases' in all such cases. So we prefer to say that a noun phrase (henceforth NP) normally consists of a noun with or without various dependents. (In other words, the head is accompanied by ZERO OR MORE dependents.)

It's much the same with other categories of phrase, e.g., verb phrases. *Complained* in [2], just like *complained about it* in [3], can be regarded as a verb phrase (VP). And the same general point will hold for the rest of the categories we introduce below: although they CAN contain more, they sometimes contain just a head and nothing else.

3   Subject and predicate

Basic clauses can be analysed as a construction consisting of subject plus predicate, as in [2] and [3]. The predicate typically describes a property of the person or thing referred to by the subject, or describes a situation in which this person or thing plays some role. In elementary clauses describing an action, the subject normally indicates the actor, the person or thing performing the action, while the predicate describes the action, as in *Kim left* and *People complained* in [2]. But this is rather vague: meaning doesn't give much guidance in distinguishing the subject from the predicate.

Syntactically, however, the subject is quite sharply distinguished from other elements by (among others) the following properties:

- It usually has the form of an NP.
- Its **default** position is before the verb.

- In interrogative clauses it typically occupies a distinctive position just after the verb.

The last two of these points are illustrated by contrasts of the following kind:

[4]   BASIC   INTERROGATIVE
  i a. _The clock has stopped._   b. _Has the clock stopped?_
  ii a. _Kim is downstairs._   b. _Is Kim downstairs?_
  iii a. _Some customers complained._   b. _Did some customers complain?_

Here the [a] version represents the basic form while the [b] version is **interrogative** (a type of clause characteristically used to ask questions). The constructions differ with respect to the position of the subject: it precedes the verb in [a], but follows it in [b]. In [iii] the interrogative differs also in that it contains the verb **do**, which is absent from [a]. This **do** is often added to form interrogatives, but the general point is nonetheless clear: the subject precedes the verb in the basic version and follows it in the interrogative. One useful test for finding the subject of a clause, therefore, is to turn the clause into an interrogative and see which expression ends up after the (first or only) verb.

4   Two theoretical distinctions

Before we continue with our survey we pause to introduce two theoretical distinctions frequently needed in the rest of the book. One (§4.1) is the distinction between functions and categories, which is implicit in the elementary description of the clause that has already been given. The second (§4.2) is a clarification of two senses of the term 'word'.

4.1   Functions and categories

In our example _Some people complained about it_ we have said that _some people_ is subject and that it is an NP. These are two quite different kinds of concept. Subject is a **function**, while NP is a **category**. Function is a relational concept: when we say that _some people_ is subject we are describing the relation between it and _complained_, or between it and the whole clause. It is THE SUBJECT OF THE CLAUSE, not simply a subject. A category, by contrast, is a class of expressions which are grammatically alike. An NP is (setting aside a narrow range of exceptions) simply a phrase with a noun as head (it's not the NP of anything, it's just an NP). The class of NPs thus includes an indefinitely large set of expressions like the following (where underlining marks the head noun): _some people, all things, Kim, people_ (as used in _People complained_), _the people next door, the way home_, and so on.

The reason we need to distinguish so carefully between functions and categories is that the correspondence between them is often subtle and complex. Even though there are clear tendencies (like that the subject of a clause is very often an NP), a single function may be filled by expressions belonging to different categories, and expressions belonging to a single category may occur in different functions. We can see this in the following examples:

[5]   ONE FUNCTION, DIFFERENT   ONE CATEGORY, DIFFERENT
        CATEGORIES   FUNCTIONS
   i a. *His guilt was obvious*.   b. *Some customers complained*.
  ii a. *That he was guilty was obvious*.   b. *Kim insulted some customers*.

- In the left-hand column the underlined expressions both function as subject: they stand in the same relation to the predicate *was obvious*. But while *his guilt* is an NP (having the noun *guilt* as head), *that he was guilty* isn't – it's a clause, with its own subject (*he*) and its own predicate (*was guilty*).
- In the right-hand column *some customers* is in both cases an NP, but it has different functions. It is subject in [ib], but in [iib] it has the function of 'object', which we explain in §6 below.

4.2   Words and lexemes

The term 'word' is commonly used in two slightly different senses. The difference can be seen if we ask how many DIFFERENT words there are in a sentence such as:

[6]   *They had two cats and a dog; one cat kept attacking the dog*.

Focus on the four we've underlined. The second and fourth are obviously instances of the same word, but what about the first and third? Are these instances of the same word, or of different words? The answer depends on which sense of 'word' is intended.

- In one sense they are clearly different: the first contains an *s* at the end.
- But there is a second sense in which they're merely different FORMS OF THE SAME WORD.

In this book we restrict **word** to the first sense and introduce a new term, **lexeme**, for the second sense. The 'lex' component of 'lexeme' is taken from 'lexicon', which has more or less the same meaning as 'dictionary' – and 'lexicography' has to do with writing dictionaries. *Cat* and *cats* are different words, but forms of the same lexeme. The idea is that they are the same as far as the dictionary is concerned: the difference is purely grammatical. They are covered under a single dictionary entry, and in most dictionaries there is no explicit mention of *cats*.

The difference between the various forms of a lexeme is a matter of **inflection**. *Cat* and *cats*, then, are different **inflectional forms** of the same lexeme – the **singular** and **plural** forms respectively. In order to distinguish the lexeme as a whole from its various forms we represent it in boldface: *cat* and *cats* are inflectional forms of the lexeme **cat**. Similarly, *take, takes, took, taking, taken* are inflectional forms of the verb lexeme **take**. And *big, bigger, biggest* are inflectional forms of the adjective lexeme **big**.

Not all lexemes show inflectional variation of this kind. For those that don't, the distinction between word and lexeme is unimportant, and we will represent them in ordinary italics, as with *the*, *and*, *very* and so on.

5   Word and lexeme categories: the parts of speech

The traditional term 'parts of speech' applies to what we call categories of words and lexemes. Leaving aside the minor category of **interjections** (covering words like *oh*, *hello*, *wow*, *ouch*, etc., about which there really isn't anything interesting for a grammar to say), we recognise eight such categories:

[7]
i	NOUN	*The dog barked.*	*That is Sue.*	*We saw you.*
ii	VERB	*The dog barked.*	*It is impossible.*	*I have a headache.*
iii	ADJECTIVE	*He's very old.*	*It looks empty.*	*I've got a new car.*
iv	DETERMINATIVE	*The dog barked.*	*I need some nails.*	*All things change.*
v	ADVERB	*She spoke clearly.*	*He's very old.*	*I almost died.*
vi	PREPOSITION	*It's in the car.*	*I gave it to Sam.*	*Here's a list of them.*
vii	COORDINATOR	*I got up and left.*	*Ed or Jo took it.*	*It's cheap but strong.*
viii	SUBORDINATOR	*It's odd that they were late.*	*I wonder whether it's still available.*	*They don't know if you're serious.*

This scheme has much in common with the traditional one, but there are also some important differences that we will point out in the brief survey below.

The two largest and most important categories are the noun and the verb, the two that we have already introduced. The most basic kind of clause contains at least one noun and one verb and, as as we have seen in [2] above, may contain just a noun and verb.

The first six categories in list [7] can function as the head of corresponding phrases (noun phrase, verb phrase, adjective phrase, etc.). The other two can't. The very small **coordinator** and **subordinator** classes do not function as head but serve as markers of **coordination** and **subordination** (we'll explain those terms below). An NP with a coordinator added to it (such as *or Jo*) is still a kind of NP; and when you add a subordinator to a clause (as with *that they were late*), you get a kind of clause. There are no such things as 'coordinator phrases' or 'subordinator phrases'.

5.1   Nouns

In any language, the **nouns** make up by far the largest category in terms of number of dictionary entries, and in texts we find more nouns than words of any other category (about 37 per cent of the words in almost any text).

(a) Meaning

Noun is the category containing words denoting all kinds of physical objects, such as persons, animals and inanimate objects: *cat*, *tiger*, *man*, *woman*, *flower*, *diamond*, *car, computer,* etc. There are also innumerable abstract nouns such as *absence, man-liness, fact, idea, sensitivity, computation,* etc.

(b) Inflection

The majority of nouns, though certainly not all, have an **inflectional form** contrast between **singular** and **plural** forms: *cat ~ cats, tiger ~ tigers, man ~ men, woman ~ women,* etc.

(c) Function

Nouns generally function as head of NPs, and NPs in turn have a range of functions, including that of **subject**, as in [2] and [3].

(d) Differences from traditional grammar

Our noun category covers **common nouns** (illustrated in (a) above), **proper nouns** (*Kim, Sue, Washington, Europe,* etc.) and **pronouns** (*I, you, he, she, who,* etc.). In traditional grammar the pronoun is treated as a distinct part of speech rather than a subclass of noun. This, however, ignores the very considerable syntactic similarity between pronouns and common or proper nouns. Most importantly, pronouns are like common and proper nouns in their function: they occur as heads of NPs. They therefore occur in essentially the same range of positions in sentences as common and proper nouns – and this is why traditional grammars are constantly having to make reference to 'nouns or pronouns'.

5.2   Verbs

(a) Meaning

We use the term **situation** for whatever is expressed in a clause, and the **verb** is the chief determinant of what kind of situation it is: an action (*I opened the door*), some other event (*The building collapsed*), a state (*They know the rules*), and so on.

(b) Inflection

The most distinctive grammatical property of verbs is their **inflection**. In particular, they have an inflectional contrast of **tense** between **past** and **present**. A past tense that is marked by inflection is called a **preterite**.

In the present tense there are two forms, depending on properties of the subject (primarily whether it is singular or plural):

[8]

PRETERITE	PRESENT	
She worked in Paris.	*She works in Paris.*	*They work in Paris.*
He knew the answer.	*He knows the answer.*	*They know the answer.*

The singular subject *she* and *he* occur here with the present tense forms *works* and *knows* while plural *they* occurs with *work* and *know*. Verbs have other inflectional forms too, such as the one marked by the ending ·*ing* seen in *They are <u>working</u> in Paris*.

(c) Function

Verbs characteristically occur as **head** of VPs that themselves function as **predicate** in a **clause**. As head of the VP, the verb largely determines what other elements are permitted in the VP. Thus English allows *She <u>left</u> the airport* but not **She <u>arrived</u> the airport*; it allows *He <u>seemed</u> mature* but not **He <u>knew</u> mature*; and so on.[2]

(d) Subclasses

There is a very important distinction between a small class of **auxiliary verbs** and the rest, called **lexical verbs**. The auxiliary verbs have a number of special properties. One is that they can sometimes precede the subject. This occurs in interrogatives:

[9]   AUXILIARY VERB   LEXICAL VERB
    a. *<u>Can</u> you speak French?*   b. **<u>Speak</u> you French?*

Although [b] is ungrammatical, there is a way of forming an interrogative corresponding to the clause *You speak French*: the auxiliary verb **do** is added, so the interrogative clause has an extra word: *Do you speak French?*

  Auxiliaries are usually followed (perhaps not immediately) by another verb, as *can* and *do* in the foregoing examples are followed by *speak*. Notice also *It <u>will</u> <u>rain</u>*; *They <u>are</u> <u>working</u> in Paris*; *She <u>has</u> <u>gone</u> home*. The words *will*, *are*, and *has* are all auxiliary verbs.

5.3   Adjectives

(a) Meaning

Adjectives characteristically express properties of people or of concrete or abstract things. Thus when they combine with the verb **be** the clause generally describes a state: *The soup is <u>hot</u>, Max was <u>jealous</u>*, etc.

(b) Function

Most adjectives can occur in either of two major functions, **attributive** and **predicative**:

[10]   ATTRIBUTIVE   PREDICATIVE
    i a. *some <u>hot</u> soup*   b. *The soup is <u>hot</u>.*
    ii a. *a <u>jealous</u> husband*   b. *He became <u>jealous</u>.*

In the attributive use the adjective functions as **modifier** to a following noun in NP structure. In the predicative use it generally occurs after the verb **be** or one of a small subclass of similar verbs such as ***become*, *feel*, *seem***, etc.

[2] Throughout this book we use an asterisk (*) to mark the beginning of a string of words that is NOT a sentence of Standard English. That's the only thing asterisks will be used for.

(c) Gradability and inflection

The most central adjectives are **gradable** – that is, they denote properties that can be possessed in varying degrees, properties like those expressed by *big, good, hot, jealous, old*, etc. The degree can be indicated by a modifier, as in *fairly big, surprisingly good, very hot, extremely jealous, three years old* – and can be questioned by *how*: *How big is it?*, etc.

One special case of marking degree is by **comparison**, and with short adjectives this can be expressed by **inflection** of the adjective:

[11]   PLAIN   COMPARATIVE   SUPERLATIVE
        Kim is old.   *Kim is older than Pat*.   *Kim is the oldest of them all*.

This inflectional system is called **grade**: *old* is the **plain** form, *older* the **comparative** form, and *oldest* the **superlative** form.

Gradability, however, is less distinctive for adjectives than the functional property (b) above, as it is not only adjectives that can be gradable.

5.4   Determinatives

(a) Definiteness

There is a class of words called **determinatives**. The two most common members are the words *the* and *a*. These function as **determiner** in NP structure. They mark the NP as **definite** (in the case of *the*) and **indefinite** (in the case of *a*). I use a definite NP when I assume you will be able to identify the referent. I say *Where's the dog?*, for example, only if I'm assuming you know which dog I'm referring to. There's no such assumption made with an indefinite NP, as in *I could hear a dog barking*.

(b) Determinative vs determiner

Notice that **determinative** is the name of a category (a class of words), while **determiner** is the name of a function. There are other determinatives besides *the* and *a*: examples include *this, that, some, any, many, few, one, two, three*, etc. They can likewise function as determiner, but that isn't their only function. In *It wasn't that bad*, for example, the determinative *that* is modifier of the adjective *bad*.

(c) Differences from traditional grammar

Traditional grammars generally don't use the term 'determinative'. The words in that class are treated as a subclass of the adjectives. But in fact words such as *the* and *a* are very different in grammar and meaning from adjectives like those illustrated in §5.3 above, so we put them in a distinct primary category.

5.5   Adverbs

(a) Relation to adjectives

The most obvious **adverbs** are those derived from adjectives by adding *·ly*:

[12]	i ADJECTIVE	*careful*	*certain*	*fortunate*	*obvious*	*rapid*	*usual*
	ii ADVERB	*carefully*	*certainly*	*fortunately*	*obviously*	*rapidly*	*usually*

Words like those in [ii] constitute the majority of the adverb class, though there are also a fair number of adverbs that do not have this form, some of them quite common: they include *almost, always, not, often, quite, rather, soon, too,* and *very.*

(b) Function

It is mainly function that distinguishes adverbs from adjectives. The two main functions of adjectives exemplified in [10] are attributive and predicative, but adverbs do not occur in similar structures: compare *a jealously husband and *He became jealously.* Instead adverbs mostly function as **modifiers** of verbs (or VPs), adjectives, or other adverbs. In the following examples the modifying adverb is marked by single underlining and the element it modifies by double underlining:

[13]	i MODIFYING A VERB OR VP	*She spoke clearly.*	*I often see them.*
	ii MODIFYING AN ADJECTIVE	*a remarkably good idea*	*It's very expensive.*
	iii MODIFYING AN ADVERB	*She spoke quite clearly.*	*It'll end quite soon.*

5.6   Prepositions

(a) Meaning

The most central members of the **preposition** category have primary meanings expressing various relations of space or time:

[14]	*across the road*	*after lunch*	*at the corner*	*before Easter*
	in the box	*off the platform*	*on the roof*	*under the bridge*

(b) Function

Prepositions occur as head of **preposition phrases** (PPs), and these in turn function as dependents of a range of elements, especially verbs (or VPs), nouns and adjectives. In the following examples we use single underlining for the preposition, brackets for the PP, and double underlining for the element on which the PP is dependent:

[15]	i DEPENDENT ON A VERB OR VP	*I sat [by the door].*	*I saw her [after lunch].*
	ii DEPENDENT ON A NOUN	*the man [in the moon]*	*the day [before that]*
	iii DEPENDENT ON AN ADJECTIVE	*keen [on golf]*	*superior [to the others]*

(c) Differences from traditional grammar

In traditional grammar the class of prepositions only contains words that combine with nouns (actually, in our terms, NPs). The examples of prepositions in [14] and [15] above all comply with that, and we'll continue to limit our choice of preposition examples the same way in the early chapters. But in Ch. 7, §2, we drop this restriction and extend the membership of the preposition category. We'll show that there are very good reasons for doing this.

5.7 Coordinators

The central members of the coordinator category are *and*, *or*, and *but* – in traditional grammar they are called 'coordinating conjunctions'. Their function is to mark the **coordination** of two or more expressions, where coordination is a relation between elements of equal syntactic status. This syntactic equality is typically reflected in the ability of any one element to stand in place of the whole coordination, as in:

[16] i   *We need a long table and at least eight chairs.*
      ii a. *We need a long table.*   b. *We need at least eight chairs.*

In [i] we have a coordination of *a long table* and *at least eight chairs*, each of which can occur in place of the whole, as evident from the two examples in [ii]. Precisely because the elements are of equal status, neither is head: coordination is not a head + dependent construction.

5.8 Subordinators

(a) Function

The most central members of the **subordinator** category are *that*, *whether*, and one use of *if* – the one that is generally interchangeable with *whether* (as in *I don't know whether/if it's possible*). These words serve to mark a clause as subordinate. Compare, for example:

[17]   MAIN CLAUSE   SUBORDINATE CLAUSE
      a. *He did his best.*   b. *I realise [that he did his best].*

He did his best in [a] is a **main clause**, one which, in this example, forms a sentence by itself. Addition of the subordinator *that* changes it into a **subordinate clause**. Subordinate clauses characteristically function as a dependent element within the structure of a larger clause. In [b] *that he did his best* is a dependent of the verb *realise*, and hence is part of the larger clause *I realise that he did his best*. *That* is often optional: in *I realise he did his best* the clause *he did his best* is still subordinate, but it is not overtly marked as such in its own structure.

(b) Differences from traditional grammar

One minor difference is that we follow most work in modern linguistics in taking subordinators and coordinators as distinct primary categories, rather than subclasses of a larger class of 'conjunctions'. More importantly, we will argue in Ch. 7, §2.1, for a redrawing of the boundaries between subordinators and prepositions – but again we will in the meantime confine our examples to those where our analysis matches the traditional one in respect of the division between the two categories.

5.9   The concept of prototype

The brief survey we've just given shows something important. Categories like noun, verb and adjective have not just one property distinguishing them from each other and from other categories: they have a cluster of distinctive properties. But while there are lots of words that have the full set of properties associated with their category, there are others which do not. Take *equipment*, for example. It's undoubtedly a noun, but it doesn't have a plural form the way nouns generally do.

We use the term **prototypical** for the central or core members of a category that do have the full set of distinctive properties.

- *Cat* and *dog* are examples of prototypical nouns, but *equipment* is a non-prototypical noun.
- *Go, know*, and *tell* (and thousands of others) are prototypical verbs, but *must* is non-prototypical, because (for example) it has no preterite form (**I musted work late yesterday* is ungrammatical), and it can't occur after *to* (compare *I don't want to go* with **I don't want to must work late*).
- *Big, old*, and *happy* are prototypical adjectives, while *asleep* is non-prototypical because it can't be used attributively (**an asleep child*).

We introduce the concept of prototype here because the parts of speech provide such clear examples of it, but it applies throughout the grammar. It applies to subjects, for instance. The NP *his guilt*, as in the clause *His guilt was obvious*, is a prototypical subject, whereas in *That he was guilty was obvious* the subordinate clause *that he was guilty* is a non-prototypical subject. It differs from *his guilt* in that it can't invert with an auxiliary verb to form an interrogative (that is, we don't find **Was that he was guilty obvious?*).

6   The structure of phrases

A phrase normally consists of a **head**, alone or accompanied by one or more **dependents**. The category of the phrase depends on that of the head: a phrase with a noun as head is a noun phrase, and so on.

We distinguish several different kinds of dependent, the most important of which are introduced in the following subsections.

6.1   Complement and modifier

The most general distinction is between **complements** and **modifiers**, as illustrated for VPs and NPs in [18], where complements are marked by double underlining, modifiers by single underlining:

[18]   i VP   *He [kept her letters for years]*.
       ii NP   *She regularly gives us [very useful advice on financial matters]*.

Complements are related more closely to the head than modifiers. In the clearest cases, complements are obligatory: we cannot, for example, omit *her letters* from [i]. In [ii] the complement is optional, but its close relation to the head is seen in the fact that the particular preposition *on* which introduces it is selected by *advice*: *advice* takes *on*, *fear* takes *of*, *interest* takes *in*, and so on. A more general account of the distinction between complements and modifiers will be introduced when we come to look at clause structure in Ch. 4.

6.2 Object and predicative complement

The next distinction applies primarily within the VP. Two important subtypes of complement are the **object** and the **predicative complement**, illustrated in [19]:

[19] OBJECT   PREDICATIVE COMPLEMENT
   i a. *I met a friend of yours.*   b. *She was a friend of yours.*
  ii a. *Sam appointed a real idiot.*   b. *I felt a real idiot.*
 iii a. [*very friendly* can't be an object] b. *They seemed very friendly.*

Objects are found with a great number of verbs, while predicative complements occur with a quite limited number of verbs, with **be** by far the most frequent. The constructions differ in both meaning and syntax.

- A prototypical object refers to a person or other entity involved in the situation. In [ia] there was a meeting between two people, referred to by the subject and object, while in [iia] we have a situation involving Sam and a person described as a real idiot. A predicative complement, by contrast, typically expresses a property ascribed to the person or other entity referred to by the subject. In [ib] *a friend of yours* gives a property of the person referred to as *she*, while in [iib] *a real idiot* doesn't refer to a separate person but describes how I felt.
- The most important syntactic difference is that a predicative complement can have the form of an adjective (or AdjP), as in [iiib], whereas an object cannot. Thus we cannot have, say, **I met very friendly* or **Sam appointed very friendly.*

6.3 Determiner

This type of dependent is found only in the structure of NPs, where it serves to mark the NP as definite or indefinite. Certain kinds of singular noun usually require the presence of a determiner. In *The dog barked* or *I need a key*, for example, the determiners *the* and *a* are obligatory.

The determiner function is usually filled by determinatives (see §5.4 above), but it can also have the form of a **genitive** NP, as in *Fido's bone* or *the dog's owner*, where *'s* is the marker of the genitive.

7   Canonical and non-canonical clauses

There is a vast range of different clause structures, but we can greatly simplify the description if we confine our attention initially to **canonical clauses**, those which are syntactically the most basic or elementary. The others, **non-canonical clauses**, can then be described derivatively, in terms of how they differ from the canonical ones.

Canonical clauses consist of a subject followed by a predicate, as illustrated in [2] and [3]. The subject is usually (but not invariably) an NP, while the predicate is always – in canonical clauses – a VP.

Non-canonical clauses contrast with canonical ones on one or more of the dimensions reviewed in §§7.1–7.5. below.

7.1   Polarity

Polarity is the name of the system contrasting **positive** and **negative** clauses.

[20]   POSITIVE   NEGATIVE (non-canonical)
    a. *He is very careful.*   b. *He isn't very careful.*

Canonical clauses are positive, while negative clauses are non-canonical. The grammar will have a special section describing how negation is expressed. In [b] the negation is marked on the verb; it can also be marked by *not* (*He is not very careful*) or by some other negative word (*Nobody liked it*).

7.2   Clause type

Canonical clauses are **declarative**. Clauses belonging to any other clause type are non-canonical. We illustrate here two of these other clause types, **interrogative** and **imperative**.

(a) Interrogative

[21]   DECLARATIVE   INTERROGATIVE (non-canonical)
    a. *She can mend it.*   b. *Can she mend it?*

Declaratives are characteristically used to make **statements**, while interrogatives are associated with **questions**. Syntactically, the subject *she* of interrogative [b] follows the verb instead of occupying the default position before the verb (see §3 above).

(b) Imperative

[22]   DECLARATIVE   IMPERATIVE (non-canonical)
    a. *You are patient.*   b. *Be patient.*

- Imperatives are characteristically used to issue what we call **directives**, a term covering requests, commands, instructions, etc.

- Syntactically, the most important difference between imperatives and declaratives is that they usually contain no subject, though there is a covert subject understood: [b] is interpreted as "You be patient".
- There is also a difference in the inflectional form of the verb: *are* in [a] is a present tense form, but *be* in [b] is not.

7.3   Subordination

The distinction between **subordinate** and **main** clauses has already been introduced in connection with our discussion of subordinators as a word category. All canonical clauses are main clauses. Subordinate clauses characteristically function as a dependent within a larger clause, and very often they differ in their internal structure from main clauses, as in the following examples:

[23]   MAIN   SUBORDINATE (non-canonical)
  i a. *She's ill.*   b. *I know that she's ill.*
  ii a. *We invited the Smiths.*   b. *Inviting the Smiths was a mistake.*
  iii a. *Some guy wrote the editorial.* b. *He's [the guy who wrote the editorial].*

- In [ib] the subordinate clause is complement of the verb *know*. It is marked by the subordinator *that*, though in this context this is optional: in *I know she's ill* the subordinate clause does not differ in form from a main clause.
- In [iib] the subordinate clause is subject of the larger clause. Its structure differs more radically from that of a main clause: the subject is missing and the verb has a different inflectional form.
- The subordinate clause in [iiib] is called a **relative clause**. The most straightforward type of relative clause functions as modifier within the structure of an NP and begins with a distinctive word such as *who*, *which*, *when*, *where*, etc., that 'relates' to the head of the NP – *who* in our example relates to *guy*.

7.4   Coordination

One clause may be **coordinated** with another, the relation usually being marked by means of a **coordinator** such as *and* or *or*. Again, canonical clauses are non-coordinate, with coordinate clauses described in terms of the structural effects of coordination. Compare:

[24]   NON-COORDINATE   COORDINATE (non-canonical)
          That's Bill.
                                  That's Bill or I'm blind.
          I'm blind.

Here the coordination is marked by *or* in the second clause. In this example there is no marking in the first clause: coordinate clauses do not necessarily differ from non-coordinate ones, just as subordinate clauses do not necessarily differ from main ones.

7.5   Information packaging

The grammar makes it possible, in many cases, to say essentially the same thing by means of syntactically different constructions. It allows us to present – or **package** – the information in a variety of ways. Canonical clauses always present the information in the syntactically most elementary way. In Ch. 15 we review a fair number of constructions which differ from canonical clauses on this dimension; here we illustrate with just three: passive, preposing, and extraposition.

(a) Passive clauses

[25]   ACTIVE   PASSIVE (non-canonical)
      a. *The dog bit me.*   b. *I was bitten by the dog.*

These have the same meaning; they describe the same situation and if used in the same context it would be impossible for one to be true while the other was false.

The terms **active** and **passive** reflect the fact that in clauses describing an action the subject of the active version (in [a] *the dog*) denotes the active participant, the performer of the action, while the subject of the passive version (in [b] *I*) denotes the passive participant, the undergoer of the action. Syntactically the passive version is clearly more complex than the active by virtue of containing extra elements: the auxiliary verb *was* and the preposition *by*. It is for this reason that we take the passive as a non-canonical construction.

(b) Preposing

[26]   BASIC ORDER   PREPOSING (non-canonical)
      a. *I gave the others to Kim.*   b. *The others I gave to Kim.*

Here the two versions differ simply in the order of elements – more precisely, in the position of the object *the others*.

- In [a] the object occupies its **default** position after the verb.
- In [b] it is **preposed**, placed at the beginning of the clause, before the subject.

Canonical clauses have their elements in the basic order, with departures from this order being handled in our account of various types of non-canonical clause, such as the preposed complement construction in [b].

(c) Extraposition

[27]   BASIC (no extraposition)   EXTRAPOSITION (non-canonical)
      a. *That I overslept was unfortunate.*   b. *It was unfortunate that I overslept.*

- In [a] the subject is a **subordinate clause** – occupying the usual **subject** position.
- In [b] the subject position is occupied by the pronoun *it* and the subordinate clause appears at the end: it is called an **extraposed subject**.

In pairs like this, the version with extraposition is much more frequent than the basic one, but we still regard version [a] as syntactically more basic. The extraposition construction is virtually restricted to cases where the basic subject is a subordinate clause. It's the [a] version that matches the canonical structure of clauses with NPs as subject, e.g., _The delay was unfortunate_. And [b] is (slightly) more complex in structure: it contains the extra word _it_.

7.6   Combinations of non-canonical features

Non-canonical clause categories can combine, so that a clause may differ from a canonical one in a number of different ways at once:

[28]   CANONICAL   NON-CANONICAL
  i a. _Sue can swim._   b. _He says that Sue can't swim._
  ii a. _Kim took the car._ b. _I wonder whether the car was taken by Kim._

The underlined clause in [ib] is both **subordinate** and **negative**. The one in [iib] is **interrogative** and **passive** as well as subordinate. (In subordinate clauses, an interrogative clause of this type is marked by the subordinator _whether_, not by putting the subject after the verb.)

8   Word structure

We have space for very little material on word structure here, but we need to point out that words are made up of elements of two kinds: **bases** and **affixes**. For the most part, bases can stand alone as whole words whereas affixes can't. Here are some examples, with the units separated by a decimal point, bases double-underlined, and affixes single-underlined:

[29]   _en·danger slow·ly un·just work·ing black·bird·s un·gentle·man·ly_

The bases _danger_, _slow_, and _just_, for example, can form whole words. But the affixes can't: there are no words *_en_, *_ly_, *_un_. Every word contains at least one or more bases; and a word may or may not contain affixes in addition.

Affixes are subdivided into **prefixes**, which precede the base to which they attach, and **suffixes**, which follow. When citing them individually, we indicate their status by putting · after prefixes (_en·_, _un·_) and before suffixes (_·ly_, _·ing_).

Exercises

1. Divide the main clauses of the following examples into **subject** and **predicate**. Underline the subject and double-underline the predicate. (For example: _This is the house that Jack built_.)
   i _I think it's a disgrace._

ii _The guy in that house over there works for the city._

iii _Most of the mistakes he made were very minor._

iv _The thing that puzzles me is why no one called the police._

     v *One of her daughters is training to be a pilot.*

2. The underlined expressions in the following examples are all NPs. State the **function** of each one (either **subject** or **direct object** or **predicative complement**).

    i *I've just seen <u>your father</u>.*
    ii *<u>The old lady</u> lived alone.*
    iii *Sue wrote <u>that editorial</u>.*
    iv *She's <u>the editor of the local paper</u>.*
    v *It sounds <u>a promising idea</u> to me.*

3. Assign each word in the following examples to one of the part-of-speech categories: **noun** (N), **verb** (V), **adjective** (Adj), **determinative** (D), **adverb** (Adv), **preposition** (Prep), **subordinator** (Sub), **coordinator** (Co).

    i *She lives in Moscow.*
    ii *The dog was barking.*
    iii *Sue and Ed walked to the park.*
    iv *I met some friends of the new boss.*
    v *We know that these things are extremely expensive.*

4. Construct a plausible-sounding, grammatical sentence that uses at least one word from each of the eight categories listed in the previous exercise (and in [7] in the text of this chapter).

5. Is it possible to make up an eight-word sentence that contains exactly ONE word of each category? If it is, do it; if not, explain why.

6. Classify the underlined clauses below as **canonical** or **non-canonical**. For the non-canonical ones, say which non-canonical clause category or categories they belong to.

    i *<u>Most of us enjoyed it very much</u>.*
    ii *<u>Have you seen Tom recently</u>?*
    iii *<u>He tends to exaggerate</u>.*
    iv *Who said <u>she was ill</u>?*
    v *<u>I've never seen anything like it</u>.*
    vi *They invited me, <u>but I couldn't go</u>.*
    vii *<u>This house was built by my grandfather</u>.*
    viii *<u>It's a pity you live so far away</u>.*
    ix *<u>I'm sure she likes you</u>.*
    x *<u>Tell me what you want</u>.*

3 Verbs, tense, aspect, and mood

1 Verb inflection

Verbs are **variable lexemes**. That is, they have a number of different inflectional forms that are required or permitted in various grammatical contexts. For example, the lexeme *fly* has a form *flown* that is required in a context like [1a], where it follows the verb **have**, and a form *flew* that is permitted in a context like [1b], where it is the only verb in a canonical clause:

[1]   a. *Kim has <u>flown</u> home.*   b. *Kim <u>flew</u> home.*

Notice that we said that *flown* is REQUIRED in contexts like [1a], but that *flew* is PERMITTED in contexts like [b]. This is because in [b] we could have *flies* instead of *flew*. And there is of course a difference in meaning between *Kim flew home* and *Kim flies home*: the former locates the situation in past time, while the latter locates it in present or future time.

We see from this that there are two kinds of inflection: in some cases an inflectional contrast serves to convey a meaning distinction, while in others (like the *flown* of [1a]) the occurrence of a particular inflectional form is simply determined by a grammatical rule.

1.1 The verb paradigm

The set of inflectional forms of a variable lexeme (together with their grammatical labels) is called its **paradigm**. In some languages the verb paradigms are extremely complex, but in English they are fairly simple. The great majority of verbs in English have paradigms consisting of six inflectional forms. As illustration, we give in [2] the paradigm for the verb **walk**, with sample sentences exemplifying how the forms are used:

[2]

	PARADIGM		EXAMPLE SENTENCE
PRIMARY FORMS	**preterite**	walked	She *walked* home.
	3rd singular present	walks	She *walks* home.
	plain present	walk	They *walk* home.
SECONDARY FORMS	**plain form**	walk	She should *walk* home.
	gerund-participle	walking	She is *walking* home.
	past participle	walked	She has *walked* home.

Inflectional form vs shape

We explain below the various grammatical terms used to classify and label the inflectional forms. But first we must note that *walked* and *walk* each appear twice in the paradigm. To cater for this we need to draw a distinction between an inflectional form and its **shape**.

By shape we mean spelling or pronunciation: spelling if we're talking about written English, pronunciation if we're talking about spoken English.

The preterite and the past participle are different inflectional forms but they have the same shape *walked*. Similarly for the plain present and the plain form, which share the shape *walk*.

In the case of the preterite and the past participle there is a very obvious reason for recognising distinct inflectional forms even though the shape is the same: many common verbs have DIFFERENT shapes for these inflectional forms. One is *fly*, as shown in [1]: its preterite form has the shape *flew*, while its past participle has the shape *flown*.

The reason for distinguishing the plain present from the plain form is less obvious. We take up the issue in §1.2 below.

Primary vs secondary forms

With one isolated exception that we take up in §8.4, **primary** forms show inflectional distinctions of tense (preterite vs present) and can occur as the sole verb in a canonical clause. **Secondary** forms have no tense inflection and cannot occur as the head of a canonical clause.

Preterite

The term **preterite** is used for an **inflectionally marked past tense**. That is, the past tense is marked by a specific inflectional form of the verb rather than by means of a separate auxiliary verb. By a **past** tense we mean one whose most central use is to indicate past time. The preterite of **take** is *took*, and when I say *I took them to school* I am referring to some time in the past. The relation between tense and time in English, however, is by no means straightforward, as we saw in Ch. 1, §3, and it is important to be aware that preterite tense does not always signal past time. For example, in the more complex construction *It would be better if I took them to school next week* we have the same preterite form *took*, but here the time is future. We'll look into this a bit more in §5.2 below. Right now we simply want to point out that although making a reference to past time is the central use of the preterite (which is why we call it a past tense), a preterite doesn't ALWAYS signal past time.

Present tense

The central use of **present** tense forms is to indicate present time. For example, *The door opens inwards* describes a state of affairs that obtains now, at the moment of speaking. This explains why the present tense forms are so called, but here too it must be emphasised that they are not invariably used for referring to present time. In *The exhibition opens next week*, for example, we again have the same verb-form, but here the exhibition is claimed to open at some time in the future.

3rd singular present vs plain present

Almost all verbs have two present tense forms, such as *walks* and *walk* in [2]. The choice between them depends on the subject of the clause: the verb **agrees** with the subject. The 3rd person singular form occurs with a 3rd person singular subject (e.g. *She walks home*), and the plain present tense form occurs with any other kind of subject (e.g. *They walk home*).

The agreement involves the categories of **person** and **number**, which apply in the first instance to NPs and hence are discussed more fully in Ch. 5, §§2, 8.2. Number, contrasting singular and plural, needs no further commentary at this point. Person contrasts 1st person (*I* and *we*), 2nd person (*you*) and 3rd person (all other NPs). Thus the 3rd person singular present form occurs with 3rd person singular subjects and the plain form with any other subject – whether plural (*My parents walk home*), 1st person (*I walk home*) or 2nd person (*You walk home*).

We call this *walk* the 'plain' present tense (in preference to the cumbersome 'non-3rd person singular') because it is identical with the **lexical base** of the lexeme. The lexical base is the starting-point for the rules of morphology which describe how the various inflectional forms are derived. The 3rd person singular present tense *walks* is formed from the lexical base by adding ·*s*, the gerund-participle is formed by adding ·*ing*, while the plain present tense involves no such operation on the lexical base.

The plain form

The **plain form** is likewise identical with the lexical base of the verb. But it is not a present tense form, so we call it simply 'plain form' in contrast to 'plain present'. The distinction between these two inflectional forms is discussed in §1.2 below.

The plain form is used in three syntactically distinct clause constructions: **imperative**, **subjunctive**, and **infinitival**. Infinitival clauses have two subtypes, the *to*-infinitival and the bare infinitival. These constructions are illustrated in [3] with the plain form of *keep*:

[3]   i   IMPERATIVE   *Keep us informed tonight.*
      ii SUBJUNCTIVE   *It's essential [that he keep us informed].*
      iii INFINITIVAL { a. *TO*-INFINITIVAL   *It's essential [(for him) to keep us informed].*
                       { b. BARE INFINITIVAL   *He should [keep us informed].*

- Imperatives are normally main clauses, and are typically used as directives – the term we have given for various ways of getting people to do things, such as requests, orders, instructions and so on. They usually have the subject *you* understood rather than overtly expressed.

- Subjunctives occur as main clauses only in a few more or less fixed expressions, as in *God bless you*, *Long live the Emperor*, etc. Their most common use is as subordinate clauses of the kind shown in [ii]. Structurally these differ only in the verb inflection from subordinate clauses with a primary verb-form – and many speakers would here use a present tense in preference to the slightly more formal subjunctive: *It's essential that he keeps us informed.*

- *To*-infinitivals, as the name indicates, are marked by *to*. The subject is optional, and usually omitted. If present it is preceded by *for*, and if a pronoun such as *I*, *he*, *she*, etc., it appears in a different inflectional form from that used for subjects in canonical clauses and also in subjunctives: compare *him* in [iiia] with *he* in [ii].

- Bare infinitivals lack the *to* marker and almost always have no subject. They mostly occur after various auxiliary verbs such as *should*, *can*, *may*, *will*, etc.

The gerund-participle

Traditionally (for example, in the grammar of Latin), a **gerund** is a verb-form that is functionally similar to a noun, whereas a **participle** is one that is functionally similar to an adjective. English verb-forms like *walking* are used in both ways, and no verb has different forms corresponding to the two uses, so we have only a single inflectional form with the shape *walking* in our paradigm, and we call it the **gerund-participle**. These examples show what we mean about its two main kinds of function:

[4]   i   a. *She argued against [buying any more of them].*   [gerund-participle]
          b. *She argued against [any further purchases].*   [noun]
      ii a. *People [earning $50,000 a year] don't qualify*   [gerund-participle]
             for the rebate.
          b. *[Moderately affluent] people don't qualify for*   [adjective]
             the rebate.

In the [i] examples the bracketed parts function as complement to the preposition *against*. In [ia] the bracketed part is a clause, with the verb *buying* as its head; in [ib] the bracketed part is an NP with the noun *purchases* as head. The similarity between the verb-form *buying* and the noun *purchases* is simply this: they head expressions with the same function.

In the [ii] examples the bracketed parts are alike in that they both modify the head noun *people*. In [iia] the brackets surround a clause with the verb *earning* as head; in [iib] we have an adjective phrase with the adjective *affluent* as head. Again, *earning* and *affluent* are thus functionally similar in that each heads an expression modifying a noun.

The past participle

There is a second inflectional form of the verb that contains the term 'participle' as part of its name: the **past participle**. It occurs in two major constructions, perfect and passive, illustrated here with the past participle of the verb *fly*:

[5]   i   a. *She has flown from Dallas.*   } [perfect]
        b. *She may have flown to Brussels.*
    ii   a. *The Brussels–Dallas route is flown by only two airlines.* } [passive]
        b. *A route [flown by only two airlines] is bound to be expensive.*

The **perfect** is usually marked by the auxiliary ***have*** with a following past participle, as in [i]. The **passive** is a non-canonical clause construction (introduced in Ch. 2, §7.5). The most central type is illustrated in [iia], which corresponds to the active clause *Only two airlines fly the Brussels–Dallas route*. The bracketed sequence in [iib] is a subordinate passive clause with no subject and without the auxiliary verb ***be*** that appears in [iia].

The 'participle' component of the name is based on the use of the form in constructions like [5iib], which is comparable to [4iia] above. *Flown* in [5iib] is the head of a subordinate clause modifying the noun *route*, which makes it functionally similar to an adjective, such as *unpopular* in *A [very unpopular] route is bound to be expensive*. There is, however, nothing adjective-like about the use of *flown* in the perfect [i], or indeed in the central passive construction [iia].

The 'past' component of the name, on the other hand, derives from its use in the perfect construction. The perfect is a kind of past tense, and in [5i], for example, the flying is located in past time. But there is no past time meaning associated with *flown* in passive clauses like those in [5ii].

1.2   Verb-forms and shape sharing

We have seen that different inflectional forms of a verb may share the same shape. In our example paradigm for ***walk*** given in [2], this applies to the preterite and the past participle (both *walked*) and to the plain present and the plain form (both *walk*). We look further at these two major cases of shape sharing in this section; there are also certain minor cases that will be left to Ch. 16, where we present a systematic description of English inflectional morphology.

(a) Shape sharing between preterite and past participle

Walk is an example of a **regular** verb, i.e. one whose inflectional forms are all predictable by general rule. An **irregular** verb, by contrast, is one where the shape of at least one inflectional form has to be specified for that particular verb. **Show**, for example, has an irregular past participle: a dictionary needs to tell us that it has the shape *shown*. And for *fly*, both preterite (*flew*) and past participle (*flown*) are irregular.

All regular verbs have identical shapes for the preterite and the past participle, and so indeed do most of the 200 or so irregular verbs. Nevertheless, there are a good number like *fly* which have distinct shapes.

We can set out the paradigms for **walk** and *fly* in chart form, with lines indicating distinctions in shape (the order of presenting the forms is chosen purely to make it easy to represent where shape-sharing occurs):

[6] Regular verbs like **walk**

PRIMARY	SECONDARY
3rd sing present *walks*	gerund-participle *walking*
plain present plain form *walk*	
walked preterite past participle	

Irregular verbs like *fly*

PRIMARY	SECONDARY
3rd sing present *flies*	gerund-participle *flying*
plain present plain form *fly*	
flew preterite	*flown* past participle

When preterite and past participle share the same shape, we can tell which one we have in any given sentence by a **substitution** test: we select a verb in which preterite and past participle are distinct and substitute it in the example to see which shape is required. The following examples will illustrate the idea:

[7]   EXAMPLES WITH **walk**   *fly* SUBSTITUTED FOR **walk**
    i a. *She usually underlined walked there.*   b. *She usually underlined flew there.*
    ii a. *It would be better if we walked more.*   b. *It would be better if we flew more.* } [preterite]

[8]   i a. *She has walked a lot.*   b. *She has flown a lot.*
        ii a. *We were walked to the door.* b. *We were flown to New York.* } [past participle]

We can see that the *walked* of [7] is a preterite form, because the experiment of substituting *fly* in these constructions requires *flew*. *Flown* would be quite impossible here: **She usually flown there* and **It would be better if we flown more*. Notice that in [ii] we have again chosen a construction where the preterite does not indicate past time. You can't decide whether a form is preterite or not by asking whether it refers to past time: the matter has to be determined grammatically.

Similarly, we can see that the *walked* of [8] is a past participle, since in these constructions (the perfect in [i] and the passive in [ii]) the form *flown* is required. The [b] examples would be ungrammatical with *flew*: **She has flew a lot*, **We were flew to New York*.

(b) Shape sharing between plain present and plain form

Almost all verbs have a present tense form that is identical in shape with the plain form. The only verb with a plain form distinct from all its present tense forms is **be**: it has three present tense forms (*am*, *is*, and *are*), all different in shape from its plain form, *be*. We can therefore use a substitution test involving **be** to distinguish plain present forms and plain forms of other verbs. Consider, for example, the following forms of the verb **write**:

[9]   EXAMPLES WITH **write**   **be** SUBSTITUTED FOR **write**
    i   a. *They write to her.*   b. *They are kind to her.*   [present tense]
   ii   a. *Write to her.*   b. *Be kind to her.*
  iii   a. *It's vital that he write to her.*   b. *It's vital that he be kind to her.*
   iv   a. *It's better to write to her.*   b. *It's better to be kind to her.*   [plain form]
    v   a. *He must write to her.*   b. *He must be kind to her.*

The underlined verbs in [i] are present tense forms, while those in [ii–v] are plain forms. It is this contrast between *are* in [ib] and *be* in the other [b] examples that provides the main justification for saying that there are two inflectional forms with the shape *write*, not just one.

Note, however, that even with **be**, we have the same form in all of [9ii–v] (that is, in the imperative, the subjunctive, the *to*-infinitival, and the bare infinitival). The difference between these constructions is purely syntactic: they are different kinds of clause, but they all require the same inflectional form of the verb.

The present tense forms in [9i] contrast in the tense system with preterite forms, and show agreement with the subject, as we see in [10]:

[10]   i   a. *They wrote to her.*   b. *They were kind to her.*   [preterite]
       ii   a. *He writes to her.*   b. *He is kind to her.*   [3rd sing present]

No such contrasts apply to the plain form verbs in [9ii–v]. For example, the construction in [9iv] doesn't allow either the preterite or the 3rd singular present:

[11]   i   a. **It's better to wrote to her.*   b. **It's better to was kind to her.*
       ii   a. **It's better to writes to her.*   b. **It's better to is kind to her.*

The plain present tense and the plain form thus enter into quite different sets of contrast within the verb paradigm. And this is the basis for the different names we have given to the forms: the *write* of [9ia] is a present tense form, but that of [9iia–va] is not.

2   Finite and non-finite clauses

There is an important distinction between two kinds of clause, related to the distinction between main and subordinate clauses. Clauses may be either **finite** or **non-finite**. Finite clauses may be either main or subordinate; non-finite clauses are always subordinate.

Traditional grammars classify VERBS as finite or non-finite, and then classify CLAUSES according to whether or not they contain a finite verb. But historical change has reduced the number of inflectionally distinct verb-forms in such a way that the distinction between finite and non-finite clauses can no longer be satisfactorily defined purely in terms of verb inflection. There is one verb-form, the **plain form**, that occurs in both finite and non-finite clauses, while the other forms are restricted to just one or other of the two classes of clause. In Present-day English the relation between clause finiteness and verb inflection can be stated as follows:

[12] i   If the verb is a primary form, the clause is finite.
      ii   If the verb is a gerund-participle or a past participle, the clause is
            non-finite.
      iii   If the verb is a plain form, the clause may be finite or non-finite;
            specifically:
            a. Imperative and subjunctive clauses are finite.
            b. Infinitival clauses are non-finite.

That gives us a partial fit between finiteness and verb inflection that looks like this:

[13]

VERB-FORM	CONSTRUCTION	EXAMPLE	FINITENESS
i PRIMARY FORMS		*She <u>brings</u> her own food.*	FINITE
ii	IMPERATIVE:	*<u>Bring</u> your own food.*	
iii PLAIN FORM	SUBJUNCTIVE:	*We insist [that she <u>bring</u> her own food].*	
iv	INFINITIVAL:	*It's rare [for her to <u>bring</u> her own food].*	
v GERUND-PARTICIPLE		*She regrets [<u>bringing</u> her own food].*	NON-FINITE
vi PAST PARTICIPLE		*This is the food [<u>brought</u> by my sister].*	

The structure of non-finite subordinate clauses differs more radically from that of main clauses than does that of finite subordinate clauses. That is why we draw the line between finite and non-finite after [iii] in [13] rather than after [i].

- Imperatives belong in the finite category because they occur as main clauses: the non-finite constructions in [iv–vi] are always subordinate.
- Subjunctives occur predominantly as subordinate clauses (in main clauses they are restricted to more or less fixed expressions like *God bless you*, etc.,

mentioned above). Nevertheless, subordinate subjunctives like [iii] are structurally very like subordinate clauses with primary verb-forms: compare *We insist* [*that she _brings_ her own food with her*] (and, as we noted in §1.1 above, many speakers use this instead of [iii]). The subordinate clauses in [iv–vi], however, differ quite markedly in their structure from clauses with primary verb-forms. In [iv] the clause is introduced by *for* rather than *that*, and the subject pronoun appears in the form *her* rather than *she*. And in [v–vi] there is no subject.

3   Auxiliary verbs

We turn now to an important division within the category of verbs between roughly a dozen **auxiliary verbs** and all the rest, which we call **lexical verbs**. The auxiliary verbs (or more briefly, **auxiliaries**) differ sharply in grammatical behaviour from lexical verbs, and figure crucially in a number of common constructions.

Within the auxiliaries there are also major differences between the special subclass known as **modal** auxiliaries and the rest of the class, which we will call **non-modal**; the significance of the term 'modal' will be explained in §8, when we consider the meanings expressed by these verbs. The classification is like this:

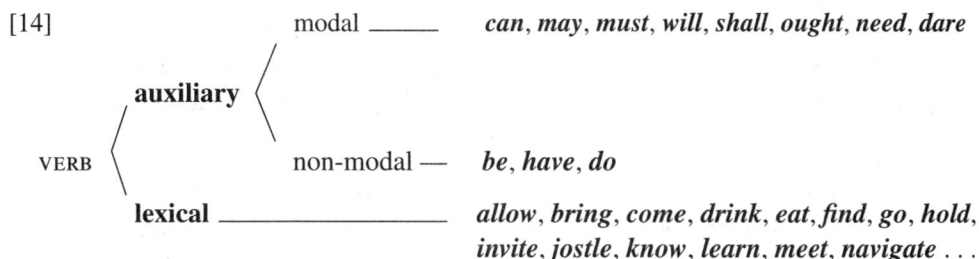

[14]

modal ——— *can, may, must, will, shall, ought, need, dare*

auxiliary

VERB

non-modal — *be, have, do*

lexical ————————— *allow, bring, come, drink, eat, find, go, hold, invite, jostle, know, learn, meet, navigate* . . .

The forms *could, might, would, should* are the preterite forms of the modals *can, may, will,* and *shall*, respectively. They differ very considerably in their uses from ordinary preterites, however, and thus may not at first appear to be preterites (see §8.3).

We begin by looking at some of the most important grammatical properties distinguishing auxiliaries from lexical verbs. We then turn in §3.2 to the distinctive properties of the modal auxiliaries. There is some overlap between auxiliary and lexical verbs and in §3.3 we examine four such cases: ***need, dare, have*** and ***do***. Finally, §3.4 gives a general definition of auxiliary verb.

3.1   Distinctive properties of auxiliary verbs

Auxiliary verbs behave differently from lexical verbs in a number of ways. The two most important ways involve **subject–auxiliary inversion** and **negation**.

▨ (a) Subject–auxiliary inversion

We have seen that interrogative clauses differ from declaratives in the position of the subject. In interrogatives the subject follows a primary verb-form, instead of preceding the verb as it always does in canonical clauses. This inversion of positions between subject and verb is permitted only with auxiliary verbs. It is referred to as **subject–auxiliary inversion**. Compare:

[15]   AUXILIARY VERB   LEXICAL VERB
   i a. *She <u>has</u> taken the money.*   b. *She <u>takes</u> the money.*   [declarative]
  ii a. *<u>Has</u> she taken the money?*   b. **<u>Takes</u> she the money?*   [interrogative]

Interrogative clauses with lexical verbs have to be constructed in a different way. To form the interrogative of *She takes the money* we add the auxiliary verb ***do***. This has no meaning of its own – it simply permits compliance with the grammatical requirement that this kind of interrogative clause should contain an auxiliary verb. We refer to it therefore as the **dummy** auxiliary ***do***. It cannot be used in combination with another auxiliary verb, so the [b] example in [16] is ungrammatical. The present tense in [a] is marked on ***do***; *take* is a plain form.

[16]   DUMMY ***do*** + LEXICAL VERB   DUMMY ***do*** + AUXILIARY VERB
      a. *Does she take the money?*   b. **Does she have taken the money?*

▨ (b) Negation

There are two ways in which auxiliaries differ from lexical verbs with respect to negation. In the first place, the simplest type of negative clause construction, where the negation is associated with a primary verb-form, is permitted with auxiliary verbs, but not with lexical verbs:

[17]   AUXILIARY   LEXICAL VERB
   i a. *She <u>has</u> taken the money.*   b. *She <u>takes</u> the money.*   [positive]
  ii a. *She <u>has</u> not taken the money.* b. **She <u>takes</u> not the money.* [negative]

To form the negative of *She takes the money* we have to add dummy ***do***, just as we did to form the interrogative, and again this ***do*** cannot combine with another auxiliary verb:

[18]   DUMMY ***do*** + LEXICAL VERB   DUMMY ***do*** + AUXILIARY VERB
      a. *She does not take the money.*   b. **She does not have taken the money.*

In the second place, auxiliaries have negative inflectional forms. They all end in *n't*, and are found in the preterite and present tense:

[19]   i PRETERITE   *He <u>couldn't</u> swim.*   *She <u>wouldn't</u> help us.*   *They <u>hadn't</u> finished.*
    ii PRESENT   *He <u>can't</u> swim.*   *She <u>won't</u> help us.*   *They <u>haven't</u> finished.*

No lexical verb has forms of this kind: **tookn't*, **taken't*, etc., are completely impossible. Historically the negative forms arose through contraction, with *could* + *not* being reduced to *couldn't*, and so on. But in Present-day English they are best regarded as inflectional forms, for two reasons.

- Some of them are quite irregular. There is, for example, no general rule of contraction that would yield *won't* from *will + not*: we simply have to note that *won't* is an irregular negative form, just as *would* is an irregular preterite form. Similarly for *can't* and *shan't*.
- In subject–auxiliary inversion constructions they occur in positions where verb + *not* would generally be impossible. We have, for example, *Isn't it ready?*, but not **Is not it ready?*

3.2   Modal auxiliaries

There are two inflectional properties that distinguish the modal auxiliaries from all other verbs. They also share a purely syntactic property that distinguishes the prototypical ones from nearly all other verbs.

(a) Lack of secondary inflectional forms

Modals have only primary forms and hence simply cannot occur in constructions requiring a secondary form – a plain form, gerund-participle or past participle. We can see this clearly when we contrast the modal auxiliary ***must*** with ***have***, which can have a very similar meaning but is not a modal auxiliary:

[20]	MODAL AUXILIARY	NOT MODAL AUXILIARY	
i	a. *I <u>must</u> work late tonight.*	b. *I <u>have</u> to work late tonight.*	[primary form]
ii	a. **I will <u>must</u> work late.*	b. *I will <u>have</u> to work late.*	[plain form]
iii	a. **I am <u>musting</u> work late.*	b. *I am <u>having</u> to work late.*	[gerund-participle]
iv	a. **I've often <u>must</u> work late.*	b. *I've often <u>had</u> to work late.*	[past participle]

(b) No distinct 3rd singular agreement form in the present tense

The modal auxiliaries show no agreement with the subject, having a single present tense form. There are no special 3rd singular forms (**cans, *mays, *musts, *wills*, etc.). Note again, then, the contrasting behaviour of ***must*** and ***have***:

[21]			
i	a. *I <u>must</u> leave now.*	b. *I <u>have</u> to leave now.*	[1st singular subject]
ii	a. *She <u>must</u> leave now.*	b. *She <u>has</u> to leave now.*	[3rd singular subject]

(c) Bare infinitival complement

The prototypical modal auxiliaries take a single complement with the form of a bare infinitival clause. Nearly all other verbs that select infinitival complements take the *to*-infinitival kind: here again we can note the contrast between ***must*** and ***have*** in [20–21]. There are some verbs that take bare infinitivals (one is ***help***, as in *We <u>helped</u> wash up*), but very few. There is also one verb that qualifies as a modal auxiliary by criteria (a)–(b) but takes (for most speakers) an infinitival with *to*. This is **ought**, as in *You ought to be more careful.*

3.3   Dually-classified verbs

A few verbs belong to both auxiliary and lexical verb classes, exhibiting auxiliary behaviour under certain circumstances and lexical verb behaviour elsewhere. The main ones are **do**, **have**, **need** and **dare**.

(a) *Do*

Dummy **do** is an auxiliary, but in other uses – e.g. in *She did her best*, etc. – **do** is a lexical verb. This is evident from the fact that to form the interrogative or negative in such cases we use dummy **do**, just as with other lexical verbs:

[22]   WITHOUT DUMMY **do**   WITH DUMMY **do**
      a. **Does she her best?*   b. *Does she do her best?*

(b) *Have*

- **Have** is always an auxiliary when it marks perfect tense (where it normally occurs with a following past participle).
- When it occurs in clauses describing states, expressing such meanings as possession (*He has enough money*) or obligation (*You have to sign both forms*), usage is divided. Most speakers treat it as a lexical verb, but some treat it as an auxiliary, especially in the present tense. Those speakers accept *%Has he enough money?* and similar examples. We refer to this use as 'static **have**'.[1]
- 'Dynamic **have**', by contrast, occurs in clauses describing events, like *He had a fit*. Dynamic **have** is a lexical verb for all speakers.

These facts are illustrated in [23]:

[23]   AUXILIARY USAGE   LEXICAL VERB USAGE
   i a. *Have you told her?*   b. **Do you have told her?*   [perfect]
   ii a. *%Has he enough money?*   b. *Does he have enough money.* ⎫
  iii a. *%Have I to sign both forms?* b. *Do I have to sign both forms?* ⎬ [static]
   iv a. **Has he a fit when you do that?* b. *Does he have a fit when*   [dynamic]
                                              you do that?

(c) *Need*

Need behaves as an auxiliary (a modal auxiliary) when it has a bare infinitival complement (overt or understood). Elsewhere, it is a lexical verb. Auxiliary **need** has only present tense forms, and occurs only in **non-affirmative contexts** – i.e. in negatives, interrogatives and related constructions:

---

[1] Static **have** as an auxiliary is used more by older than by younger speakers, and is more characteristic of BrE than AmE.

[24]   AUXILIARY USAGE   LEXICAL VERB USAGE
    i a. *Need we tell anyone?*   b. *Do we need to tell anyone?*
    ii a. *She needn't go.*   b. *She doesn't need to go.*
    iii a. **Need she any help?*   b. *Does she need any help?*

Note that in [i–ii] auxiliary **need** takes a bare infinitival complement (*tell anyone* and *go*), whereas lexical **need** takes a *to*-infinitival.

(d) *Dare*

Auxiliary **dare** (again, a modal) is very much like auxiliary **need**, in that it occurs only in non-affirmative contexts and takes a bare infinitival complement. Lexical **dare** mostly occurs in non-affirmative contexts too, but is not restricted to them.

[25]   AUXILIARY USAGE   LEXICAL VERB USAGE
    i a. *I daren't tell anyone.*   b. *I didn't dare to tell anyone.*
    ii a. *Dare they accept her challenge?*   b. *Do they dare to accept her challenge?*
    iii a. [no auxiliary counterpart]   b. *She had dared to contradict him.*

There is no auxiliary counterpart to [iiib], for two reasons. In the first place, *dared* is a past participle whereas modal auxiliaries have only primary forms. Secondly, this is not a non-affirmative context.

3.4   The general concept of auxiliary verb

The grammatical properties outlined in §3.1 serve to distinguish auxiliary verbs from lexical verbs in English. There are many languages, however, that have auxiliary verbs, so we need to shift focus at this stage and consider what is meant by auxiliary verb as a general term.

A general definition of auxiliary verb can be given along the following lines. Auxiliary verbs form a small subclass of verbs whose members are characteristically used to mark **tense**, **aspect**, **mood** or **voice**. These categories are also often marked in languages by inflection, so auxiliary verbs tend to convey meanings which elsewhere are expressed by inflection of the verb.

The subclass of verbs in English with the distinctive properties concerning inversion and negation clearly satisfies this general definition. Most members of the class do serve to mark tense, aspect, mood or voice, as shown in [26]:

[26]   AUXILIARY VERB   CATEGORY MARKED   EXAMPLE
    i   *have*   **perfect tense**   *Sue has written the preface.*
    ii *be*   **progressive aspect** *Sue is writing the preface.*
    iii *may*, *can*, *must*, etc. **mood**   *Sue may write the preface.*
    iv *be*   **passive voice**   *The preface was written by Sue.*

What is meant by the general terms tense, aspect, mood and voice will be explained as we describe these categories for English. The full set of verbs for [iii] comprises the modal auxiliaries listed in [14]: 'modal' is the adjective corresponding to the category 'mood'.

It is worth emphasising again, however, that a general definition of a category does not provide criteria for deciding which expressions in English belong to that category: it provides a principled basis for naming a category that has grammatically distinctive properties in a range of languages (see Ch.1, §3). To determine which verbs in English are auxiliaries we need to apply the grammatical criteria relating to subject–auxiliary inversion and negation.

In the first place this excludes verbs like *begin*, *continue*, *keep*, *stop* even though in constructions like *They began/continued/kept/stopped interrupting her* the meaning belongs in the same family as that of progressive *be* in *They were interrupting her* – and indeed a good number of traditional grammars do analyse these verbs as auxiliaries of aspect.

Conversely, *be* qualifies as an auxiliary verb not just when it is marking progressive aspect or passive voice, but also when it is the only verb in the clause, taking a complement with the form of an AdjP, NP, etc. Its behaviour with respect to inversion and negation is the same in this construction as in those where it is marking progressive aspect or passive voice. This is shown in [27], where this use of *be* is compared with the one marking progressive aspect:[2]

[27]   ***be* AS ASPECT MARKER**   ***be* AS ONLY VERB**
   i a. *He is acting strangely.*   b. *He is insane.*
  ii a. *Is he acting strangely?*   b. *Is he insane?*
 iii a. *He isn't acting strangely.*   b. *He isn't insane.*

4   Perfective and imperfective interpretations

In the remainder of this chapter we examine the meaning and use of four systems associated with the verb that are marked by the formal devices described above – by inflection or by auxiliary verbs. There are two systems of tense to consider: a 'primary' one marked by the inflectional contrast between preterite and present tense, and a 'secondary' one marked by the the perfect auxiliary *have*. The other two systems we shall be dealing with are progressive aspect, marked by the progressive auxiliary *be*, and mood, marked by the modal auxiliaries.[3] The four systems are shown with examples in [28]:

[28]
	SYSTEM	TERMS	MARKING	EXAMPLE
i	Primary tense	Preterite	preterite inflection	*went*
		Present	present tense inflection	*goes*
ii	Secondary tense	Perfect	***have*** with past participle	*has gone*
		Non-perfect	[no special marking]	*goes*
iii	Aspect	Progressive	***be*** with gerund-participle	*is going*
		Non-progressive	[no special marking]	*goes*
iv	Mood	Modal	modal with plain form	*can go*
		Non-modal	[no special marking]	*goes*

---

[2] Traditional grammar does not analyse the *be* of the [b] examples as an auxiliary, but since it does not provide syntactic criteria for determining what verbs are auxiliaries in English, membership of the class is ill defined and varies from one grammar to another.

[3] The use of auxiliary *be* in *It was written by Kim* is not covered in this chapter. It marks passive voice. The passive is one of the constructions described in the chapter on information packaging (see Ch. 15, §2).

The preterite and the perfect are different kinds of past tense: note that both *She went home* and *She has gone home* locate her going home in past time.

Before we begin our survey of the four systems listed in [28] we need to introduce an important semantic distinction that is relevant to all of them. We use **situation** as a cover term for the kinds of things that are described by a clause – actions like publishing a novel, processes like growing tall, states like being a student, etc. – and we distinguish two kinds of clause interpretation that look at situations in different ways.

- When a clause describes a situation in a way that considers it as a whole, in its totality, without reference to any internal temporal structure or subdivision it might have, we say that the clause has a **perfective** interpretation.
- When a clause describes a situation in a way that makes reference to its internal temporal structure or subdivisions, we say that the clause has an **imperfective** interpretation.

The following examples illustrate the distinction:

[29]   PERFECTIVE   IMPERFECTIVE
  i a. *She wrote a novel.*   b. *She was writing a novel.*
  ii a. *She spent last summer with her parents.* b. *She still lived with her parents.*

The natural interpretation of [ia] is perfective: it simply describes an event that took place in the past. Example [ib], by contrast, has an imperfective interpretation: we are not concerned with the total event of her writing a novel, but with just part of it, some part in the middle during the process of its composition. Note that it does not follow from [ib] that she ever actually completed the novel. This clause has progressive aspect, and clauses with this form are almost always interpreted imperfectively.

But imperfective interpretations are not confined to progressive clauses. While [iia] is perfective – it talks about the summer as a whole – [iib] has an imperfective interpretation (despite not being in the progressive aspect). In [iib], just as in [ib], we are not concerned with any situation in its totality. The situation of her living with her parents obtained at the time in the past that is being talked about, and the *still* indicates that it had also obtained at an earlier time, and there is nothing to say that it ended. She might still live with her parents now, at the time of speaking.

Perfective vs perfect

It is important to distinguish the term 'perfective' from 'perfect', which we introduced earlier in the chapter.

- **Perfect** is the name of a grammatical category, a type of past tense;
- **Perfective** applies, as far as English is concerned, to a kind of semantic interpretation.

The potentially confusing similarity between the terms reflects the fact that both are derived from a Latin word meaning "complete". There are, however, two entirely different kinds of completeness involved. With the perfect the key concept is that of past time. In examples like *She has written a novel*, the novel-writing is a completed event in the past. With the perfective it is a matter of viewing the situation as a complete whole, but it need not be in the past. In *She will write a novel*, for example, the novel-writing situation is still perfective, but it is in future time, not the past. It is best to think of the two terms as quite independent, with the similarity between them being based on their historical origin rather than being indicative of any close correlation between them.

5   Primary tense

The primary tense system contrasts the **preterite**, an inflectionally marked past tense, with the **present tense**:

[30]   PRETERITE   PRESENT TENSE
      a. *She <u>was</u> in Bonn.*   b. *She <u>is</u> in Bonn.*

A tense system is a system associated with the verb where the basic contrasts in meaning have to do with the **location in time** of the situation, or the part of it under consideration. This clearly applies to the system illustrated in [30]. The clauses are interpreted imperfectively, and the preterite in [i] indicates that the state in question obtained at a time in the past, while the present tense in [ii] indicates that it obtains in the present. Past and present time are relational concepts. Usually past time is understood as time preceding the time of speaking and present time is time simultaneous with the time of speaking.

The examples in [30] illustrate the most central use of the two primary tenses, but both have a range of other uses too: the relation between tense and time in English is not at all straightforward. We'll show this for each of the two tenses in the primary system.

5.1   The present tense

(a) Present time

The most basic use of the present tense is to indicate present time – more specifically, time that coincides with the time of utterance, as in [30b].

But the time of utterance is of course very short. It often takes only a second or two to utter a sentence. So naturally there are severe restrictions on the use of the present tense in clauses with perfective interpretations. Compare these two examples:

[31]   i *I <u>promise</u> to be back for lunch.*   [perfective]
       ii *Sue <u>mows</u> the lawn.*   [imperfective]

- The salient interpretation of [i] is perfective: there is a single act of promising which is performed by uttering the sentence. The act of promising and the uttering of the sentence thus occupy the same brief period of time (two or three seconds).
- But [ii] cannot under any normal circumstances be interpreted in terms of a single act of mowing the lawn at the time of speaking. It takes much longer to mow a lawn than to utter a sentence, so the present time cannot be the time of the situation considered as a totality. The natural interpretation, then, is an imperfective one: we take the sentence to describe a state of affairs where Sue regularly or habitually mows the lawn. This state – like that in [30b] – holds at the time of speaking, but began before then and will (presumably) continue after it.

To talk about a single act of mowing the lawn while it is going on we would normally use the progressive aspect version: *Sue is mowing the lawn*. Here the progressive picks out a point within the total duration of the act, which means the interpretation is an imperfective one.

(b) Future time, I: the futurate

The present tense is often used for situations located in future time. In main clauses this is restricted to cases where it can be assumed that we have present knowledge of a future event, as in:

[32] i *The next high tide is at 4 o'clock.*   *The sun rises tomorrow at 6.10.*
      ii *Exams start next week.*   *We arrive home two days before Easter.*

This construction is called the **futurate**. The future time is usually specified by a time adjunct, marked here by double underlining. The two most common cases involve:

- recurrent events in nature whose time can be calculated scientifically (as in [i]);
- events that are arranged or scheduled in advance (as in [ii]).

(c) Future time, II: subordinate clauses

The present tense is used with future time reference without the above restrictions in certain types of subordinate clause. Three cases of this kind are illustrated in [33]:

[33] i *Please bring the washing in if* [*it rains*].
      ii *I'll give it to you before* [*I leave*].
      iii *I hope* [*you are feeling better soon*].

The underlined verbs are present tense but clearly make future time references.

- In [i] the subordinate clause is complement within a conditional adjunct;
- In [ii] it is complement within a temporal adjunct;
- In [iii] it is complement of the verb **hope**.

(d) Past time: the historic present

In certain types of narrative, especially in informal style, the present tense is used instead of the preterite for past time events, even in discourses that have begun in the preterite:

[34]   *I was waiting at the bus-stop when this guy <u>drives</u> up and <u>offers</u> me a lift in his BMW, so I <u>say</u> 'Well, I don't know,' and he <u>says</u> 'You can trust me, I'm a grammarian,' so I <u>get</u> in, and off we <u>go</u>.*

5.2   The preterite

(a) Past time

The central use of the preterite is to locate the situation, or the part of it under consideration, in past time. Compare the present tense examples in [31] with their preterite counterparts:

[35]   i   *I <u>promised</u> to be back for lunch.*   [perfective]
        ii *Sue <u>mowed</u> the lawn.*   [imperfective or perfective]

Here [i] again has a perfective interpretation: it reports a promise made in the past. Example [ii], however, can be interpreted either imperfectively or perfectively. In the former case it is the past time analogue of [31ii], with Sue habitually or regularly mowing the lawn. This state of affairs held at the time that's being referred to.

We noted above that perfective interpretations of present tense clauses with present time reference are restricted to situations of very short duration, since they have to be co-extensive with the act of utterance. No comparable constraint applies with the preterite, however, and thus [35ii], unlike [31ii], can readily be used perfectively to denote a single act of mowing the lawn located as a whole in past time.

(b) Modal remoteness: the modal preterite

There is a second important use of the preterite where the meaning has to do not with time but with **modality**. We call this the **modal preterite** use. Modality is a type of meaning that is characteristically associated with mood rather than tense and is explained further in §8. At this point it's enough to say that it covers various kinds of case where the situation described in a clause is not presented as factual. The modal preterite is used to present the situation as, in varying degrees, modally **remote**. What this means can best be understood by comparing the modal preterite with the present tense in such examples as those in [36], where in each pair the time is the same in [b] as in [a].

[36]   PRESENT TENSE   MODAL PRETERITE
        i a. *I'm glad they <u>live</u> nearby.*   b. *I wish they <u>lived</u> nearby.*
        ii a. *I hope she <u>arrives</u> tomorrow.*   b. *I'd rather she <u>arrived</u> tomorrow.*
        iii a. *If he <u>loves</u> her, he'll change his job.*   b. *If he <u>loved</u> her, he'd change his job.*
        iv a. *If you <u>leave</u> now, you'll miss the*   b. *If you <u>left</u> now, you'd miss the*
              rush-hour traffic.   *rush-hour traffic.*

- Because of the contrasting meanings of *glad* and *wish*, we understand from [ia] that they do in fact live nearby, and from [ib] that they don't. In [ib] *they lived nearby* is thus interpreted **counterfactually**, i.e. as contrary to fact, or false: this is the highest degree of modal remoteness.

- A lesser degree of modal remoteness is seen in [iib]: this doesn't imply that she definitely won't arrive tomorrow, but it suggests that it may well be that she won't (perhaps I'm proposing a change to current arrangements where she's arriving at some other time). In these two examples the modal preterite is grammatically obligatory, for **wish** requires a preterite form of the verb in a finite complement, and so does the idiom *would rather*.

- In [iii–iv], we find something different again: here there is a choice between present tense and preterite. These examples illustrate an important distinction between two kinds of conditional construction, **open**, as in [iiia/iva], vs **remote**, as in [iiib/ivb].

  - The open type characteristically leaves it open as to whether the condition is or will be fulfilled: he may love her or he may not; you may leave now or you may not.

  - The remote type, by contrast, generally presents the fulfilment of the condition as a more remote possibility. So [iiib] suggests a readiness to believe that he doesn't love her; this is the version I'd use, for example, in a context where he's not planning to change his job and I'm arguing from this that he doesn't love her. Similarly, [ivb] presents your leaving now as somewhat less likely than in the case of [iva]: it would generally be preferred, for example, in a context where your current plans or inclinations are to leave later.

(c) Backshift

A third use of the preterite shows up in indirect reported speech. Notice the contrast between *has* and *had* in this pair:

[37] i *Kim has blue eyes.*   [original utterance: present tense]
       ii *I told Stacy that Kim had blue eyes.*   [indirect report: preterite]

If I say [i] to Stacy, I can use [ii] as an indirect report to tell you what I said to Stacy. I'm repeating the content of what I said to Stacy, but not the exact wording. My utterance to Stacy contained the present tense form *has*, but my report of it contains preterite *had*. Nonetheless, my report is entirely accurate. This kind of change in tense is referred to as **backshift**.

The most obvious cases of backshift are with verbs of reporting that are in the preterite, like *told* or *said*. It would not occur with present tense verbs of saying; in the present tense, my report would have been *I tell Stacy that Kim has blue eyes*. In fact, even with preterite reporting verbs backshift is often optional: you can keep the original present tense instead of backshifting it. Instead of [37ii], therefore, we can have:

[38]   *I told Stacy that Kim has blue eyes.*

Although indirect reported speech represents the most obvious case, backshift also happens quite generally in constructions where one clause is embedded within a larger one containing a preterite verb:

[39]   i *Stacy didn't know that Kim had blue eyes.*
       ii *I wondered at the time whether they were genuine.*
      iii *I wish I knew if these paintings were genuine.*

All the underlined verbs have backshifted tense. Notice in particular that the *knew* of [iii] is actually a modal preterite, and doesn't refer to past time at all; but it still provides a context in which backshift can take place. So backshift can't be understood at all on the basis of some simple idea about preterite tenses referring to past time; it's a special grammatical principle about the use of the preterite tense inflection.

6   The perfect

The **perfect** is a past tense that is marked by means of an auxiliary verb rather than by inflection, like the preterite. The auxiliary is **have**, which is followed by a past participle. Examples are given in [40] along with their non-perfect counterparts:

[40]   PERFECT   NON-PERFECT
       i a. *She has been ill.*   b. *She is ill.*
      ii a. *She had left town.*   b. *She left town.*
     iii a. *She is said to have spoken fluent Greek.*   b. *She is said to speak fluent Greek.*

In [ia] and [iia] the auxiliary **have** is itself inflected for primary tense, *has* being a present tense form, *had* a preterite. These constructions thus have **compound tense**: [ia] is a **present perfect**, [iia] a **preterite perfect**. In [iiia] **have** is in the plain form, so this time there is no primary tense, no compound tense.

In all three cases the perfect encodes past time meaning. This is very obvious in [i] and [iii] where the [a] examples refer to past time and the [b] ones to present time – but we will see below that it also holds for [ii].

The present perfect is the most frequent of the constructions in [40], and we will begin with this even though the combination of present and past tenses makes it the most complex of the three.

6.1   The present perfect

The present perfect, like the simple preterite (the non-perfect preterite) in its central use, locates the situation, or part of it, in past time:

[41]   PRESENT PERFECT   SIMPLE PRETERITE
       a. *She has read your letter.*   b. *She read your letter.*

The difference in meaning results from the fact that the present perfect is a compound tense combining past and present, whereas the simple preterite is purely a past tense. The former includes explicit reference to the present as well as the past, whereas the latter does not. We can see the significance of the present tense component in two ways.

(a) Time adjuncts

Under certain conditions the present perfect allows time adjuncts referring to the present. The preterite does not. And conversely, the present perfect more or less excludes time adjuncts referring to the past, since they divorce the situation from present time. So we have these contrasts:

[42]   i   a. *We have <u>by now</u> finished most of it.*   b. **We <u>by now</u> finished most of it.*
       ii a. **She has finished her thesis <u>last week.</u>*   b. *She finished her thesis <u>last week</u>.*

(b) Current relevance

With the present perfect the past time situation is conceived of as having some kind of current relevance, relevance to the present, whereas the preterite does not express any such relationship. Compare:

[43]   i   a. *She has lived in Paris for ten years.*   b. *She lived in Paris for ten years.*
       ii   a. *She has met the President.*   b. *She met the President.*
       iii a. *The premier has resigned.*   b. *The premier resigned.*
       iv   a. *You've put on some weight.*   b. *You put on some weight.*

- In [ia] the connection with the present is that she is still living in Paris. In [ib], by contrast, the period of her living in Paris is located wholly in the past.
- In [iia], a natural interpretation would be that we are concerned with her **past experience** as it affects her status now: some past experience of hers at some indefinite time puts her in the present state of being among the relatively small class of people who have met the President. If I use [iib], on the other hand, I'm simply reporting a past event, and it will typically be clear from the context what time period I am talking about.
- In [iiia] we see an example of the present perfect as used to report **hot news**. Examples like [iiia] are very common in radio and TV news broadcasts (and, of course, not at all common in history books).
- Example [iva] illustrates the common use of the present perfect where the concern is with **present results** of past events. The salient context is one where you are now somewhat heavier than you were before. In [ivb] there is no such connection with the present: it simply describes a past event, and it could well be that the extra weight was subsequently lost.[4]

---

[4] On the last point, colloquial AmE differs somewhat from BrE. The adjunct *already* calls attention to the early occurrence and present results of an event; but American speakers will often say *I did that already* where a BrE speaker would say *I've already done that.* AmE speakers understand the use of the perfect in such contexts, but use it less frequently.

6.2   The preterite perfect

In §5.2 we distinguished three main uses of the preterite, and all three of them are found in the preterite perfect, i.e., the construction where the perfect auxiliary is in the preterite form *had*:

[44]   i   *She <u>had gone</u> to bed.*   [past time]
         ii   *It would have been better if she <u>had gone</u> to bed.*   [modal remoteness]
       iii   *You said she <u>had gone</u> to bed.*   [backshift]

- The central use of the preterite is to indicate past time, and when the preterite combines with the perfect we then have two components of past time. So in [i] her going to bed is located in the past relative to some other past time – such as the time of our arrival in *She had already gone to bed when we arrived.*
- In [44ii] the preterite indicates not past time but modal remoteness. In this example the conditional has a counterfactual interpretation: she didn't go to bed. Because the preterite is marking modal remoteness, it can't also indicate past time, so the perfect has to be used for this purpose. (Compare the non-perfect *It would be better if she went to bed*, where the time is the immediate future, not the past.)
- For [44iii], a natural context would be to report you as having said *She went to bed* or *She has gone to bed*. Here the preterite or the present perfect of the original utterance is backshifted to a preterite perfect.

6.3   The perfect in clauses without primary tense

The third case to consider is where auxiliary ***have*** appears in a secondary form, so that there is no primary (inflectional) tense. The perfect in this case serves to locate the situation in past time, just like the preterite in clauses that do have primary tense. Compare the following pairs:

[45]   PRIMARY TENSE: PRETERITE   NO PRIMARY TENSE: PERFECT
     i a. *We believe that she <u>was</u> in Bonn*   b. *We believe her to <u>have been</u> in Bonn*
              at the time.   *at the time.*
    ii a. *As we <u>reached</u> agreement yesterday,*   b. *<u>Having reached</u> agreement yesterday,*
              we don't need to meet today.   *we don't need to meet today.*

In each pair, there is reference to past time in both [a] and [b]. The past time is expressed by the preterite in [a] and the perfect in [b].

Examples like these show why we refer to the preterite as the primary past tense and the perfect as the secondary one. The preterite represents the most common, or default, way of locating the situation in past time, but it can't be used in clauses without inflectional tense, such as the non-finite clauses in [45ib/iib]: the perfect is then called into service to perform the job that in the [a] examples is performed by the preterite. The same point applies to examples like [44ii] above. As we noted, this is a conditional construction with the preterite expressing modal remoteness: this means that the preterite can't also serve to locate the situation in past time, so this has to be done by the perfect.

6.4   The continuative perfect

One difference between the perfect and the preterite is that we can use the perfect to indicate that the situation lasted over a period starting before a certain time and continuing up to that time. We call this the **continuative** use of the perfect, as opposed to the **non-continuative** use:

[46]   NON-CONTINUATIVE PERFECT   CONTINUATIVE PERFECT
    i a. *She has already gone to bed.*   b. *She has been in bed for two hours.*
   ii a. *She had already gone to bed when*   b. *She had been in bed for two hours*
       we arrived.   *when we arrived.*

- In the [a] examples the perfect simply locates her going to bed in the past – relative to the time of speaking in the present perfect [ia] and to the time of our arrival in the preterite perfect [iia].
- In the [b] examples, however, her being in bed continued over a period of time: in [ib] it began two hours before the time of speaking, lasting until now, while in [iib] this period began two hours before we arrived, lasting until then. The continuative interpretation is imperfective, so there is no implication in [ib/iib] that the situation of her being in bed ended at the time of utterance or when we arrived. (Similarly for [43ia], which is also continuative.)

The continuative use of the perfect is much less common than the non-continuative one, and is usually marked explicitly by a duration expression giving the length of the period in question, such as *for two hours* in [46].

7   Progressive aspect

The **progressive** is formed by means of auxiliary *be* followed by a gerund-participle. Compare:

[47]   PROGRESSIVE   NON-PROGRESSIVE
    a. *She <u>was writing</u> a novel.*   b. *She <u>wrote</u> a novel.*

The concept of aspect

A grammatical form or construction qualifies as an **aspect** if its main use is to indicate how the speaker views the situation described in the clause with respect not to its location in time but to its temporal structure or properties.

Thus in [47] the time referred to is past in both [a] and [b], but the situation is viewed in different ways. In [b] it is considered in its totality, as a complete event, whereas in [a] the situation is presented as being in progress at a certain time. The two clauses have the same tense – the preterite – but they differ in aspect.

The progressive and imperfectivity

Clauses with progressive form usually have **imperfective** interpretations. We have just noted, for example, that while [47b] is concerned with her writing a novel as a whole, [47a] is not: the former has a perfective interpretation, the latter an imperfective one. Not all clauses with imperfective interpretations, however, have progressive form – cf. the discussion of [29] in §4. The characteristic meaning of progressive aspect involves a specific kind of imperfectivity – it presents the situation as being in progress. This implies that the situation has the following two properties:

- it has **duration**, rather than being instantaneous, or 'punctual';
- it is **dynamic**, rather than static: states don't progress, they simply hold or obtain.

Clauses describing punctual or static situations thus generally appear in the non-progressive:

[48]   i a. *I finally found my key.*   b. *At last it has stopped raining.*   [punctual]
        ii a. *She has blue eyes.*   b. *This jug holds two pints.*   [static]

Finding one's key (as opposed to searching for it) is punctual, and one wouldn't say **I was finally finding my key.* Having blue eyes is a state – hence the striking peculiarity of **She is having blue eyes.* It's the same with the other examples.

Contrasts between non-progressive and progressive

The basic meaning of the progressive is to present the situation as being in progress, but this general meaning tends to interact with features relating to the kind of situation being described to yield a more specific interpretation, a more specific difference between a progressive clause and its non-progressive counterpart. Writing a novel, for example, is a situation with a determinate endpoint (when the novel is completed), and thus while [47b] entails that the novel was indeed completed, [47a] does not: she may or may not have gone on to complete it. But there is no such sharp difference in the pair *They watched TV* and *They were watching TV*. Watching TV (as opposed to watching a particular programme) does not have a determinate endpoint, and so we find that if *They were watching TV* is true, so is *They watched TV*.

Here are four contrasting pairs of examples where the grammatical difference is purely that one is non-progressive and the other is progressive:

[49]   NON-PROGRESSIVE   PROGRESSIVE
     i a. *He nodded.*   b. *He was nodding.*
    ii a. *He is very tactful.*   b. *He is being very tactful.*
   iii a. *She lives with her parents.*   b. *She is living with her parents.*
    iv a. *She reads the 'New Scientist'.* b. *She is reading the 'New Scientist'.*

- A salient interpretation of [ia] is that there was just one nod. But a nod is punctual, so [ib] cannot normally involve a single nod: it conveys the idea of a
  sequence of nods.
- The default interpretation of [iia] is as a state: we take it to describe his charac-
  ter/personality. The progressive requires a dynamic component of meaning, and
  we interpret [iib] in terms of behaviour rather than character: "He is behaving
  very tactfully".
- Non-progressive [iiia] again describes a state, while the progressive [iiib] conveys
  that the situation is a relatively temporary one – it is progressing towards its end.
- The usual interpretation of [iva] is as a state, with regular, habitual reading of
  the 'New Scientist': reading it takes too long to permit an interpretation with
  a single reading in present time. The most salient interpretation of [ivb]
  (though not the only one) is then of a single reading in progress at the present
  moment.

The progressive futurate

There are certain cases where clauses with progressive form do not have the usual "in
progress" meaning. The most important involves the futurate construction (see §5.1):

[50]   a. *I see my broker today.*   b. *I'm seeing my broker today.*

In both clauses we are concerned with a future act of seeing someone. Version [ia]
is an ordinary futurate use of the present tense, and conveys that an appointment has
been set up or is regularly scheduled, whereas [ib] may suggest simply that I intend
to go and see my broker today.

8   Mood

Mood is a grammatical category associated with the semantic dimension of **modality**. Mood is to modality as tense is to time: tense and mood are categories of grammatical form, while time and modality are the associated categories
of meaning.

Modality deals mainly with two related contrasts: **factual** vs **non-factual**, and
asserted vs **non-asserted**. The meaning differences seen in [51i] and [51ii] are dif
ferences in modality.

[51]   NON-MODAL | MODAL
    i a. *She saw him.* | b. *She must have seen him.*   c. *She may have seen him.*
    ii a. *He leaves today.* | b. *He must leave today.*   c. *He can/may leave today.*

In [i] the [a] version presents her seeing him as a matter of fact, whereas in [b] it is
an inference and in [c] simply a possibility. In [ii] the [a] version has the force of an
assertion, whereas [b] can be used as a kind of directive, imposing an obligation,
and [c] can be used to give permission.

Modality can be expressed by a great variety of formal means. The possibility meaning of [51ic], for example, could also be expressed by means of an adverb (_Perhaps_ she saw him), an adjective (_It's possible_ that she saw him), a noun (_There's a possibility_ that she saw him), and so on. But for English at least the term 'mood' is restricted to grammatical systems associated with the verb.

In §8.1 we look at the kinds of meaning expressed by the modal auxiliaries. Then in §8.2 we take up the issue of the relation between modality and future time in the context of an examination of the auxiliary _will_. In §8.3 we look at the preterite forms of the modals. The final section, §8.4, deals with the use of _were_ in constructions like _I wish she were here_ – a relic of an earlier system of mood marked by inflection, rather than by auxiliaries.

8.1   Uses of the modal auxiliaries

There are three main families of meanings that the modal auxiliaries express: **epistemic**, **deontic** and **dynamic**. The first two, illustrated in [51i–ii] respectively, are the most central ones, and we will take these two together in order to bring out the important contrast between them. We will then conclude the section with a discussion of dynamic modality.

The epistemic vs deontic contrast

Epistemic modality expresses meanings relating primarily to what is necessary or possible given what we know (or believe): the term derives from the Greek word for "knowledge". **Deontic** modality expresses meanings relating primarily to what's required or permitted: this term derives from the Greek word for "obligation". The two kinds of meaning are illustrated in the following pairs:

[52]   EPISTEMIC   DEONTIC
    i a. _He must have overslept._   b. _He must apologise._
    ii a. _She may be ill._   b. _She may take as many as she needs._
    iii a. _The storm should be over soon._   b. _We should call the police._

- In the [a] examples the modals are interpreted **epistemically**: the varying degrees of non-factuality that they convey reflect limitations on the speaker's knowledge. In [ia], I may not know that he overslept, but I'm inferring that he did. In [ib], I don't know that she's ill, but I also don't know that she isn't, and am countenancing it as a possibility. In [ic], I don't know how long the storm will last, but the probability or expectation is that it will be over soon.
- The [b] examples are interpreted **deontically**: the meanings have to do with **obligation** or **permission** of various kinds. More specifically, the operative notion in [ib] is obligation, in [iib] permission, and in [iiib] a milder kind of obligation where it is a matter of what is the right thing to do. These notions all have to do with authority and judgement rather than knowledge and belief. Very often

declarative clauses with deontic meanings of modals are used to try and influence what happens rather than simply to make assertions.

The link between the two families of meanings is that the concepts of necessity and possibility – the key concepts in modal logic – apply to both. But with epistemic modality, necessity and possibility relate to whether or not something is the case, is true, whereas with deontic modality they relate to whether or not something happens, or is done. In [52i], for example, I'm saying in [a] that it is necessarily the case that he overslept, and in [b] that it is necessary for him to apologise: in neither do I countenance any other possibility.

Epistemic and deontic meanings are not in general associated with different expressions. Many examples are ambiguous, allowing either kind of interpretation for the modal:

[53]   *You __must__ be very tactful.*   [epistemic or deontic]

There is an epistemic interpretation of this under which it means I have evidence that leads me to believe you're very tactful. And there is also a deontic one that I might use to tell you there is an obligation or need for you to be very tactful (and perhaps thus to tell you to behave with tact).

Dynamic interpretations

Some of the modals have uses concerned with **properties** or **dispositions** of persons or other entities involved in the situation:

[54]   i   *She __can__ speak five languages.*
        ii *I've asked him to help us but he __won't__.*
        iii *I __daren't__ tell you any more.*

These are called **dynamic** interpretations, and are somewhat peripheral to the concept of modality. In [i], *can* is used to describe an ABILITY of hers; in [ii], the negative form of *will* talks about VOLITION (his unwillingness to help us); in [iii], *dare* says something about whether my COURAGE is sufficient for me to tell you any more. (*Dare* is unique among the modals in that it has ONLY a dynamic use.)

With *can* we find clear cases of ambiguity between a dynamic and either an epistemic or a deontic interpretation:

[55]   i   *You __can't__ be serious.*   [epistemic or dynamic]
        ii *She __can__ drive.*   [deontic or dynamic]

- The epistemic interpretation of [i] denies the possibility that you are being serious: it suggests a context where you have said something that I take to be absurd. The dynamic interpretation says something about your personality: you are incapable of being serious.
- In [ii] the deontic reading is that she has permission to drive, while the dynamic one attributes an ability to her – she knows how to drive.

> **Prescriptive grammar note**
>
> Some people insist that *can* is not to be used in a deontic sense – that permission should be expressed by *may* instead. There is absolutely no truth to this claim about *can*, which is used frequently in all of the three types of meaning we have distinguished, and has been for centuries. No evidence whatever supports the view that the deontic use is in some way incorrect.

8.2 Futurity, modality, and *will*

In this section we treat a special feature of the meaning of one modal, *will*. There are some languages that have a three-term tense system contrasting past, present and future. Contrary to what is traditionally assumed, English is not one of them: it has no future tense. It does have several ways of talking about future time, and the most basic one does involve the auxiliary *will*. Nonetheless, *will* belongs grammatically and semantically with the auxiliaries that mark mood rather than with the various markers of tense.

There is an intrinsic connection between future time and modality: we don't have the same kind of knowledge about the future as we do about the past and the present, so it isn't possible to be fully factual about future events or situations. It shouldn't be too surprising, then, that a modal auxiliary might be used for talking about the future.

The close association between *will* and modality may be illustrated with the following sets of contrasts:

[56] i a. *She beat him in under an hour.*   b. *She will beat him in under an hour.*
      ii a. *He likes you.*   b. *He will like you.*

[57] i a. *She left Paris yesterday.*   b. *She will have left Paris yesterday.*
      ii a. *That is the plumber.*   b. *That will be the plumber.*

[58]   a. *Australia meets Sweden in the*   b. *Australia will meet Sweden in the*
            Davis Cup final in December.   *Davis Cup final in December.*

- The examples in [56] illustrate the difference that is commonly found between statements about the past or present and those about the future: [ia] and [iia] will be construed as statements of fact, whereas [ib] and [iib] have more of the character of predictions.

- In [57], *will* is used in the [b] versions with situations located in past and present time, and the difference between them and the [a] versions is clearly one of modality, not time. The [a] versions are presented as statements of fact, the [b] ones as inferences.

- Both versions of [58] locate the situation in future time, so again the difference between them is one of modality, not time reference. The [a] version is more assured, and appropriate only in a context where the finalists have been determined; the [b] version could be used to make a prediction earlier in the competition (when it isn't clear who will survive until December without being knocked out of the tournament).

In all three cases, the version without a modal is more assured than the one that has *will*. The differences are related to the speaker's knowledge. The meanings contributed by *will* therefore belong in the **epistemic** family.[5]

8.3   The preterite forms of the modals

Four of the modal auxiliaries, **can**, **may**, **will** and **shall** have preterite forms – *could*, *might*, *would* and *should* respectively. It is quite clear that they are preterites, but it must also be stressed that they are highly exceptional in their behaviour. We'll look briefly at both the similarities and the differences between the preterites of the modals and other preterites.

(a) Similarities with ordinary preterites

Could and *would* can be used with past time meaning and in the subordinate part of a remote conditional, and all four preterites are found in backshift:

[59]   i   *I asked him to help me, but he <u>couldn't</u>/<u>wouldn't</u>.*   [past time]
       ii   *We'd save a lot of money if you <u>could</u>/<u>would</u> cycle to work.*   [remote conditional]
       iii *I thought I <u>could</u>/<u>would</u>/[%]<u>should</u>/<u>might</u> see her yesterday,*
            but I had to work late at the office.   [backshift]

Note that backshift is obligatory in the context of [iii], so that it would be ungrammatical to replace the preterite forms by present tense *can*/*will*/[%]*shall*/*may*.[6]

(b) Differences from other preterites

With other verbs the modal remoteness use of the preterite is restricted to a few subordinate constructions, but with the modals it occurs freely in main clauses, in examples like these:

[60]   i   *I <u>could</u>/<u>would</u>/[%]<u>should</u>/<u>might</u> do it if they offered to pay me.*
       ii   *You <u>could</u>/<u>might</u> have been killed!*
       iii *You <u>should</u> apologise.*
       iv   *<u>Could</u>/<u>Would</u> you help me move these boxes?*

* Example [i] is a remote conditional construction (the open counterpart being *I can*/*will*/[%]*shall*/*may do it if they offer to pay me*). Both the modal auxiliary and *offered* are modal preterites, but while any modal preterite can occur in the subordinate clause, only a modal auxiliary can occur in the main clause.

---

[5] With some predictions there isn't much doubt – e.g., when I say *She'll be two tomorrow* on the day before a child's birthday. But there's no grammatical distinction between cases like this and cases like the ones in [56]. In some varieties of English, especially BrE, **shall** is used with 1st person subjects as an alternant of **will** for future time situations, so we get [%]*I shall be glad when it's all over.* This use is epistemic. But the most common use of **shall** is in interrogative clauses like *Shall I pick you up at six?* This **shall** is deontic because I'm asking you to tell me what to do.

[6] Actually, some speakers do allow *may* here, which shows that for them the two forms have become separated – *might* is no longer the preterite form of **may** for these speakers, so it isn't substituted for *may* in backshifting.

- The salient interpretation of [ii] is that you have done something reckless, putting you at risk of being killed – but in fact you weren't killed.
- In [iii] you owe someone an apology: the right thing for you to do is to apologise. In Present-day English, this use of preterite *should* is not perceived as semantically related to present tense *shall*: neither BrE nor AmE speakers normally say %*You shall apologise*.
- In [iv], interrogative clauses are used as directives: I'm asking for your help (cf. Ch. 9, §4.4). The preterites here sound more polite and diffident than present tense *can* and *will*.

8.4   Irrealis *were*

English once had an inflectional mood system applying, like tense, to all verbs. Over the centuries this has been almost entirely lost. The meaning distinctions are now conveyed by tense. We noted earlier the difference in meaning contrasts between preterite and present in [61i] and [61ii]:

[61]   PRETERITE TENSE   PRESENT TENSE
   i a. *He loved her.*   b. *He loves her.*
   ii a. *If <u>he loved her</u> he'd change his job.*   b. *If <u>he loves her</u> he'll change his job.*

In [i] the contrast is straightforwardly one of time: [ia] refers to past time, [ib] to present time. In [ii], however, the contrast is one of modality: [iia] presents his loving her as a somewhat more remote possibility than [iib]. It is for this reason that we refer to *loved* in [iia] as a **modal preterite** – a use of the preterite where the meaning has to do with modality, not time.

Now consider what happens when the verb concerned is **be**, and the subject is 1st or 3rd person singular. One possibility is that we have a set of relationships just like those in [61]:

[62]   PRETERITE TENSE   PRESENT TENSE
   i a. *He was in love with her.*   b. *He is in love with her.*
   ii a. *If <u>he was in love with her</u> he'd go.*   b. *If <u>he is in love with her</u> he'll go.*

Was in [ia] has the central preterite meaning of past time; *was* in [iia] is a modal preterite.

It is also possible, however, to have the form *were* in place of *was* in [iia] but not [ia]. In this case the temporal and modal meanings are not different meanings of a single form: they are meanings of different forms. *Was* is a tense form, but this *were* is a mood form. We call it **irrealis**, indicating that it conveys varying degrees of remoteness from factuality:

[63]   IRREALIS MOOD   PRESENT TENSE
   a. *If <u>he were in love with her</u> he'd*   b. *If <u>he is in love with her</u> he'll*
     change his job.   *change his job.*

The difference between [63a] and [62iia] is one of style level: *were* is here somewhat more formal than *was*.

This use of *were* is highly exceptional: there is no other verb in the language where the modal remoteness meaning is expressed by a different inflectional form from the past time meaning. The irrealis mood form is unique to *be*, and limited to the 1st and 3rd person singular. It is an untidy relic of an earlier system, and some speakers usually, if not always, use preterite *was* instead.

Be is also unique in having three different present tense forms (instead of the usual two) and two different preterite forms (instead of one). This is by far the most irregular verb in the entire English vocabulary. Here is its full paradigm:

[64]   PRIMARY FORMS

	NEUTRAL			NEGATIVE		
	1st sg	3rd sg	Other	1st sg	3rd sg	Other
Present	*am*	*is*	*are*	*aren't*[7]	*isn't*	*aren't*
Preterite	*was*		*were*	*wasn't*		*weren't*
Irrealis	*were*		—	*weren't*		—

SECONDARY FORMS

PLAIN FORM	PAST PARTICIPLE	GERUND-PARTICIPLE
be	*been*	*being*

We include the irrealis forms among the primary forms, because there is a negative irrealis form, and also because of the close relation with preterite *was* and *wasn't*. This is why we distinguish the two major subsets of inflectional forms as 'primary' vs 'secondary' rather than by the more transparent (and more usual) terms 'tensed' and 'non-tensed'.[8]

---

[7] *Aren't* appears with 1st person singular subjects only in clauses where it precedes the subject: we get *Aren't I?*, but not **I aren't*. The form %*amn't* is restricted to certain regional British dialects, and '*ain't* is definitely (notoriously) non-standard, so there isn't a standard ·*n't* form of *be* for the 1st person singular present when the subject precedes. However, *I'm not* is available, using the reduced '*m* form of *am* with the separate word *not* instead of a negative form of *be*.

[8] The non-negative forms in [64] are labelled 'neutral' rather than 'positive' because they occur in both positive and negative clauses (e.g. *That is true* and *That is not true*). Traditional grammar calls our irrealis a 'past subjunctive', contrasting with 'present subjunctive' *be*. But there are no grounds for analysing this *were* as a past tense counterpart of the *be* that we find in constructions like *It's vital that he be kind to her*. We don't use 'subjunctive' as a term for an inflectional category, but for a syntactic construction employing the plain form of the verb (cf. §1.1).

Exercises

1. For some but not all of the following verb lexemes, the **preterite** and **past participle** forms have distinct shapes. Say for each whether the shapes are the same or different, and make up examples to show that you are right.

   i *burn*   vi *forget*
   ii *buy*   vii *hold*
   iii *draw*   viii *ride*
   iv *drink*   ix *run*
   v *fall*   x *sing*

2. The underlined verbs below are forms of lexemes whose **preterite** and **past participle** have the same shape. Use the substitution test to determine which form occurs in these instances, citing the evidence you use.

   i *I don't think they <u>found</u> anything suspicious.*
   ii *That's not the edition I <u>recommended</u>.*
   iii *She wasn't one of those <u>arrested</u>.*
   iv *Do you think we'll get <u>charged</u>?*
   v *Haven't you seen the mess they <u>made</u>?*
   vi *Get it <u>repaired</u> without delay.*
   vii *Who <u>said</u> it was mine?*
   viii *I don't want anyone <u>hurt</u>.*
   ix *I <u>met</u> him on a Monday.*
   x *I don't believe we've <u>met</u>.*

3. Determine whether the underlined verbs below are **plain forms** or **plain present** tense forms. Again, present the evidence on which you base your decision.

   i *The twins, he says, <u>seem</u> quite distraught.*
   ii *It would be best not to <u>say</u> anything about it.*
   iii *He thinks they didn't <u>like</u> him.*
   iv *They wouldn't help me <u>change</u> the tyre.*
   v *Let's <u>go</u> to the movies.*
   vi *We <u>have</u> written to the editor.*
   vii *They <u>appreciate</u> what you're doing for them.*
   viii *<u>Tell</u> me what you want.*
   ix *I doubt whether you really <u>know</u> her.*
   x *Do you <u>know</u> what time it is?*

4. The verb *beware* (as in *Beware of the dog*) is highly exceptional in its inflection. Construct example sentences containing the following kinds of clause with a form of *beware* as verb, marking the ones that turn out to be ungrammatical with *.

   i a clause with 3rd person singular subject and present tense verb;
   ii a clause with plural subject and present tense verb;
   iii an imperative clause;
   iv a subjunctive clause;
   v an infinitival clause;
   vi a gerund-participial clause;
   vii a past-participial clause.

   On the basis of your data give a paradigm for *beware*, leaving blank any position where the inflectional form is missing for this verb.

5. Classify the underlined clauses below as **finite** or **non-finite**.

   i *Everyone <u>arrested at the demonstration</u> has now been released.*
   ii *It is essential <u>that he complete the course</u>.*
   iii *I think <u>they may not have read the instructions</u>.*
   iv *<u>Having been through a similar experience myself,</u> I sympathise.*
   v *I'd advise you <u>not to take it too seriously</u>.*
   vi *<u>Hurry up,</u> or we'll be late.*

6. Change the following declarative clauses into **interrogatives**, write out the result, and say on this basis whether the underlined verbs are **auxiliaries** or **lexical** verbs.

   i *They <u>were</u> informed of the change.*
   ii *She <u>would</u> rather we met later.*
   iii *They <u>ought</u> to accept the offer.*
   iv *They <u>used</u> to live together.*
   v *We <u>have</u> to keep them informed.*
   vi *They <u>need</u> to replace the cartridge.*
   vii *I <u>should</u> inform the police.*
   viii *They <u>had</u> it repaired.*
   ix *You usually <u>help</u> clear up.*
   x *They <u>keep</u> telling her that.*

7. Use the two **negation** tests to determine the status of the underlined verbs as auxiliaries or lexical verbs. Cite the evidence on which you base your answer.

i *You must get involved.*
ii *It is going to rain.*
iii *They tend to disagree.*
iv *She would like to see them.*
v *I saw them leave.*
vi *He wants to tell her.*
vii *He might have told her.*
viii *I'm going to solve it.*
ix *They can sardines to preserve them.*
x *They can preserve sardines.*

8. In the uses illustrated in the following examples, the three underlined verbs bear some semantic and/or syntactic similarity to the modal auxiliaries, though syntactically they're not similar enough to modals to be included in the class.

i *You are to report for duty at 8 a.m.*
ii *We have to ask what's best for the child.*
iii *They don't like it.*

Take the three verbs in turn and determine which, if any, of the three **modal auxiliary properties** described in this chapter apply to them. Construct examples where necessary, and explain your reasoning.

9. Determine whether the underlined verb-forms in the following examples are instances of the auxiliary lexemes *have*, *need* and *dare* or instances of the corresponding lexical verbs.

i *They had better hurry or they'll miss it.*
ii *They had their house burgled.*
iii *They had to call the police.*
iv *I had the staff do a thorough search.*
v *I have an idea about that.*
vi *I doubt whether we needed to see it.*
vii *We need more time to finish the work.*
viii *I don't think you need have any worries.*
ix *Did anyone dare remind him of his promise?*
x *Not one of them dare voice any criticism.*

10. During a 1954 Senate committee hearing, US Army attorney Joseph Welch addressed to US Senator Joseph McCarthy a famous pair of rhetorical questions: *Have you no shame?* and *Have you no shred of decency?* What does the syntax of these interrogative clauses tell you about American English of that period?

11. Which of the following allow a **perfective** interpretation? Consider just the main clauses, ignoring any subordinate ones embedded within them.

i *I think it's a disgrace.*
ii *I suggest you give up the idea.*
iii *I now add a sprinkling of pepper.*
iv *I want to get out of here.*
v *I do my own shopping.*

12. We have seen in this chapter that subordinate clauses functioning as complement of *before*, *if* and *hope* can have a **future time** interpretation. For example, *if it rains* in *We'll postpone the match if it rains* doesn't mean "if it is raining now", it means "if rain falls at some future time". For each of the following five prepositions and five verbs, construct an example to show whether or not it permits a future time interpretation of a present tense in its complement.

PREPOSITIONS		VERBS	
i	*after*	vi	*bet*
ii	*although*	vii	*expect*
iii	*because*	viii	*realise*
iv	*unless*	ix	*regret*
v	*until*	x	*wish*

(You should avoid examples with a futurate interpretation like *I know that we leave for Berlin next Tuesday*. For these, subordination is irrelevant: the interpretation is the same as for the main clause *We leave for Berlin next Tuesday*. Thus futurate examples don't provide relevant evidence.)

13. Classify the following conditional constructions as **open** or **remote**. For the open ones, give their remote counterparts, and conversely for the remote ones give their open counterparts.

i *It won't matter if I'm a little late.*
ii *He could easily get a job if he wanted one.*
iii *It would be disastrous if they saw the files.*
iv *If you don't pay up they'll call the police.*
v *You can stay here if you're stuck.*

(Note that some open conditionals lack remote counterparts, and some remote conditionals lack open counterparts. Here we are considering only cases where the two constructions are in contrast.)

14. For each of the following statements, imagine that someone called Jill made that statement yesterday. Write reports of the speech events in question, in the form *Jill said that* . . . For each one give a **backshifted** report, and in those cases where backshift is optional give a non-backshifted report too. (For example, given *It's too late* you would supply *Jill said it was too late* and *Jill said it's too late*.)

  i *My father has a weak heart.*
  ii *Ed is arriving this evening.*
  iii *I have a terrible headache*
  iv *I'm moving to Florida this month.*
  v *Everyone thinks I'm overreacting.*

15. For the following examples, give counterparts in which the clause with the underlined verb has been put in the **perfect tense**.

  i *I hope to <u>finish</u> soon.*
  ii *You should <u>tell</u> her the truth.*
  iii *They <u>mislaid</u> the file.*
  iv *He admitted <u>being</u> an alcoholic.*
  v *She <u>is</u> very helpful.*

16. Describe, as carefully as you can, the difference in meaning or use between the [a] and [b] members of the following pairs.

  i a. *I've been in the army for two years.*
    b. *I was in the army for two years.*
  ii a. *Have you seen Jill?*
    b. *Did you see Jill?*
  iii a. *It was the best meal I've had all week.*
    b. *It was the best meal I had all that week.*
  iv a. *She has gone to Moscow.*
    b. *She went to Moscow.*
  v a. *I've got the milk.*
    b. *I got the milk.*

17. As in Exercise 13, classify the following conditionals as **open** or **remote**, and give the counterpart of the opposite category. These examples differ from the earlier ones in that they all involve the perfect construction.

  i *If she hadn't sold her shares she would be very rich.*

  ii *If the secretary hadn't called the police someone else would have.*
  iii *If Ed has gone on holiday you can stay in his room.*
  iv *If Jill didn't report the fault, Max may have.*
  v *If you had finished your work yesterday, you could come with us tomorrow.*

18. Give **progressive aspect** counterparts to the following examples.

  i *She lived in Berlin.*
  ii *He may regret his impulsiveness.*
  iii *They neglect their children.*
  iv *I have read the newspaper.*
  v *He didn't pay any attention.*

19. Discuss the difference in meaning or use between the [a] and [b] members of the following pairs.

  i a. *I cycle to work.*
    b. *I'm cycling to work.*
  ii a. *When Tom called she phoned me.*
    b. *When Tom called she was phoning me.*
  iii a. *The train arrived.*
    b. *The train was arriving.*
  iv a. *You annoy me.*
    b. *You're annoying me.*
  v a. *He wrote an editorial.*
    b. *He was writing an editorial.*

20. Discuss the interpretation of the following examples with respect to the distinction between **epistemic**, **deontic**, and **dynamic** modality, bearing in mind that some of them are ambiguous.

  i *You needn't bother to answer.*
  ii *It must surely rain soon.*
  iii *They should be in Paris by now.*
  iv *She can't live with her parents.*
  v *It may easily be shown that this is false.*
  vi *These animals can be dangerous.*
  vii *It needn't have been Jill that wrote the note.*
  viii *Bill is one of those people who must always have the last word.*
  ix *There could be some other reason.*
  x *Could I have another beer, please?*

4 Clause structure, complements and adjuncts

In this chapter we investigate the structure of **canonical clauses**, the syntactically most elementary type of clause. Various kinds of non-canonical clause will be introduced from time to time, but solely for the purpose of illuminating the structure of canonical clauses. Very often the best evidence for analysing one construction is provided by a comparison between it and a different but related construction.

Canonical clauses have the potential to stand alone as sentences, and we therefore follow the standard convention of citing examples with the punctuation of sentences, i.e. with an initial capital letter and final full stop.

1   Introduction

Every canonical clause has a **head** element with the form of a **verb phrase** (**VP**). Every VP in turn has as its head a **verb** (**V**). Thus a canonical clause always contains a V which is the head of a VP which is the head of the clause. The verb is the most important element in determining what the rest of the clause is like. From now on we'll refer to the verb as the **head word** of the clause.

Predicates and predicators

The term 'head' was not introduced into grammatical theory until the latter half of the twentieth century, and in talking about clause structure we will generally use the traditional, long-established terminology where the two major elements in the clause are called **subject** and **predicate**. In *Cats like water*, the NP *cats* is subject and the VP *like water* is predicate. The idea is that in elementary examples like this the predicate represents what is 'predicated of' – i.e. said about – the referent of the subject. 'Predicate', therefore, is a more specific term than 'head' when the construction concerned is a clause. Similarly, **predicator** is used for the head of the VP, i.e. for the verb *like* in this example.

Diagramming clause structure

The structure of a clause like *Cats like water* can be represented in diagram form as shown in [1].

[1]

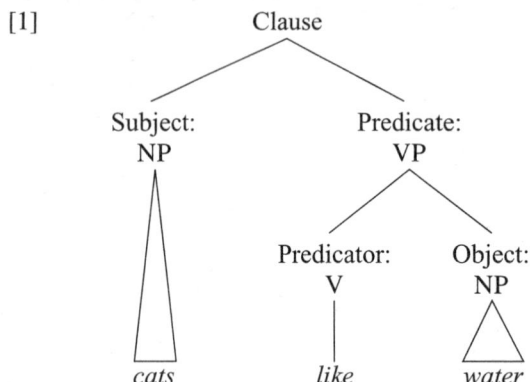

This diagram expresses in graphic form information about the function and category of the various units or **constituents** (i.e. words, phrases, clauses, etc.):

- *cats like water* belongs to the category 'clause';
- the clause is divided into two constituents functioning as subject and predicate;
- the subject precedes the predicate;
- the subject takes the form of a noun phrase (NP), and the predicate is a VP;
- the VP contains a predicator and an object;
- the predicator precedes the object;
- the predicator is a **v** and the object is an NP.

No function is assigned to the clause itself because it is not part of any larger construction; the other units, however, are given two labels: the first indicates their function in the construction containing them, the second gives their category.

The diagram omits, deliberately, some information that is irrelevant here: it does not show anything about the internal structure of the two NPs. The parts of the diagram under the NP labels are just shown as triangles, which indicates that the details of the internal structure (like what is the head of the NP) have been left out to simplify things since it is not the focus of interest and we have not yet covered the structure of NPs (that is done in Ch. 5). In this chapter we are interested merely in how phrases combine to make clauses.

Predicators select key content of clauses

What can occur in a clause is very largely determined by the predicator. For example, it is a crucial property of the verb *like* that it permits occurrence of an object (indeed, it normally requires one in canonical clauses).

A large percentage of the verbs in English allow or require an object. Some do not: examples include *elapse*, *fall*, *lie*, *mew*, *vanish*, etc. Thus *Cats mew water* is not a grammatical clause, though *Cats mew* is.

Some verbs allow or require not only an object but also some other phrase. For example, *give* allows an object and a preposition phrase (PP) with the preposition *to* as head, so we have clauses like *Lucy gave the key to the landlord*, where the NP *the key* is an object and the PP *to the landlord* is also included in the VP. We show the structure of that clause in [2], again without bothering to show details of the internal structure of the NPs or the PP.

[2]

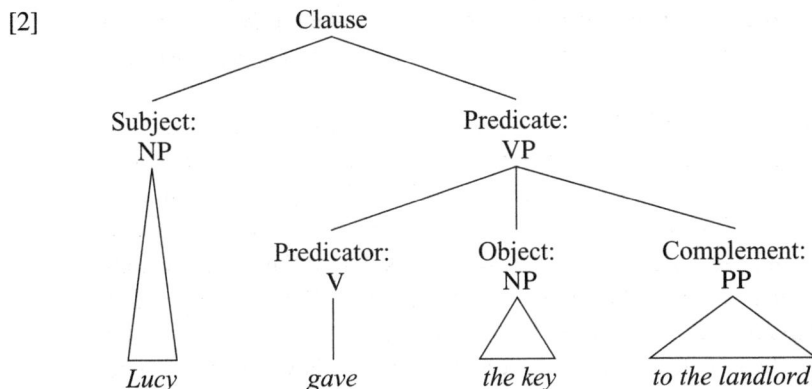

The important point to note is that in order to tell whether some object or complement is allowed in a clause, you have to know what specific verb is serving as the predicator of the clause.

Complements and adjuncts

The dependents of the predicator in the VP are of two main kinds: **complements** and **adjuncts**. The admissibility of a complement depends on the predicator belonging to a particular subclass of verbs. The term we use for this is **licensing**: complements have to be licensed by their head.

The object is one kind of complement, and we can illustrate the concept of licensing by considering the occurrence of an object with the three verbs shown in [3]:

[3] i a. *Sue <u>used</u> the cheese.*   b. **Sue <u>used</u>.*   [object obligatory]
     ii a. *Sue <u>ate</u> the cheese.*   b. *Sue <u>ate</u>.*   [object optional]
    iii a. **Sue <u>disappeared</u> the cheese.*   b. *Sue <u>disappeared</u>.*   [object excluded]

An object such as *the cheese* is admissible with, hence licensed by, the verbs *use* and *eat*, but not *disappear*: [iiia] is ungrammatical, as is any other clause with *disappear* as head and an object as dependent. There is a further difference between *use* and *eat*. With *eat* the object is optional whereas with *use* it is obligatory: [iib] is grammatical, but [ib] is not. The status of a dependent as a complement is most obvious when it is obligatory for at least some heads. But this is not essential: the crucial feature of licensing is that the admissibility of the element depends on the presence of an appropriate head.

The occurrence of adjuncts is not restricted in this way. They occur more freely, essentially without regard to what the predicator is.

The examples in [4] illustrate the difference between complements (marked by double underlining) and adjuncts (single underlining).

[4]   i   *The box was <u><u>useless</u></u> <u>because it had a hole in it</u>.*
       ii *I saw <u><u>your father</u></u> <u>this morning</u>.*
       iii *They <u>still</u> think <u><u>they were right</u></u>.*

- In [i], *useless* (an **adjective phrase**, or **AdjP**) is a complement, since it has to be licensed by the predicator. Again this can be shown by replacing **be** with a verb such as **leak**, which gives us the ungrammatical **The box leaked useless because it had a hole in it*.
- On the other hand, *because it had a hole in it* is an adjunct in [i]. We cannot find two different subclasses of verb that differ in whether they accept a *because* phrase as dependent. *The box leaked because it had a hole in it*, for example, is just as grammatical as [4i]. It doesn't make sense, of course, to say #*She spoke excellent French because it had a hole in it*, but that is due to the semantic content of this particular *because* phrase. *She spoke excellent French because she had spent a year in Paris as a student* is clearly impeccable. Licensing is a matter of grammar, and when we test by making replacements we have to be prepared to make adjustments of this kind to the semantic content. There are no verbs that exclude *because* phrases in general.
- In [ii], *your father* is a complement licensed by **see**. If **see** were replaced by **fall**, say, we would have an ungrammatical sentence. *This morning* in [ii], by contrast, is an adjunct; a temporal NP of this kind is compatible with any verb.
- In [iii], *still* is an adjunct, again because it is compatible with any verb. But the subordinate clause *they were right* is a complement, licensed by **think**. Again it is easy to find verbs like **alter** or **lose** or **work** that are incompatible with a subordinate clause of this kind, whatever its particular semantic content.

The subject as a kind of complement

We have shown that the object is a kind of complement since it satisfies the licensing requirement. The subject is rather different: all canonical clauses contain a subject, so in a sense subjects are compatible with any verb. However, certain syntactic kinds of subject are restricted to occurrence with particular kinds of verb, so the concept of licensing applies here too. Take, for example, the subject of [5i]:

[5]   i   *<u>Whether we will finish on time</u> depends primarily on the weather.*
       ii **<u>Whether we will finish on time</u> ruined the afternoon.*

The underlined expression in [5i] is a subordinate clause functioning as subject of the larger clause that forms the whole sentence. It is, more specifically, a subordinate interrogative clause: the main clause counterpart is *Will we finish on time?* A subject of this syntactic form has to be licensed by the verb (or VP). It is admissible with **depend**, but there are innumerable other verbs such as **ruin**, **see**, **think**, **yearn**, etc., that do not accept subjects of this form; so [5ii], for example, is ungrammatical.

Subjects do satisfy the condition for being complements, therefore. But they are different from other types of complement in an obvious way: they are positioned outside the VP. We will refer to the subject as an **external** complement. The other complements that are internal to the VP will be referred to as **internal** complements.

2   The subject

2.1   Distinctive syntactic properties of the subject in English

It is typical for the subject of a clause to be an NP. The only other form of subject common enough to merit mention here is a subordinate clause, as illustrated in [5i].

The subject is sharply distinguished from other elements in clause structure by the combination of a number of syntactic properties. The following survey covers four particularly important ones.

(a) Basic position before the verb

The basic position of the subject – the position it occupies in canonical clauses – is before the V (and the whole VP). This is the most obvious feature that distinguishes the subject from the object in English:

[6]   a. *Sue loved Max.*   b. *Max loved Sue.*

Only the conventional English order of elements tells us that *Sue* is subject in [a], while *Max* is subject in [b] – and thus that in [a] we are talking about Sue's feelings, and in [b] we are talking about Max's. There are non-canonical constructions where the subject does not occur in this position but, overall, location before the verb is the major overt property that picks out the subject.

(b) Case

For just a handful of NPs, there is an inflectional distinction of **case** that separates subjects from most non-subjects. The NPs concerned are mainly those consisting of the pronouns listed in [7].

[7]						
	i	NOMINATIVE	*I*	*he*	*she*	*we*	*they*
	ii	ACCUSATIVE	*me*	*him*	*her*	*us*	*them*

As subjects of finite clauses, these pronouns have to appear in the **nominative** case-form, while in object function they appear in the **accusative** case-form:

[8]   a. *She loved him.*   b. *He loved her.*

She and *he* are marked as subjects by having nominative form, while accusative *him* and *her* are objects.

With NPs that don't themselves have a contrast between nominative and accusative forms, we can generally use the case property indirectly by asking which form is required when we substitute one of the pronouns in [7]. In *The dogs barked at the visitors*, for example, *the dogs* could be replaced by nominative *they* and *the visitors* by accusative *them*. This shows that the subject is *the dogs*, not *the visitors*.

▨ (c) Verb agreement

As explained in Ch. 3, §1.1, all verbs other than the modal auxiliaries agree with the subject in the present tense, while *be* also shows agreement in the preterite:

[9]   i a. *Sue <u>loves</u> the children.*   b. *<u>The children</u> <u>love</u> Sue.*
       ii a. *Sue <u>was</u> fond of the children.*   b. *<u>The children</u> <u>were</u> fond of Sue.*

This property of determining the form of the verb is another key property of the subject. The inflectional form of the doubly underlined verbs shows that *Sue* (3rd person singular) is subject of the [a] examples, while *the children* (3rd person plural) is subject of the [b] ones.

In clauses where the verb does not show agreement, we can again use the test indirectly by changing to a construction where the verb does agree. *Kim must sign both forms*, for example, where the modal auxiliary *must* is invariable, can be changed to *Kim has signed both forms*, where *has* agrees with the subject *Kim*.

▨ (d) Subject–auxiliary inversion

In a number of constructions, including most kinds of **interrogatives**, the subject appears after rather than before the verb, which has to be an auxiliary. This enables us to confirm that *Sue* is subject of the [a] examples in [9], and *the children* is subject of the [b] ones. We just compare these clauses with their interrogative counterparts:

[10]   i a. *Does <u>Sue</u> love the children?*   b. *Do <u>the children</u> love Sue?*
        ii a. *Was <u>Sue</u> fond of the children?*   b. *Were <u>the children</u> fond of Sue?*

In [ii] we have simply inverted the subject and the auxiliary verb *be*, whereas in [i], where the declarative contains no auxiliary verb, we have inserted *do* and this is inverted with the subject (see Ch. 3, §3.1). In either case, the subject ends up in the distinctive post-auxiliary position.

2.2   Traditional errors in defining the subject

There are two semantic observations that can be made about subjects. They are sound enough in themselves, but they have been used as the basis for definitions of the subject that suffer from the shortcomings we discussed in Ch. 1, §3. The two observations are these:

* In canonical clauses that describe an action, the subject of the clause normally corresponds semantically to the **performer** of the action. For example, when we say *Oswald assassinated Kennedy*, the subject is *Oswald*, and the person it refers to (Lee Harvey Oswald) is the actor, the alleged performer of the assassination.

- The subject NP commonly (but by no means invariably) identifies a **topic** for the clause, i.e. what the clause is primarily about, and the predicate makes some sort of **comment** about that topic. For example, *Paris is lovely in the spring* has *Paris* as the subject, and it is likely to be interpreted as saying something about Paris; *Spring is a great time to visit Paris* has *spring* as the subject, and it is likely to be interpreted as saying something about spring.

Many definitions of the subject given in grammars and dictionaries represent a massive overgeneralisation of the first point: the subject is simply defined as the performer of the action expressed in the verb. Less commonly, it is defined as the topic of the sentence, the part that identifies what the sentence is about – a similarly massive overgeneralisation of the second point. There is something in both of these that is relevant to a definition of the subject at the general level: many languages have a function in the clause that is often associated with the semantic role of actor or with the topic and that shows other signs of primary syntactic importance in the clause (though some languages seem to be organised rather differently). But the correlation in English between subject and actor or topic is far too complex for the above definitions to work at the **language-particular** level. Let us examine the two definitions in turn.

(a) Subject and actor

The old-fashioned definition of the subject as the performer of the action expressed in the verb works well enough with a sentence like *We wandered down the street*; but it fails completely with examples like those in [11]:

[11]   i   *She knows him well.*
    ii   *Ernie suffered a heart attack.*
    iii   *My mother was attacked by the neighbour's dog.*

- *She* is the subject of [i], but knowing isn't an action. Notice that [i] can't be used in answer to a ***do*** question (such as *What does she do?*), so nothing in [i] talks about anyone performing an action. If we took the old-fashioned definition seriously we would have to say that there is no subject here. But *she* has all four of the syntactic properties that are the relevant ones for English: it's before the verb, it's in nominative case, the verb agrees with it, and it follows the auxiliary in the corresponding interrogative (*Does she know him well?*).
- In [ii] we do have a description of an event (rather than a state, as in [i]), but that still doesn't mean there is a performer of an action. Suffering isn't an action that Ernie performed on the heart attack. Again, then, the referent of the syntactic subject doesn't have the semantic role of actor.
- Example [iii] does describe an action, but it's a passive clause (the corresponding active clause would be *The neighbour's dog attacked my mother*), and the actor role is associated not with the subject, *my mother*, but with the complement of the preposition *by*, namely the NP *the neighbour's dog*.

So the subject of an English clause certainly cannot be identified on the basis of semantic role: it can be associated with a range of roles, depending on the kind of situation described and whether the clause is active or passive.

▒ (b) Subject and topic

In *Paris is lovely in the spring* it is natural to take the subject as expressing the topic, and in *Spring is a great time to visit Paris* we would be inclined to say that *spring* is the topic; but it is easy to find examples where it would be completely implausible to take the subject to be a topic:

[12]   i *Something is wrong with this disk drive.*
    ii *In space, <u>nobody</u> can hear you scream.*[1]
    iii *<u>It</u>'s time these kids were in bed.*

- In [i], the subject NP is *something*, but it would be nonsensical to suggest that *something* tells us what the topic is. The topic is obviously the disk drive, and the comment is that it has a fault.
- In [ii], the topic is obviously not expressed by the subject *nobody*. The clause is about what it's like in the airless void of space, and if any phrase identifies that topic it's the preposed adjunct *in space*.
- And in [iii], the subject *it* is a dummy pronoun with no identifiable meaning. It can't possibly pick out a topic. In fact this kind of main clause isn't properly described in terms of a distinction between a topic and a comment at all. Not all clauses have topic phrases.

English does not indicate the topic of a clause by any grammatical marker (though some languages do), and it certainly does not always make topics subjects. There is very often no clear-cut single answer to the question of what the topic of a clause is: it will depend very much on the context.

In English, then, there is nothing like a one-to-one relation either between subject and actor or between subject and topic. The lesson is that, at the language-particular level, we cannot define the syntactic term 'subject' in terms of the partially correlated semantic concepts 'performer of the action' or 'topic of the clause'.

3   The object

3.1   Distinctive syntactic properties of the object in English

The object in a clause almost always has the form of an NP. Unlike the subject, it is normally located within the VP, and is not so sharply distinguished from other dependents as is the subject. Nevertheless, there are a number of syntactic properties that make it fairly easy to identify in all but a small minority of cases. We summarise them in [13]:

[13]   i An object is a special case of a complement, so it must be **licensed** by the verb.
    ii With some verbs, the object is **obligatory**.

---

[1] This may look familiar: it's a famous film slogan, from the posters for *Alien* (1979).

iii The object typically corresponds to the subject of an associated PASSIVE clause.

iv The object can normally take the form of a PRONOUN (which must be in accusative if it is one of those listed in [7]).

v The basic object position is IMMEDIATELY AFTER THE VERB.

Consider how these properties distinguish the object NP in [14a] from the adjunct NP in [b]:

[14]

	OBJECT				ADJUNCT	

a. | Ed | told | *the manager.* | b. | Ed | arrived | *last week.* |

- The object *the manager* is licensed by the verb **tell**: it could not occur with a verb like **arrive** (*Ed arrived the manager* is ungrammatical). But every verb is compatible with the adjunct *last week*.
- With **tell** it is possible to omit the object (*Ed won't tell* is grammatical), but some verbs have to have an object when they occur in a canonical clause: attempting to use verbs like **accost**, **delineate**, **entail** or **force** without an object always yields ungrammatical results. But no verb requires that an adjunct like *last week* be present in the clause.
- Example [14a] has an associated passive clause with *the manager* as subject: *The manager was told* (*by Ed*). This is not possible for [b]: **Last week was arrived* (*by Ed*).
- *The manager* in [a] can be replaced by an appropriate pronoun: e.g. *Ed told her*. No such replacement is possible for *last week* in [b]: **Ed arrived it* is quite impossible.
- In [a] we cannot in general insert elements between the verb and its object: compare **Ed told unexpectedly the manager*. (Instead we have *Ed unexpectedly told the manager* or *Ed told the manager unexpectedly*.) There is no such restriction in [b]: *Ed arrived unexpectedly last week*.

3.2   Direct and indirect objects

There are two subtypes of object: **direct** and **indirect** objects. We represent them as O^d and O^i when labelling examples. The two kinds may occur together, and when they co-occur in canonical clauses, the indirect object precedes the direct object:

[15]

	S	P	O^i	O^d			S	P	O^i	O^d

a. | Sue | gave | Max | *the photo.* | b. | I | bought | them | *some shoes.* |

The traditional labels 'direct' and 'indirect' are based on the idea that in clauses describing an action the referent of the direct object is apparently more directly involved in being acted on in the situation than the referent of the indirect object. In [a], for example, it is the photo that actually changes hands and becomes one of

Max's possessions. And in [b] it is the shoes that are directly acted on by being pur-
chased and taken away.

The indirect object is characteristically associated with the semantic role of recipient, as in these examples. But it may have the role of beneficiary (the one for whom
something is done), as in *Do me a favour* or *Call me a taxi*, and it may be interpreted
in other ways, as seen from examples like *This blunder cost us the match*, or *I envy
you your good fortune*.

Alternation with prepositional construction

Most (but not all) verbs that license two objects also admit a different construction
where there is a direct object and a PP complement (C) headed by *to* or *for*.
Compare [15] with [16]:

[16]

	S	P	O^d	C			S	P	O^d	C
a.	*Sue*	*gave*	*the photo*	*to Max.*	b.		*We*	*bought*	*shoes*	*for them.*

Although the meanings are the same as in [15], the syntactic structure is different.
The PPs *to Max* and *for them* are complements (they are licensed by **give** and **buy**,
respectively), but they are not objects: they don't have properties [13iii–v]. And
since they are not objects, they can't be indirect objects.[2]

Syntactic distinction between direct and indirect object

The main syntactic property distinguishing the two kinds of object is position: when
both occur within the VP – as in canonical clauses – the indirect object precedes the
direct object. Compare [15] above with the ungrammatical orders **Sue gave the
photos Max* and **I bought some shoes them*.

In addition, the direct object readily undergoes fronting in various non-canonical
constructions, whereas the indirect object is quite resistant to it. Judgements about
the acceptability of clauses with fronted indirect objects vary considerably, depending in part on the construction, in part on the verb – and in part on the speaker making the judgement. But there is no doubt that in general the acceptability of fronted
indirect objects is significantly lower than that of direct objects. In [17] we illustrate
with four non-canonical constructions:

[17]   FRONTED DIRECT OBJECT   FRONTED INDIRECT OBJECT
  i a. *Everything else, she gave him.*   b. %*Him, she gave everything else.*
  ii a. *What did she buy him?*   b. **Who did she buy these shoes?*
  iii a. *He kept the gifts [which she*   b. %*They interviewed everyone [whom*
          had given him].   *she had given gifts].*
  iv a. *What a lot of work he gave them!*   b. **What a lot of them he gave work!*

---

[2] Nevertheless, traditional grammars analyse *to Max* and *for them* (or just *Max* and *them*) in [16] as
indirect objects. The similarity between between these elements and the corresponding ones in [15],
however, is purely semantic: there is no justification for equating them in terms of syntactic function.

- In [i] we have **preposing** of a complement: the canonical version is *She gave him everything else*. The [a] version is completely acceptable, the [b] version rare and marginal, at least for many speakers.
- In [ii] we have a type of interrogative clause differing from those considered so far in that it begins with an interrogative word. In [a] *what* is direct object (cf. *She bought him some shoes*), and in [b] *who* is indirect object (cf. *She bought Tom these shoes*). The difference in acceptability in this pair is very sharp.
- The bracketed clauses in [iii] are relative clauses. *Which* is direct object (cf. *She had given him the gifts*), while *whom* is indirect object (cf. *She had given everyone gifts*). Construction [b] is not so bad here, but still considerably less common and natural than [a].
- In [iv] we have a type of construction not encountered so far. They are **exclamative** clauses, with a fronted exclamative phrase. Again the fronted phrase in [a] is direct object (cf. *He gave them a lot of work*) and indirect object in [b] (cf. *He gave a lot of them work*). This construction is one where the fronted indirect object seems particularly bad.

4   Predicative complements

The next kind of dependent of the verb we consider is the **predicative complement** (PC in labels of example displays). A predicative complement commonly has the form of an NP, and in that case it contrasts directly with an object (O). Look at these [a] and [b] pairs:

[18]

		PC				O	
i a.	*Stacy*	*was*	*a good speaker.*	b.	*Stacy*	*found*	*a good speaker.*
ii a.	*Lee*	*became*	*a friend of mine.*	b.	*Lee*	*insulted*	*a friend of mine.*

There is a sharp semantic distinction in elementary examples of this kind. The object NPs refer to PARTICIPANTS in the situation: in each of [ib] and [iib] there are two people involved. The predicative NPs, however, do not refer to participants like this. There is only a single person involved in the [a] examples, the one referred to by the subject NP. The predicative complement NP denotes a PROPERTY that is ascribed to this person.

PCs are most clearly illustrated by examples like [18ia]. The verb *be* here has basically no semantic content. It is quite common in other languages for the verb to be completely missing in this kind of construction. The most important thing that *be* does in this example is to carry the preterite tense inflection that indicates reference to past time. The meaning of the clause is really just that Stacy spoke in an entertaining manner. So although *a good speaker* is syntactically an NP complement, it is semantically comparable to a predicate like *spoke well*. This is the basis for the term 'predicative complement': the complement typically represents what is predicated of the subject-referent in a way that is similar to that in which a whole predicate does.

A few verbs can take either a PC or an O, but with obvious differences in meaning:

[19]

	PC				O		
i a.	*This*	*proved*	*a great asset.*	b.	*This*	*proved*	*my point.*
ii a.	*He*	*sounded*	*a decent guy.*	b.	*He*	*sounded*	*the gong.*

Again, the objects denote participants but the predicative complements don't. This is perhaps made clearer by examples contrasting a reference to one person with a reference to two:

[20]   i *Honestly, I felt a fool standing there alone on the platform.*   [*a fool* = PC]
       ii *Suddenly, I felt a fool pushing in front of me on the platform.*   [*a fool* = O^d]

The obvious meaning of [i] involves just me, feeling foolish alone on the platform; but [ii] refers to two people: me, and the fool I could feel pushing in front of me on the platform.

4.1   Syntactic differences between predicative complements and objects

The two functions PC and O are distinguished syntactically in a number of ways. Our survey covers four of them.

(a) PC can have the form of AdjP

Both O and PC can have the form of an ordinary NP, but only PC can also have the form of an **adjective phrase** (AdjP):

[21]

	PC				O		
i a.	*He*	*seemed*	*a very nice guy.*	b.	*He*	*met*	*a very nice guy.*
ii a.	*He*	*seemed*	*very nice.*	b.	**He*	*met*	*very nice.*

- With **seem**, *a very nice guy* is PC and hence can be replaced by the AdjP *very nice*.
- With **meet**, no such replacement is possible because *a very nice guy* is object.

(b) PC can have the form of a bare role NP

A bare role NP is a singular NP that is 'bare' in the sense of lacking the determiner which would elsewhere be required, and that denotes some kind of role, office, or position. A PC can have the form of a bare role NP, but an O can't:

[22]

	PC					O		
i a.	*She*	*became*	*the treasurer.*	b.		*She*	*knew*	*the treasurer.*
ii a.	*She*	*became*	*treasurer.*	b.	**She*	*knew*	*treasurer.*

- In [i] both the [a] and [b] examples are fine because an ordinary NP like *the treasurer* can be either a PC or an O.
- In [ii], *treasurer* is a bare role NP, so it is permitted with **become**, which takes a PC, but not with **know**, which takes an object.

(c) PC does not correspond to the subject of a passive clause

We noted earlier that a typical object in an active clause corresponds to the subject of the passive clause that has the same meaning. A PC shows no such relationship:

[23] ACTIVE   PASSIVE
    i a. *Ed insulted a friend of mine.* b. *A friend of mine was insulted by Ed.*
    ii a. *Ed became a friend of mine.* b. **A friend of mine was become by Ed.*

- In [ia] *a friend of mine* is a direct object, and accordingly can be subject in a passive clause with the same meaning, [ib].
- But in [iia], *a friend of mine* is a PC, and so there is no corresponding passive, as evident from the ungrammaticality of [iib].

(d) PC can have the form of a nominative pronoun

There is a rather formal style of English in which the pronouns listed in [7] can appear in the nominative case when functioning as PC, while objects allow only accusative case:

[24]   PC   O

a.	*It*	*was*	*he*	*who said it.*	b.	*They*	*accused*	*him*	*of lying.*

The point here is not that nominative case is **required** on pronouns in PC function. Some older prescriptive grammars say that, but it is not true. A question like *Who's there?* is normally answered *It's me*; it sounds very stiff and formal to say *It is I*. Many speakers of Standard English would say *It was him who said it* rather than [24a]. So NPs in PC function can be accusative pronouns. What separates PC from O, however, is that no matter whether you use nominative or accusative case on PC pronouns, nominative case is absolutely impossible for O pronouns. No native speaker, even in the most formal style, says **They accused I of saying it*, or **Please let I in*.[3]

---

[3] We are concerned here with clauses where the pronoun constitutes the whole of the object: when there is coordination within the object some speakers do have nominatives, as in *%They invited Kim and I to lunch* (see Ch. 5, §8.3).

This provides further evidence that English grammar distinguishes the PC and O functions – though it is not as generally applicable a test as the other three, because *be* is really the only verb that accepts these pronouns as predicative complement.

4.2   Subjective and objective predicative complements

In the examples given so far the predicative complement relates to the subject. Most predicative complements are of this kind, but there is also a second kind in which they relate to the object:

[25]   SUBJECT + SUBJECTIVE PC   OBJECT + OBJECTIVE PC
     a. *Max seems highly untrustworthy.*   b. *I consider Jim highly untrustworthy.*

In [a] the PC relates to the subject, *Max*: the property of being highly untrustworthy is ascribed to Max. In [b] the same property is ascribed to Jim, but in this case *Jim* is a direct object.

The element to which a PC relates is called its **predicand**. Where the predicand is subject, the PC is said to be **subjective**, or to have **subject orientation**. Where the predicand is object, the PC is said to be **objective**, or to have **object orientation**.

4.3   Ascriptive and specifying uses of the verb *be*

There is an important distinction to be made between two uses of the verb *be*, as illustrated in [26]:

[26]   ASCRIPTIVE   SPECIFYING
     i a. *Mike was a loyal party member.*   b. *The last person to leave was Jane.*
    ii a. *What they gave me was useless.*   b. *What they gave me was a gold pen.*

- In the **ascriptive** construction the predicative complement denotes a property that is **ascribed** to the referent of the predicand. In [ia] *a loyal party member* denotes a property that Mike is claimed to have had – it doesn't specify who Mike was, it only ascribes party membership and loyalty to him. And in [iia], *useless* denotes a property that I claim is possessed by their gift to me – but it doesn't specify what the gift was.
- In the **specifying** construction there is a relation of **identity** between the two elements. In [ib] *Jane* specifies the identity of the last person to leave, and similarly in [iib] *a gold pen* implicitly answers the question *What did they give you?*

Ambiguities

There may be ambiguity between ascriptive and specifying uses of *be*. Example [27] has this kind of ambiguity:

[27]   *I thought he was a friend of mine.*

One salient context for this is where I am reporting a mistake I made. But it could be a mistake about either the PROPERTIES he has or his IDENTITY.

- In the first case, *a friend of mine* is ascriptive. I might be talking about someone I had thought of as a friend but who let me down. The mistake was in believing he had the properties one expects of a friend.
- In the second case, *a friend of mine* is specifying. Here I might be talking about someone who looked like my old friend Bob, so I gave him a big hug, and then realised that I was hugging a total stranger. The mistake in this case was believing him to be Bob.

Predicative complements with verbs other than *be* are ascriptive

With verbs other than *be*, predicative complements are almost always ascriptive. Notice, for example, that such verbs as *seem* and *become* could replace *be* in the [a] examples of [26], but not in the [b] ones (e.g., *Mike seemed a loyal party member* is fine, but **The last person to leave seemed Jane* is not). And when we said in the discussion of [18] that predicative complements do not refer to people or other kinds of participant in a situation, we were considering only the ascriptive use: predicative complements of the specifying type can be referential, as *Jane* in [26ib] clearly is.

Syntactic differences

The semantic difference illustrated in [26] is reflected in the syntax in various ways. The most important concerns the effect of reversing the order of the expressions in subject and predicative complement position. Compare:

[28]   ASCRIPTIVE   SPECIFYING
     i a. *The next point is more serious.*   b. *The one they arrested was Max.*
     ii a. *More serious is the next point.*   b. *Max was the one they arrested.*

- When we reverse the order in the specifying construction we change the functions. Thus while *Max* is predicative complement in [ib], that is not true in [iib]: there *Max* is subject. This can be demonstrated by applying the interrogative test for subjects: the interrogative of [iib] is *Was Max the one they arrested?*, with *Max* in the distinctive subject position following the auxiliary.
- With the ascriptive construction it is often not possible to reverse the two elements, but when reversal is acceptable the effect is merely to reorder them, not to change their functions. Thus *more serious* is predicative complement in non-canonical [iia] just as it is in [ia]. Note, for example, that we cannot invert it with the auxiliary verb to form an interrogative (cf. **Is more serious the next point?*).

5   Five canonical clause structures

As we have seen, all canonical clauses contain a subject and a predicator, but the presence of complements of different sorts (objects and predicative complements, for example) depends on the choice of verb. We can now distinguish five

major structures for canonical clauses on the basis of which internal complements
are present:

[29]   NAME   STRUCTURE   EXAMPLE
     i   ORDINARY INTRANSITIVE   S–P   *We hesitated.*
    ii   COMPLEX-INTRANSITIVE   S–P–PC   *We felt happy.*
   iii   ORDINARY MONOTRANSITIVE   S–P–O^d *We sold our house.*
    iv   COMPLEX-TRANSITIVE   S–P–O^d–PC   *We made them happy.*
     v   DITRANSITIVE   S–P–O^i–O^d *We gave them some food.*

There are two partially independent dimensions of contrast involved here: whether
there are objects (and, if so, how many), and whether there are predicative
complements.

- The dimension that relates to the number of objects in the clause is called **tran-sitivity**. An **intransitive** clause has no objects, a **monotransitive** clause has one
object, and a **ditransitive clause** has two objects, indirect and direct. In canoni-cal clauses an indirect object cannot occur without a following direct one, so the
single object of a monotransitive is always a direct object.
- The other dimension concerns the presence or absence of a predicative comple-ment. We give compound names to clauses containing a predicative complement:
complex-intransitive for an intransitive one and **complex-transitive** for a tran-sitive one. Those without predicative complements are **ordinary** intransitives
and transitives, but since the compound names are used when the clause is not
ordinary, we can normally omit the word 'ordinary'.

The labels apply to clause, verb phrase, and verb alike: *We hesitated* is an intransi-tive clause, *hesitated* is an intransitive VP, and **hesitate** is an intransitive verb. It
should be borne in mind, however, that most verbs occur in more than one of the
clause constructions. For example, **make** occurs in monotransitive clauses (*We
made lunch*) and ditransitive clauses (*We made them lunch*) as well as complex-transitive clauses, like [29iv]. When the terms are used for verbs, therefore, they
typically apply to particular USES of the verbs.

   This concludes our discussion of complements for this chapter. There are other
kinds besides those we have examined – notably complements with the form of PPs
or subordinate clauses – but these are best dealt with in the chapters dealing with
those categories: see Ch. 7, §7, for complements with the form of PPs, Ch. 10 for
finite subordinate clauses, and Ch. 13, §§3–4, for non-finite subordinate clauses.

6   Adjuncts

   The crucial distinction between complements and adjuncts is that the for-mer have to be licensed by the particular head verb whereas adjuncts do not.
Adjuncts are thus less closely dependent on the verb, and their occurrence is in gen-eral less constrained by grammatical rules. There is a great range of different kinds
of adjunct, and we have space here only to deal with them very summarily.

6.1   Semantic kinds of adjunct

Grammars traditionally classify adjuncts on the basis of meaning – as adjuncts of place, time, reason, and so on. Because this classification is based on meaning rather than grammatical form, it is inevitably open-ended and the boundaries between the different kinds are often quite fuzzy. There isn't really an answer to questions about exactly how many kinds of adjunct there are. In [30] we illustrate a number of the most frequent and obvious categories:

[30]			
	i	MANNER	*He drove <u>quite recklessly</u>.*
	ii	PLACE	*They have breakfast <u>in bed</u>.*
	iii	TIME	*I saw her <u>last week</u>.*
	iv	DURATION	*We lived in London <u>for five years</u>.*
	v	FREQUENCY	*She telephones her mother <u>every Sunday</u>.*
	vi	DEGREE	*We <u>very much</u> enjoyed your last novel.*
	vii	PURPOSE	*I checked all the doors <u>to make sure they were shut</u>.*
	viii	RESULT	*It rained all day, <u>with the result that they couldn't work</u>.*
	ix	CONDITION	*<u>If it rains</u> the match will be postponed.*
	x	CONCESSION	*<u>Although he's rich</u>, he lives very simply.*

6.2   The form of adjuncts

The adjunct function can be filled by expressions belonging to a range of different categories, as illustrated in [31]:

[31]			
	i	ADVERB (PHRASE)	*He thanked us <u>profusely</u>. We <u>quite often</u> have tea together.*
	ii	PP	*I cut it <u>with a razor-blade</u>. I'll help you <u>after lunch</u>.*
	iii	NP	*We saw her <u>several times</u>. They arrived <u>this morning</u>.*
	iv	FINITE CLAUSE	*I couldn't do it, <u>however hard I tried</u>.*
	v	NON-FINITE CLAUSE	*I kept my mouth shut, <u>to avoid giving any more offence</u>.*

- Adverbs, or AdvPs, and PPs are found in adjuncts belonging to more or less all of the semantic types of adjunct.
- NPs, by contrast, occur in a very limited range of adjunct types. The semantic type depends heavily on the head noun: *several times*, for example, indicates frequency, *this morning* indicates time. NP adjuncts cannot have the form of pronouns: we couldn't replace those in [iii], for example, by *them* and *it* – and we couldn't question them with *what*.
- For adjuncts with the form of subordinate clauses, see Ch. 10, §4.4, Ch. 13, §3.

6.3   Modifiers and supplements

We use the term **adjunct** to cover both **modifiers** of the verb or VP and **supplements**. Modifiers are tightly integrated into the structure of the clause, whereas supplements are only loosely attached. In speech the distinction is marked by intonation. Supplements are set apart intonationally from the rest of the clause: they are spoken as separate units of intonation, typically marked off by what is perceived as a slight pause. Modifiers, by contrast, are intonationally unified with the verb or VP. In writing, supplements are typically set apart by punctuation – commas, or stronger marks such as dashes or parentheses. There is, however, a good deal of variation in the use of punctuation, so that the distinction between modifiers and adjuncts is not as clearly drawn in writing as in speech.

The distinction is illustrated in the following examples:

[32]   MODIFIER   SUPPLEMENT
    i   a.   *They were playing <u>happily</u> outside.*   b.   <u>*Happily*</u>*, they were playing outside.*
    ii   a.   *I did it <u>because they told me to</u>.*   b.   *I did it – <u>because they told me to</u>.*

- In [ia] *happily* is understood as an adjunct of manner, indicating how they were playing. In [ib], however, where it is set apart at the beginning of the clause, it doesn't belong in any of the semantic types illustrated in [30], but gives the speaker's evaluation of the situation. The meaning in this case is much the same as that of *fortunately* – perhaps I was glad that they were playing outside as this enabled me to do something I didn't want them to know about.
- In [ii] there is no such difference in the semantic type: the *because* phrase indicates reason in both. But in [i] it is presented as part of a larger item of information, whereas in [ii] it is set apart as a piece of information on its own. In [iia] it could be that you already know I did it, and I'm here simply telling you why. But in [iib] I'm informing you that I did it, and then adding as supplementary information what my reason was.

We will not develop this distinction between modifiers and supplements further at this point, but there are other places where it is relevant. In particular, we will take it up again in our discussion of relative clauses in Ch. 11.

Exercises

1. Use the **licensing** criterion to determine whether the ten underlined expressions in the examples below are **complements** or **adjuncts**. In the case of complements, cite three verbs that license such a complement, and three that do not. (There are ten expressions in all; for reference, they're labelled with small roman numeral subscripts.)
   They <u>suddenly</u>[i] ran <u>to the gate</u>[ii].
   I wonder <u>if he'll be safe</u>[iii] all the time.
   I'm keeping <u>the dog</u>[iv], <u>whatever you say</u>[v].
   You'd better put <u>the cat</u>[vi] <u>out</u>[vii] now.
   It's always been easy <u>for you</u>[viii], hasn't it?
   They swam <u>in the sea</u>[ix] <u>even though it was raining</u>[x].

2. In the following examples, show how either **case** or **agreement** can be used to provide evidence that the underlined expression is subject.
      i   <u>*This letter*</u> *embarrassed the government.*
     ii   <u>*Sue*</u> *will lend you her car.*
     iii   <u>*Everything*</u> *will be OK.*
     iv   <u>*It*</u> *must be the twins he's referring to.*
      v   <u>*One of the twins*</u> *took the car.*

3. Identify the **subject** in each of the examples below (ignoring the subordinate clause in [iv]). Present the reasoning that tells you it is the subject. Use the syntactic

tests that are appropriate, and explain why the other tests are not appropriate.

  i *Tomorrow Pat will be back from skiing.*
  ii *Is today some kind of holiday?*
  iii *Down the road ran the crazy dog.*
  iv *It isn't the program that's at fault.*
  v *Dan got bitten on the neck by a bat.*

4. For which of the following clauses would it be implausible to say that the subject identifies the performer of an **action**? Give reasons for your answer.

  i *She's very like her mother.*
  ii *The decision was made by my aunt.*
  iii *My father closed the door.*
  iv *I've just received a letter from the mayor.*
  v *She underwent surgery.*

5. For which of the following is it implausible to say that the subject identifies the **topic**? Give reasons for your answer.

  i *At this time of year you're likely to get violent thunderstorms.*
  ii *Any fool could make a better job of it than that.*
  iii *My sister has just won the marathon.*
  iv *Close tabs were kept on all the directors.*
  v *Their house is worth a million and a half.*

6. In each of the following pairs pick out the one in which the underlined expression is **object**. Give syntactic reasons for your answer.

  i a. *We all enjoyed <u>that summer</u>.*
    b. *We all worked <u>that summer</u>.*
  ii a. *She fasted <u>a very long time</u>.*
    b. *She wasted <u>a very long time</u>.*
  iii a. *He seemed <u>an amazingly bad film-maker</u>.*
    b. *He screened <u>an amazingly bad film</u>.*

7. For each of the verbs below, determine (citing relevant examples) which of the following three structures they can occur in: (a) a structure with two NPs, like [15]; (b) a structure with one NP and a PP headed by *to*; (c) a structure with one NP and a PP headed by *for*.

  i **award**   vi **obtain**
  ii **borrow**   vii **owe**
  iii **envy**   viii **return**
  iv **explain**   ix **send**
  v **fine**   x **transfer**

8. Determine whether the underlined expressions below are **objects** or **predicative complements**. Give syntactic evidence in support of your answers.

  i *They arrested <u>a member of the party</u>.*
  ii *She remained <u>a member of the party</u>.*
  iii *It looks <u>a bargain</u> to me.*
  iv *He proposed <u>a bargain</u> to me.*
  v *They continued <u>the investigation</u>.*

9. Recall the classification of canonical clause types into (a) **ordinary intransitive**; (b) **complex-intransitive**; (c) **monotransitive**; (d) **complex-transitive**; and (e) **ditransitive**. For each of the verbs below, determine which of the five constructions it can enter into, and construct relevant illustrative examples.

  i **appear**   iii **judge**
  ii **consider** iv **keep**
  v **promise** viii **show**
  vi **save**   ix **turn**
  vii **send**   x **wish**

10. Explain the ambiguities of the following two sentences (they can each be understood either as **complex-transitive** or as **ditransitive**):

  i *I found her a good lawyer.*
  ii *He called me a nurse.*

5 Nouns and noun phrases

1   Introductory survey

Distinctive properties of prototypical noun phrases

(a) Function. The main functions in which NPs occur are these four:

[1]   i In clause structure:

SUBJECT	*A student* helped us.
OBJECT	They elected *a student*.
PREDICATIVE COMPLEMENT	She is *a student*.

     ii In PP structure:

COMPLEMENT	We were talking [to *a student*].

(b) Form. A typical NP consists of a **noun** serving as head word and (possibly) various accompanying dependents.

Distinctive properties of prototypical nouns

(a) Inflection. Nouns typically inflect for **number** (singular or plural) and **case** (plain or genitive):

[2]

	SINGULAR	PLURAL
PLAIN CASE	*student*	*students*
GENITIVE	*student's*	*students'*

(b) Function. Nouns can normally fill the head position in phrases with any of the four functions listed in [1].

(c) Dependents. There are various kinds of dependent that occur exclusively or almost exclusively with nouns as head. Examples of such items are underlined in [3].

[3] i CERTAIN DETERMINATIVES   *the door, a year, every book, which paper*
     ii PRE-HEAD ADJECTIVES   *young children, a big dog, recent events*
    iii RELATIVE CLAUSES   *the guy who fainted, the book I'm reading*

Nouns and concrete objects

The noun category includes words denoting all kinds of physical objects (people, animals, places, things) and substances: *apple, dog, fire, London, sister, water*, etc. We can't use this as the criterion for identifying English nouns, though, because there are also large numbers of nouns denoting abstract entities: *absence, debt, fear, love, silence, work*, etc. But we can use it as the basis for a general definition applying across languages:

[4]   NOUN: a grammatically distinct category of words which includes those denoting all kinds of physical objects, such as persons, animals and inanimate objects.

Types of dependent

Dependents in the structure of the NP are of three main types. We introduce them briefly here, and then deal with them in more detail in §§3–6.

[5] i DETERMINERS   *the news, a pear, some cheese, two new films, no reason*
     ii COMPLEMENTS   *the loss of blood, a ban on smoking, the fact that she's alive*
    iii MODIFIERS   *a young woman, a friend from Boston, people who complained*

- The determiner is a kind of dependent found only in NP structure. It is normally an obligatory element in NPs with certain types of singular noun as head. Compare *The door is open* and **Door is open*, or compare *I bought a book* and **I bought book*.
- Complements have to be licensed by the head noun – as complements in clause structure have to be licensed by the head verb. Compare *his loss of blood* with *He was losing blood*. Note that nouns like *fact, knowledge*, or *suggestion* can be accompanied by such subordinate clauses as *that she's alive*, but nouns like *boy, madness*, or *inquiry* cannot.
- Modifiers are the default type of dependent, lacking the above special features; there is no limit to the number of modifiers that can occur in an NP. Those in [iii], for example, can combine in a single NP: *a young woman from Boston who complained*.

Nominals

In clause structure we have recognised a unit intermediate between the clause and the verb, namely the verb phrase. In the same way we recognise a unit intermediate between the noun phrase and the noun, which we call a **nominal**. In *the guy who* *fainted* or *a young woman*, for example, the first division is between the determiner and the rest, with *guy who fainted* and *young woman* each forming a nominal. Simplified structures are as shown in [6]:

[6]

a. NP — Determiner: Determinative / Head: Nominal → Head: Noun, Modifier: Relative clause — *the guy who fainted*

b. NP — Determiner: Determinative / Head: Nominal → Modifier: Adjective, Head: Noun — *a young woman*

Here the noun is head of the nominal, and not directly of the NP, but we will often simplify by talking of NPs with various kinds of noun as head.

Internal and external dependents

Dependents in the structure of the NP may be distinguished as **internal** or **external**, according as they fall inside or outside the head nominal. **Complements** (with the exception of the type discussed in §9.1) are always internal, and **determiners** are always external. All the **modifiers** illustrated so far are internal, but there are also external modifiers. Compare the following examples, where underlining marks the dependent and brackets surround the head nominal:

[7]   i COMPLEMENT   **internal**   *a [knowledge of Latin], the [idea that he liked it]*
      ii DETERMINER   **external**   *these [old papers], some [people I met]*
      iii MODIFIER   **internal**   *a [big dog], the [book I'm reading]*
                      external   *almost the [only survivor], even a [young woman]*

Subclasses of noun

The three major subclasses of noun are **pronouns, proper nouns**, and **common nouns**:

[8]   i PRONOUNS   *I, me, my, mine, myself, you, he, she, it, who, what, . . .*
      ii PROPER NOUNS   *Kim, Jones, Beethoven, Boston, Canada, Nile, Easter, . . .*
      iii COMMON NOUNS *cat, day, furniture, window, fact, truth, perseverance, . . .*

● Pronouns constitute a fairly small class of words distinguished from other nouns most clearly by their inability to combine with determiners (cf. *the me, *a myself*, etc.). The most central ones differ inflectionally from other nouns – e.g. in having a contrast between nominative and accusative forms (*I* vs *me, he* vs *him*, etc.).

- Proper nouns characteristically function as the head of NPs serving as proper names, names individually assigned to particular people, places, festivals, etc. They also occur, derivatively, in other kinds of NP (cf. *Let's listen to [some Beethoven]*).
- Common nouns represent the default subclass, lacking the special properties of pronouns and proper nouns.

2   Number and countability

Number is the name of the system contrasting **singular** and **plural**. In the first instance, it applies to noun inflection: nouns typically have contrasting singular and plural forms. Thus *cat* and *cats* are the singular and plural forms of the noun **cat**, and so on.

2.1   Nouns with fixed number

Although most nouns have variable number, there are nevertheless many that do not – nouns which are invariably singular or invariably plural.

(a) Singular-only nouns

Examples of nouns which have a singular form but no plural are given in [9]:

[9]   i *crockery, dross, footwear, harm, indebtedness, nonsense, perseverance*
       ii *italics, linguistics, mumps, news, phonetics, physics*

Those in [ii] look like plurals, but the final *s* is not in fact a plural marker, like that in *cats*. This is evident from the fact that we say *The news is good* (not *are*), and so on.

(b) Plural-only nouns

Nouns with a plural form but no singular are illustrated in [10]:

[10]   i *alms, auspices, belongings, clothes, genitals, scissors, spoils, trousers*
        ii *cattle, police, vermin*

Those in [i] contain the plural suffix ·*s*, but it cannot be dropped to form a singular. In most cases there is some fairly transparent connection to plurality in the ordinary sense of "more than one": *belongings* denotes things that belong to someone, *clothes* is a cover term for articles of clothing, while *scissors* and *trousers* denote objects with two main parts. The nouns in [ii] have no inflectional marking of plurality, but behave syntactically as plurals. Note, for example, that we say *these cattle*, not **this cattle*; *The police have arrived*, not **The police has arrived*.

2.2   Count and non-count nouns

Closely related to the distinction between nouns of variable and invariable number is that between **count** nouns and **non-count** nouns. As the names imply, count nouns can take **cardinal** numerals (*one, two, three,* etc.) as dependent, while non-count nouns cannot.

Non-count nouns that are invariably singular

Non-count nouns are usually invariably singular. The possibilities for *furniture*, for example, are shown in [11], where it is contrasted with the count noun *chair*:

[11]

	SINGULAR WITH DETERMINER *THE*	SINGULAR WITH NUMERAL *ONE*	PLURAL WITH NUMERALS
COUNT NOUN	*the chair*	*one chair*	*two chairs*
NON-COUNT NOUN	*the furniture*	**one furniture*	**two furnitures*

Furniture cannot combine with any numeral, not even *one*, which goes with singular forms. The same restrictions apply to such nouns as **clothing, equipment, footwear** or the abstract nouns **eagerness, perseverance, wetness.**

Non-count nouns that are invariably plural

There are a fairly small number of non-count nouns that are invariably plural. Compare the possibilities for count *corpse* and non-count *remains* shown in [12]:

[12]

	PLURAL WITH DETERMINER *THE*	SINGULAR WITH NUMERAL *ONE*	PLURAL WITH NUMERALS
COUNT NOUN	*the corpses*	*one corpse*	*two corpses*
NON-COUNT NOUN	*the remains*	**one remain*	**two remains*

Remains is invariably plural, but even so, it cannot combine with numerals like *two* or *three*, etc. Other nouns of this kind include **credentials, genitals, proceeds,** etc.

Nouns with count and non-count uses

Nouns that have **only** a count interpretation or **only** a non-count interpretation are in a minority. Most nouns can be used with either kind of interpretation. The [a] and [b] pairs in [13] are fairly typical.

[13]   COUNT INTERPRETATION   NON-COUNT INTERPRETATION
   i a. *Would you like a <u>cake</u>?*   b. *Would you like some more <u>cake</u>?*
   ii a. *I'll have to borrow your <u>football</u>.* b. *I'm going to play <u>football</u>.*
   iii a. *The <u>cover</u> of this book is torn.*   b. *The awning provides some <u>cover</u>.*
   iv a. *I suggested a few <u>improvements</u>.*   b. *There's been little <u>improvement</u>.*

When we speak of count and non-count nouns, therefore, we are referring to nouns as used with a count and non-count interpretation. Thus *cake* is a count noun in [ia] but a non-count noun in [ib], and so on.

The meaning distinction between count and non-count

A count noun generally denotes a **class** of individual entities of the same kind. The count noun *table*, for example, denotes the whole class of tables (*one table* provides a way of referring to a single member of the class, *two tables* talks about two members, and so on). An individual member of this class cannot be divided into smaller entities of the same kind as itself. That is, a table can be chopped up into smaller parts, but those parts are not themselves tables. Likewise, if you cut a loaf in half, what you have is not two loaves, but two halves of a loaf.

Non-count nouns typically have the opposite property. A good number of them denote physical substances that can be divided into smaller amounts of the same kind. If you cut up some bread, the pieces can still be described by the non-count noun *bread*. If you take some wood and cut it into shorter lengths, these can still be referred to by means of the non-count noun *wood* – the same noun is applicable to the same stuff in smaller quantities.

Marking of the count vs non-count distinction

In many but by no means all cases, grammatical features of the NP force or strongly favour either a count or a non-count interpretation.

(a)   Plurality favours the count interpretation

A plural head noun will generally indicate a count interpretation. In *She described the improvements they had made*, for example, we interpret *improvements* in a count sense like that of [13iva] (*I suggested a few improvements*) rather than the non-count sense of [13ivb] (*There's been little improvement*). That is, it implies a set of separable, individual improvements that you could count. As noted above, there are some non-count plural nouns, like *remains*, but they are restricted to a relatively small number of particular lexemes.

(b)   Singular common noun head with no determiner favours the non-count interpretation

In general, common nouns can occur in the singular without a determiner only if they have a non-count interpretation. That's why we get these contrasts:

[14]   i a. *She was reading <u>book</u>.   b. *She was drinking <u>water</u>.*
     ii a. *We made <u>table</u>.*   b. *We made <u>progress</u>.*

Book and *table* normally have count interpretations, and so the [a] examples are inadmissible, whereas non-count *water* and *progress* occur readily without a determiner because they're interpreted in a non-count sense. Count nouns are found without determiners only in a very limited range of special syntactic constructions. Two of them are illustrated in [15]:

[15]   i a. *Who wants to be <u>treasurer</u>?*   b. *Who wants to be <u>millionaire</u>?*
     ii a. *They were living together as*   b. *I've met <u>husband</u>, but I don't think*
                   <u>husband</u> and <u>wife</u>.   *I've ever seen him with <u>wife</u>.*

● *Treasurer* in [ia] is what we have called a **bare role NP** (one without a determiner: see Ch. 4, §4.1). Nouns that do not denote some kind of role or office cannot occur without a determiner in predicative complement function, as evident from the contrast between *treasurer* and *millionaire* in [i]: *treasurer* is a role in an organisation, but *millionaire* is just a status that anyone has as soon as their net worth reaches a million dollars, pounds, etc.

● In [iia] we have two closely related nouns in a coordination construction, which sometimes allows omission of the determiner. But the same nouns need determiners when they are not in a coordination, as we see from [iib].

(c) Certain determinatives are generally restricted to one or other interpretation

Determinatives such as *the*, *this*, *that*, *what*, and *no* occur with either type of noun, but in singular NPs the determinatives listed in [16] are generally restricted to one or the other, as illustrated in [17]:

[16] i COUNT   *one, another, each, every, either, neither*; also to some extent *a*
      ii NON-COUNT   *much, little, a little, enough, sufficient*; also to some extent *all*

[17] i a. *Every table* was inspected.   b. **Every furniture* was inspected.
      ii a. **He didn't read much book.*   b. *He didn't drink much water.*

We have set aside *a* and *all* at the end of the lists because with these determinatives there are some exceptions, as in *He has a high regard for them* (where *regard* is non-count) and *He spent all day* at the races (where *day* is count).

2.3   Subject–verb agreement

Number is the major factor involved in subject–verb agreement. Compare:

[18]   SINGULAR SUBJECT   PLURAL SUBJECT
      i a. *Their dog eats a lot.*   b. *Their dogs eat a lot.*
      ii a. *Their dog was eating.*   b. *Their dogs were eating.*

As we change from a singular subject in [a] to a plural subject in [b] the inflectional form of the verb changes too, and the verb is accordingly said to **agree** with the subject. The agreement applies in the present tense with all verbs except the modal auxiliaries. In the preterite, only the verb *be* displays agreement: other preterites such as *ate* occur in the same form with all kinds of subject.

Subject–verb agreement involves person as well as number, for 1st person *I*, although singular, requires *eat*, not *eats*. *Eats* occurs with 3rd person singular subjects and *eat* with all others: i.e. plurals, 1st person *I*, or 2nd person *you*. But most of the complexities regarding agreement arise with respect to number, and that is why we will now focus on number in more detail. There are four special cases to be noted.

Measure expressions

Expressions like *ten days*, *twenty dollars*, *five miles*, etc., are plural in form but the quantity or measure they denote can be conceptualised as a single abstract entity, and this singular conceptualisation can override the plural form in determining the form of the verb. So the following examples have plural subjects with a singular agreement form of the verb:

[19] i a. *Ten days is a long time to be on your own.*
      b. *Twenty dollars seems far too much to pay for a takeaway pizza.*
    ii a. *That ten days we spent together in Paris was wonderful.*
      b. *Another three eggs is all we need.*

Ten days can be seen as a single block of time; twenty dollars is a price; three eggs can be viewed as a single quantity of food. Note that in the [ii] cases the measure expression not only takes a singular verb, it even occurs with a determiner that normally selects a singular head (cf. *that day*, *another egg*).

Quantificational nouns

There are a few nouns expressing quantification which can occur in the singular as head of an NP whose number for agreement purposes is determined by a smaller NP embedded within it:

[20]

SINGULAR	PLURAL
[A *lot* of *money*] *was* wasted.	[A *lot* of *things*] *were* wasted.
[The *rest* of *the meat*] *is* over there.	[The *rest* of *the eggs*] *are* over there.
(not possible)	[A *number* of *faults*] *were* found.

The head of the bracketed NP in each case is marked by double underlining. Notice that each head is singular, but the form of the verb depends on the single-underlined NP that is complement to the preposition *of*. The meaning of *number* is such that the embedded NP must be plural, so the bottom left position in the table can't be filled.

Collective nouns

Nouns such as *board*, *committee*, *jury*, *staff*, *team* are **collective** nouns in that they denote a collection, or set, of individuals. When they occur in the singular as head of the subject NP the verb can, especially in BrE, be either singular or plural, though AmE clearly favours the singular:

[21]   SINGULAR VERB   PLURAL VERB
    i a. *The committee has interviewed her.*   b. [%]*The committee have interviewed her.*
   ii a. *The jury is still deliberating.*   b. [%]*The jury are still deliberating.*
  iii a. *The board consists entirely of men.*   b. *The crew are all over forty.*

The choice of a plural verb focuses on the individuals that make up the collection, on the members of the committee or jury or whatever, rather than on the collection as a unit, the official body that the members constitute.

The examples in [iii] are cases in which variation would be less likely. In [iiia], the property of consisting entirely of men can only apply to the board as a whole; it can't apply to any individual member of the board, so a plural verb is much less likely (though not all BrE speakers would dismiss %*The board consist entirely of men* as impossible). In [iiib], by contrast, the property of being forty or older can apply only to the individual members of the crew, not the crew as a whole, and the adjunct *all* reinforces the focus on the individuals; so [iiib] with its plural agreement is much more likely than %*The crew is all over forty* (though in AmE the latter might nonetheless occur).

Any, no, none, either, neither

We also find alternation between singular and plural verb agreement in examples like [22]:

[22] i a. [*None* of *the objections*] *was* valid.   b. [*None* of *the objections*] *were* valid.
     ii a. [*Neither* of *them*] *seems* valid.   b. [*Neither* of *them*] *seem* valid.

Subjects with *any*, *no*, and *none* occur freely with either singular or plural agreement. With *neither*, and even more with *either*, singular agreement is usual; plural agreement is informal, and condemned by prescriptivists. The difference is that *any* and *no* can function as determiner to both singular and plural nouns: both *No objection was valid* and *No objections were valid* are grammatical. *Either* and *neither* occur only with singulars: *Neither objection was valid* is grammatical, but **Neither objections were valid* is definitely not.

3   Determiners and determinatives

The **determiner** position in an NP is usually filled by one of two kinds of expression.

- In all the examples so far it has been a **determinative**, and some of these can be accompanied by their own modifiers, making a **determinative phrase**, abbreviated **DP**.
- In addition, the determiner may have the form of a **genitive NP**.

Examples, with the determiners underlined, are given in [23]:

[23]   DETERMINATIVE   *the* city   *some* rotten eggs
      DP   *almost all* politicians   *very few* new books
      GENITIVE NP   *her* income   *the senator's* young son

In this section we focus on determinatives and DPs. Genitive determiners are discussed in §9.1.

The determiner is generally an obligatory element with count singular common nouns, as discussed in connection with [14–16] above. It is, by contrast, incompatible with pronouns: we have *I am ready*, not **The I am ready,* and so on.

3.1   Definiteness

The main semantic contribution of the determiner is to mark the NP as **definite** or **indefinite**. *The* is known as the **definite article** and *a* as the **indefinite article** since these are the most basic and elementary markers of definite and indefinite NPs, but all NPs can be classified as definite or indefinite.

Definite article

What is meant by definite here can best be understood by looking at some examples containing the definite article. In the following the definite NP is enclosed in brackets; the part following *the* is the head.

[24] i [*The President of France*] *has appointed a new prime minister.*
    ii *Where did you put* [*the key*]?

The indicates that the head of the NP is considered SUFFICIENT IN THE CONTEXT TO IDENTIFY THE REFERENT.

- Only one person can be President of France at a given time, so using that description in [i] uniquely identifies a person.
- Although any number of keys might exist, [ii] will be used only in a context that makes clear which one I'm talking about (e.g., the key to the car you just told me to unload).

Use of *the* can be thought of as pre-empting a *which* question. It would obviously be inappropriate for you to respond to [i] with *Which President of France?* because there is only one. And in [ii], my use of *the* reflects my assumption that you won't need to ask *Which key?*

The unique identification can be more indirect, and it can depend on the meaning of the rest of the sentence or other linguistic context, as these examples illustrate:

[25] i [*The father of one of my students*] *emailed me yesterday.*
    ii [*The only language she spoke*] *was Tzotzil.*

- In the case of [i] you won't know precisely who I am referring to because I don't identify the student. But a *which* question consisting of *which* + the head of the NP would still make no sense. You can't ask *Which father of one of your students?*, because nobody has more than one father. So if you let *one of my students* serve to pick out a certain student (you just imagine a certain student *X* that so far you don't know much about), then the nominal *father of one of my students* can provide a uniquely identifying description: the unique person who is the father of *X*.
- You can see this limited kind of identifiability in [25ii] as well. The nominal *only language she spoke* must pick out a single language, so the question *Which only language she spoke?* would be nonsense. But of course I don't assume that you can name the language, since the whole point of the rest of the sentence is to tell you its name. The head nominal describes a unique entity, but at the moment

when you hear that nominal you know very little about it. The predicate of the clause then goes on to give a fuller identification of it.

Indefinite article

The indefinite article does not indicate that the description in the head is defining. The description is not presented as unique in the context. Take these examples:

[26] i [*A cabinet minister*] *has been arrested.*
      ii *I'll give you* [*a key*].

- A cabinet contains a number of ministers, and if I don't know (or am not bothering to say) which one of them got arrested I will use *a* rather than *the*. Here, of course, a *which* question is perfectly appropriate: *Which one?* would be a natural response to [i].
- The context for [ii] is likely to be one where it is clear which lock you'll be using the key in, but it will be a lock for which there are multiple keys, and if I haven't decided (or don't care) which of them I'll give you, I will again use the indefinite article.

Articles with plural NPs

Article use has been illustrated so far with singular NPs, but of course *the* also occurs in plurals:

[27] i [*The Presidents of France and Italy*] *will be meeting again tomorrow.*
      ii *Where did you put* [*the keys*]?

These are very much like the singulars. Again a *which* question would be inappropriate.

- In [i] the head uniquely defines a set of two people, so the referent is clearly identifiable.
- In [ii] I'm talking about a bunch of keys, and the context is assumed to make clear which bunch.

Which determiners are definite and indefinite

The words that mark the NP as definite or as indefinite when they serve as determiners are given in [28i] and [28ii].

[28] i DEFINITE   *the*; **this**, **that**; *all*, *both*; relative *which*, *whichever*, *what*, *whatever*[1]
      ii INDEFINITE   *a*; *each*, *every*; *some*, *any*; *either*, *neither*; *no*; *another*; *a few*, *a little*, *several*; *many*, *much*, *more*, *most*, *few*, *fewer*, *little*, *less*; *enough*, *sufficient*; interrogative *which*, *whichever*, *what*, *whatever*; *one*, *two*, *three*, *four*, *five*, . . .

---

[1] Relative *which*, *whichever*, etc., occur in relative clauses: see Ch. 11, §§2, 4.

Apart from the interrogatives, all the indefinite markers have to do with **quantification**. Among the definite markers, *all* and *both* are also quantificational, but illustrate the special case of quantification that involves totality.

This and **that** are unique among the determinatives in that they inflect for number, in agreement with the head noun: compare *this book* and *these books*, *that day* and *those days*.

3.2 Determinatives as modifiers

It should be borne in mind that although **determinatives** are a class of words that most commonly function as **determiners** (hence the similarity of the terms), many are also found in other functions, particularly **modifier**.[2] Compare, for example:

[29]   DETERMINER   MODIFIER
 i a. [*The younger son*] *had died.*   b. *I feel* [*all the better*] *for my holiday.*
 ii a. *Who's* [*that tall guy over there*]*?*   b. *He shouldn't have driven* [*that fast*].
 iii a. [*Many people*] *were offended.*   b. *He listed* [*its many failings*].

While the underlined determinative is determiner in NP structure in the [a] examples, it is a modifier in the others: a modifier in an AdjP in [ib], in an AdvP in [iib], and in an NP in [iiib].

3.3 Determinative phrases

A number of the quantificational determinatives accept dependents of their own. A determinative with dependents functions as the head of a phrase which we call a **determinative phrase (DP)**. In most cases the dependents are modifiers preceding the head of the DP. In the following examples, brackets enclose the NP, with underlining marking the DP inside it:

[30] i a. [*Not many people*] *turned up.*   b. *There were* [*at most fifty applications*].
 ii a. [*Almost every copy*] *was torn.*   b. *We have* [*hardly any milk*] *left.*
 iii a. [*Some thirty paintings*] *were stolen.* b. *I haven't* [*very much money*] *on me.*

4 Complements

One striking difference between nouns and verbs is that NOUNS DON'T TAKE OBJECTS. With nouns that are morphologically related to transitive verbs, as

---

[2] We use 'determiner' for the function term and 'determinative' for the category term since the suffix ·*er* matches that in the function term 'modifier', while ·*ive* matches that in the category term 'adjective'.

criticism is related to *criticise*, the complement of the noun that corresponds to the object of the verb has the form of a PP:

[31]   VERB + OBJECT   NOUN + PP COMPLEMENT
   i   a. *I criticised her decision*.   b. *my criticism of her decision*
  ii   a. *He abandoned his ship*.   b. *his abandonment of his ship*
 iii   a. *Sandy married Pat*.   b. *Sandy's marriage to Pat*

The preposition is usually *of*, as in [ib] and [iib], but with certain nouns other prepositions are selected, as in [iiib].

Complements in NP structure are therefore virtually restricted to PPs and subordinate clauses.

PP complements

Dependents with the form of PPs qualify as complements when they are licensed by the particular head noun. The clearest cases have one or more of the following properties.

(a) They correspond to object or subject NPs in clause structure. The object case has been illustrated in [31], while correspondence with a subject is seen in [32]:

[32]   SUBJECT + VERB   NOUN + PP COMPLEMENT
   i   a. *The warriors returned*.   b. *the return of the warriors*
  ii   a. *The premier attacked*.   b. *an attack by the premier*

This type of PP complement can combine with one corresponding to the object in a clause, as in *the removal of the files by the secretary* – cf. *The secretary removed the files*. (For the construction with a genitive NP, as in *the warriors' return* or *the premier's attack*, see §9.1.)

(b) The choice of preposition is specified by the head noun. Many nouns take complements headed by a particular preposition:

[33]   *their belief in God, its effect on the audience, familiarity with the data, the introduction to the book, a request for more staff, secession from the alliance*

(c) The PP is obligatory because the noun makes little sense without it.

[34]   *the advent of the steam engine, the abandonment of sensible budgetary policies, a dearth of new ideas, the feasibility of the proposal, a paucity of reliable data*

The nouns in [34] almost always occur with a PP headed by *of*, and even if someone did say something like *What's the feasibility?*, we would have to understand them as having asked about the feasibility of some particular planned action that they had left to be understood from the context.

▨ Subordinate clause complements

Subordinate clauses may be finite or non-finite, and both types are found as complements to nouns:

[35]   i FINITE   *the claim <u>that he was ill</u>, a suspicion <u>that it was a hoax</u>*
       ii NON-FINITE   *her ability <u>to complete the task</u>, his eagerness <u>to redeem himself</u>*

For discussion of these constructions, see the chapters on subordinate clauses, Ch. 10 and Ch. 13.

▨ Indirect complements

Consider now the following examples, where brackets enclose the NP and underlining marks the complement.

[36]   i   *We had to put up with [a longer delay <u>than we had bargained for</u>].*
       ii *He gave [so complicated an explanation <u>that I was completely baffled</u>].*
       iii *It was [too serious a problem <u>for us to ignore</u>].*

We call these **indirect complements** because although they follow the head noun it is not the head noun that licenses them.

● In [i] the complement is licensed by the comparative adjective *longer*: if we drop this the NP becomes ungrammatical (**a delay than we had bargained for*).
● Similarly, in [ii] the complement is licensed by the *so* that modifies *complicated*.
● In [iii] it is licensed by *too*. This time we could drop *too serious* without loss of grammaticality – but it would have a dramatic effect on the interpretation of the infinitival clause. *A problem for us to ignore* means "a problem that we can/should ignore", whereas the NP in [iii] means "a problem that was so serious that we could/should not ignore it".

5   Internal modifiers

Nouns accept a very wide range of **modifiers** within the nominal. Because they are inside the nominal they are called **internal** modifiers. Some precede the head of the NP, while others follow.

▨ (a) Pre-head modifiers

[37]   i   ADJP   *a <u>long</u> letter, this <u>latest</u> problem, some <u>very irate</u> customers*
       ii DP   *another <u>two</u> candidates, the <u>more than thirty</u> candidates*
       iii NOMINAL   *a <u>brick</u> wall, <u>high octane</u> petrol, a <u>United States</u> warship*
       iv VP   *the <u>condemned</u> man, a <u>sleeping</u> child, a <u>recently discovered</u> fossil*

● The most common type of pre-head modifier is an **adjective**, either alone or with its own dependents, as in [37i].

- **Determinatives**, again alone or with dependents, are modifiers when they FOLLOW a determiner rather than functioning as one themselves, as in [ii].
- The modifiers in [iii] are nominals consisting of **nouns**, either alone or (as in the second and third examples) with their own internal dependents. Note that a modifier cannot contain its own determiner: it is a nominal, not an NP. We cannot have, for example, *a the United States warship.*
- VP modifiers as in [iv] have either a gerund-participle or a past participle form of the verb as head.

Dependents within a pre-head modifier almost always precede the head of that modifier. To take the last phrase in [37iv] as an example, we can say *This fossil was discovered recently* (where *discovered recently* is a complement of the verb *be*), but we cannot refer to it with the phrase *a discovered recently fossil.* We have to place the adverb dependent *recently* before the verbal head *discovered*, to make the NP *a recently discovered fossil.*

(b) Post-head modifiers

[38]	i	PP	*the tree by the gate, food for the baby, a hut in the forest, a house of ill repute, a man without scruples*
	ii	ADJP	*people fond of animals, the ones most likely to succeed*
	iii	APPOSITIVE NP	*the opera 'Carmen', my wife Lucy, our friend the mayor*
	iv	NON-APPOSITIVE NP	*a woman my age, someone your own size, a rug this colour*
	v	FINITE CLAUSE	*the guy who spoke first, the knife with which he cut it, the money that he gave me, some people I met on the train*
	vi	NON-FINITE CLAUSE	*the person for you to consult, students living on campus, a letter written by his uncle*

- The **PPs** in [i] are NOT syntactically licensed by the head like those in [31–34] above.
- **AdjPs** in post-head position usually contain their own dependents, especially post-head ones; the AdjPs shown in [ii] would not be possible before the head noun.
- **Appositive NP** modifiers are distinguished from the non-appositive ones by their ability to stand alone in place of the whole NP: instead of *They invited my wife Lucy* we could have simply *They invited Lucy.*
- **Finite** clause modifiers are all **relative** clauses.
- **Non-finite** clauses may be **infinitival, gerund-participial,** or **past-participial.**

Combinations of modifiers

There is no grammatical limit to the number of modifiers that can occur within a single NP. The following examples contain two, three, four and five respectively:

[39]	i	*a big black dog*
	ii	*the two French novels we had to study*
	iii	*an old Italian woman with six kids who was complaining bitterly*
	iv	*that nice little old man at the library with the umbrella*

There are preferences as to relative order, especially among pre-head modifiers. *A big black dog*, for example, will be strongly preferred over *a black big dog*. Numeral modifiers usually precede adjectives, as in *the three young nurses*, but under restricted conditions the reverse order is found, as in *an enjoyable three hours*.

6   External modifiers

External modifiers in an NP are located within the NP but outside the head nominal. There are various subtypes, all highly restricted with respect to the range of expressions admitted. Here we illustrate just three of these subtypes:

[40]   i *all the children, both her sons, half a day, twice the amount we'd asked for*
    ii *such a disaster, too risky a venture, so difficult an assignment*
    iii *even the children, only a politician, the prime minister alone, the boss herself*

- Those in [i] are quantificational expressions that occur before various determiners.
- Those in [ii] are adjectives or AdjPs which occur as external modifier only before the indefinite article *a(n)*.
- Those in [iii] do not require the presence of a determiner: they occur, for example, with proper nouns, as in *even Kim, Julia herself*, etc.

7   The fused-head construction

In all the NP examples so far the head element has been distinct from the dependents and filled by a noun. We turn now to a construction where the head is combined, or **fused**, with a dependent element, usually the determiner or an internal modifier. That is, a single word is at the same time a determiner or modifier and also the head. We call this the **fused-head** construction.

7.1   Three kinds of fused head

We distinguish three subtypes of the fused-head construction, illustrated in [41], where square brackets enclose the NP and underlining marks the fused head:

[41]   i SIMPLE   *Kim has lots of friends, but Pat doesn't seem to have [any].*
    ii PARTITIVE   *[Some of his remarks] were quite flattering.*   [explicit]
                      I have two photos of her, but [both] are out of focus.   [implicit]
    iii SPECIAL   *[Many] would disagree with you on that point.*

In all these examples the underlined word is a determinative combining the functions of determiner and head.

The simple subtype

Here it is possible to expand the fused-head NP into an ordinary NP with a separate head – one retrieved from the context. Thus in [41i] we could replace *any* by *any friends*.

The partitive subtype

Partitive is intended to suggest denoting a part rather than the whole thing.

● In an **explicit** partitive, the fused head is followed by a **partitive PP complement,** such as *of his remarks* in our example. The NP *some of his remarks* is partitive in the sense that it denotes a subset of the set consisting of his remarks: we
understand it to mean "some remarks from the set of his remarks". Note, however, that in this case we cannot expand into a construction with a separate head:
we can't say **some remarks of his remarks.*
● In the **implicit** partitive the *of* complement is understood rather than being
overtly expressed. Thus in the second example of [41ii] *both* is understood
as "both of them" (i.e. "both of the two photos of her"). This case is accordingly
different from the simple fused-head construction: *any* in [i] is understood as
"any friends", not "any of them".

The special subtype

● In [41iii] *many* is understood as "many people", but this represents a special
interpretation of fused-head *many*: *people* is not retrievable from the surrounding
text – or even from the presence of people in the situation of utterance.
● In *I don't think [much] has happened while you've been away* fused-head *much*
has an inanimate, abstract interpretation.

7.2   Fused determiner-heads

Further examples of fused determiner-heads, with the determinatives
eight, *several*, and **this**, are given in [42]:

[42] i SIMPLE   *They sent six copies though I had ordered [eight].*
     ii PARTITIVE   *They sent twenty copies but [several] were damaged.*
    iii SPECIAL   *[This] is infuriating.*

Almost all determiners can occur in this construction, the main exceptions being
the two articles *the* and *a*, together with *every* and *what*.

The, a, every

These have substitutes in fused structures: *the* is replaced by the appropriate form of
that; *a* is replaced by *one*; and *every* is replaced by *every one*:

[43] i a. **The impact of war is more serious than the of drought.*
        b. *The impact of war is more serious than that of drought.*
     ii a. **I need a pen, but I haven't got a.*
        b. *I need a pen, but I haven't got one.*
    iii a. **He inspected a dozen cars, but every (of them) was defective.*
        b. *He inspected a dozen cars, but every one (of them) was defective.*

What

In the case of *what* we need to distinguish carefully between two items: the **determinative** *what* and the **pronoun** *what*. The determinative functions as **determiner** the way other determinatives do, while the pronoun functions as (non-fused) **head** the way other pronouns do:

[44]   i [*What* course] *are you taking?*   [determinative functioning as determiner]
       ii [*What*] *do you want?*   [pronoun functioning as head]

The way we can tell that there are two items here is that there is a clear difference in meaning between them.

- The pronoun *what* is **non-personal**: it does not apply to human beings (we need personal *who* instead: *Who do you want?*).
- The determinative *what*, on the other hand, is **neutral** with respect to the personal vs non-personal distinction: in [i] it accompanies a head that does not denote a human being, but in *What philosophers have you read?* it accompanies a human head noun. (Compare the impossibility of **What wrote this article?*)

With *what*, then, we do not get a fused determiner-head structure: *what* is either the determiner or the head, and we can tell which by checking the possibility of human denotation.

No

Unlike the determinatives discussed above, *no* does occur in the fused determiner-head construction, but we find a difference in inflection, with the form *none* occurring in the fused-head construction, and *no* everywhere else:

[45]   *Kim had [no money], and Pat also had [none].*

7.3   Fused modifier-heads

Fusion of **modifier** and head of an NP is seen in the following examples, where an adjective serves as modifier and as head at the same time:

[46]   i   SIMPLE   *Should I wear the red shirt or [the blue]?*
       ii PARTITIVE   [*The youngest of their children*] *was still at school.*
       iii SPECIAL   [*The French*] *don't take these things too seriously.*

- In [i] we understand *the blue* to mean "the blue shirt".
- In [ii] the reference is to the youngest member of the set consisting of their children.
- In [iii] *the French* has a special interpretation: it means French people in general.

Modifiers cannot fuse with the head as readily as determiners can. Examples like these are not grammatical:

[47]   i   **Kim had hoped for a favourable review, but Pat wrote [a critical].*
       ii **That mattress is very soft: I'd prefer [a hard].*
       iii **Look through this box of screws and pick out [some small].*

Instead of the fused-head construction in cases like these we use an NP with **one** as head: *a critical one, a hard one, some small ones*.

The modifiers which most readily fuse with the head include these:

- **determinatives** used in modifier function following a determiner (e.g. *these two*)
- **superlatives** and **comparatives** (*the best, the most important of them, the taller of them*)
- **ordinal** numeral words (*the second, the eighth*)
- certain semantic categories of **adjective**, e.g. colour adjectives as in *the blue* and nationality adjectives that aren't also count nouns, as in *the French, the English, the Dutch* (we don't get **The Belgian are very courteous* because we use the count noun instead: *The Belgians are very courteous*).

7.4   Compound forms

There are a number of forms where the fusion of determiner and head has become a morphological fact: *every, some, any, no* have formed compound words with nouns like *body, one,* and *thing*, making words like *everybody, someone,* and *nothing*. (*Body* and *one* have the special meaning "person" in these compounds.) There is a simple way to tell that the determiner is fused with the head: it is not possible to insert a modifier between them. Adjectival modifiers follow the head instead of appearing in the usual pre-head position. The contrasts between the [a] and [b] cases in [48] show this:

[48]   FUSED HEAD   SEPARATE HEAD
   i   a. *somebody famous*   b. *some famous person*
   ii a. *nothing harmful*   b. *no harmful thing*

Notice that *no one* is a compound although it is usually written with a space as if it were two words (it is sometimes written as *no-one*, but not as **noone*). The test just mentioned shows that it is a compound: *No one famous showed up at the premiere* cannot be expressed in the form **No famous one showed up at the premiere*.

8   Pronouns

Pronouns form a subclass of nouns distinguished syntactically from common nouns and proper nouns by their inability to take determiners as dependent. We say *I am ill*, not **This I am ill*; we say *She likes him*, not **The she likes the him*. They nevertheless occur as head of NPs functioning in the main NP positions of subject, object, predicative complement, complement of a preposition. They form a subclass of nouns rather than being a separate category.

There are several different kinds of pronoun, illustrated in [49]:

[49]   i   PERSONAL   *I like them*   *Your sister underestimates herself.*
    ii RECIPROCAL   *They dislike each other* *We were helping one another.*
    iii INTERROGATIVE   *Who saw them leave?*   *What do you want?*
    iv RELATIVE   *the guy who helped us*   *the book which you recommended*

In this section we deal with just the first two types: the others will be covered in the chapters that deal with interrogative and relative clauses: see Ch. 9, §2.4, and Ch. 11, §§3–4.

8.1   Deictic and anaphoric uses of pronouns

Most pronouns are characteristically used either **deictically** or **anaphorically**.

(a) Deictic uses of pronouns

The term **deixis** applies to the use of expressions in which the meaning can be traced directly to features of the act of utterance – when and where it takes place, and who is involved as speaker and as addressee. In their primary meaning, for example, *now* and *here* are used **deictically** to refer respectively to the time and place of the utterance. Similarly, *this country* is likely to be interpreted deictically as the country in which the utterance takes place. Several of the pronouns are predominantly used deictically, with *I* and *we* referring to the speaker and a group including the speaker, *you* to the addressee(s) or a set including the addressee(s).

(b) Anaphoric uses of pronouns

The term **anaphora** applies to the use of expressions in which the meaning is derived from another expression in the surrounding linguistic material. That other expression is called the **antecedent**. The pronouns in [50] are underlined and their antecedents are doubly underlined.

[50]   i *Liz said she was unavailable.*
       ii *The victim's daughter didn't come to the meeting. Liz said she was unavailable.*
      iii *When I last saw her, Liz seemed to be extremely busy.*

- In the most obvious interpretation for [i], *she* refers to Liz – and it does so by virtue of its **anaphoric** relation to the antecedent *Liz* in the main clause.
- That is not the only interpretation, however. In [ii], the same sentence occurs in a context where *she* is much more likely to be interpreted as referring to the victim's daughter. The antecedent is located in an earlier sentence.
- The antecedent usually precedes the pronoun (the Latin prefix *ante·* means "before"), but under certain conditions it can follow, as in [iii].

The traditional term 'pronoun' has a Latin origin (like 'antecedent'), and the meaning suggests it serves for or on behalf of a noun. This is based on the anaphoric use, but it unfortunately suggests that a pronoun is used in place of a noun, which is not correct. An anaphoric pronoun stands in place of a full **noun phrase**. In [ii], for example, *she* could be replaced by the antecedent NP (*Liz said the victim's daughter was unavailable*), but not by the head noun (**Liz said daughter was unavailable*).

The examples of deixis given above included not only pronouns but also other kinds of expression (*this country*, *here*, *now*), and it is likewise not only pronouns that are used anaphorically. In *I warned <u>Jack</u> about that, but <u>the fool</u> wouldn't listen*, for example, the NP *the fool* is anaphorically related to the antecedent *Jack*.

8.2   Personal pronouns

The prototypical members of the set of personal pronouns are as follows:

[51]		SINGULAR	PLURAL
	1ST PERSON	*I*	*we*
	2ND PERSON	*you*	*you*
	3RD PERSON	*he*, *she*, *it*	*they*

The term 'personal' should not be thought to imply that these pronouns are used to refer to persons: obviously, this doesn't apply to almost all cases of *it* and many of *they*. This subclass is called 'personal' because it is the one to which the grammatical distinction of **person** applies.

The category of person

- **1st person** indicates reference to the **speaker**. We follow the widespread practice in linguistics of using this term to cover the writer of written language as well as the speaker of spoken language.
- **2nd person** usually indicates reference to the **addressee(s)** – not everyone who hears (or reads) the utterance, but the person or persons addressed by the speaker.
- **3rd person** is the default term in the system, giving no indication that the speaker or the addressee is included, and thus typically excluding them. Notice that ALL NPs headed by a common or proper noun or a pronoun other than *I*, *we*, or *you* are 3rd person.

The terms '1st', '2nd' and '3rd' reflect a **hierarchical ordering**. We can see this clearly by looking at how we select plural pronouns:

- We first ask whether the set of people being referred to **includes the speaker(s)**.[3] If so, the 1st person plural *we* is the pronoun to use. That might include the addressee(s) too (*Let's leave now, so <u>we</u> don't have to rush*) or it might not (*<u>We</u>'re better off without you*).
- Next, if the set being referred to does not include the speaker(s), we ask whether it **includes the addressee(s)**. If so, then the 2nd person *you* is the right pronoun. That might include someone other than the addressee(s) (*When your husband*

---

[3] Note that there may be more than one speaker: in writing this arises with joint letters, jointly authored works, etc., in speech in communal prayer, chants, etc.

comes out of hospital <u>you</u> should take a holiday together) or it might not (*Will <u>you</u> now please turn to page 58*).

- Last, if both questions get a negative answer, a 3rd person form is used. That means any 3rd person NP will normally be taken to refer to people (or things) other than the speaker and addressee, though in a few cases we find the speaker or addressee being referred to in the 3rd person. For example, in formal writing, expressions like *the writer* or *the reader* are sometimes used instead of 1st or 2nd person pronouns.

Non-deictic use of *you*

There is a secondary, non-deictic, use for 2nd person *you* in which it does not refer to any particular person(s): *You could hear a pin drop* or *You can't do that kind of thing when you're pregnant* (which could be addressed to a man no less than to a woman). Here it is used to talk about people generally, and is equivalent to the slightly formal *one*, a less prototypical member of the personal pronoun category.

Gender

The 3rd person singular pronouns contrast in **gender**, which is a classification of NPs that has a variety of dimensions in some languages but in English revolves mainly around sex.

- The **masculine** gender pronoun *he* is used for males – humans or animals that have salient enough sexual characteristics for us to think of them as differentiated (certainly for gorillas, usually for ducks, probably not for rats, certainly not for cockroaches).
- The **feminine** gender pronoun *she* is used for females, and also, by extension, for certain other things conventionally treated in a similar way: political entities (*France has recalled <u>her</u> ambassador*) and certain personified inanimates, especially ships (*May God bless <u>her</u> and all who sail in <u>her</u>*).
- The **neuter** pronoun *it* is used for inanimates, or for male or female animals (especially lower animals and non-cuddly creatures), and sometimes for human infants if the sex is unknown or considered irrelevant: *The baby grunted again, and Alice looked very anxiously into <u>its</u> face to see what was the matter with <u>it</u>.*

Choice of a singular human pronoun without sex specification

No singular 3rd person pronoun in English is universally accepted as appropriate for referring to a human when you don't want to specify sex. The need for such a pronoun is often acute, especially where no particular person is referred to and the antecedent is indefinite and applicable to both males and females. The pronoun most widely used in such cases is *they*, in a secondary use that is interpreted semantically as singular. (In its primary use, of course, it refers to groups and has plural antecedents.) Examples of semantically singular **they** are given in [52]:

[52]   i   *Nobody in their right mind would do a thing like that.*
       ii *Everyone has told me they think I made the right decision.*
       iii *We need a manager who is reasonably flexible in their approach.*
       iv *In that case the husband or the wife will have to give up their seat on the board.*

Notice that this special interpretation of *they* doesn't affect verb agreement: we have *they think* (3rd plural) in [ii], not *they thinks (3rd singular). Nonetheless, **they** can be INTERPRETED as if it were 3rd person singular, with human denotation and unspecified gender.

The pronoun **he** used to be recommended for these uses. That would give us *%Nobody in his right mind would do a thing like that* instead of [52i]. However, this now seems inappropriate to a large proportion of speakers, who systematically avoid the use of **he** in such contexts (hence the per cent sign on the example just given).

This avoidance of **he** can't be dismissed as just a matter of political correctness. The real problem with using **he** is that its primary sense unquestionably colours the interpretation, sometimes inappropriately. If *his* were used in place of *their* in [52iii], it would suggest that the speaker assumes the manager will be a man. And **he** is impossible for just about all speakers in cases like [52iv], where the antecedent is a coordination of a masculine and a feminine NP joined by *or*: you could hardly say *?In that case the husband or the wife will have to give up his seat on the board.* This shows that **he** doesn't have a genuinely sex-neutral sense.

Some speakers use disjunctive locutions like *he or she* in preference to the sexist use of **he**: *We need a manager who is reasonably flexible in his or her approach.* But this sounds absurd when there are repeated occurrences: examples like *?Everyone agreed he or she would bring his or her lunch with him or her* are far too cumbersome for use. And **Everyone's here, isn't he or she?* is flatly ungrammatical, because the interrogative component in this construction is required to contain just an auxiliary and a pronoun. The only natural non-sexist alternative would be: *Everyone's here, aren't they?*

Among younger speakers today, semantically singular **they** is extending its scope: people use it even with definite NP antecedents, sidestepping any presumptions about the sex of the person referred to, as in *You should ask your partner what they think,* or *The person I was with said they hated the film.*

There is just one problem area for **they** with singular antecedents: what to use in the **reflexive** construction (the one containing compound forms like *myself, ourselves,* etc.). *Everybody enjoyed themselves* seems fine, because we're talking about a number of people; but *?Somebody here obviously considers themselves above the law,* with the visibly plural *selves,* sounds odd given that there's just one person involved and the verb is a 3rd person singular form. The obvious solution would be to have a singular form *themself.* This is found, and has a long history in English, but at the moment it is quite rare, and can't really be regarded as standard.

Prescriptive grammar note

Usage manuals vary considerably in their attitude to semantically singular *they*. The more factually based ones treat it as acceptable, recognising that it has been in the language for several hundred years, used by writers of impeccable standing – Chaucer, Shakespeare, Milton, Austen, Wilde, and large numbers of other authors. The more conservative manuals, however, insist that the conflict between the primarily plural form and the singular meaning makes this use of *they* incorrect. In fact there are manuals still in print that directly recommend the use of *he*. But defenders of this advice must face an awkward question: why should an extension from plural to singular sense for *they* be unacceptable, if extension from masculine to sex-neutral sense for *he* is supposed to be all right?

We don't think there is any way to answer this question, or to defend the conservative position. Semantically singular *they* is well established in fine literature and completely natural in both conversation and writing.

8.3   Inflection

The personal pronouns exhibit a greater amount of inflectional variation than other nouns. In the first place there is a distinction between **reflexive** and **non-reflexive** forms, and secondly they have up to four different **case-forms**. The following table displays in full the forms of the central personal pronouns.

[53]

		NON-REFLEXIVE				REFLEXIVE
		Nominative	**Accusative**	**Genitive**		**Plain**
		Plain		**Dependent**	**Independent**	
i	*I*	*I*	*me*	*my*	*mine*	*myself*
ii	*you*	*you*		*your*	*yours*	*yourself*
iii	*he*	*he*	*him*	*his*		*himself*
iv	*she*	*she*	*her*	*her*	*hers*	*herself*
v	*it*	*it*		*its*		*itself*
vi	*we*	*we*	*us*	*our*	*ours*	*ourselves*
vii	*you*	*you*		*your*	*yours*	*yourselves*
viii	*they*	*they*	*them*	*their*	*theirs*	*themselves*

Reflexive forms

The **reflexive** pronouns have two main uses: one where they function as **complement**, and an **emphatic** use where they function as **modifier** in clause or NP structure:

[54]   COMPLEMENT USE   EMPHATIC USE
  i a. _Sue hurt herself._   b. _Sue designed the house herself._
  ii a. _Sue was talking to herself._   b. _Sue herself admitted it was a mistake._

- In the complement use the reflexive forms generally contrast with non-reflexive ones: [ia] contrasts with *Sue hurt her*, and so on. In [ia], *Sue* is the antecedent for the pronoun, so the meaning is that the person hurt was the same as the one who caused the hurt: "Sue hurt Sue". In *Sue hurt her*, by contrast, *Sue* cannot be the antecedent, and hence we understand that Sue hurt some other female. Complement reflexives occur in a close syntactic relation to the antecedent. In the simplest and most common case, illustrated here, the antecedent is subject of the clause containing the reflexive as complement of the verb, as in [ia], or of a preposition, as in [iia].
- In the emphatic use only reflexive forms are permitted: we can't say **Sue designed the house her*. In [ib] the reflexive emphasises that it was Sue who designed the house: she didn't have someone else do it. In [iib] it emphasises that Sue made the admission: perhaps she was the one who made the mistake.

The nominative–accusative contrast of case

The grammatical category of case applies to a system of inflectional forms whose primary use is to mark various syntactic functions. This is clearly the major factor determining the choice between nominative and accusative forms in English, but style level is an important secondary factor. Compare:

[55]　i　*They wrote the editorial.*　　　　　　　　　[subject: nominative]
　　　ii　*Kim met them in Paris.*　　　　　　　　　[object of verb: accusative]
　　　iii　*I was talking to them yesterday.*　　　　[object of prep: accusative]
　　　iv　*It was they/them who complained.*　　　[PC: nominative or accusative]

- When the pronoun is subject of a finite clause it appears in nominative form, and when it is object – of the verb, as in [ii], or of a preposition, as in [iii] – it appears in accusative form.
- When the pronoun is predicative complement both forms are found – though the nominative is largely restricted to constructions of the form *it* + *be* + pronoun, as in [iv]. Here the nominative is quite formal in style, with the accusative somewhat informal. However, in constructions like *The only person who didn't complain was me* a nominative could hardly replace the underlined accusative.

Case in verbless constructions

There is also alternation between the two case-forms in certain verbless constructions:

[56]　　a. *She's a year younger than I.*　　b. *She's a year younger than me.*

Again, the nominative in [a] is strongly formal in style, and the accusative is much more common in ordinary conversation.

> ### Prescriptive grammar note
>
> The more authoritarian and conservative manuals claim that only a nominative is grammatically correct in [55iv], where the pronoun is predicative complement, and [56], where it is understood as subject of an elliptical clause (cf. *younger than I am*). But that is to confuse correctness with formality, as we pointed out in Ch. 1, §2: the accusative variants are unquestionably grammatical in Standard English.

Plain case

In Present-day English the contrast between nominative and accusative forms is found only with personal pronouns and with interrogative and relative **who** (discussed in Ch. 9, §2.4, Ch. 11, §3). Other nouns appear in the same form in all the above constructions: cf. *The <u>minister</u> wrote the editorial, Kim met the <u>minister</u> in Paris*, and so on. We use the term **plain form** here: to say that *minister* was nominative in the first and accusative in the second would be to make the mistake of confusing INFLECTIONAL CASE with GRAMMATICAL FUNCTION.

Case in coordinations

For many speakers the above rules extend to constructions where the pronoun is coordinated, but there are also many who use special rules for coordinative constructions. Note the status markers on the following examples:

[57] i a. *Kim and <u>I</u> went over there.*   b. ¹*Kim and <u>me</u> went over there.*
      ii a. *They invited Sandy and <u>me</u>.*   b. ᵒ*They invited Sandy and <u>I</u>.*

The whole coordination is subject in [i] and object in [ii], so in the absence of coordination we would have nominative *I* in [i] (*I went over there*) and accusative *me* in [ii] (*They invited me*). Construction [ib] is not accepted as Standard English, though it is very common in non-standard speech. Construction [iib], however, is used by many highly educated people with social prestige in the community; it should be regarded as a variant Standard English form.

> **Prescriptive grammar note**
>
> The pattern in [iib] is heard constantly in the conversation of people whose status as speakers of Standard English is clear, but it is nevertheless condemned as incorrect or illiterate by many usage manuals. For this reason it is not so common in print: editors will often 'correct' it. Nonetheless, examples are certainly found. Those who condemn it simply assume that the case of a pronoun in a coordination must be the same as when it stands alone. Actual usage is in conflict with this assumption. (Note that we have already come across another instance of coordinated NPs differing in form from non-coordinated ones: recall the discussion of *husband and wife* in [15iia].)

Genitive case

While the nominative–accusative contrast is found only with a handful of pronouns, **genitive** case applies to nouns quite generally – and hence is discussed in a separate section below (§9). The distinction between **dependent** and **independent** forms of the genitive, however, is restricted to personal pronouns. Compare:

[58]   DEPENDENT FORM   INDEPENDENT FORM
      i a. *I've lost <u>my</u> key.*   b. *This is <u>mine</u>.*
      ii a. *He objected to <u>my</u> taking notes.*   b. *Your proposal is better than <u>mine</u>.*

- The dependent form usually functions in NP structure as determiner to a following head, as in [ia]. It also occurs as subject of a gerund-participial clause, as in [iia], where it is a dependent of the VP head; this latter use is somewhat formal in style, with accusative *me* as an informal alternant.
- The independent form occurs as head in NP structure – a pure head in [ib], a fused determiner-head in [iib], where we understand "my proposal".

8.4   Reciprocal pronouns

There are two reciprocal pronouns, *each other* and *one another*. They are written with a space as if they were two words, but the parts are inseparable and they are best regarded as single pronouns. There is no difference in meaning between them.

The reciprocal pronouns are similar to the reflexives (in their complement use) in that they have to be in a close syntactic relation to their antecedent. Compare:

[59]   REFLEXIVES   RECIPROCALS
    i a. *Lee and Pat* cursed *themselves*.   b. *Lee and Pat* cursed *each other*.
    ii a. **Lee and Pat knew that I would   b. **Lee and Pat knew that I would
            curse *themselves*.   curse *each other*.

Usually, the antecedent is subject of the clause containing the pronoun, as in [i]. It cannot normally be in a different clause, as shown in [ii]. It should be clear that lack of meaning is not the problem. Just as [ib] means that Lee cursed Pat and Pat cursed Lee (as the term 'reciprocal' suggests), so [iib] could have meant (if it were grammatical) that Lee knew that I would curse Pat and Pat knew that I would curse Lee.

The reciprocals differ from the reflexives, however, in two major respects.

- First, they do not display person agreement with their antecedent.
- Second, they have genitive forms, as seen in *Lee and Pat blamed each other's parents*.

9   Genitive case

Leaving aside interrogative and relative *whose* and the personal pronouns (which have the irregular forms listed in [53]) the genitive is marked in writing by ·*'s* (*dog's*) or by the apostrophe alone (*dogs'*): for the distinction between these, see Ch. 16, §4.2.

9.1   Genitive NPs as subject-determiner

The most frequent use of genitive case is to mark a dependent in the structure of an NP:

[60]   i a. [*The teacher's* car] was stolen.   b. *They phoned* [*my* mother].
       ii a. [*These people's* fate] is unknown.   b. *I met* [*the Secretary of State's* son].

Underlining here marks the genitive dependent, while brackets enclose the NP in which it functions. The genitive dependent is an NP: we have one NP functioning in the structure of another. Thus the first division of the bracketed NP in [ia], for example, is *the teacher's* + *car* (not *the* + *teacher's car*). This is particularly clear in examples like those in [ii].

* In [iia] plural *these* obviously belongs with plural *people*, not singular *fate*.
* And in [iib] the person I met was the son not of the State but of the Secretary of State.

The ·*'s* suffix occurs at the end of the genitive NP; the latter usually has the head in final position, as in [ia] and [iia], but it can contain a relatively short post-head dependent, like *of State* in [iib]. Compare, similarly, *someone else's responsibility* or *the guy next door's voice*.

Dual function of the genitive NP

The genitive NPs in [60] combine the functions of determiner and complement. The construction is semantically equivalent to one where the two functions are realised separately, by a definite determiner and a post-head *of* phrase complement. Compare:

[61] i a. *the patient's condition*   b. *the condition of the patient*
      ii a. *one patient's father*   b. *the father of one patient*

The single dependent of the [a] examples does the work of the two dependents of the [b] examples.

* As a determiner, the genitive is always definite. Note, for example, that [iia] corresponds to *the father of one patient*, not *a father of one patient*.
* As a complement, the genitive is comparable to the subject of a clause. It occurs before the head nominal as a clause subject occurs before the head VP. And where the noun is morphologically related to a verb the genitive has the same role as a clause subject. Compare *Kim's criticism of the report* and *Kim criticised the report*, and so on.

For this reason we refer to the genitive NPs in [60–61] as **subject-determiners**.

'Genitive' vs 'possessive'

The term 'possessive' is often used instead of 'genitive', especially for pronouns, but it is important to see that the semantic relation between the genitive NP and the following head is by no means limited to that of possession. Consider these cases, and think about which of them (if any) could possibly be said to have something to do with possessing:

[62]   *her father, her friends, her birth, her infancy, her anger, her lack of money, her acceptance of your offer, her refusal to compromise, her rapid action*

Not one of these permits a natural paraphrase with **possess**, in the way that *her car* can be paraphrased as *the car she possesses*. Often there will be a range of interpretations available. *Her letter* might be the letter she wrote or the letter she received, and there are other possibilities available in special contexts. In the context of a language-teaching class, for example, it could be the letter that has been assigned to her to translate.

9.2   Other uses of the genitive

Genitive case is also used in the following constructions:

[63]   i   SUBJECT   *She didn't approve of [his being given a second chance].*
      ii   FUSED HEAD   *They accepted Kim's proposal but not Pat's.*
     iii   OBLIQUE   *The argument was sparked by a casual remark of Kim's.*
      iv   PREDICATIVE   *Everything in this room is Mary's.*
       v   ATTRIBUTIVE   *They've just moved to an old people's home.*

- In formal style the **subject of a gerund-participial clause** that is functioning as complement (of a verb or preposition) appears in genitive case, as in [i].
- Like most other determiners, a genitive can **fuse** with the head, as in [ii], understood as "Pat's proposal".
- The **oblique genitive** occurs as complement to *of* in a post-head dependent. Note the contrast between *a casual remark of Kim's* in [iii], which is marked as indefinite by the article *a*, and *Kim's casual remark*, which is marked as definite by the genitive subject-determiner.
- The **predicative genitive** functions as complement of *be*, *become*, etc., and here it does indicate possession, as in [iv].
- The **attributive genitive** functions as internal modifier in NP structure. Note that in [v] *an* is determiner to the larger nominal (*old people's home*), not the genitive one (*old people's*); this contrasts with [60iia] above.

Exercises

1. Write out or type the following passage (it's the opening paragraph of the preface to Steven Pinker's book *The Language Instinct*) with the **nouns** underlined and the **NPs** enclosed in square brackets. (Don't forget that one NP can occur within another: in a phrase like *I met the father of the bride*, for example, *the bride* is an NP within the larger NP *the father of the bride*, so you would write [*the father* of [*the bride*]].)

   I have never met a person who is not interested in language. I wrote this book to try to satisfy that curiosity. Language is beginning to submit to that uniquely satisfying kind of understanding that we call science, but the news has been kept a secret.

2. There are a number of nouns that are **plural-only** in some of their senses, but not in all. For example:

   PLURAL-ONLY   *Eat more greens.*
   ORDINARY   *Those greens don't match.*

   For the first nine of the following give two examples containing the word in an appropriate context, one where it has its plural-only sense, and one where it is an ordinary plural with a contrasting singular form. For the last item, *people*, give one example where it is a plural-only noun, and one where it is a singular:

i *arts*
ii *beginnings*
iii *brains*
iv *compliments*
v *customs*
vi *holidays*
vii *letters*
viii *spectacles*
ix *spirits*
x *people*

3. Say whether the underlined nouns in the following examples have a **count** or a **non-count** interpretation. In each case construct another example in which the noun has the opposite interpretation.

i *You needn't have gone into so much <u>detail</u>.*
ii *I've run out of <u>paper</u>.*
iii *Can I have another <u>sausage</u>?*
iv *He has jet-black <u>hair</u>.*
v *They treat their new <u>help</u> appallingly.*

4. Are the underlined NPs below **definite** or **indefinite**? Give reasons for your answer.

i *<u>Those shoes</u> are filthy.*
ii *<u>Both copies of the report</u> are missing.*
iii *I need <u>two copies of your report</u>.*
iv *<u>Either time</u> would be OK for me.*
v *We found <u>several big mushrooms</u>.*

5. In the following examples give (a) the **function** within NP structure, and (b) the **category**, of the underlined expressions (there are twenty in all; for reference they're labelled with small roman numeral subscripts).

<u>her</u>[i] interest <u>in language</u>[ii]
<u>a</u>[iii] <u>brick</u>[iv] wall
<u>the</u>[v] people <u>who need most help</u>[vi]
<u>three</u>[vii] <u>Canadian</u>[viii] soldiers
<u>its</u>[ix] <u>many</u>[x] virtues
a <u>very useful</u>[xi] discussion <u>of the problem</u>[xii]
a person <u>of impeccable taste</u>[viii]
<u>even</u>[xiv] the director <u>herself</u>[xv]
<u>several</u>[xvi] things <u>you forgot to say</u>[xvii]
a <u>Vietnam war</u>[xviii] veteran
<u>that large</u>[xix] a <u>deficit</u>[xx]

6. Classify the **fused heads** in the following examples as (a) **simple**; (b) **partitive**; or (c) **special**:

i *Jill has two children and her sister <u>three</u>.*
ii *<u>Which</u> of her arguments did you find the most convincing?*
iii *Thousands of people saw it, and <u>most</u> thought it was first-class.*
iv *You've made progress, but <u>much</u> still remains to be done.*
v *There were several slices, and as usual Tom took the <u>largest</u>.*
vi *The show verges on the <u>obscene</u>.*
vii *There are wolves out there; I saw <u>several</u>.*
viii *The first letter is P and the <u>second</u> is Q.*
ix *The <u>good</u> die young.*
x *Many are called but <u>few</u> are chosen.*

7. Select an appropriate **case-form** of the pronoun *I* for the blank positions in the following examples. If more than one case-form is admissible in Standard English, list them all and comment on the difference between them.

i *Your father and __ have been considering this matter.*
ii *In the other photo, the guy in the middle of the front row is __.*
iii *They've arranged for you and __ to meet with Dr Jackson this evening.*
iv *They went to the same school as __.*
v *They're seeing Kim before you and __.*

8. What kind of genitive do we have in the following examples: (a) **subject-determiner**; (b) **subject**; (c) **fused-head**; (d) **oblique**; (e) **predicative**; or (f) **attributive**?

i *A friend of <u>mine</u> told me you're leaving the country.*
ii *<u>Your</u> application has been approved but <u>Jill's</u> is still being considered.*
iii *This book belongs to Pat, but the rest are <u>yours</u>.*
iv *Do you know if there's a <u>men's</u> toilet around here?*
v *He objects to <u>your</u> being paid more than everybody else.*

6   Adjectives and adverbs

1   Adjectives

1.1   Distinctive properties of prototypical adjectives

Adjectives typically denote **properties** of objects, persons, places, etc.: properties relating to age (*old*, *young*), size (*big*, *small*), shape (*round*, *flat*), weight (*heavy*, *light*), colour (*black*, *blue*), merit or quality (*good*, *bad*), and so on. Syntactically, prototypical adjectives in English have the following three properties.

(a) Function

They have **attributive** and **predicative** uses. Attributive adjectives function as internal pre-head **modifier** to a following noun; predicative adjectives function mainly as **predicative complement** in clause structure:

[1]   i   ATTRIBUTIVE USE   *an <u>old</u> car*   <u>black</u> *hair*   <u>good</u> *news*
       ii PREDICATIVE USE   *The car is <u>old</u>.*   *Her hair is <u>black</u>.*   *The news is <u>good</u>.*

(b) Grade

They either inflect for **grade**, showing a contrast between **plain**, **comparative** and **superlative** forms, or else form comparative and superlative adjective phrases (AdjPs) marked by *more* and *most*:

[2]   PLAIN   COMPARATIVE   SUPERLATIVE
       i *She is <u>tall</u>.*   *She is <u>taller</u> than you.*   *She is the <u>tallest</u> of them all.*
       ii *This is <u>useful</u>* *This is <u>more useful</u> than that.* *This is the <u>most useful</u> one.*

(c) Modification

They can be modified, usually by adverbs, as in [3] (the adverbs are double-underlined):

[3]   <u>*too*</u> *<u>old</u>*   <u>*remarkably*</u> *<u>tall</u>*   <u>*extremely*</u> *<u>useful</u> to us*

112

1.2   Adjectives vs nouns

The properties given above make it a generally easy matter to distinguish adjectives from **nouns**, especially when taken together with the properties of nouns presented in Ch. 5, §1.

In this section we pick out a selection of the most decisive properties that do distinguish between nouns and adjectives. We use *judge*, *size*, and *silk* as examples of words that occur as nouns but not as adjectives, and *wise*, *big*, and *smooth* as examples of words that occur as adjectives but not as nouns.

(a) Inflection

Nouns typically have **plural inflected forms**; adjectives (in English) never do. Conversely, many adjectives have **comparative** and **superlative inflected forms**, but no nouns do:

[4]   PLURAL FORMS WITH ·s OR ·es   SUPERLATIVE FORMS WITH ·est
  i a. N   *judges   sizes   silks*   b. **judgest *sizest   *silkest*
  ii a. ADJ **wises *bigs *smooths*   b. *wisest   biggest   smoothest*

Not all nouns have plural forms and not all adjectives have comparative and superlative forms, but where the forms do exist the difference between nouns and adjectives is particularly clear.

(b) Determiners

Nouns take **determiners** as dependent but adjectives do not. Some of the determinatives that function as determiner in NP structure, however, can also function as modifier in AdjP structure, so in applying this test we need to select items which cannot modify adjectives. This can be done by picking genitives, or the determinatives *which* and *some*:

[5]   i N   *which judge?*   *my size*   *some silk*
      ii ADJ   **which wise?*   **my big*   **some smooth*

(c) Modifiers

Nouns and adjectives take different kinds of **modifiers**. Most importantly, NOUNS TAKE ADJECTIVES as modifier, but adjectives don't normally take other adjectives as modifier. Adjectives most often take adverbs. There are enormous numbers of adjective–adverb pairs that differ just by the presence of the suffix ·ly on the adverb, as in *remarkable* vs *remarkably*, and in those cases it is the word without the ·ly that modifies a following noun, and the one with ·ly that modifies a following adjective, as the examples in [6] show:

[6]   i N   *a remarkable judge*   *its incredible size*   *this wonderful silk*
      ii ADJ   *remarkably wise*   *incredibly big*   *wonderfully smooth*

Switching adjectives and adverbs makes ungrammatical phrases in every case: **a remarkably judge*, **remarkable wise*, etc.

(d) Function

The attributive and predicative uses of adjectives do not provide a good test for distinguishing them from nouns because nouns can also function as attributive modifiers or predicative complements. But there is a function-based test that separates nouns from adjectives fairly well: the ability of nouns to head phrases in **subject** and **object** position. We illustrate in [7].

[7]		SUBJECT	SUBJECT	OBJECT
	i N	*The judge arrived.*	*Its size amazed me.*	*I like silk.*
	ii ADJ	**Wise arrived.*	**Big amazed me.*	**I like smooth.*

Overlap between the categories

It should be borne in mind that there are a good many lexemes that belong to both noun and adjective categories. They have the positive properties of both. One example is *cold*:

- it can be an adjective denoting a low temperature (*This soup is cold*);
- It can also be a noun denoting a minor illness (*I caught a bad cold*).

Compare, then:

[8]			ADJECTIVE	NOUN
	i	INFLECTION	*colder, coldest*	*colds*
	ii	DETERMINERS		*my cold, which cold?*
	iii	MODIFIERS	*terribly cold*	*a terrible cold*
	iv	FUNCTION		*The cold was nasty. Don't catch a cold.*

- The adjective has comparative and superlative forms while the noun has a plural.
- The noun takes determiners as dependent.
- The modifier contrast is evident in [iii], with the adjective taking an adverb and the noun an adjective as modifier.
- The noun occurs as head of a phrase in subject or object function.

The fused modifier-head construction

One complication in distinguishing between adjectives and nouns is that a limited range of adjectives can appear as **fused modifier-head** in an NP, as described in Ch. 5, §7. Further examples are given in [9].

[9]	i	SIMPLE	*The first version wasn't very good but [the second] was fine.*
	ii	PARTITIVE	*I couldn't afford [even the cheapest of them].*
	iii	SPECIAL	*This tax cut will benefit [only the rich].*

Precisely because they are in head position in NP structure, the underlined words might at first glance be thought to be nouns. But they're not nouns: they're adjectives. In the **simple** and **partitive** constructions this is fairly easy to see:

- Note the possibility of adding a repetition of the noun *version* in [i].
- In [ii] we have a superlative form, *cheapest*, which certainly can't be a noun.

Less obvious, however, is the construction in [iii] with its **special** interpretation. In most cases, nevertheless, the form in the special construction can be clearly identified as an adjective.

- This is shown first of all by the modifier test: *the extremely rich* provides evidence that *rich* is an adjective because it is preceded by a modifying adverb (a noun would be modified by an adjective).
- Notice also that in this special fused modifier-head use, the only determiner permitted is *the* – a person who is rich can't be referred to as **a rich* or **some rich*. And although the NP *the rich* is plural (hence the verb agreement in *The rich are the beneficiaries*), it doesn't have plural inflection on *rich* – two rich people can't be referred to as **two riches*. *Rich* thus behaves very differently from a noun.

Overall, there is strong evidence that *the rich* in [9iii] contains an adjective but no noun.

1.3   Adjectives vs verbs

The properties given in §1.1 together with those presented in Ch. 3, §1 for the verb enable us to distinguish adjectives from **verbs** in a similar way. We'll apply a selection of the most decisive properties to distinguish the adjectives *fond*, *sad*, *appreciative* from the verbs *love*, *regret*, *enjoy*.

(a) Inflection and grade

Verbs have a richer system of inflection than any of the other parts of speech. Most distinctive are the **preterite** and **3rd person singular** forms. As already mentioned, **comparative** and **superlative** inflection is found with adjectives but not verbs. We illustrate in [10] with preterite and comparative forms:

[10]			PRETERITE FORMS				COMPARATIVE FORMS		
i	a.	V	*loved*	*regretted*	*enjoyed*	b.	**lover*	**regretter*	**enjoyer*
ii	a.	ADJ	**fonded*	**sadded*	**appreciatived*	b.	*fonder*	*sadder*	[n/a]

The asterisks in [ib] mark impossible comparative forms (*lover* is of course established in a quite different sense as a noun, but the point here is that it's not the comparative of **love**). We wouldn't expect a comparative inflectional form for *appreciative*, because adjectives of this length don't take grade inflection, but even with *appreciative* there is a comparative marked by *more*. And that suffices to distinguish it from a verb, since when *more* combines with a verb it doesn't precede it:

[11]	i	V	**I more <u>love</u> you.*	*I <u>love</u> you more.*
	ii	ADJ	*I'm more <u>appreciative</u> than you.*	**I'm <u>appreciative</u> than you more.*

(b) Modifiers

Unlike nouns, verbs take largely the same modifiers as adjectives: compare *Kim loved Pat <u>immensely</u>* and *Kim was <u>immensely</u> fond of Pat*. Nevertheless there are some adverbs that can modify adjectives but not verbs. They include *very; pretty*, in the sense "fairly, quite"; and *too*, in the sense "excessively". The adverb *too* can also mean "as well", and in this sense it can modify verbs, so in the following examples we add the subscript 'x' to make explicit that we are concerned with *too* in the "excessively" sense:

[12] i   V   { *I very <u>love</u> her.   *He pretty <u>regrets</u> it.   *She too_x <u>enjoyed</u> it.
      ii   { *I <u>love</u> her very.   *He <u>regrets</u> it pretty.   *She <u>enjoyed</u> it too_x.
      iii ADJ   I'm very <u>fond</u> of her.   He's pretty <u>sad</u>.   She was too_x <u>appreciative</u>.

Not all adjectives are semantically compatible with the degree modifiers *very*, *too* and *pretty*. They have to denote a property that can hold to a greater or lesser extent – what we will call a **scalar** property. For those adjectives that do denote scalar properties, the degree modification seen in [12iii] provides a very clear indication of their status as adjectives as opposed to verbs.

(c) Function

A major difference between verbs and adjectives is that verbs function as predicator (head of a VP) in clause structure whereas adjectives do not. In their predicative use, adjectives occur not as predicator but as complement to a verb such as *be*, *become*, *seem*, etc.:

[13] i V   They <u>love</u> you.   We <u>regret</u> it.   You <u>enjoy</u> it.
      ii ADJ They <u>are</u> <u>fond</u> of you.   We <u>became</u> <u>sad</u>.   You <u>seem</u> <u>appreciative</u>.

The predicator in each case in [ii] is the double-underlined word, not the adjective.

Overlap between the categories

Again we need to bear in mind that there are some items that belong to both categories. **Tame**, for example, is a verb in *We tame them* but an adjective in *They are tame*. In pairs like this, where the adjective is identical with the plain form and plain present tense of the verb, it is very easy to distinguish between them in terms of the above criteria.

- The verb has the preterite form *tamed* and the 3rd person singular present tense *tames*. And it can't take *very* as modifier: *We very tame them* or *We tame them very*.
- The adjective has the comparative form *tamer* and the superlative *tamest*. And it can be modified by *very*: *They are very tame*.

When the verb-form involved is a gerund-participle or past participle form, things are not so obvious, because these verb-forms can occur after *be* in the progressive and passive constructions. That means there can be ambiguity between verb and adjective interpretations, as in [14]:

[14]   a. *They are entertaining.*   b. *The clock was broken.*

- For [a], the verbal interpretation is "They are currently receiving guests", while the adjectival interpretation is "They are enjoyable". The former is excluded if

we add *very* (*They are very entertaining* can only mean "They are very enjoyable") or replace *be* by *seem* or *become* (e.g., *They became entertaining*). The
adjectival interpretation is excluded if we add an object for the verb (*They are
entertaining some colleagues*), since virtually no adjectives take objects.

- For [b] the verbal interpretation describes an event: "Someone or something
  broke the clock". The adjectival interpretation, by contrast, describes a state:
  "The clock was in an inoperative condition". Brokenness tends to be thought of
  as a yes-or-no property, so in general the adjective *broken* doesn't take *very* as
  modifier, but it certainly can (in fact *very broken* is a common phrase among
  computer programmers). And the *seem* test is also relevant: *It seemed broken* can
  only be adjectival.

1.4   Adjectives vs determinatives

The distinction between adjectives and **determinatives** is not as sharply
drawn as those between adjectives and nouns or adjectives and verbs. Nevertheless,
the definite article *the* and the indefinite article *a* differ strikingly from prototypical
adjectives with respect to both syntax and meaning:

- The articles can be obligatory: in most cases NPs with a count singular noun as
  head must have some kind of determinative, so in *The dog barked* or *A dog
  barked*, the article is required: **Dog barked* is not grammatical.
- The articles are non-gradable.
- The articles cannot be used predicatively.
- The articles serve to mark the NP as definite or indefinite rather than denoting
  some property of the referent.

Other items can then be assigned to the determinative category by virtue of having one or more of the following properties:

[15]   i They don't occur with articles, and articles don't occur with them.
       ii They can occur as the only pre-head dependent of a count singular noun.
       iii They can occur as fused head in a partitive construction.

The examples in [16] show how these properties distinguish the determinative *some*
from the adjective *good*:

[16]   DETERMINATIVE   ADJECTIVE
      i a. *She gave me the <u>some</u> apples.   b. *He gave me the <u>good</u> apples.*
      ii a. *<u>Some</u> guy called to see you.*   b. **<u>Good</u> guy called to see you.*
      iii a. *I took <u>some</u> of the books.*   b. **I took <u>good</u> of the books.*

- In [i], [a] is inadmissible because *some* cannot follow *the*.
- In [ii], *guy* is a count singular noun and requires a determiner, such as *some*.
- In [iii] *some* is fused head with a partitive complement, a construction which
  does not admit adjectives except for comparative and superlatives (*the younger of
  the two, the best of the lot*).

1.5   Gradable and non-gradable adjectives

We have said that prototypical adjectives have comparative and superlative forms and take degree modifiers such as *very, too* ("excessively") and *pretty*. Adjectives of this kind are said to be **gradable**. They denote scalar properties that can apply in varying degrees. *Good, old, big* and so on denote properties of this kind – and one can ask about the degree to which the property applies with *how*: *How big is it?*, etc.

Not all adjectives are of this kind. There are also **non-gradable** adjectives, as in *an alphabetical list*. It makes no sense to ask how alphabetical a list is, or to say that one list is more alphabetical than another. *Alphabetical* thus denotes a **non-scalar** property. Other examples of non-gradable adjectives are seen in [17]:

[17]   the *chief* difficulty   *federal* taxes   *glandular* fever   my *left* arm
         a *medical* problem   *phonetic* symbols   *pubic* hair   their *tenth* attempt

Some adjectives can be used in either way: like the distinction between count and non-count in nouns, the gradable vs non-gradable distinction applies to uses rather than lexemes as such. Compare:

[18]   NON-GRADABLE USE   GRADABLE USE
   i   a. *in the public interest*   b. *a very public quarrel*
  ii   a. *the British government*   b. *a very British response*
 iii   a. *The motorway is now open.*   b. *He was more open with us than the boss.*

Typically, as in these examples, the non-gradable sense is the basic one, with the gradable sense representing an extended use.

1.6   The structure of adjective phrases

An **AdjP** consists of an adjective as **head**, alone or accompanied by one or more **dependents**. The dependents may be **complements**, licensed by the head, or **modifiers**, less restricted in their occurrence.

(a) Complements

The complements are almost always PPs, as in [19], or subordinate clauses, as in [20]:

[19]   afraid *of the dark*   bent *on revenge*   conversant *with it*   good *at chess*
         kind *to children*   remote *from reality*   unaltered *by heat*   unfit *for use*

[20]   glad *it was over*   uncertain *what to do*   eager *to win*   hard *to grasp*
         busy *making lunch*   difficult *for us to see*   thankful *that no one had been hurt*

● The choice of preposition in [19] depends on the head adjective: we couldn't have, for example, **afraid on the dark* or **bent of revenge*. With certain adjectives (in particular senses) the PP is obligatory: the sense of *bent* shown here, for example, requires a PP complement with *on* (or *upon*); and *conversant* cannot occur at all without a complement.

* The kind of subordinate clause likewise depends on the adjective: we couldn't have *glad what to do, **busy to make lunch*, and so on.

(b) Modifiers

The most common type of modifier is an adverb (or AdvP), as underlined in [21i], but other categories are also found: determinatives (underlined in [21ii]), PPs (as in [21iii]), and in a very limited range of cases, NPs (as in [21iv]):

[21]   i *extremely* hot   *morally* wrong   *very* useful   *almost completely* watertight
       ii *this* young   *that* old   *no* different   *much* better   *any* smaller   old *enough*
       iii cautious *to excess*   dangerous *in the extreme*   an [*in some respects* good] idea
       iv *five years* old   *two hours* long   *a great deal* smaller   *a bit* overpowering

PPs generally follow the head, but in attributive AdjPs they normally precede, as in the last example of [iii], where we have put brackets round the whole AdjP.

1.7   Predicative complements and predicative adjuncts

In their predicative use, adjectives (or AdjPs) generally function as complement in clause structure. As we saw in Ch. 4, §5, predicative complements occur in complex-intransitive and complex-transitive clauses:

[22]   COMPLEX-INTRANSITIVE CLAUSE   COMPLEX-TRANSITIVE CLAUSE

   a. | *The suggestion* | *is* | *ridiculous.* | b. | *I* | *consider* | *the suggestion* | *ridiculous.* |
         S   P   PC   S   P   O   PC

The adjective is related to a **predicand** (*the suggestion*), which is subject in the complex-intransitive construction, and object in the complex-transitive construction.

In addition to being complements, licensed by the head, predicative AdjPs can be adjuncts. Compare, for example:

[23]   i PREDICATIVE COMPLEMENT   *Max was unwilling to accept these terms.*
       ii PREDICATIVE ADJUNCT   *Unwilling to accept these terms, Max resigned.*

In [i] the AdjP is a complement licensed by the verb (*be*), but in [ii] it is an adjunct, with no such licensing – it is, more specifically, a supplement, detached by intonation or punctuation from the rest of the clause. It is nevertheless still predicative, in that it is related to a predicand. We understand in [ii], no less than in [i], that the unwillingness to accept these terms applies to Max.

1.8   Adjectives restricted to attributive or predicative function

Although most adjectives can be used both attributively and predicatively, there are nevertheless many that are restricted to one or other of these two uses:

[24]   ATTRIBUTIVE USE   PREDICATIVE USE
    i a.   *a huge hole*   b. *The hole was huge.*
   ii a.   *utter nonsense*   b. **That nonsense was utter.*
  iii a.   **the asleep children* b. *The children were asleep.*

- *Huge* illustrates the default case, where the adjective appears both attributively and predicatively.
- *Utter* is an exceptional case: an **attributive-only** adjective, which can't be used predicatively (as shown in [iib]).
- *Asleep* is the opposite kind of exception, as evident from [iii]; it can occur predicatively but not attributively: it is a **never-attributive** adjective.

(a) Attributive-only adjectives

NPs containing a sample of other adjectives that are **attributive-only** are given in [25]:

[25]   *these damn budget cuts*   *the eventual winner*   *her former husband*
        our future prospects   *the main problem*   *a mere child*
        the only drawback   *their own fault*   *the principal advantage*
        the putative father   *the sole survivor*   *a veritable jungle*

(b) Never-attributive adjectives

Here are some further examples of predicative uses of **never-attributive** adjectives:

[26]   *The house was ablaze.*   *The boy seemed afraid.*   *The child was alone.*
        Something was amiss.   *It was devoid of interest.* *Corruption was rife.*
        It is liable to flood.   *The baby looked content.*   *I was utterly bereft.*

Restrictions may apply to senses rather than lexemes

As with the gradable vs non-gradable distinction, the restrictions often apply just to certain senses of a lexeme. In [27], for example, it is ONLY IN THE SENSES ILLUSTRATED that the underlined adjectives in [i] are attributive-only, and those in [ii] never-attributive:

[27]   i *a certain country*   *the late queen*   *the lawful heir*
      ii *I feel faint*   *He was glad to see her.* *I'm sorry you missed it.*

Structural restrictions on attributive adjectives

Attributive AdjPs mostly cannot contain dependents that follow the head. The typical case is as in [28], where the underlined adjective licenses a post-head dependent (double-underlined), and the AdjP is allowed only predicatively as in the [a] cases, not attributively as in the [b] cases.

[28]   PREDICATIVE   ATTRIBUTIVE
    i a. *She was <u>devoted</u> <u>to her children</u>.*   b. **a <u>devoted</u> <u>to her children</u> mother*
    ii a. *She was <u>cautious</u> <u>to excess</u>.*   b. **a <u>cautious</u> <u>to excess</u> manager*

There are a few post-head dependents that can occur with attributive adjectives, though, as seen in [29].

[29]   i a. *The house was <u>big</u> <u>enough</u>.*   b. *a <u>big</u> <u>enough</u> house*
    ii a. *The result was <u>better</u> <u>than expected</u>.*   b. *a <u>better</u> <u>than expected</u> result*
    iii a. *It was <u>better</u> <u>than anyone expected</u>.*   b. *a <u>better</u> result <u>than anyone expected</u>*

- *Enough* is allowed quite generally after gradable adjectives, as in [i].
- *Than expected* in [iib] is a short comparative complement that is permitted within an attributive AdjP.
- A longer phrase would have to be located after the head noun, as in [iiib], where it functions as **indirect** complement (see Ch. 5, §4).

1.9   Other functions of AdjPs

Besides the two major functions discussed above, there are two relatively minor functions in which adjectives and AdjPs are found.

(a) Postpositives

Postpositive adjectives function in NP structure as post-head internal modifier. There are three cases to consider:

[30]   i *everything <u>useful</u>   somebody <u>rich</u>   somewhere <u>safe</u>   those <u>responsible</u>*
    ii *children <u>keen on sport</u>   a report <u>full of errors</u>   a suggestion <u>likely to offend</u>*
    iii *the only modification <u>possible</u>   the ones <u>asleep</u>   the president <u>elect</u>*

- The examples in [i] have fused determiner-heads, making it impossible for the adjectives to occur in the usual pre-head position – compare *everything useful* with *every useful thing*.
- The modifiers in [ii] would be inadmissible in pre-head position because the adjective has its own post-head dependents; the postpositive construction provides a way of getting around the fact that such AdjPs cannot be used as attributive modifiers.
- A limited number of adjectives can occur postpositively without their own dependents and with a non-fused head noun, as in [iii]: *possible* can also be attributive whereas *asleep* (as we have seen) cannot. *Elect* (meaning "recently elected but not in office yet") is one of a very small number of exceptional adjectives that occur only postpositively.

(b) External modifiers

Certain forms of AdjP occur right at the beginning of the NP, before the indefinite article *a*:

[31]   i a. *[<u>How long</u> a delay] will there be?*   b. *He'd chosen [<u>too dark</u> a colour].*
    ii a. *It seemed [<u>such</u> a bargain].*   b. *[<u>What</u> a fool] I was.*

- One type are AdjPs containing *how, as, so, too, this* or *that* as modifier, as in [i].
- There are two adjectives that can appear by themselves in this position: *such* and the exclamative word *what*, shown in [ii].

2   Adverbs

The **adverb** is the fourth and last of the categories of lexemes that we call **open** – the categories with huge and readily expandable membership. Noun and verb are the major open categories. Every canonical clause, even the simplest, must contain at least one of each (*Kim laughed, Clouds formed, They moved*). Such elementary constructions can be expanded by adding adjectives and adverbs as modifiers. Nouns take adjectives as their simplest and most typical modifiers, while verbs take adverbs.

The main thing that makes the adverb category open is that such a high proportion of adverbs are morphologically derived from adjectives by adding the suffix ·*ly*. It is with these related adjective–adverb pairs that we can see most clearly the contrast between the modifiers of nouns and the modifiers of verbs:

[32]   MODIFICATION OF NOUN   MODIFICATION OF VERB
   i a. *a <u>happy</u> <u><u>family</u></u>*   b. *They all <u><u>lived</u></u> <u>happily</u> ever after.*
   ii a. *a <u>greedy</u> <u><u>child</u></u>*   b. *The child <u><u>devoured</u></u> it <u>greedily</u>.*
   iii a. *a <u>passionate</u> <u><u>lover</u></u>*   b. *They <u><u>loved</u></u> each other <u>passionately</u>.*

Here double underlining marks the head word, and single underlining marks the modifier – an adjective in [a], an adverb in [b].

2.1   Adverbs as modifiers of categories other than the noun

The term 'adverb' is based on the function of these words as modifiers of verbs. But to a very large extent the words that are used for modifying verbs also function as modifiers to adjectives; and a good many modify other adverbs as well:

[33] i   a. *a <u>virtual</u> <u><u>disaster</u></u>*   b. **his <u>almost</u> <u><u>death</u></u>*   [noun]
    ii a. *It <u>virtually</u> <u><u>evaporated</u></u>.*   b. *He <u>almost</u> <u><u>died</u></u>.*   [verb]
    iii a. *It was <u>virtually</u> <u><u>impossible</u></u>.*   b. *He was <u>almost</u> <u><u>dead</u></u>.*   [adjective]
    iv a. *He spoke <u>virtually</u> <u><u>inaudibly</u></u>.*   b. *He was wounded <u>almost</u> <u><u>fatally</u></u>.*   [adverb]

The annotations on the right give the category of the (double-underlined) head word.

- In the [a] set, on the left, we have the adjective *virtual* modifying the noun, with the corresponding adverb *virtually* modifying the other three heads.
- In the [b] set the adverb *almost* modifies a verb, adjective or adverb; but since it isn't derived from any adjective there is no matching noun modifier to complete [ib].

Not only do adverbs modify verbs, adjectives and other adverbs, they also modify determinatives, PPs and NPs. Again we double-underline the head that is modified in [34].

[34] i a. _Virtually_ _all_ copies are torn.   b. I have _almost_ _no_ money left.   [determinative]
      ii a. I did it _virtually_ _by myself._   b. It lasted _almost_ _until midnight._   [PP]
      iii a. I'm _virtually_ _his only friend._   b. I bought _almost_ _the last copy._   [NP]

Note that in [iii] the adverb functions as external modifier, not internal modifier like _virtual_ in [33ia] (see Ch. 5, §6).

The basic division, then, is between words that modify nouns, and words that modify other categories (categories of words or of larger constituents). The noun-modifiers are adjectives, and the others are adverbs.[1] By no means all adverbs can modify all of this wide range of head elements, but there is a significant amount of overlap. Moreover, in all of these positions we find adverbs that are recognisable as such by virtue of being derived from an adjective by the addition of _·ly_.

2.2   Adverbs vs adjectives

In §1.1 we listed three major properties of adjectives, having to do with **function**, **grade** and **modification**. The last two apply to adverbs as well as adjectives.

Prototypical members of the adverb category enter into the system of grade, though the _·er_ and _·est_ suffixes are incompatible with the _·ly_ suffix (we find neither *_quicklier_ nor *_quickerly_), so for the most part comparatives and superlatives are formed by means of _more_ and _most_ rather than by inflection, as in _quickly_, _more quickly_, _most quickly_. And adverbs, like adjectives, take adverbs as modifier, as illustrated in [33]. The crucial distinction between adverbs and adjectives is thus a matter of function.

One aspect of this has already been discussed: adjectives modify nouns whereas adverbs modify other categories. But there is another functional difference that is no less important. Most adjectives can function as predicative complement as well as noun modifier, but adverbs do not normally occur in this function. Again the difference is most easily seen by taking adjective–adverb pairs related by _·ly_:

[35]   MODIFIER   PREDICATIVE COMPLEMENT
      i a. an _impressive_ performance   b. Her performance was _impressive._   [adjective]
      ii a. She performed _impressively._   b. *Her performance was _impressively._   [adverb]

---

[1] This is slightly oversimplified. There is a construction where we find an adverb modifying a noun, as in _Industrial action resulted in the_ _withdrawal_ _indefinitely of the vehicular ferry service_ or _A_ _shortage_ _of timber_ _internationally_ _led to a steep rise in prices._ The construction is subject to severe constraints; most importantly, adverbial modifiers of nouns are restricted to **post-head** position – compare _the_ _indefinite_ _withdrawal_ _of the vehicular ferry service,_ where the pre-head modifier is required to be an adjective. There are also constraints on the kind of adverb permitted. Manner adverbs, for example, are normally excluded, so that we have _his_ _angry_ _reaction,_ but not *_his_ _reaction_ _angrily._

Impressive and *impressively* can both function as modifier (here of noun and verb respectively), but only the adjective can be used predicatively. The same applies to those adverbs that are not derived from adjectives – they cannot be used as predicative complements:

[36]   a. *She <u>almost</u> succeeded.*   b. **Her success was <u>almost</u>.*

Overlap between the categories

We do find some overlap between the adjective and adverb categories – items that belong to both by virtue of occurring in both sets of functions.[2] Compare:

[37]   i ADJ   *their <u>early</u> departure*   *that <u>very</u> day*   *I don't feel <u>well</u>.*
        ii ADV   *They departed <u>early</u>.*   *It's <u>very</u> good.*   *I didn't play <u>well</u>.*

With some items, such as *early*, the meaning is the same, while in others it is different.

- The adjective *very*, for example, means something like "particular": it emphasises the identity of the day (that one, not any other). The adverb *very*, on the other hand, means approximately "extremely".
- The adjective *well* means "in good health", while the adverb means "in a good way" or "to a good standard".

Warning: addition of ·*ly* sometimes forms adjectives, not adverbs

Although the addition of ·*ly* usually forms an adverb from an adjective, it does not invariably do so. In particular, there are some adjectives that are formed from nouns in this way; examples are given in [38]:

[38]   i N   *beast*   *coward*   *death*   *father*   *friend*   *prince*   *woman*
        ii ADJ   *beastly*   *cowardly*   *deathly*   *fatherly*   *friendly*   *princely*   *womanly*

It is clear that despite the ·*ly* ending the words in [ii] are adjectives, not adverbs. They can function attributively and predicatively, but do not modify verbs, as illustrated for *friendly* in [39]:

[39]   ATTRIBUTIVE USE   PREDICATIVE USE   MODIFYING VERB
        a <u>friendly</u> old man   *He seems quite <u>friendly</u>.*   **He behaved <u>friendly</u>.*

2.3   The structure of AdvPs

The structure of AdvPs is similar to that of AdjPs, but somewhat simpler. Dependents can again be divided into complements and modifiers.

---

[2] The overlap is much greater in some non-standard varieties than in Standard English: a well-known non-standard feature, for example, omits the ·*ly* in many adverbs modifying verbs, as in ¹*They pay the rent regular.*

Complements

A few adverbs formed with the ·*ly* suffix license complements:

[40] i *Purchase of State vehicles is handled <u>similarly</u> <u>to all State purchases</u>.*
  ii *<u>Happily</u> <u>for the boys</u>, the class was cancelled.*

- In one type, the adverb licenses the same kind of complement as the adjective from which it is formed. Compare [i], for example, with *Purchase of State vehicles is <u>similar</u> <u>to all State purchases</u>*. Other adverbs of this kind (with the preposition they go with shown in parentheses) include *separately* (*from*), *independentiy* (*of*), and *equally* (*with*).
- A very few adverbs, such as *happily* in [ii], take complements that are not licensed by a corresponding adjective with a matching sense: compare **The cancellation of the class was happy for the boys.*

Modifiers

Modifiers are mostly AdvPs (as in [41i]), but again determinatives ([ii]), PPs ([iii]) and certain NPs ([iv]) are also found:

[41] i *She sang <u>very</u> <u>well</u>.   I did it <u>rather</u> <u>hurriedly</u>.   He spoke <u>remarkably</u> <u>clearly</u>.*
  ii *I didn't do it <u>that</u> <u>well</u>.   They arrived <u>much</u> <u>sooner</u> than we had expected.*
  iii *They behaved <u>badly</u> <u>in the extreme</u>.   He didn't answer <u>at all</u> <u>convincingly</u>.*
  iv *We arrived <u>three hours</u> <u>late</u>.   It had all happened <u>a bit</u> <u>suddenly</u>.*

Exercises

1. For each of the following adjectives, decide whether it can be used in **attributive** function, whether it can be used in **predicative** function, and whether it can be used in **postpositive** function. Give your evidence in detail.

   i *alone*   vi *latter*
   ii *available*   vii *marine*
   iii *ersatz*   viii *previous*
   iv *galore*   ix *prime*
   v *immune*   x *sleepy*

2. Classify the underlined words below as adjectives or nouns, justifying your answer by reference to the criteria given in Chs. 5 and 6.
   i *She is <u>secretary</u> of the Film Society.*
   ii *I've always admired the <u>Irish</u>.*
   iii *That's not a <u>government</u> responsibility.*
   iv *I want the <u>original</u>, not a copy.*
   v *What they say is <u>nonsense</u>.*
   vi *That sounds <u>stupid</u>.*
   vii *It verges on the <u>obscene</u>.*
   viii *She's quite a <u>comic</u>.*
   ix *Do it the <u>French</u> way.*
   x *He's learning <u>French</u>.*

3. Among younger generation speakers, especially in AmE, we find not only *That was a lot of fun, How much fun will we have?*, and *I thought it was fun*, but also some constructions that older-generation speakers do not use, like these:
   %*It was so fun.*
   %*I can think of a lot of things funner than that.*
   %*It's the funnest thing I've ever done.*
   What is the change that has occurred to separate the two age groups' dialects?

4. Which of the underlined words below are **adjectives**, which are **verbs**, and which are

ambiguous between the two categories in the examples given? Give evidence for your answers.

i *The trains aren't _running_ today.*
ii *What we said was simply _ignored_.*
iii *She sounded quite _impressed_.*
iv *It was a _rewarding_ experience.*
v *His act is not _amusing_.*
vi *His act is not _amusing_ the crowd.*
vii *We were _surrounded_.*
viii *The bill was _paid_.*
ix *He was _shot_ in the leg.*
x *Let _sleeping_ dogs lie.*

5. For each of the following adjectives say whether it is (a) **gradable**; (b) **non-gradable**; or (c) **ambiguous**, usable in two senses of which one is gradable and the other is not. In case (c), give examples of the two uses, commenting on the difference in meaning.

i *certain*   vi *philosophical*
ii *Christian*   vii *true*
iii *feminine*   viii *worthy*
iv *latter*   ix *primary*
v *main*   x *childlike*

6. For each of these examples, identify the **predicand** of the underlined predicative AdjP.

i *We found your suggestion _very helpful_.*
ii *The problem was thought _insoluble_ by many.*
iii *_Unable to contain his anger_, Max stormed out of the room.*

iv *We find the accused _guilty_, your honour.*
v *Eventually, _too tired to cry_, the two children fell asleep.*

7. Which of the following adjectives license **PP complements** with a particular preposition as head? Give examples for those that do. If you cannot find any example in which the adjective has a PP complement, just write 'none'.

i *able*   vi *easy*
ii *capable*   vii *free*
iii *careful*   viii *intent*
iv *clever*   ix *long*
v *concise*   x *responsible*

8. Classify the underlined words below as **adjectives** or **adverbs**, giving your reasons in each case.

i *_Fortunately_, he had plenty of time.*
ii *He was going far too _fast_.*
iii *She seemed a very _kindly_ old soul.*
iv *We were annoyed at their _late_ arrival.*
v *They're becoming _increasingly_ unruly.*
vi *I was feeling quite _poorly_.*
vii *She works extremely _hard_.*
viii *We made _too_ many concessions.*
ix *_Kindly_ refrain from smoking.*
x *That was very _ungentlemanly_.*

9. Construct convincing examples in which the adverb *quite* modifies: [i] a **verb**; [ii] an **adjective**; [iii] an **adverb**; [iv] a **PP**; and [v] an **NP**.

7 Prepositions and preposition phrases

1   The traditional class of prepositions

Prepositions make up a much smaller class of lexemes than the open categories of verb, noun, adjective and adverb. There are only about a hundred prepositions in current use. Traditional grammars list even fewer than that, but we don't follow the tradition on this point. Although all words traditionally classified as prepositions are classified as prepositions in our treatment too, we recognise a good number of other prepositions, formerly classified as adverbs, or as 'subordinating conjunctions'. We begin this chapter with an account of the category of prepositions as traditionally understood, and then explain why we have chosen to expand it.

We give in [1] a sampling of the words that (in at least some of their uses) belong to the category of prepositions.

[1]	*above*	*across*	*after*	*against*	*at*	*before*	*behind*
	below	*between*	*beyond*	*by*	*down*	*for*	*from*
	in	*into*	*of*	*off*	*on*	*over*	*round*
	since	*through*	*to*	*under*	*up*	*with*	*without*

These words share the following properties.

▨ (a) They take NPs as complement

In general, words are traditionally analysed as prepositions only if they have complements with the form of NPs. In the following pairs, for example, traditional grammar accepts the underlined words in [a] as prepositions, but not those in [b]:

[2]   TRADITIONALLY A PREPOSITION   TRADITIONALLY NOT A PREPOSITION
   i a. *The sun sank [below the horizon].*   b. *I went [below].*
  ii a. *I haven't seen her [since Easter].*   b. *I haven't seen her [since she left town].*
 iii a. *They set off [despite the rain].*   b. *We stayed indoors [because of the rain].*
  iv a. *%He jumped [out the window].*   b. *He jumped [out of the window].*

- *Below* fails to qualify in [ib] because it has no complement at all.
- The other items in [b] fail because they have complements that are not NPs: a clause in [iib] and a PP headed by *of* in [iiib/ivb].
- With *out* there is divided usage. In AmE it can sometimes take an NP complement, as in [iva], but in BrE it requires *of* – so it can be a preposition in AmE but not in BrE.

(b) No inflection

The prepositions of traditional grammar do not inflect. We have just *at*, for example: there are no forms *atter*, *ats*, or whatever.

(c) Meaning: relations in space or time

Most traditional prepositions have meanings to do with relations in space or time: *at the post office* identifies a spatial location, *into the garden* fixes a direction of travel, *after lunch* locates a time period as following lunchtime, etc. Not all prepositions have this kind of meaning (for example, *despite* in [2iiia] doesn't), so this can't be used as a condition for belonging to the class of prepositions; but it is relevant to a general definition of prepositions, and we will take it up again in §4.

(d) Function: head of wide range of dependents

Prepositions head phrases that characteristically occur in a range of functions, notably dependents of either nouns or verbs, including as a special case the complement of the verb **be**. In the following examples single underlining marks the PP, double underlining the head on which it is dependent:

[3]   DEPENDENT OF NOUN   DEPENDENT OF VERB   COMPLEMENT OF *BE*
   i *a house at the beach*   *He saw her at school.*   *He is at lunch.*
  ii *the chair in the corner*   *She fell in the pool.*   *We were in the pool.*
 iii *the woman from Paris*   *She comes from Paris.*   *She is from Paris.*
  iv *a bottle of milk*   *I don't approve of it.*   *That is of interest.*

2   Extending the membership of the class

The reason why we extend the membership of the preposition class beyond the words that traditional grammar calls prepositions is that we see no justification for restricting it to words that have NP complements. That is, we don't think the condition discussed under (a) in §1 should be regarded as essential.

Notice first the effect of the NP complement condition on how we have to classify the word *before* in the three constructions shown in [4]. We compare *before* with the verb **know**:

[4]	TYPE OF COMPLEMENT	*before* AS HEAD	**know** AS HEAD
i	NP	*We left <u>before</u> <u>the last act.</u>*	*We <u>know</u> <u>the last act.</u>*
ii	CLAUSE	*That was <u>before</u> <u>he died.</u>*	*I <u>know</u> <u>he died.</u>*
iii	NO COMPLEMENT	*I had seen her once <u>before</u>.*	*Yes, I <u>know</u>.*

In [i] the complement of *before* or *know* (marked by double underlining) is an NP; in [ii] it is a subordinate clause; and in [iii] there is no complement. Everyone agrees that this difference in the complements has no bearing on the classification of **know**: it is a verb in all three examples. **Know** happens to be a verb that licenses either an NP or a clause as complement, and where the complement is optional.

But traditional grammar treats *before* in a completely different way. It is treated as a preposition in [i], a 'subordinating conjunction' in [ii], and an adverb in [iii]. We see this triple assignment as an unnecessary complication. It is much simpler to give *before* a uniform analysis, treating it as a preposition in all three, just as **know** is a verb in all three.

Notice in the first place that *before* has the same meaning in all of [i–iii]. Secondly, it takes the same modifiers in these three contexts. We could, for example, insert such items as *long, shortly, an hour, a short while* in front of *before* in all three examples in [4]. The difference between the three instances of *before* is thus solely a matter of the complement. Nowhere else in the grammar is a part-of-speech distinction based purely on a difference of this kind.

Our extension of the preposition category involves redrawing the boundaries between prepositions and subordinators, and between prepositions and adverbs. We take up these two pairs in turn.

2.1   Prepositions vs subordinators

The traditional class of subordinating conjunctions contains (among others) the words in [5]:

[5]	i	*after*	*before*	*since*	*till*	*until*			
	ii a.	*although*	*because*	*if*_c	*lest*	*provided*	*though*	*unless*	
	b.	*if*_i	*that*	*whether*					

We need to distinguish two words with the shape *if*.

- One has a **conditional** meaning, as in *I'll help you <u>if I can</u>*: we show this above as if_c.
- The other occurs in subordinate **interrogative** clauses like *See <u>if there are any</u> <u>vacancies</u>*, corresponding to main clause *Are there any vacancies?*: we show it as if_i. This is a variant of *whether*: compare *See <u>whether there are any</u> <u>vacancies</u>*.

The words in [i] traditionally belong to the preposition class as well, whereas those in [ii] do not. We have argued against a dual classification treatment of the [i] words, analysing them simply as prepositions that license different kinds of complement. But once we reconsider the distinction between prepositions and subordinators we find there are good reasons for reassigning the words in [iia] as well to the preposition class. This leaves a very small subordinator class, with *that*, *whether* and *if* as its main members.

The major argument for drawing the boundary between prepositions and subordinators between [iia] and [iib] is that *that*, *whether* and *if*ᵢ function as **markers of subordination** whereas the other words in [5] function as **heads** of the constituents they introduce. Consider the following examples:

[6]   i a. *I think [(that) she's probably right].*
         b. *I don't know [whether they have received our letter yet].*
        ii a. *She stayed behind for a few minutes [after the others had left].*
         b. *They complained [because we didn't finish the job this week].*

- In [i] the bracketed constituents are subordinate clauses with *that* and *whether* simply marking the subordination: the main clause counterparts are *She is probably right* (declarative) and *Have they received our letter yet?* (interrogative). In this context the *that* is optional (as indicated by the parentheses): the clause is in the position of complement to *think*, so it is not obligatory to mark its subordinate status in its own structure. *Whether* is not omissible because it marks the clause as interrogative as well as subordinate: it is just with the default declarative type that the subordinator is often optional.
- *After* and *because* in [ii] by contrast are not grammatical markers of subordination. They have independent meaning, and it is by virtue of this meaning that we interpret the bracketed constituents as adjuncts of time and reason respectively. This makes them like heads – just as *after* is head in the time adjunct *after the departure of the others*. They are not themselves part of the subordinate clause; rather, the subordinate clauses are just *the others had left* and *we didn't finish the job this week*, and these function as complement within the phrases headed by *after* and *because*.

2.2   Prepositions vs adverbs

Prepositions with optional NP complements

We begin the task of redrawing the boundaries between prepositions and adverbs by looking further at words like *before* in [4], which can occur either with an NP complement or without a complement. There are a fair number of words of this kind; a sample are listed in [7]:

[7] | *aboard* | *above* | *across* | *after* | *along* | *behind* | *below* |
        | *beneath* | *beyond* | *by* | *down* | *in* | *off* | *outside* |
        | *over* | *past* | *round* | *since* | *through* | *under* | *up* |

As we have noted, these are traditionally analysed as prepositions when they have an NP complement but as adverbs when they have no complement:

[8]   TRADITIONAL PREPOSITION   TRADITIONAL ADVERB
    i a. *She went <u>aboard</u> the liner.*   b. *She went <u>aboard</u>.*
    ii a. *He sat <u>outside</u> her bedroom.*   b. *He sat <u>outside</u>.*

It has often been suggested that the traditional adverb category has something of the character of a classificatory wastebasket, a dumping ground for words that don't belong in any of the other more clearly defined categories. This criticism certainly seems valid in the present case. *Aboard* in [ib] and *outside* in [iib] don't, on the traditional account, qualify as prepositions because prepositions are defined in such a way that they require NP complements. They are obviously not nouns, verbs, adjectives or conjunctions, so there is nowhere to put them except in the adverb category.

We put it this way because it is important to see that these words do not in fact satisfy the definition that traditional grammar gives to the adverb category: 'An adverb is a word that modifies a verb, an adjective or another adverb'. They typically occur, for example, in the three functions given in [3] for PPs:

[9]   DEPENDENT OF NOUN   DEPENDENT OF VERB   COMPLEMENT OF *BE*
    i   *the <u>conditions aboard</u>*   *She <u>went aboard</u>.*   *She <u>is</u> still <u>aboard</u>.*
    ii *the <u>temperature outside</u>*   *He <u>sat outside</u>.*   *He <u>is</u> outside.*

(Contexts for the first example in each set might be *I won't attempt to describe* [*the conditions aboard*] and [*The temperature outside*] *was over 40°*.)

The first and third of the functions illustrated in [9] are characteristic of prepositions, but not of adverbs. Let us consider them in turn.

(a)   Dependents of nouns

Adverbs do not normally occur as dependents of nouns: in related adjective–adverb pairs it is the adjective that appears in this function. No such restriction applies to prepositions. Compare:

[10]   PP   ADVERB
    i a. *She criticised them <u>with tact</u>.*   b. *She criticised them <u>tactfully</u>.*
    ii a. [*A manager <u>with tact</u>*] *is needed.* b. *[A manager <u>tactfully</u>] is needed.*

- The underlined expressions in [i] modify the verb, and we see that both PP and adverb are admissible.
- In [ii], however, they modify the noun *manager* and here the PP is admissible but the adverb is not; instead we need an adjective: *a tactful manager*.

(b)   Complement of the verb *be*

Adverbs cannot normally function as complement to *be* in its ascriptive sense: here we again have adjectives, in their predicative use. As with (a) above, there is no comparable constraint applying to prepositions. Compare:

[11]   PP AS COMPLEMENT OF *BE*   AdvP AS COMPLEMENT OF *BE*
    i a. *The key is <u>under the mat</u>.*   b. **Lucy was <u>enthusiastically</u> today.*
    ii a. *The meeting is <u>on Tuesday</u>.*   b. **Rain is <u>again</u>.*

The [a] examples, with a PP functioning as complement of *be*, are impeccable, but the [b] ones, with an adverb in this function, are ungrammatical.

- Instead of [ib] we have *Lucy was enthusiastic today*, with the corresponding adjective.
- Since the adverb *again* has no adjective counterpart we cannot correct [iib] in the same way; for this particular example we could have *It is raining again*, with *again* now functioning as modifier to the verb **rain**.

The classification of words like *aboard* and *outside* as adverbs is thus inconsistent with the traditional definition of that category. The best way to remove this inconsistency is to amend the definition of prepositions so that they are no longer required to have an NP complement. *Aboard, outside* and similar words will then be prepositions both when they have NP complements and when they occur alone. This revision simultaneously gets rid of the complication of a dual classification for these words and removes from the adverb class words which differ radically in their syntactic properties from genuine adverbs, thus making it a significantly more coherent class. Notice in particular that with our more restricted class of adverbs, but not with the larger class of traditional grammar, all functions that can be filled by adverbs accept some of the most central type, the type formed from adjectives by adding ·*ly*.

This revision of the traditional analysis is not an original idea of ours. The core of it was first put forward as early as 1924 by the great Danish grammarian Otto Jespersen, and it is adopted in much work in linguistics since the 1970s.

One reason why traditional grammarians have not taken it up may have to do with the etymology, or historical source, of the term 'preposition'. This suggests a word placed in front of another word – the traditional preposition is a word placed in front of a noun (or NP, in our analysis). It may therefore seem undesirable to apply the term to a word which is not positioned in front of an NP. But there are three points to be made in favour of doing so.

- First, prepositions do not always precede their complements: in *What are you looking for?* the preposition *for* does not precede its complement *what* (see §5 for more discussion of this construction).
- Second, no one worries that the etymology of 'adverb' suggests a word dependent on a verb, although the term applies also to words modifying adjectives, other adverbs, and so on.
- Third, the term 'preposition' is so deeply ingrained in the grammatical tradition that there would inevitably be a great deal of opposition to a newly invented replacement; it is better just to recognise that words often change their meanings, and to accept a change in the meaning of 'preposition'. The property of being placed before an NP will still apply in central cases, but not in all.

Further extensions of the preposition category

Once we remove the requirement that a preposition must have an NP complement, the way is open for us to reassign to this category a number of other words that are traditionally analysed as adverbs. There are a good number of words that behave like prepositions, not adverbs, with respect to one or both of constructions (a) and (b) above, but which NEVER take NP complements. We list in [12] a number of those that occur both as dependents of nouns and as complement to *be*, as illustrated in [13]: these are words which should very clearly be reassigned to the preposition category.

[12] i *abroad   downstairs   here   outdoors   overboard   overseas   there*
      ii *ahead   because   instead*

[13]   DEPENDENT OF NOUN   COMPLEMENT OF *BE*
      i a. *You can use* [*the office <u>downstairs</u>*].   b. *The spare chairs are <u>downstairs</u>.*
      ii a. [*Water <u>instead</u> of wine*] *won't do!*   b. *This is <u>instead</u> of your usual lunch.*

- The words in [12i] normally occur without complements; four are compounds incorporating a core preposition (*down, out, over*) as the first element.
- Those in [12ii] take complements with the form of PPs: *ahead <u>of us</u>, because <u>of the weather</u>*, etc.

3   Further category contrasts

The differences between prepositions and nouns are too obvious to merit further discussion, but it may be helpful to compare the syntactic properties of prepositions with those of adjectives and verbs – not so much with a view to redrawing the boundaries between these categories, but simply to clarify the differences between them.

3.1   Prepositions vs adjectives

We deal here with the main features that distinguish between the preposition and adjective categories in the great mass of clear cases, setting aside a very small number of highly exceptional words whose status as adjective or preposition is problematic and controversial.

(a) NP complements

Prototypical members of the preposition class license NP complements. Adjectives do not.

(b) Inflection and gradability

Prototypical adjectives inflect for grade (with plain, comparative and superlative forms such as *big, bigger, biggest*) or else have comparatives and superlatives marked by the modifiers *more* and *most* (e.g. *useful, more useful, most useful*). More generally, they are **gradable**, accepting a range of degree modifiers including, most distinctively, *very* and *too* ("excessively") – cf. Ch. 6, §1.3.

Prepositions, by contrast, are normally **non-gradable**. There are, however, some PPs with specialised meanings that do permit certain kinds of grading – PPs such as those in [14]:

[14]   *at home with X* ("familiar with X, knowledgeable about X"), *in control, in the know* ("informed"), *on top of the world* ("extremely happy"), *out of order* ("inappropriate"), *out of sorts* ("unwell, discontented")

Thus I might say *You're more at home with trigonometry than I am* or *I feel more in control of the situation than I used to*. The gradability, however, doesn't apply to the preposition by itself but to the larger expression, and hence comparison in these cases is not marked inflectionally: we don't say **You're atter home with trigonometry than I am*.

(c) The predicand requirement for adjectives

An important difference between adjectives and prepositions is revealed by certain facts about **adjuncts**. We have seen that in their predicative use adjectives are related to a **predicand**, and this applies not only with predicative complements but also with predicative adjuncts (see Ch. 6, §1.7). All prepositions, on the other hand, can head adjuncts that are unassociated with any predicand. The contrast is seen in the following examples:

[15]   EXAMPLES WITH *anxious* (ADJECTIVE)   EXAMPLES WITH *after* (PREPOSITION)
  i a. [*Anxious to make amends*], the   b. [*After the end of the semester*], the
         dean threw a party for the students.   *dean threw a party for the students.*
  ii a. *[*Anxious to make amends*],   b. [*After the end of the semester*],
         there was a party for the students.   *there was a party for the students.*

The bracketed constituents are adjuncts: an AdjP adjunct in [a] and a PP adjunct in [b]. The difference in grammaticality of the examples in [ii] shows that the AdjP is subject to a constraint that does not apply to the PP: THE ADJP MUST BE RELATED TO A PREDICAND. This requirement is satisfied in [ia], where the predicand is the subject *the dean*: we understand that the dean was anxious to make amends. But it's not satisfied in [iia]: the adjunct is not related to a predicand, and hence there's no indication of who was anxious to make amends.

Notice, the claim is NOT that adjuncts with the form of a PP CANNOT be related to a predicand. They certainly can be. The crucial point, though, is that there is no general constraint that they MUST be. Compare, for example:

[16]   i [*In control of the situation at last,*] *Sue began to feel more relaxed.*
       ii [*In this country*] *there is less than 5% unemployment.*

In [i] *Sue* is predicand for the bracketed adjunct: we understand that Sue was in control of the situation at last. But there is no such relation in [ii]. So the preposition *in* can be the head of an adjunct that is not related to a predicand. And this holds quite generally for prepositions, but not for adjectives.

This gives us a test for prepositions: they differ from adjectives in ALWAYS being able to head phrases in adjunct function which have no semantic relation to a predicand.

▓ (d) Complement of *become*

One of the main functions in which AdjPs appear is that of predicative complement – complement to such verbs as *be*, *appear*, *become*, *feel*, *seem*, etc. A high proportion of prepositions can head PPs functioning as complement to *be*, but they occur less readily with the other verbs. Most importantly, they do not normally occur with *become*. So in general, if you take a PP that can be the complement of *be*, you will find it cannot be the complement of *become*, but with AdjPs there is no such restriction:

[17] AdjP complements   PP complements
    i a. *We <u>are</u> grateful to you.*   b. *We <u>are</u> in your debt.*
    ii a. *We <u>became</u> grateful to you.*   b. **We <u>became</u> in your debt.*

Even PPs like *in a bad temper*, which are semantically very like adjectives, do not appear with *become*: we get *The boss became angry* but not **The boss became in a bad temper*.

Adding a modifier to a PP complement to *become* may improve acceptability a great deal. Compare, for example, **They became in love*, which is ungrammatical or at best marginal, with *They became more and more in love*, which is acceptable. We therefore need to formulate the distinction in this way: adjectives can normally head complements to *become*, whereas prepositions without modifiers normally cannot.

3.2   Prepositions vs verbs

In general, there is little difficulty in distinguishing verbs from prepositions. Verbs usually function as predicator in clause structure, and in finite or infinitival clauses they are easily recognisable as verbs by this function. There is, for example, no doubt about the status of *follow* as a verb in [18]:

[18]   a. *We always <u>follow</u> the manual.*   b. *I advise you to <u>follow</u> the manual.*

There are, however, a number of prepositions which have the same shape as the gerund-participle or past participle forms of verbs. These are cases where historical change led to a word taking on the properties of a preposition in addition to its original verbal properties, so that it now belongs to both categories. Three examples, with the relevant word underlined, are given in [19]:

[19]   PREPOSITION   VERB
    i   a. *<u>Following</u> the meeting, there   b. *<u>Following</u> the manual, we tried to*
           will be a reception.*   *figure out how to assemble the unit.*
    ii a. *<u>Owing</u> to the drought, many   b. *<u>Owing</u> so much to the bank,*
           farms are going bankrupt.*   *farmers can't afford any luxuries.*
    iii a. *Liz did remarkably well, <u>given</u>   b. *Liz was <u>given</u> only three months*
           her inexperience.*   *to live.*

The difference is very similar to the predicand requirement that we discussed above in connection with the difference between prepositions and adjectives. Predicative adjectives have to be related to a predicand, and verbs in predicator function have to be related to a subject, either overt or understood.

- In [ib] *following* is predicator in a gerund-participial clause functioning as adjunct; this clause itself has no overt subject, but an understood subject is retrievable from the subject of the main clause: the sentence implies that WE were following the manual.
- *Owing* in [iib] is interpreted in a similar way: we understand that it is farmers who owe so much to the bank. (See Ch. 13, §2.2, for further discussion of this construction.)
- Example [iiib] is a passive clause, and *Liz* is the subject – compare the active version *They gave Liz only three months to live.*

But in the [a] examples, there is no such predicational relationship to a subject. The underlined words derive historically from verbs, but they have developed meanings distinct from the verbal ones, and in this use these words belong to the preposition category. *Following* means "after"; *owing to X* means "because of X"; and *given X* means roughly "if we take X into account".

4   Grammaticised uses of prepositions

An important property that applies to about a dozen of the most frequent prepositions is that they have what we call **grammaticised** uses, as illustrated in these examples:

[20]   i   *The article was written by a first-year student.*
      ii   *[The sudden death of the president] stunned the nation.*
     iii   *I [transferred several hundred dollars to them].*
      iv   *[Their request for assistance] was ignored.*
       v   *They all seem [quite keen on the idea].*

The role of the underlined prepositions here is not to express spatial relations as prepositions often do, but just to mark certain grammatical functions.

- Example [i] is a passive clause, and *by* marks the NP (*a first-year student*) that corresponds to the subject of the corresponding active (*A first-year student wrote the article*).
- The bracketed sequence in [ii] is an NP within which *of* marks the NP (*the president*) that corresponds to the subject of the corresponding clause (*The president suddenly died*) or the genitive subject-determiner in an equivalent NP (*the president's sudden death*).
- *To, for*, and *on* in the PPs in [iii–v] mark the complements of a verb (***transfer***), a noun (***request***), and an adjective (***keen***), respectively. These words license a PP complement containing a particular preposition: we say that the preposition is **specified** by the head (double-underlined) of the bracketed construction.

What makes 'grammaticised' an appropriate term for such prepositions is that where they are placed in sentences depends not on what they mean but entirely on rules of the grammar. The underlined prepositions in [20] don't have any identifiable meaning of their own, and there is no possibility of replacing them by any other preposition.

In other examples, these same prepositions do have meaning, of course. In a sentence like *I sat by the door*, the word *by* expresses a relation of being fairly close to the door. In a sentence like *He went to Paris*, the word *to* indicates the endpoint in a process of movement. And so on. But in these cases we can replace them with prepositions of different meaning while keeping everything else the same: we could say *I sat opposite the door*, or *He went across Paris*. But it is not possible to make changes like this in [20] without changing the grammatical construction.

Only a few prepositions have grammaticised uses, the main ones being the single-syllable words *as, at, by, for, from, in, of, on, than, to,* and *with*. These make up only a small minority of the words belonging to the preposition category, but their grammaticised uses account for a considerable proportion of the actual occurrences of prepositions in texts.

The property of occurring in grammaticised uses helps to distinguish the category as a whole from other categories. We can now give a fairly useful general definition of 'preposition', one that provides a basis for using the same term in different languages:

[21]   The term **preposition** applies to a relatively small category of words, with basic meanings predominantly having to do with relations in space and time, containing among its prototypical members grammaticised words that serve to mark various grammatical functions.[1]

5   Preposition stranding

In certain non-canonical clause constructions the complement of a preposition may be fronted so that it precedes the preposition (usually with intervening material) instead of occupying the basic complement position after the preposition. In the following examples the preposition is marked by double underlining, the complement by single underlining:

[22]   i *Who did they vote for?*   [interrogative]
       ii *I can't find the book [which she was referring to]*   [relative]

The preposition is here said to be **stranded**, i.e. located before a site from which its understood complement is missing.

---

[1] In some languages, e.g. Japanese, words corresponding to English prepositions occur AFTER their NP complements. In such languages the category is generally called 'postposition' rather than 'preposition'. The difference in position is not really important, though. Japanese verbs, for example, are normally at the end of the clause (i.e., transitive verbs follow their objects), but that doesn't cast doubt on their being verbs. We might therefore want to apply the same general term to both languages. For this reason our general definition (unlike standard dictionary definitions) makes no reference to position. The intention is that the definition and the term should be applicable in both kinds of language, just as with 'verb'.

Prescriptive grammar note

A stranded preposition quite often occurs at the end of the sentence. Prescriptive manuals generally discuss preposition stranding in terms of sentences that end with a preposition, and some of the more old-fashioned ones still state that ending a sentence with a preposition is incorrect or at least inelegant. This is a case of a particularly silly prescriptive rule that is clearly and massively in conflict with actual usage. All fluent users of English use stranded prepositions, and most usage books now recognise that. Nonetheless, some schoolbooks still seem to be trying to teach students to avoid stranded prepositions, and some speakers who mistakenly believe in the old rule struggle to obey it. The truth is that the construction illustrated in [22] has been grammatical and commonplace in English for hundreds of years.

An alternative to the stranding construction of [22] is available. It places the preposition at the beginning of the clause so it accompanies the NP that is understood as its complement. We call it preposition **fronting**. The fronting alternatives to the sentences in [22] are shown in [23].

[23]   i   *For whom did they vote?*   [interrogative]
         ii   *I can't find the book [to which she was referring].*   [relative]

The choice between the stranding and fronting constructions

There are some factors that influence the choice between stranding and fronting, and in certain cases one or the other is not grammatical. Two kinds of factor are involved, one having to do with style, the other with particular syntactic features of the clause concerned.

(a)   Style

The fronted construction is more formal than the stranded one. This can be seen in such a pair of interrogative clauses as:

[24]   STRANDED PREPOSITION   FRONTED PREPOSITION
         a. *Where did this come from?*   b. *From where did this come?*

Version [a] is by far the more natural of the two, with [b] sounding stiff and strange to most speakers. Interrogatives with preposition fronting are heard in prepared and organised speech, as in a planned interview (*To what do you attribute this trend?*), but in ordinary conversation the stranding construction is strongly preferred.

(b)   Syntactic factors that disfavour or exclude the stranded version

Although the traditional prescriptive warning about preposition stranding is nonsense, there are some syntactic circumstances (hardly ever mentioned in the books that say stranding is bad grammar) that can make preposition stranding almost or completely impossible. We list a small sample of such circumstances in [25]:

[25]   STRANDED PREPOSITION   FRONTED PREPOSITION
  i a. *This is the safe [which the   b. This is the safe [to which the key
       key to was stolen].   was stolen].
 ii a. *I have a lecture ending at two   b. I have a lecture ending at two
       [which I'll be free all day after].   [after which I'll be free all day].
iii a. *What way am I annoying you in?   b. In what way am I annoying you?

- In [ia] the stranded preposition occurs within a subject NP (the subject of *was stolen*). That is fairly clearly ungrammatical.
- In [ii] the PP is in adjunct rather than complement function, specifically an adjunct of time. There is a tendency for the stranding construction to be avoided in adjuncts generally. With adjuncts of place it is not so strong, so you may hear sentences like ?*That's the town [which I first met her in]*; but the tendency is quite strong for many other adjuncts, like adjuncts of time or duration.
- This is more than just a tendency with some fixed adjunct expressions: the manner adjunct *in what way*, as in [iiib], can never be split up by stranding.

(c)   Syntactic factors that disfavour or exclude the non-stranded version

One thing that is never made clear in the books that recommend against stranding prepositions is that there are also syntactic circumstances that make the non-stranded version, with preposition fronting, almost or completely impossible. Again we illustrate with just a few examples:

[26]   STRANDED PREPOSITION   FRONTED PREPOSITION
  i a. That depends on [who I give it to]. b. *That depends on [to whom I give it].
 ii a. What did you hit me for?   b. *For what did you hit me?
iii a. Which metals does it consist of?   b. ?Of which metals does it consist?

- In [i] the clause containing the preposition (bracketed) is a subordinate interrogative clause functioning as **complement to a preposition** (*on*); here stranding is obligatory.
- In [ii] we have the idiom *what for* meaning "why", where *for* is never fronted.
- The verb **consist** in [iii] is one of those that license a PP complement with a specified preposition (like **transfer** in [20iii]), and there is a fairly strong preference for the stranding construction with such verbs. The [b] version isn't grammatically forbidden, but it sounds very stiff and formal.

6   The structure of PPs

Prepositions function as heads of phrases, and as such can take various dependents, both complements and modifiers.

6.1   Complements

Prepositions take a range of complement types comparable to that of verbs:

[27]	i	OBJECT NP	*I was talking [to a friend].*	*I'm looking [for my glasses].*
	ii	PREDICATIVE	*I regard her [as a friend].*	*I took him [for dead].*
	iii	PP	*I stayed [until after lunch].*	*[According to Ed,] it's a hoax.*
	iv	ADVP	*It won't last [for long].*	*I hadn't met her [till recently].*
	v	CLAUSE	*I left [because I was tired].*	*We agreed [on how to proceed].*

(a) Object and predicative

As with verbs, we need to make a distinction between objects and predicative complements: the *friend* examples above contrast in the same way as those in [28]:

[28]	i	OBJECT NP	*I was visiting a friend.*
	ii	PREDICATIVE	*I consider her [a friend].*

The crucial syntactic difference is again that a predicative can have the form of an AdjP (*I regard her as very bright*, where *as* is the preposition) or a bare role NP (*They elected her as treasurer*); see Ch. 4, §4.1 for discussion.

Almost all predicatives in PP structure occur with *as*, but one or two verbs, such as **take**, license PP complements consisting of *for* + predicative.

(b) PPs

PP complements to prepositions are of two kinds.

- First, there are PPs denoting times or places which occur with a few prepositions that usually take NPs – compare *I stayed until after lunch* with *I stayed until the afternoon*. Other examples of this type are *from behind the curtain* and *since before lunch*.
- Second, there are prepositions that take complements with a specified preposition as head: *to* is selected by *according, due, owing, prior, pursuant*, etc.; *of* is selected by *ahead, because, instead, out*, etc.; *from* is selected by *away, apart, aside*, etc.

(c) AdvPs

There are a handful of PreP + AdvP combinations, which could be seen as prepositions taking adverb phrases as complements. But there are very few: in addition to the ones in [27iv], we find *before long, for later, until recently*, and a very few others. They are basically fixed phrases (for example, we get *before long* but not **after long*).

(d) Subordinate clauses

A good number of prepositions take various kinds of **subordinate clause** as complement. These include the prepositions that were traditionally classified as 'subordinating conjunctions': see [5i/iia] above.

Prepositions with no complement

Although most PPs contain a complement, there are some prepositions that take no complement: they can occur on their own. We discussed some of these above: *She went aboard* ([8ib]), *The spare chairs are downstairs* ([13ib]), and so on.

The exceptional preposition *ago*

There is one preposition that is strikingly exceptional in that it invariably FOLLOWS its complement. This is *ago*, as in *She arrived two weeks ago*, where *two weeks* is complement of *ago*. The order here reflects the historical origin of *ago*: it derives from the form *agone*, containing the past participle of *go*. Originally *two weeks ago* meant something like "two weeks gone", i.e., located at a point in time that is now two weeks gone by into the past.

Dictionaries classify *ago* as an adverb, but there is compelling evidence that it is a preposition, exceptional only in its position relative to its complement. Consider the following data:

[29] i a. *I spent two weeks in Paris.*   b. **I spent two weeks ago in Paris.*
      ii a. **She arrived two weeks.*   b. *She arrived two weeks ago.*
      iii a. *I recall his behaviour two weeks ago.* b. *That was two weeks ago.*

- Examples [i–ii] show that *ago* is head of the phrase *two weeks ago*: the distribution of the whole phrase is quite different from that of *two weeks* alone.
- In [iii] we see that *ago* phrases readily modify nouns or function as predicative complement to verbs like *be*: these functions are characteristic of PPs, not AdvPs, as we noted in §2.2.

6.2   Modification

Some of the main types of modification in the structure of PPs are illustrated in [30], where the modifiers are underlined:

[30] i   *We had to leave [a few minutes before the end].*
      ii *It landed [way behind us].*
      iii *We went [straight home].*
      iv *It all seemed [completely out of this world].*

- NPs measuring extent commonly occur with temporal and spatial prepositions, as in [i].
- Measurement of extent can also be expressed, as in [ii], by adverbs like *just, directly, soon, shortly, way*, etc.
- The words *straight* and *right* occur as adjectives, but they can also occur as adverbs in modifier function. But they only modify prepositions: we find *It flew right under the bridge*, but in Standard English we don't have **It was right large* or **We drove right slowly*.

- A number of PPs with metaphorical or idiomatic meanings are gradable, and these accept degree modifiers such as *completely, quite, very much*, etc. So we get *completely out of his mind, quite in tune with my ideas, very much within the spirit of our policy*, etc.

7   PP complements in clause structure

PPs function as complement or modifier to a wide range of heads – verbs, nouns, adjectives, and so on. In this section we focus on those functioning as complement of a verb, elaborating on the description of clause structure that was begun in Ch. 4.

7.1   Goal, source and location

PPs are the most usual form for complements indicating **goal, source** and **location**. Goal and source are found in clauses expressing motion (or anything viewed metaphorically as motion). The goal is the place to which something moves, and the source the place from which it moves:

[31] i *We drove from Boston to New York.* ⎫
      ii *He jumped off the table into her arms.* ⎭   [source + goal]
      iii *She fell into the pool.*   [goal]

Goal and source PPs clearly qualify as complements since they need to be licensed by the verb – normally, a verb of motion. PPs expressing location complements are seen in examples like these:

[32] i *The suitcase is underneath my bed.*
      ii *She stayed in her bedroom all morning.*

7.2   The complements of prepositional verbs

We have seen that a dozen or so prepositions have grammaticised uses, and prominent among them are those where a particular preposition is **specified** by the head of the larger construction, by a verb, noun or adjective.

There are many verbs that take a PP complement of this kind. They are called **prepositional verbs,** and occur in a range of constructions, as illustrated in [33]:

[33] i *She abided by their decision.   He asked for water.   I'm counting on her help. We came across some errors.   The meal consists of fruit and vegetables.*
      ii *He accused her of fraud.   I won't hold it against you.   He'll treat me to lunch. She convinced us of her innocence.   They supplied us with weapons.*
      iii *That counts as satisfactory.   He had passed for dead.   I served as secretary.*
      iv *I regard that as unfair.   They rated it as a success.   He took me for a fool.*

The prepositions that begin the underlined PPs are not in contrast with other prepositions like those in [31–32]. The complement-licensing properties of the verbs specifically mention the particular preposition that heads the complement.[2]

- The examples in [33i] are all intransitive.
- Those in [ii] are transitive – the PP complement follows an NP object.
- In [iii–iv] the complement of the preposition is predicative – again, this is evident from the possibility of its having the form of an AdjP or bare role NP.

Fossilisation

Some verb + preposition combinations are **fossilised**, in the sense that they don't permit any variation in their relative positions. An example of such a fossilised combination is ***come*** + *across*, meaning "find by chance", as in *I came across some letters written by my grandmother*. It is contrasted in [34] with the non-fossilised combination ***ask*** + *for*, "request":

[34]   NON-FOSSILISED   FOSSILISED
   i a. *I asked for some information.*   b. *I came across some letters.*
  ii a. *the information [which I asked for]* b. *the letters [which I came across]*
 iii a. *the information [for which I asked]* b. *the letters [across which I came]*

The difference is illustrated in the relative clause construction enclosed in brackets in [ii–iii]. These examples include relative clauses containing the relative pronoun *which* functioning as complement to a preposition. As we saw in §5, there are ordinarily two variants of this construction:

- In the **stranded** preposition construction, *which* occupies front position in the clause, and the preposition occurs after the verb, separated from its complement. This is the variant shown in [ii].
- In the **fronted** preposition construction, the preposition is fronted along with its complement *which*, as in [iii], so it appears immediately before its complement as normal.

Both variants are permitted with ***ask for***, but only the first is permitted with ***come across***: [iiib] is not grammatical. The reason is that the second type of relative clause construction separates the preposition from the verb which specifies it, whereas fossilisation doesn't allow any departure from the fixed order of verb + preposition. The fronted preposition construction is not grammatically compatible with the fossilised ***come across*** that means "find by chance".

---

[2] Some verbs occur with more than one specified preposition. But the resultant preposition–verb combinations generally have very different meanings. For example, we get *He was looking after me*, *He was looking at me*, and *He was looking for me*, involving utterly different notions – caring, watching, and searching, respectively.

The same kind of fossilisation is found in transitive clauses. Compare:

[35]   NON-FOSSILISED   FOSSILISED
    i   a. *He <u>accused</u> her <u>of</u> a crime.*   b. *I <u>let</u> him <u>off</u> some work.*
    ii a. *the crime [which he <u>accused</u> her <u>of</u>]* b. *the work [which I <u>let</u> him <u>off</u>]*
    iii a. *the crime [<u>of</u> which he <u>accused</u> her]* b. **the work [<u>off</u> which I <u>let</u> him]*

Let *+ off*, meaning "allow not to do", is fossilised in that the preposition must follow the verb, with only the object intervening. Again, then, the stranded preposition
construction is permitted in both [iia] and [iib], whereas the fronted preposition
construction is permitted in [iiia] but is quite inadmissible in [iiib].

7.3   Particles

Particles are the only complements which can freely come between the
verb and its direct object. Compare, for example, the particle *down* with the non-
particle *downstairs* in [36]:

[36]   PARTICLE   NON-PARTICLE
    i   a. *She took the suitcase <u>down</u>.*   b. *She took the suitcase <u>downstairs</u>.*
    ii a. *She took <u>down</u> the suitcase.*   b. **She took <u>downstairs</u> the suitcase.*

Both *down* and *downstairs* can follow the object, but only *down* can occur between
verb and object, as in [ii]. *Down* is a particle, but *downstairs* is not.

Particles are short words (one or two syllables) that with just one or two exceptions are all prepositions unaccompanied by any complement of their own. Some of
the most common prepositions belonging to the particle category are listed in [37]:

[37]   *along   away   back   by   down   forward   in*
        off   on   out   over   round   under   up

Particles can never precede an unstressed personal pronoun object

One general constraint on the order 'particle + object' is that it is inadmissible if the
object has the form of an **unstressed personal pronoun**. For example, we can
replace *the suitcase* by unstressed *it* in [36ia] but not in [iia]:

[38]   a. *She took <u>it</u> <u>off</u>.*   b. **She took <u>off</u> it.*

7.4   Verbal idioms

An **idiom** is a combination of words whose meaning is not predictable
from the meanings of the components. A **verbal idiom** is an idiom beginning with a
verb. ***Kick*** *the bucket*, with the sense "die", is a familiar example: you can't guess
the meaning just by knowing the meanings of the words (it has nothing to do with
kicking or buckets).

There are huge numbers of verbal idioms in English, and many of them contain
prepositions. Some of the examples used earlier in this section contain verbal
idioms – e.g. *hold* NP *against* NP in [33ii]; *come across* NP in [34]; *let* NP *off* NP in

[35]; and so on. Two other constructions that often contain such verbal idioms are illustrated in [39]:

[39]   i   *He finally <u>backed down</u>.   Her father <u>passed away</u>.   When will you <u>grow up</u>?*
           Kim and Pat have <u>fallen out</u>.   Do you think the idea will <u>catch on</u>?
       ii *This <u>ties in with</u> your first point.   I'm not going to <u>put up with</u> this any longer.*
           Liz just <u>gets by on</u> her pension.   You should <u>stand up to</u> him.

* Those in [i] consist of a verb and a preposition without a complement. Non-idiomatic examples of this construction are seen in *She came in* or *She went out*, where *in* and *out* are goal complements.

* The idioms in [ii] consist of a verb + a preposition with no complement + a preposition with an NP complement. *In* in **tie in with**, for example, has no complement while *with* has *your first point* as its complement. A non-idiomatic example of this construction is *She came in with her uncle*.

Idioms need not be syntactic constituents

Idiom is a lexical concept. Idioms have to be listed and described in a dictionary of the language, because of their particular form and special **idiomatic meanings**. But it would be a mistake to assume that what counts as a lexical unit will necessarily form a syntactic unit as well. This is not so. The underlined expressions in [39i] do happen to be syntactic constituents: they are VPs with the verb as head and the PP as complement. But those in [39ii] are not; here the lexical and syntactic units do not match up.

Take as an example the sentence *This ties in with your first point*. As we have said, *with* is a preposition taking *your first point* as its complement, so *with your first point* forms a PP. Syntactically, the VP consists of three constituents (*ties + in + with your first point*), not two (*ties in with + your first point*). This is evident from the way the idiom behaves in the relative clause construction discussed above. For alongside the stranded preposition version *a point which this ties in with* we have the more formal version with preposition fronting *a point with which this ties in*, where the fronted *with which* clearly forms a PP. Note also the possibility of inserting a clause adjunct after *in*: *This ties in well with your first point*.

More obvious are examples like *hold* NP$_1$ *against* NP$_2$ from [33ii], since here the verb has an object which separates it from the preposition and isn't part of the idiom. For example, in *I won't <u>hold</u> it <u>against</u> you if you refuse*, there is a special idiomatic meaning associated with the use of **hold** together with *against* (roughly, "I won't judge you adversely if you refuse"), but there is no syntactic constituent consisting solely of *hold* and *against*: they aren't even adjacent in the sequence of words.

The important thing about idioms, then, is that they have special and unpredictable meanings, but that is the only respect in which they are special. They do not also constitute special syntactic units with peculiar structure. In syntactic structure they are generally quite ordinary, and often identical to the structure the same sequence of words has when the meaning is the literal and predictable one.[3]

8   Prepositional idioms and fossilisation

In the last section we were concerned with verbal idioms – idioms beginning with a verb. There are also a large number of prepositional idioms – idioms beginning with a preposition. In particular, we examine here a sample of expressions with the form preposition + noun + preposition that are idiomatic in meaning and largely or wholly fossilised in syntax. Examples are given in [40i–ii], which contrast with the ordinary sequences in [iii]:

[40] i *by means of* hard work   *on behalf of* my son   *with effect from* today
      ii *by virtue of* her age   *in front of* the car   *in league with* the devil
      iii *in photos of* their parents   *to questions of* ethics   *with knowledge of* his goals

Fossilisation means that the parts cannot be varied independently as freely as in ordinary sequences. One reflection of this is that we cannot drop the first preposition in [i–ii], to yield NPs that can be used elsewhere, though we can do this in [iii]:

[41] i *Means of hard work enabled her to pass the exam.*
      ii *Virtue of her age led them to drop the charges.*
      iii *Photos of their parents were lying on the table.*

The expressions *photos of their parents*, *questions of ethics* and *knowledge of his goals* are obviously NPs which in [40iii] happen to be functioning as complement of a preposition but which can also appear in the normal range of NP functions, such as subject in [41iii].

The analysis of [40i–ii], however, is much less obvious. Many writers treat the underlined sequences here as syntactic units, commonly called 'complex prepositions'. The motivation for this lies in the meaning: *in front of the car* is semantically comparable to *behind the car*, and this tempts grammarians to see *in front of* as an element of the same kind as *behind*, only more complex in its internal structure. It is a mistake, however. Semantic relations of this kind do not provide a reliable guide to syntactic analysis.

For examples like those in [40i] there is compelling evidence that the structure is the same as for [40iii], with the first preposition taking an NP as complement. Notice that the noun can take pre-head dependents:

[42]   by *similar* means   on *my son's* behalf   with *immediate* effect

These show that the fossilisation is only partial. The changes made here to the sequence following the first preposition demonstrate clearly that it has the status of

---

[3] Many grammars use the term 'phrasal verb' for some or all of the expressions we have been considering in §§7.3–4. We have not adopted this term. It is thoroughly misleading. It's not the whole expressions **fall** *out*, **tie** *in with*, etc., that are verbs; it's just the lexemes **fall**, **tie**, etc.

an NP. If *by means of* were really a single preposition, we wouldn't expect to be able to insert *similar* after the first part of it and drop the last part to get *by similar means*.

Changes of this kind are not possible in [40ii], where the degree of fossilisation is greater. A case can be made for treating the first two words as forming a unit that takes the remainder as its complement. *In front of the car*, for example, will have a unitary preposition *in front* as head, and *of the car* will be its complement.

That, however, is very different from taking *in front of* as a whole as a complex preposition. The *of* in *in front of the car* actually belongs with *the car*, not with the head *in front*. This is evident from the fact that if we omit *the car* when it is retrievable from the context, we must also drop the *of*. Compare, for example:

[43]   i a. *She stood in front of the car.*   b. *She stood in front.*
         ii a. *She stood behind the car.*   b. *She stood behind.*

You can't say **She stood in front of*. From a syntactic point of view, therefore, it is clearly not *in front of* that behaves like *behind*, but just *in front*; it differs from *behind* in that it takes an optional complement with *of*, rather than an NP.

The same general point applies to the second preposition in the other sequences in [40ii].

- Take *in league with*. We can have *The two of them are in league with the devil* or just *The two of them are in league* (understood as "in league with each other"). This shows that from a syntactic point of view *with* belongs in the first instance with the following NP, not with *league*.
- In *by virtue of her age* we cannot omit *of her age*, but we can still show that *of* forms a PP with *her age*. One piece of evidence is that the *of* can be repeated in coordination, as in *by virtue of her age and of her family commitments*. The coordinator *and* here is linking the two constituents that are underlined. They are PPs. And that means *by virtue of* is not a preposition, not a syntactic unit of any sort.

Exercises

1. For each of the following sentences (all from the opening pages of Mary Shelley's novel *Frankenstein*), underline the **complement** of the doubly underlined **preposition** – all the words that make up the complement, but no other words. In each case give the category of the complement.
   i *What may not be expected in a country of eternal light?*
   ii *Six years have passed since I resolved on my present undertaking.*
   iii *I commenced by inuring my body to hardship.*

   iv *My life might have been passed in ease and luxury.*
   v *They fly quickly over the snow in their sledges.*

2. List ten word sequences other than the ones discussed in this chapter that are standardly described (or could plausibly be taken) as '**complex prepositions**'. Provide evidence for their degree of fossilisation, classifying them as **less fossilised** (like the cases in [40i] of this chapter, e.g., *by means of*) or **more fossilised** (like those in [40ii]).

3. Determine which of the verbs below belong to the class of **prepositional verbs**. For those that do, identify the preposition(s) they select and provide relevant examples. (Do this exercise with the help of a good dictionary.) For each verb + preposition sequence say whether or not it is **fossilised**, and provide evidence that your claim about fossilisation is correct.

   i *bank*   vi *hope*
   ii *believe*   vii *see*
   iii *convince*   viii *stand*
   iv *fall*   ix *treat*
   v *feel*   x *wait*

4. The word *up* is a **particle** in *We folded up the map* but not in *We climbed up the mountain*. What syntactic differences can you find between the two constructions? Use these differences to say for each of the following which of the two kinds of construction it belongs to.

   i *I looked <u>over</u> my shoulder.*
   ii *We must bring <u>in</u> the washing.*
   iii *We'd better run <u>off</u> some more copies.*
   iv *I knocked <u>over</u> the vase.*
   v *He never got <u>over</u> his disappointment.*

5. For each of the following words, decide whether it is a **preposition** or an **adjective**, and give arguments to support your view: [i] *about*; [ii] *ahead*; [iii] *aloof*; [iv] *aloft*; [v] *around*.

6. Construct an example, complete with as much context as necessary, to show that when the context is right a pronoun can FOLLOW the particle in a **verb + particle** construction like *rip you off* or *call him out* or *turn them down*, if it is contrastively stressed.

7. Which of the following **prepositions** can occur in **declarative main clauses** either with or without an NP complement? Give examples to illustrate both uses, noting those which occur without an NP complement only in a restricted subset of their uses/meanings:

   i *against*   vi *throughout*
   ii *between*   vii *to*
   iii *despite*   viii *underneath*
   iv *inside*   ix *until*
   v *opposite*   x *within*

8. The following examples have **stranded** prepositions. Construct corresponding examples with a fronted preposition. If you find any of your examples ungrammatical, mark them with * in the usual way.

   i *They couldn't agree on who it referred to.*
   ii *What am I supposed to cut this thing with?*
   iii *He's the man I showed the photo to.*
   iv *The place we're going to is so informal they don't have table cloths.*
   v *It was the only proposal which every department member agreed with.*

9. The following examples have **fronted** prepositions. Construct corresponding examples with a **stranded** preposition. If the example turns out to be ungrammatical, mark it with *.

   i *Under what circumstances would you agree?*
   ii *In what year was she born?*
   iii *He came to the bed in which Goldilocks had been sleeping.*
   iv *It appealed to everyone with whom he discussed it.*
   v *It was a situation in which it would have been hard for anyone to form a judgement concerning what to do.*

10. Classify the following words as **adverbs** or **prepositions**, basing your answers on the criteria discussed in Ch. 7 and citing the relevant evidence: [i] *ahead;* [ii] *always;* [iii] *indoors;* [iv] *often;* [v] *overseas.*

8 Negation and related phenomena

1 Negative and positive clauses

Negation is marked by individual words (such as *not, no, never*) or by affixes within a word (such as *·n't, un·, non·*). Very often, however, there is an effect on the whole clause. In pairs like those in [1], for example, we have a contrast between a **positive clause** and the corresponding **negative clause**:

[1]   POSITIVE CLAUSE   NEGATIVE CLAUSE
    a. *He has signed the agreement.*   b. *He hasn't signed the agreement.*

The grammatical system in which positive and negative contrast is called **polarity**: clause [a] has **positive polarity**, while [b] has **negative polarity**.

Semantically, a simple pair of positive and negative clauses like these are related in such a way that they cannot both be true, but they also cannot both be false. One of them has got to be true: either he has signed the agreement or he hasn't.

Syntactically, positive is the default polarity. All canonical clauses are positive. Negative clauses are marked as such by the presence of a specific negative element, like the negative verb-form *hasn't* in [1b]. And positive and negative clauses differ in the way they combine with other expressions in the structure of larger units. Here are the three major differences.

(a) Addition of *not even*

After a negative clause we can add a constituent introduced by *not even*, and it makes sense. This is not possible with positive clauses:

[2]   i POSITIVE CLAUSE: *I have read your book, not even the introduction.*
       ii NEGATIVE CLAUSE: *I haven't read your book, not even the introduction.*

The addition in [ii] is interpreted as "I haven't even read the introduction". The *not* isn't obligatory (cf. *I haven't read your book, even the introduction*) but the crucial point is that it can occur in the negative clause [ii] but is impossible in the positive [i].

(b) The connective adjuncts *so* and *neither* or *nor*

When we add a related clause of the same polarity, the positive pair may be linked by *so*, the negative pair by *neither* or *nor*:

[3]   i POSITIVE CLAUSE: *I have read your book, and <u>so</u> have my students.*
     ii NEGATIVE CLAUSE: *I haven't read your book, and <u>neither</u> have my students.*

Switching the connectives leads to ungrammaticality: **I have read your book and neither have my students*; **I haven't read your book and so have my students.*

(c) Confirmatory tags

A common device for seeking confirmation of what one says is to add a truncated interrogative clause known as a **tag**. It generally consists of just an auxiliary verb + personal pronoun subject, and its polarity is the reverse of that of the clause to which it is attached:

[4]   i POSITIVE CLAUSE + NEGATIVE TAG: *They have read my book, <u>haven't they?</u>*
     ii NEGATIVE CLAUSE + POSITIVE TAG: *They haven't read my book, <u>have they?</u>*

In [a] the negative tag (*haven't they?*) attaches to the positive clause, while in [b] the positive tag (*have they?*) attaches to the negative clause.

These **reversed polarity** tags have to be distinguished from those with **constant polarity**. These don't ask for confirmation, but suggest an attitude such as surprise, disbelief, disapproval or the like: an author might say *So they've read my book, have they? Amazing!* For many speakers constant polarity tags aren't used with negative clauses: *%So they haven't read my book, haven't they?* will be rejected by many speakers of Standard English. For those speakers, if a negative tag is acceptable on a clause, the clause must be positive.

2   Subclausal negation

We have seen that the effect of a negative element is very often to make the clause containing it negative. Negative elements don't always have this effect, however. In the cases where they don't, the negation is **subclausal**.

Affixal negation

The most obvious case where negative elements don't make a clause negative is where the negative element is an affix other than the *n't* that appears on auxiliary verbs. Take negative prefixes as in <u>dis</u>like, <u>in</u>attentive, <u>non</u>-negotiable, or <u>un</u>willing, or suffixes such as ·*less* in *home<u>less</u>*. We can use the constructions shown in [2–4] to show that these affixes don't make the whole clause negative. Compare, for example, *He was unkind*, which contains the prefix *un*·, with *He wasn't kind*, which contains a negative verb-form. The latter clause is of course negative, but the former is positive, as is evident from the following data:

[5]   SUBCLAUSAL NEGATION   CLAUSAL NEGATION

   i a. *He was unkind, _not even_ to me.   b. He wasn't kind, _not even_ to me.

   ii a. He was unkind, and _so_ was Sue.   b. He wasn't kind, and _neither_ was Sue.

   iii a. He was unkind, _wasn't he?_   b. He wasn't kind, _was he?_

- _He wasn't kind_ behaves just like the earlier _I haven't read your book_: it accepts _not even_, takes _neither_ (or _nor_) as connective, and selects a positive confirmation tag.
- _He was unkind_, by contrast, behaves like the obviously positive _I have read your book_: it doesn't accept _not even_, it does take _so_ as connective, and it selects a negative tag.

We call the negation in _He was unkind_ subclausal because it works below the level of the clause.

    Notice that there is a semantic difference between _He was unkind_ and _He wasn't kind_. If _He wasn't kind_ is false, then _He was kind_ must be true; but if _He was unkind_ is false, it doesn't follow that _He was kind_ is true: he could be neutral, neither kind nor unkind.

Other cases of subclausal negation

Some further contrasts between subclausal and clausal negation are illustrated in [6]:

[6]   SUBCLAUSAL NEGATION   CLAUSAL NEGATION

   i a. She works for _nothing_.   b. She's interested in _nothing_.

   ii a. It was _no_ mean achievement.   b. It was _no_ great deal.

   iii a. This is a _not_ uncommon mistake.   b. This is _not_ an uncommon mistake.

   iv a. _Not_ surprisingly, he complained.   b. Surprisingly, he did _not_ complain.

Again the tests differentiate clearly between the [a] and [b] examples: the right confirmation tag for [ia] would be _doesn't she?_, while the one for [ib] would be _is she?_, and so on.

- _Nothing_ and _no_ generally mark clausal negation. In [ia] and [iia] we have exceptional cases where they don't.
- The contrast in [iii] is due to the fact that the _not_ in [a] is in an attributive modifier in NP structure (_not uncommon_), whereas in [b] the _not_ is modifying the verb _is_.
- In [iva], _not_ modifies _surprisingly_, and the main predication is positive: "He complained, which wasn't surprising". In [ivb], by contrast, the negation applies to _complain_: "He didn't complain, which was surprising".

3   Clausal negation

Within clausal negation we make a further distinction between **verbal** and **non-verbal** negation:

[7]	VERBAL NEGATION	NON-VERBAL NEGATION
i	a. *She <u>didn't</u> tell me anything.*	b. *She told me <u>nothing</u>.*
ii	a. *She <u>does not</u> live here any more.*	b. *She <u>no longer</u> lives here.*

Verbal negation is marked either by **negative inflection** on the verb, as in [ia], or by **modification** of the verb by the separate word *not*, as in [iia].

3.1   Verbal negation

The grammatical significance of the distinction between verbal and non-verbal negation is that verbal negation requires the insertion of the **dummy auxiliary** *do* under certain conditions, whereas non-verbal negation never does. This difference is evident in [7] above, where *do* is required in the [a] examples but not the [b] ones.

▨   Conditions for the insertion of dummy *do* with verbal negation

(a)   In clauses with a primary verb-form

Negative clauses of this kind require the presence of an auxiliary verb. If there is no auxiliary in the corresponding positive clause, formation of the negative involves the insertion of *do* as described in Ch. 3, §3.1, and illustrated in [8]:

[8]	POSITIVE	NEGATIVE
i	a. *She is lenient with them*	b. *She <u>isn't</u> lenient with them.*
ii	a. *She rejected his offer.*	b. *She <u>didn't</u> reject his offer.*

- In [ia] *be* is an auxiliary verb, so we do NOT insert *do* when negating the clause.
- In [iia] *reject* is a lexical verb, so we must insert *do* to form the negative.

(b)   In imperative clauses

Imperative clauses with verbal negation ALWAYS require *do*:

[9]			
i	a. *Be lenient with them.*	b. *<u>Don't</u> be lenient with them.*
ii	a. *Reject his offer.*	b. *<u>Don't</u> reject his offer.*

Notice, then, the difference between [9ib] and [8ib]: *do* is added in the imperative, but not in the declarative.

▨   Inflectional verb-form vs *not*

We said that verbal negation is marked either by negative inflection on the verb itself or by using the separate word *not* to modify the verb. Inflectional negation is admissible only in those constructions where dummy *do* occurs (under the conditions described above): that is, in clauses with a primary verb-form and in imperative clauses, as illustrated in [8] and [9] respectively. Elsewhere, neither *do* nor negative inflection is permitted, as seen in the subjunctive clauses in [10]:

[10]　　　　MARKING BY INFLECTION　　　　　MARKING BY *NOT*
　　　i　a. *It is vital [*that we <u>ben't</u> disturbed*].　　b. *It is vital [*that we <u>not be</u> disturbed*].
　　　ii　a. *It is vital [*that he <u>don't</u> delay*].　　b. *It is vital [*that he <u>not delay</u>*].

Notice that where marking by *not* is the only option, the *not* normally comes before the verb rather than after it.

In constructions that permit both kinds of verbal negation, the difference between them is primarily one of style. Marking by *not* is characteristic of more formal style than inflectional negation.

3.2　　Non-verbal clausal negation

Non-verbal clausal negation is marked either by *not* modifying a constituent other than a verb, or else by various negative words that are not used for verbal negation: *nothing, never, few*, etc.

Not as a marker of non-verbal negation

Not can modify a considerable range of non-verbal elements, but by no means all. In a comprehensive grammar we would need to detail all the possibilities, but in this short introduction we will merely provide a sample, including some that illustrate the limitations on the use of *not* as a modifier.

In the following examples, single underlining highlights *not* and double underlining marks the element that it modifies – admissibly in the [a] examples, inadmissibly in the [b] examples:

[11]　　　　ADMISSIBLE　　　　　　　　　INADMISSIBLE
　　　i　a. <u>Not</u> <u>everybody</u> agrees with you.　　b. *<u>Not</u> <u>somebody</u> agrees with you.
　　　ii　a. <u>Not</u> <u>all</u> her friends supported her.　　b. *<u>Not</u> <u>each</u> of her friends supported her.
　　　iii　a. <u>Not</u> <u>even</u> Tom liked it.　　b. *<u>Not</u> <u>Tom</u> liked it.

Other markers of non-verbal negation

We confine our attention here to items that can mark clausal negation. This excludes the affixes *un-, non-, in-*, etc., which – as illustrated in [5] above – mark subclausal negation. There are two groups to consider: **absolute negators** and **approximate negators**.

(a)　Absolute negators

These are listed in [12], with some examples of clausal negation given in [13]:

[12]　i　*no, none, nobody, no one, nothing, nowhere*[1]
　　　ii　*neither, nor, never*

[13]　i　a. <u>Nobody</u> objected to her plan.　　b. <u>Neither</u> Kim <u>nor</u> Pat has arrived.
　　　ii　a. *We found <u>no</u> mistakes.*　　b. *He <u>never</u> apologises.*

---

[1] For informal AmE, *no place* (synonymous with *nowhere*) can be added to this list.

Where the negator follows the subject in clausal negation, as in [13ii], there is usually an equivalent clause with verbal negation:

[14]   NON-VERBAL NEGATION   EQUIVALENT VERBAL NEGATION
    i a. *We found <u>no</u> mistakes.* (=[13iia])   b. *We <u>didn't</u> find <u>any</u> mistakes.*
    ii a. *There is <u>no one</u> here.*   b. *There <u>isn't</u> <u>anyone</u> here.*
    iii a. *He <u>never</u> apologises.* (=[13iib])   b. *He <u>doesn't</u> <u>ever</u> apologise.*

The versions with verbal negation have forms with *any, anybody, anyone*, etc., in place of the negators in [12i], and *either, or*, and *ever* in place of those in [12ii].

(b)   Approximate negators

These are listed in [15], and in [16] we again give examples involving clausal negation:

[15]   *few, little; rarely, seldom; barely, hardly, scarcely*

[16]   i a. *<u>Few</u> of them realised it was a hoax.*   b. *He <u>rarely</u> goes to church nowadays.*
        ii a. *She <u>hardly</u> spoke a word all evening.*   b. *There's <u>scarcely</u> any food left.*

Few of them comes close in meaning to *none of them*: *none* indicates absolutely zero, while *few* puts the number within a small part of the scale down at the end close to zero. This is why we say it is an **approximate** negator. In a similar way, *rarely* approximates to *never*; *hardly spoke a word* approximates to *didn't speak a word*; and *scarcely any food* approximates to *no food*.

Although only approximate semantically, these items largely follow the pattern of the absolute negators with respect to the tests for clausal negation. In particular, the confirmation tags for the examples in [16] are those that attach to absolute negative clauses. For [ia] we have *did they?*, for [ib] *does he?*, for [iia] *did she?*, and for [iib] *is there?* Note here the contrast between *few*, which is negative, and *a few*, which is positive – witness *A few of them realised it was a hoax, didn't they?*

4   Non-affirmative items

A fair number of words or larger expressions are **polarity-sensitive** in the sense that they occur readily in clauses of one polarity but not of the other. Compare, for example:

[17]   POSITIVE   NEGATIVE
    i a. *I have <u>some</u> objections to make.*   b. **I don't have <u>some</u> objections to make.*
    ii a. **I have <u>any</u> objections to make.* b. *I don't have <u>any</u> objections to make.*

- *Some* is by no means wholly excluded from negative clauses, but it is subject to restrictions that do not apply to the positive: we say, therefore, that it has **positive orientation**.
- Conversely *any* (in the sense it has here) has **negative orientation**: it occurs freely in negatives but is excluded from positives like [iia].

The majority of polarity-sensitive items have negative orientation, and our main focus here will be on these.

What excludes *any* from [17iia] is not just that the clause is positive: it is also **declarative**. If we look instead at an **interrogative** clause, we find it is freely admitted:

[18]   a. *Have you <u>any</u> objections to make?*   b. *Who has <u>any</u> objections to make?*

We refer to items like *any*, therefore, as **non-affirmatives**. (The verb *affirm* contrasts with *question* and hence suggests declarative; the adjective *affirmative* is a synonym of *positive*.)

In general, then, the restriction on non-affirmative items is that they cannot occur in clauses that are both **declarative** and **positive**.

A sample of non-affirmative items is given in [19]. Some items are non-affirmative only in certain senses or uses (though often the most frequently occurring of their uses), and we mark those with a subscript n.

[19]   i *any$_n$, anybody$_n$, any longer/more, anyone$_n$, anything$_n$, anywhere$_n$*
       ii *at all, either$_n$, ever$_n$, long$_n$, much, till/until, whatever$_n$, yet$_n$*
      iii *dare$_n$, need$_n$, bother* (+ infinitival), *budge, can bear$_n$, can stand$_n$, give a damn/fig, have a clue$_n$, lift a finger$_n$, move a muscle$_n$, see a thing$_n$*

The following examples illustrate the differences between polarity-sensitive and non-polarity-sensitive versions of the five items *anybody, either, ever, long,* and *can stand*:

[20]   NON-AFFIRMATIVE   NOT POLARITY-SENSITIVE
      i a. *Did you see <u>anybody</u>?*   b. *<u>Anybody</u> can make promises.*
     ii a. *I didn't see <u>either</u> of them.*   b. *<u>Either</u> version would do.*
    iii a. *Will it <u>ever</u> end?*   b. *It will last for <u>ever</u>.*
     iv a. *I won't stay <u>long</u>.*   b. *It has been a <u>long</u> day.*
      v a. *No one <u>can stand</u> the pressure.* b. *Everyone <u>can stand</u> for a minute.*

Notice also that *dare* and *need* are non-affirmative as modal auxiliaries but not as lexical verbs; see Ch. 3, §3.3.

Other constructions that accept non-affirmatives

It is not only negatives and interrogatives that allow non-affirmative items to appear. They are also found in a number of other constructions, as illustrated in [21].

[21]   i *She was <u>too</u> taken aback to say <u>anything</u>.*
       ii *She ran fast<u>er</u> than she had <u>ever</u> run before.*
      iii *We slipped away <u>without</u> <u>anyone</u> noticing.*

The constructions concerned all have semantic affinities with negation.

- Because of the *too* in [i], we understand that she did NOT say anything.
- Because of the comparative, [ii] indicates that she had NEVER run that fast before.
- Because of the meaning of *without*, it follows from [iii] that NO ONE noticed.

Prescriptive grammar note

There are non-standard varieties of English – widespread in Britain, North America, and Australasia – that use **negative** items in place of Standard English **non-affirmative** items in clauses with verbal negation:

[22]   STANDARD   NON-STANDARD

   i a. *I didn't see <u>anybody</u>.*   b. *'I didn't see <u>nobody</u>.*

  ii a. *He didn't say <u>anything</u> to <u>anybody</u>.*   b. *'He didn't say <u>nothing</u> to <u>nobody</u>.*

The [b] examples here mark the negation in two or more places: once in the verb, and then again in the underlined negative words. This phenomenon is called **negative concord** ('concord' being another term for 'agreement'): selection of *nothing* and *nobody* is determined by agreement with the preceding negative.

Prescriptive manuals are right to say that the negative concord construction is not Standard English. But they also commonly condemn it as **illogical**. It isn't. To think that the non-standard dialects that use negative concord are illogical is to confuse logic and grammar.

It is true that in logic two negatives cancel each other out and make a positive: *It's not the case that he didn't speak to her* is true if and only if he spoke to her. And in Standard English *I didn't see nobody* (with stress on *nobody*) implies that I did see somebody. But that isn't what it means in the non-standard dialects: as everyone knows, there it means that I didn't see anybody. In examples like [22ib] we have two **grammatical** negatives, but only one **semantic** negative.

The kind of grammar that the non-standard dialects follow is also found in some standard languages: in Standard French, Italian, and Polish for example. There are also colloquial Standard English constructions that mark negation twice: *Pick up some cement? Not in my car you <u>won't</u>!* means "You won't pick up cement in my car", but it expresses the negation twice; this emphatic construction is informal in style, but it isn't non-standard.

Even formal Standard English has some constructions where negation is expressed more than once. One example is *I saw <u>neither</u> Kim <u>nor</u> Pat*, where *neither* expresses negation once and *nor* expresses it again – compare *I didn't see either Kim or Pat*, which means the same but has only one grammatical negative.

Negative concord as in *'I didn't see nobody* is not illogical; it just happens to be a feature of non-standard varieties that is absent from the standard variety. And of course Standard English speakers know about it: when the Rolling Stones sing *I can't get no satisfaction*, everyone understands that the meaning is "I am unable to obtain satisfaction" – not "I am unable to obtain zero satisfaction"!

5   Scope of negation

The **scope** of negation is the part of the sentence that the negative applies to semantically. Scope is best understood by examination of contrasts like the one in [23]:

[23]   NEGATION HAS SCOPE OVER *MANY*   *MANY* HAS SCOPE OVER NEGATION

     a. *<u>Not</u> many people believed him.*   b. *<u>Many</u> people did<u>n't</u> believe him.*

The difference in meaning is considerable: [a] entails that the number of people who believed him is relatively small, but certainly [b] does not (we might be talking, for example, about a major political figure in a country with a huge population, where there are many people who didn't believe him and many others who did).

● In [a] the negation applies to *many*: the number of people who believed him was not large. We say then that *many* falls within the scope of the negation – or that the negation **has scope over** *many*.

● In [b], however, the negation does not apply to *many*: it does not have scope over it. On the contrary, the quantification expressed by *many* has scope over the negation, since it gives the size of the set of people who had the property that they didn't believe him.

The same kind of contrast is found in the following pairs, where again the item with double underlining has scope over the one with single underlining:

[24]   i a. *I didn't omit my name deliberately.*   b. *I deliberately didn't omit my name.*
       ii a. *You needn't tell anyone about it.*   b. *You mustn't tell anyone about it.*

● In [ia] the negative has scope over the adjunct *deliberately*: omitting my name was not something I made a point of doing. In [ib], by contrast, *deliberately* has scope over the negation: I made a point of not omitting my name.

● In [iia] the negation has scope over the modal auxiliary *need*, expressing deontic necessity: "It isn't necessary for you to tell anyone about it". In [iib], however, modal *must*, likewise expressing deontic necessity, has scope over the negation: "It is necessary that you not tell anyone about it".

Note that in cases where some element has scope over the negation, it is normally possible to find a paraphrase in which the negative marker is located in a subordinate clause.

● For [23b], for example, we have *There were many people [who didn't believe him]*.

● For [24ib]: *I deliberately chose [not to omit my name]*.

● For [24iib], *You are required [not to tell anyone about it]*; and so on.

There is a significant degree of correlation between semantic scope and grammatical order. Very often, a negative element has scope over what follows but is within the scope of elements that precede. For example, in [23] and [24i] the negative marker in [a] precedes the element over which it has scope and in [b] follows the element which has scope over it. But the correlation is clearly only partial. In [24ii], for example, there is no difference in grammatical structure between [a] and [b]: the scope difference is attributable to specific properties of the modal auxiliaries *must* and *need*.

Exercises

1. Are the following clauses grammatically **positive** or **negative**? Give evidence for your answers.

    i   *You're so negative I want to strangle you.*

    ii *I disagree with all of you.*

    iii *They're always complaining about things of no importance at all.*

    iv *I can do nothing to help you.*

    v   *Never before had they offered such good terms.*

    vi *That's absolute nonsense, you brainless ninny.*

    vii *We finished the job in no time.*

    viii *Everybody hates lying, mealy-mouthed, pontificating little weasels like you.*

    ix *We can't just not answer their letter.*

    x   *There's hardly any chance of them changing their mind.*

2. The following examples have **non-verbal** clausal negation; construct equivalent examples with **verbal negation**.

    i   *He had told neither the boss nor her secretary.*

    ii *They were impressed by none of the candidates.*

    iii *We have nowhere to hide.*

    iv *I saw no one on the road.*

    v   *We're taking neither of them with us.*

3. Discuss the difference in meaning between the following:

    i   *He had read a few books on the subject.*

    ii *He had read few books on the subject.*

4. For each of the following words or expressions, construct one example where it behaves as a **non-affirmative** item and one where it is not polarity-sensitive: [i] *anything*; [ii] **kick** *the bucket*; [iii] **need** (verb); [iv] *whatever*; [v] *yet*.

9 Clause type: asking, exclaiming, and directing

1 Clause type and speech acts

Philosophers use the term **speech acts** for things you can do with sentences of your language – things like making **statements**, asking **questions**, issuing **commands**, or uttering **exclamations**. (All of these speech acts can of course be performed with written language too.) Which of these you can do with a given sentence depends to a large extent on its syntactic form. The syntax of English distinguishes a set of **clause types** that are characteristically used to perform different kinds of speech acts. The major types are the five illustrated in [1]:

[1] i DECLARATIVE   *You are very tactful.*
     ii CLOSED INTERROGATIVE   *Are you very tactful?*
     iii OPEN INTERROGATIVE   *How tactful are you?*
     iv EXCLAMATIVE   *How tactful you are!*
     v IMPERATIVE   *Be very tactful.*

(See §2 below for an explanation of closed versus open interrogatives.)

Although the correspondence between these clause types and the speech acts they can be used to perform is not one-to-one, speech acts do have a characteristic correlation with clause types. We show the default correlation in [2]:

[2]   CLAUSE TYPE   CHARACTERISTIC SPEECH ACT
     i declarative   making a statement
     ii closed interrogative   asking a closed question
     iii open interrogative   asking an open question
     iv exclamative   making an exclamatory statement
     v imperative   issuing a directive

- **Directive** covers commands, instructions, requests, entreaties and the like.
- A **closed question** is one with a closed set of answers. For example, there are just two answers to the closed question *Is Sue here?* – namely *Yes, she's here* and *No, she isn't here*.
- *Where is Sue?*, by contrast, is an **open question**: the set of answers is open-ended.

The correlations in [2] could provide for general definitions of the clause types. For example, the imperative clause type can be defined as a clause construction CHARACTERISTICALLY USED TO ISSUE DIRECTIVES.

However, it's important that 'imperative' and 'directive' are terms for entirely different things, and they DO NOT ALWAYS CORRESPOND. They cannot be used as language-particular definitions. This chapter is concerned with the syntactic properties of the clause types and the way in which they line up with clause meanings and speech acts. The correlation isn't anywhere near as simple as you might have expected.

Where the correlation fails

One example in [3] shows a directive that isn't expressed by an imperative, and the other shows an imperative that doesn't express a directive:

[3]   i   CLOSED INTERROGATIVE   *Could you please open the door.*
        ii IMPERATIVE   *Turn up late* *and you'll be fired.*

- Example [i] would normally be used and understood as a directive (specifically, a polite request); but it is of closed interrogative form. It's not an imperative.
- The underlined clause of [ii] has imperative form, but would not be naturally interpreted as a directive: I'm not telling you to turn up late. The whole sentence is understood as if it had a conditional adjunct: it means "If you turn up late, you'll be fired". This of course implies that you should NOT turn up late, so the sentence does the opposite of telling you to turn up late!

This shows that we have to distinguish carefully between CLAUSE TYPE and SPEECH ACT – between imperative and directive, between interrogative and question, and so on. Clause type is the major factor determining what kind of speech act will be performed, but it is not the only one.

Clause type, not sentence type

As the term makes clear, the clause types are categories of CLAUSE. In the simplest cases the terms can be applied derivatively to sentences, but in more complex cases they cannot. Consider the following examples:

[4]   i   *Kim made a mistake.*
        ii *Kim made a mistake, but does it really matter?*
        iii *Do you think* *Kim made a mistake?*

- In [i] we have a sentence with the form of a declarative clause, so this is one of the simple cases where we could say, derivatively, that [i] is a 'declarative sentence'.

- In [ii] the sentence has the form of a coordination of clauses, the first of declarative type and the second of closed interrogative type. In such cases it doesn't make sense to ask which of the five types the sentence as a whole belongs to.
- In [iii] the underlined sequence of words is a declarative clause, but it is merely a part of the larger clause that forms the whole sentence. The underlined clause isn't a sentence, and therefore it's not a declarative sentence.

Clause type in main and subordinate clauses

The reason we say that *Kim made a mistake* is a declarative clause in [4iii], when it isn't a main clause and doesn't make a statement, is that essentially the same contrasts are found in subordinate clauses as in main clauses. There is one exception: imperatives are normally confined to main clauses. But the other categories are applicable to subordinate clauses too. This is illustrated in [5], where underlining marks the subordinate clauses in the [b] examples:

[5]		MAIN CLAUSE		SUBORDINATE CLAUSE
	i	a. *It was a success.*	b.	*Sue thinks it was a success.*
	ii	a. *Was it a success?*	b.	*She didn't say whether it was a success.*
	iii	a. *How big a success was it?*	b.	*She wants to know how big a success it was.*
	iv	a. *What a success it was!*	b.	*He told me what a success it was.*

This further reinforces the need to distinguish between clause type and speech acts: by saying [ib] I don't claim it was a success, by saying [iib] or [iiib] I'm not asking questions about its success, and by uttering [ivb] I'm not making an exclamation about how successful it was.

In this chapter, though, we'll confine our attention to main clauses; clause type in subordinate clauses is dealt with in Ch. 10.

Declarative as the default clause type

The declarative type can be regarded as the default clause type – the type that all canonical clauses belong to. Declaratives simply lack the special syntactic properties of the other clause types. In this chapter, then, we can focus on the **non-declarative** clause types: closed and open **interrogatives** (§2), **exclamatives** (§3); and **imperatives** (§4), with a few other minor types illustrated in §5.

2   Interrogatives and questions

We've mentioned interrogative clauses in earlier chapters without drawing the distinction between the types that we now call **closed** and **open**. The syntactic structure of the two is significantly different.

The terms 'closed' and 'open'

These terms apply in the first instance to questions. As noted above, a **closed question** like *Is Sue here?* has just two answers, whereas an **open question** like *Where* *is Sue?* has an open-ended set of answers. The terms are then applied derivatively to interrogatives: **closed interrogatives** and **open interrogatives** are clause types characteristically used to ask closed and open questions respectively.

Note that we distinguish between an **answer** to a question and a **response** to it. A response is whatever someone says as a result of being asked some question. I might ask: *Is Sue here?*, and you might say *I'm not sure.* That would be a response, but not an answer. It was a closed question, and it has only two answers: *Yes* or *No.* (Lawyers often have to remind witnesses about this.) If I ask: *Where is Sue?*, I've asked an open question whose answer will give the location of Sue, but again, if you said: *Why do you ask?*, that would be a response, not an answer to my question.

2.1   The form of closed interrogatives

Closed interrogative form is marked by subject–auxiliary inversion: the subject occurs after the auxiliary verb, as in the [b] members of the pairs in [6].

[6]	DECLARATIVE		CLOSED INTERROGATIVE
i	a.	*It is raining.*	b.	*Is it raining?*
ii	a.	*He can't swim.*	b.	*Can't he swim?*
iii	a.	*The doctor recommended it.*	b.	*Did the doctor recommend it?*

- In [i–ii] the closed interrogative differs from its declarative counterpart by having subject and auxiliary verb in the reverse order.
- If, as in [iiia], the declarative does not contain an auxiliary, the dummy auxiliary *do* appears in the interrogative, as described in Ch. 3, §3.1.

Closed interrogatives vs other subject–auxiliary inversion clauses

Inversion is not restricted to closed interrogatives, but elsewhere it normally occurs only when certain kinds of element occupy initial position in the clause, as in [7]:

[7]	i	<u>*Never*</u> *had I seen her so furious.* ⎫	[declarative]
	ii	*Jill approved of it and* [<u>*so*</u> *did her husband*]. ⎬	
	iii	<u>*Why*</u> *are you looking at me like that?*	[open interrogative]

- In [i] and [ii], belonging to the default declarative category, the inversion is triggered by the occurrence in initial position of a negative element (*never*) and a connective (*so*).
- In [iii] the inversion is triggered by the initial interrogative element *why*, a marker of the open interrogative type.

Rising intonation as a marker of questions

A closed question can be signalled by means of a rise in the **intonation** (represented by '↗') instead of by a different syntactic form:

[8]	i	*You're sure you can afford it?* ↗
	ii	*So they offered her $50 but she refused?* ↗

These are closed QUESTIONS, but they are not closed INTERROGATIVE CLAUSES. Use of intonation to mark a question does not change syntactic clause type. This is evident from examples like [ii]. We saw above that clause type applies specifically to clauses, but here we have a coordination of clauses, and the rising intonation gives a question meaning to the coordination as a whole, not the individual clauses. The answers are *Yes, they offered her $50 but she refused* and *No, it's not the case that they offered her $50 but she refused*. The two clauses are declaratives, but INTONATION OVERRIDES CLAUSE TYPE in determining what kind of speech act is performed. As we pointed out in §1, clause type is the major factor in determining what kind of speech act is performed, but it isn't the only one. Intonation is one of the additional factors.

2.2   Polar questions and alternative questions

There are two kinds of closed question, depending on how the answers are derivable from the question: **polar** questions and **alternative** questions.

[9]   i a. POLAR QUESTION $\begin{cases} Did\ he\ read\ her\ note? \\ Didn't\ he\ read\ her\ note? \end{cases}$
       b.

      ii a. ALTERNATIVE QUESTION $\begin{cases} Is\ the\ meeting\ today,\ tomorrow,\ or\ next\ Monday? \\ Is\ the\ Kensington\ Runestone\ genuine,\ or\ is\ it\ a\ hoax? \end{cases}$
       b.

(a) Polar questions

In a **polar question** one answer is derivable directly from the question itself, while the other is its polar opposite, i.e. its negative or positive counterpart.

- In [ia] one answer is *Yes, he read it*, and the other is its negation: *No, he didn't read it*.
- These are also the answers to [ib], but here it's the negative answer, *No, he didn't read it*, that is derivable directly from the question itself.

(b) Alternative questions

An **alternative question** contains a coordination of elements linked by *or*, and the answers derive from the separate coordinated elements.

- In [iia] there are thus three answers: *It is today*; *It is tomorrow*; and *It is next Monday*.
- Similarly in [iib] there are two answers: *It is genuine*, and *It is a hoax*.

Note that the *or* in [9iib] joins whole clauses, so it's not a marker of a distinct clause type. What we have is a coordination of TWO CLOSED INTERROGATIVE CLAUSES expressing A SINGLE ALTERNATIVE QUESTION.

While an *or*-coordination is an essential component of an alternative question, it's possible to have an *or*-coordination in other kinds of speech act, which means that an *or*-coordination may occur coincidentally in a polar question. However, we can tell them apart because of an intonation difference, as seen in [10]:

[10] i *Do you want me to give it to mum ↗ or dad ↘?*   [alternative question]
    ii *Do you want me to give it to mum or dad ↗?*   [polar question]

The arrows indicate the main direction of the intonation towards the end.

- Version [i], with rising intonation on *mum* and falling intonation on *dad*, is an alternative question: I take it for granted that you want me to give it to one parent, and ask which one. The answers are thus *I want you to give it to mum* and *I want you to give it to dad.*
- Version [ii] does not have a separate intonational rise on *mum*, but has a rise at the end. It is a polar question, with the answers *Yes, I want you to give it to mum or dad* and *No, I don't want you to give it to mum or dad.*

2.3   Interrogative tags

A special case of the closed interrogative is in the **interrogative tags** that are appended to some clauses, usually declaratives:

[11] i *Your brother looked pretty embarrassed, <u>didn't he?</u>*
    ii *We haven't done anything wrong, <u>have we?</u>*

The tags here are closed interrogatives reduced to just an auxiliary verb and a pronoun subject. Everything else is left implicit, because it's recoverable from the preceding clause.

As noted in Ch. 8, §1, the most usual construction has a **reversed polarity tag**: the polarity of the tag is the reverse of that of the first clause.

- In [i], for example, the declarative is positive and the tag negative.
- In [ii], by contrast, the declarative is negative and the tag positive.

Such tags express a need for confirmation of the statement expressed in the declarative.

2.4   The form of open interrogatives

Open interrogatives are marked by the presence of one (or more) of the interrogative words given in [12]:

[12]   *who   whom   whose   what   which   when   where   why   how*

Interrogative phrases and their position

The interrogative word, alone or in combination with other words such as the head noun in *what books* or *which version*, forms an **interrogative phrase**. This can have a variety of functions in the clause, such as subject, object, predicative complement, and so on.

The important syntactic distinction is between subjects and non-subjects. Non-subjects are usually **fronted**. That is, they are placed before the subject, rather than later, where non-subject elements in canonical clauses would go.

[13]   i SUBJECT   _Who called the police?_

         ii   ⎧ _Which version_ did they recommend? ⎫

        iii NON-SUBJECT ⎨ _What_ are they?   ⎬   [fronted]

        iv   ⎩ And after that they went _where_?   [not fronted]

- In [i], the interrogative phrase _who_ is subject. It's in the usual subject position, before the predicator.
- In [ii], _which version_ is object of _recommend_, and in [iii], _what_ is predicative complement. They are non-subjects. They occur fronted, and the fronting is accompanied by obligatory subject–auxiliary inversion.
- In [iv], _where_ is a locative complement, i.e., a non-subject. It is not fronted, though. It occurs in the position where you'd expect a locative PP to be in a canonical clause.

The last construction is restricted to contexts that typically involve sustained questioning: in court, or in quizzes or game shows (_Tirana is the capital of which European country?_). In other contexts, non-subject interrogative phrases are normally fronted.

Case

Who, whom and _whose_ are respectively nominative, accusative and genitive forms of the pronoun **who**. The choice between _who_ and _whom_ – like the choice between nominative and accusative forms of the personal pronouns (Ch. 5, §8.3) – depends on two factors: **function** and **style level**. The style factor, however, applies differently than it does with the personal pronouns. With the personal pronouns the accusative form is used in certain constructions as a less formal variant of the nominative. With **who**, things are the other way round: it's the nominative form that is less formal. Compare [14] with [55] of Ch. 5:

[14]   i   _Who wrote the editorial?_   [subject: nominative]

        ii   _Whom_ / _Who_ did Kim meet in Paris? [object of verb: accusative or nominative]

        iii a. _To whom_ / *_To who_ is he talking? ⎫

             b. _Whom_ / _Who_ is he talking to?   ⎬ [object of prep: accusative or nominative]

        iv   _Who was she?_   [PC: nominative]

- When the pronoun is subject of a finite clause it again appears in the nominative, as in [i], but this is the only place where **who** follows the pattern of the personal pronouns.
- When it is object of the verb, as in [ii], both cases are found, but _whom_ is formal; _who_ is preferred in conversational spoken English by most people.
- When the pronoun is object of a preposition we need to distinguish between the two constructions discussed in Ch. 7, §5.
  - In [iiia] the preposition is fronted with **who** and forms part of the interrogative phrase. This is quite formal, and normally requires accusative _whom_.

○ In [iiib] the preposition is stranded (and hence not part of the interrogative phrase). This is very much more common except in formal style, and strongly favours *who*.

● When fronted ***who*** is a predicative complement it is always nominative, as in [iv].

Multiple interrogative phrases

It is possible to have more than one interrogative phrase in a clause; but only one can be fronted:

[15]   i   *Who went where?*
          ii *How much did you give to whom?*

2.5   Open questions and their answers

We've said that open interrogatives are characteristically used to express open questions – questions with an open-ended set of answers, derivable from the questions by replacing the interrogative phrases by appropriate non-interrogative ones which we'll call **replacement phrases**. Thus possible answers to the questions in [13] are given in [16] (the replacement phrase is underlined):

[16]   i   *Her father called the police.*
          ii *They recommended the most recent version.*
          iii *They are microscopes.*
          iv *And after that they went home.*

Very often the answer is reduced to JUST THE REPLACEMENT PHRASE, since the rest is recoverable from the question without alteration.

Appropriate replacements

What counts as an appropriate replacement phrase depends on the interrogative phrase, especially on the particular interrogative word it contains. Here are some very simple cases where the interrogative word is head of the interrogative phrase:

● *Who* and *whom* need replacements denoting **personal** entities – humans, or sometimes animals and robots (*Who is that bone for? – Rex*).
● *Whose* is personal too, but needs a genitive replacement (*Whose is this bike? – Mary's*).
● *What* is **non-personal** (*What was he wearing? – A suit*), but when it's a predicative complement its replacement can be an indication of occupation, religion, etc. (*What is Jill? – She's a Catholic*).
● *When, where* and *why* call for replacements denoting times, places and reasons, respectively (*When did they leave? – Yesterday*; *Where are you going? – To the bank*; *Why are you late? – Because I missed my flight*).
● When *how* is an adverb in adjunct function it generally questions manner or means (*How did you fix it? – By changing the battery*; *How did you sleep? – Very well*).

- *How* can also be an adjective, functioning as predicative complement. Here it permits a fairly small range of answers, typically indicating state of health or evaluation (*How are you? – Very well*; *How was the concert? – Excellent*).

There are also cases where the interrogative word is a dependent:

- When *what* and *which* function as determiner in NP structure, the replacements must be consistent with the head noun. So *What video shall we get?* and *Which video shall we get?* need replacements referring to a video. (The difference between *what* and *which* is that the latter implies selection from some definite set; in the example given, *which* suggests prior mention of a number of videos, with the question asking for a choice between them.)
- *How* can function as degree modifier of adjectives, determinatives or adverbs, and the replacement must have the right sort of meaning to fit the function: *How wide is it? – Two inches* (or *Two inches wide*); *How many copies do you need? – Fifteen*; *How fast were they going? – About fifty miles an hour*.

2.6   Information questions and direction questions

In all the questions considered so far, the answers have been statements. We call these **information questions**. There's also a less frequent type of question, **direction questions**, whose answers are directives. The questions in the [a] examples in [17] are closed (polar), those in the [b] ones open.

[17]	i	INFORMATION QUESTION	POSSIBLE ANSWER (STATEMENT)
		a. *Did you open the window?*	*Yes, I did.*
		b. *What did you give her?*	*I gave her a CD.*
	ii	DIRECTION QUESTION	POSSIBLE ANSWER (DIRECTIVE)
		a. *Shall I open the window?*	*Yes, please do.*
		b. *What shall we give her?*	*Let's give her a CD.*

2.7   Echo questions

One distinctive type of (information) question is the **echo question**, uttered in response to a preceding utterance which we call the **stimulus**:

[18]		STIMULUS	ECHO QUESTION	
	i	A: *She wrote to the minister.*	B: *She wrote to the minister?*	[closed (polar)]
	ii	A: *He invited Arthur.*	B: *He invited who?*	[open]

Echo questions serve to check or clarify a stimulus that wasn't clearly perceived or was surprising. They can be closed or open. Closed echo questions are usually of the polar type.

- A polar echo typically repeats the stimulus in full or in reduced form and has sharply rising intonation; it's used to check whether I correctly heard what you said (or meant to say).

- An open echo repeats the stimulus with a question word substituted for part of it – the part that's specifically in need of confirmation or clarification. The echo question word is never fronted: it occupies the same position as the part of the stimulus that it substitutes for.

3   Exclamatives

3.1   The structure of exclamative clauses

Exclamative clauses are marked by an exclamative phrase containing *what* or *how*. Again, this phrase may have a range of functions, the major distinction again being between subject and non-subject. An exclamative subject occupies its basic position, whereas an exclamative non-subject is obligatorily fronted:

[19] i   SUBJECT   *What unpleasant people work in this restaurant!*
      ii   { *How clever you are!*
      iii NON-SUBJECT   { *What a disaster would it be if they were to appoint his son!*

When a non-subject is fronted the subject itself usually precedes the verb, as in [ii]. It is possible to have subject–auxiliary inversion, as in [iii], but this is much less likely than the uninverted *What a disaster it would be if they were to appoint his son!*

Exclamatives and exclamations

There are many ways of conveying **exclamatory meaning** besides using exclamative clause type. Compare, for example:

[20] i   a. *Get the hell out of here.*   b. *What the hell are you doing?*
      ii a. *Look at that fantastic sunset!*   b. *Who saw that fantastic sunset?*
      iii a. *Don't be so pathetically stupid.* b. *Why are you so pathetically stupid?*

The exclamatory meaning is expressed here by *the hell* in [i], *fantastic* [ii], and *so pathetically* in [iii], but these are independent of clause type. They combine with imperative structure in the [a] examples and with open interrogatives in the [b] ones. *What* and *how* in [19], by contrast, are restricted to the particular clause type we call exclamative. Note, for example, the impossibility of inserting them in imperatives or open interrogatives:

[21]   a. **Don't be what a tyrant.*   b. **Why are you what a tyrant?*

That's why we originally gave the characteristic use of exclamatives (in [2]) as making an **exclamatory statement**, rather than simply an exclamation.

3.2   Exclamative *what* and *how*

What and *how* occur in either exclamative or open interrogative clauses, but with some differences in grammar and meaning.

▒ (a) *What*

Exclamative *what* has the syntax of an **adjective**. It always occurs in NPs with a following head, and can never be a pronoun like the interrogative pronoun *what* (as in *What was that?*). The difference between exclamative *what* and interrogative *what* is clearest in count singular NPs, where exclamative *what* precedes the indefinite article *a*. Compare:

[22]			EXCLAMATIVE		INTERROGATIVE
i	a.	COUNT SING	*What a car that was!*	b.	*What car was that?*
ii	a.	PLURAL	*What sights we saw!*	b.	*What sights did we see?*
iii	a.	NON-COUNT	*What talent she had!*	b.	*What talent did she have?*

In [i], where singular *car* has a count interpretation, we see an overt difference between exclamative *what a car* (with *a* as determiner, and *what* as external modifier) and interrogative *what car* (with *what* as determiner). In [ii–iii] the exclamative and interrogative phrases are alike, but we still have the same meaning difference as in [i].

- Interrogative *what* questions identity: answers to the [b] questions will identify the relevant car, sights and talent.
- Exclamative *what* is concerned with quality or degree: a remarkable car, remarkable sights, remarkable talent.

▒ (b) *How*

Exclamative *how* is invariably an adverb: it has no use comparable to the interrogative predicative adjective *how* of *How was the concert?*, etc. Exclamative and interrogative uses of adverbial *how* are contrasted in [23]:

[23]		EXCLAMATIVE		INTERROGATIVE
i	a.	*How old he is!*	b.	*How old is he?*
ii	a.	*How they deceived us!*	b.	*How did they deceive us?*

- In [i], the adverb *how* is a degree modifier in AdjP structure. The exclamative use in [ia] indicates a notably high degree – it comments on his being amazingly old. The interrogative use in [ib] merely asks what his age is (he may be very young).
- In [ii], *how* is an adjunct in clause structure, but of two different semantic types. The exclamative use in [iia] suggests some really major deception. The interrogative use in [iib] merely questions the manner (it means "In what way did they deceive us?").

4   Imperatives and directives

4.1   The form of imperative clauses

The major syntactic features distinguishing imperative clauses from declaratives are as stated in [24]. Examples are given in [25].

[24]   i   A 2nd person subject is omissible.
      ii   The verb is in the plain form.
     iii   Auxiliary *do* is required in verbal negation even with *be*.

[25]   DECLARATIVE   IMPERATIVE
      i a. *You told her the truth.*   b. *Tell her the truth.*
     ii a. *You are more tolerant.*   b. *Be more tolerant.*
    iii a. *Everybody follows me.*   b. *Everybody follow me.*
     iv a. *You aren't impetuous.*   b. *Don't be impetuous.*

- In [ia] the subject is obligatory, whereas [ib] illustrates the usual form of imperatives, with the subject *you* understood. It's possible to include *you* (*You tell her the truth!*), but this is much less common.
- Examples [ii] and [iii] show the verb-form difference: *are* and *follows* are present tense forms; *be* and *follow* are plain forms. As we noted in Ch. 3, §1.2, plain present tense forms and plain forms are nearly always the same; as a result, the verb in an imperative is distinct from that of a present tense declarative in just two cases: with the verb *be* as in [ii], and with a 3rd person singular subject, like the *everybody* of [iii].
- In [iv] we see the difference with respect to auxiliary *do*: it's not permitted in the declarative version but it's required in the imperative.

4.2   First person imperatives

Most imperative clauses have a 2nd person subject, either overtly expressed as *you* or understood that way. In some cases 3rd person subjects are found, like *everybody* in [25iii] (it means "everybody among you"). But there is also a distinct subtype of imperative construction understood as **1st person plural**. It is marked by a specialised use of the verb *let*, differing from the ordinary verb *let* ("allow") in four ways:

[26]   ORDINARY *LET*   1ST PERSON IMPERATIVE *LET*
      i a. *They let us have our ball back.*   b. *Let's get our ball back.*
     ii a. *He didn't let us attend the meeting.*   b. *Don't let's attend the meeting.*
    iii a. *He let us not attend the meeting.*   b. *Let's not attend the meeting.*

- The specialised *let* CANNOT HAVE A SUBJECT (cf. **You let's get our ball back*). It's the verb FOLLOWING *let* that is understood with a 1st person plural subject.
- There's a clear meaning difference between [iia] and [iiia]: [iia] means "He refused us permission to attend" (*let* is WITHIN the scope of negation), while

[iiia] means "He gave us permission to stay away" (*let* is OUTSIDE the scope of negation). There's no such difference between [iib] and [iiib]: *let* is just a marker of the construction, with no independent meaning, so the question of whether or not it falls within the scope of the negation doesn't arise.

● Specialised *let* allows **reduction** to *'s* for the pronoun *us* (in fact it's almost always reduced; spelling it out as *us* is very formal style). This is not possible with ordinary *let*.

● Normally *us* can refer to either you and me or me and someone else (see Ch. 5, §8.2). But in 1st person imperatives the *us* (or *'s*) is always understood as INCLUSIVE OF THE ADDRESSEE(S): in [ib], for example, it's a matter of me and you getting our ball back.

4.3   Uses of the imperative

(a) Imperatives as directives

Issuing directives is the characteristic use of imperatives. Directives include a wide range of more specific types of speech act:

[27]   i   ORDERS: *Stand up. Keep off the grass. Get out of my way. Take aim!*
        ii REQUESTS: *Please pass the salt. Kindly tell Sir Randolph we're here.*
        iii INSTRUCTIONS: *Shake well before using. Press TUNE MODE and select 'Manual'.*
        iv ADVICE: *Sell now while prices are high. Watch your step.*
        v   INVITATIONS: *Come and have lunch. Step this way. Feel free to contact me.*
        vi PERMISSIONS: *Come in. Make yourself at home. Take as many as you need.*

What kind of directive an utterance is understood to issue will depend on such factors as context and tone of voice, though there are some linguistic devices that serve to distinguish requests from orders, such as *please* and *kindly* in [ii].

(b) Imperatives as wishes

Imperatives can be used to express certain kinds of wish:

[28]   *Sleep well.   Have a great week-end.   Get well soon.*

These differ from directives in that the situations concerned are generally not regarded as being under your control. I'm not instructing you to sleep well, have a great weekend, recover: I'm expressing a hope. This usage is restricted to a quite narrow range of situations like being comfortable, having fun, getting well.

(c) Imperatives as conditions

[29]   i   *Invite one without the other* and there'll be trouble.
        ii *Help me this once* and I'll never ask you again.

Here the imperative clauses (underlined) are the first element in a coordination construction that has a conditional interpretation: "If you invite one without the other, there'll be trouble", "If you help me this once I'll never ask you again". The second element in the coordination indicates the consequence of fulfilling the condition that is indirectly expressed in the imperative. The interpretation of the whole depends on whether the consequence is assumed to be undesirable or desirable.

- In [i], trouble is undesirable, so you certainly won't take the imperative as a directive.
- In [ii], however, the consequence (my never asking you for help again) is desirable, so the imperative retains its force as a request.

4.4   Non-imperative directives

The imperative construction can be used for various kinds of directive, both telling (where I expect compliance) and asking (where you may decline). But other clause types are often used to make the speaker's intentions somewhat clearer.

(a) Interrogatives as directives

It is particularly common for closed interrogatives to be used for requests:

[30]   i   *Will you feed the cat.*
       ii *Could you help me with the washing-up.*
       iii *Would you mind turning your radio down a little.*

In many contexts directives of this form are considered more polite than imperatives.

(b) Declaratives as directives

[31]   i   *I order/beg you to leave while there's still time.*
       ii *You will drive her to the airport and then report back to me.*
       iii *I want you to mow the lawn this week-end.*

- In [i] the verbs **order** and **beg** denote speech acts and hence make explicit what kind of directive is intended: an order or an entreaty.
- In [ii] I'm telling you what you will be doing, but since the situation is under your control (you're the driver), in effect I'm giving you an order, though indirectly and implicitly.
- In [iii] I'm saying what I want you to do, and in a context where I have some relevant kind of authority or control over you I am indirectly or implicitly telling you to do it.

5   Minor clause types

Most main clauses fall into one or other of the five clause types listed in [1] at the beginning of this chapter. But there are a few other minor patterns, mostly involving fixed formulae or fragmentary structures. The following is a small sample, the examples in [i] being main clause subjunctives, as mentioned in Ch. 3, §2:

[32]   i   *Long live the Queen.   Suffice it to say that the matter is being investigated.*
           So be it.   God help you if you do this again.   God bless America.
       ii *May you be forgiven.   Would to God I had never heard of Enron.*
       iii *Out of my way!   Off with his head!   Hands up!   Into the bin with it!*
       iv *The more the merrier.   No pain, no gain.   Out of sight, out of mind.*

Exercises

1. Classify the following according to **clause type**, and say what kind of speech act they would most likely be used to perform.
   i *Please turn the light on.*
   ii *I advise you to accept their offer.*
   iii *I advised her to accept their offer.*
   iv *Can you close that door please.*
   v *You're leaving already?*
   vi *Where shall I put my coat?*
   vii *What a senseless waste of human life it was.*
   viii *Have a nice day.*
   ix *Aren't we lucky!*
   x *Allow me to congratulate you.*

2. Form **open interrogatives** from the following **declaratives**, replacing the underlined phrase with a corresponding interrogative phrase such as *who, what, when*, etc.
   i *She said __something__ to them.*
   ii *__Someone__ has taken my umbrella.*
   iii *He sold his car to __someone__.*
   iv *He thinks they'll appoint __someone__.*
   v *They left early __for some reason__.*
   vi *You told her I was going __somewhere__.*
   vii *You first suspected he was the murderer __at some time__.*
   viii *Things have changed for you __in some way__ since last year.*
   ix *You think __someone__ has the most influence with these people.*
   x *We can get __somebody__ to clear up this mess.*

3. Attach the proper **reverse polarity tags** to the following declaratives.
   i *You don't know where to put it.*
   ii *She believes everything you say.*

   iii *Everyone thought it was impossible.*
   iv *They used to live in Baltimore.*
   v *There is no future for us.*

4. **Interrogative tags** can also be attached to **imperative** clauses, as in *Don't tell anyone, will you?* What tags could naturally be added to the following? (Where both reversed and constant polarity tags can be used, give them both, and comment on any difference between them.)
   i *Give this letter to Angela.*
   ii *Don't show the letter to Angela.*
   iii *Take your feet off the sofa.*
   iv *Let's take a break.*
   v *Let's not waste any more time.*

5. The following clauses are given without any final punctuation mark to avoid prejudicing things, so they don't conform to normal written English. For each one, say whether it is (a) an **open interrogative**; (b) an **exclamative**; or (c) **ambiguous** between open interrogative and exclamative. If your answer is (a) or (b), explain what grammatical factors make the clause unambiguous. If your answer is (c), comment on the difference in meaning.
   i *Who thinks it was awesome*
   ii *How much remains to be done*
   iii *How did you convince them*
   iv *What a disappointment it was*
   v *How often have I told you to lock up*
   vi *What idiot devised this plan*
   vii *Who cares about your stupid project*
   viii *What kind of fool do you take me for*
   ix *How geeky I look in that propeller hat*
   x *Why don't you give them a chance*

10 Subordination and content clauses

1 Subordinate clauses

Subordinate clauses characteristically function as dependent within some larger construction. The next higher clause in the structure is called the **matrix clause**.

Subordinate clauses often differ in their internal structure from main clauses. Some typical differences are illustrated in [1]:

[1]   MAIN CLAUSE   SUBORDINATE CLAUSE
    i a. *Sue is the best candidate.*   b. *I agree <u>that Sue is the best candidate</u>.*
    ii a. *He was looking at a book.*   b. *This is the book <u>he was looking at</u>.*
   iii a. *I gave him my address.*   b. *I made a mistake in <u>giving him my address</u>.*

- The underlined clause in [ib], a dependent in clause structure, is marked as subordinate by its introductory word *that*, which is a **subordinator**.
- The underlined clause in [iib], a dependent in NP structure, is marked as subordinate by having a missing NP, the understood object of the preposition *at*.
- The underlined clause in [iiib], a dependent in PP structure, is marked as subordinate by having its subject left understood and its verb in gerund-participle form.

The differences are generally greater in non-finite clauses than in finite ones, so in this and the next two chapters we focus on finite subordinate clauses (such as those in [ib/iib]), returning to non-finites (such as [iiib]) in Ch. 13.

Content clause as the default kind of finite subordinate clause

There are three major subclasses of finite subordinate clause, illustrated in [2]:

[2]   i RELATIVE CLAUSE   *They weren't among the people <u>who had been invited</u>.*
       ii COMPARATIVE CLAUSE   *More people came than <u>had been invited</u>.*
      iii CONTENT CLAUSE   *I don't think <u>that these people had been invited</u>.*

- The relative clause underlined in [i] has as its subject a relative pronoun *who* with the preceding noun *people* as its antecedent.
- The comparative clause underlined in [ii] has no overt subject at all.
- Content clauses lack special properties of this kind. We can regard them as the default kind of finite subordinate clause, from which relative and comparative clauses differ in certain distinctive ways described in Ch. 11 and Ch. 12.

The content clause in [iii] is introduced by the subordinator *that*, but the rest of the clause does not differ from that of the main clause *These people had been invited*. And the subordinator is in fact optional here: *I don't think these people had been invited* is also grammatical.

Content clauses function predominantly as complement within the larger construction: the one cited here, for example, is complement of the verb **think**.

2   Clause type in content clauses

The system of clause type described for main clauses in Ch. 9 applies also to content clauses, except that imperatives are normally restricted to main clauses. In [3] we illustrate main clause and content clauses of the other four types:

[3]		MAIN CLAUSE	CONTENT CLAUSE
i	DECLARATIVE	*Liz is in Paris.*	*He says <u>that Liz is in Paris</u>.*
ii	CLOSED INTERROGATIVE	*Is she ill?*	*I wonder <u>whether she is ill</u>.*
iii	OPEN INTERROGATIVE	*What do you want?*	*Tell me <u>what you want</u>.*
iv	EXCLAMATIVE	*What a bargain it is!*	*Tell her <u>what a bargain it is</u>.*

In the following three sections we survey declarative, interrogative and exclamative content clauses respectively.

3   Declarative content clauses

3.1   The subordinator *that*

The major feature that can distinguish declarative content clauses from their main clause counterparts is the subordinator *that*. It is sometimes obligatory, sometimes optional, and sometimes inadmissible:

[4]		WITH SUBORDINATOR *that*	WITHOUT SUBORDINATOR *that*
i	OBLIGATORY	*<u>That I need help</u> is clear.*	*<u>*I need help</u> is clear.*
ii	INADMISSIBLE	*<u>*I left before that he arrived</u>.*	*I left before <u>he arrived</u>.*
iii	OPTIONAL	*I know <u>that it's genuine</u>.*	*I know <u>it's genuine</u>.*

- The main place where *that* is obligatory is where the content clause is subject of the matrix clause, as in [4i]. It is likewise obligatory if the content clause is preposed so as to precede the subject, as in *<u>That I need help</u> I can't deny.*

- *That* is inadmissible in a clause that is complement to a preposition like *before* in [ii]. Most prepositions exclude *that*; there are only a very few (such as *notwith-standing*, *in order*, and *provided*), which allow it.
- Elsewhere, *that* is in general optional, as we see in [iii]. It is more likely to be omitted in informal than in formal style, and it is more likely to be omitted after short and common verbs than after longer and less frequent ones. For example, in *This will demonstrate that it is genuine* the subordinator would probably not be omitted.

3.2   Declaratives as complement

Declarative content clauses mostly function as **complement** of a verb, noun, adjective, or preposition. The range of complement functions is illustrated in [5]:

[5]			
	i	SUBJECT	*That they refused* didn't surprise us.
	ii	EXTRAPOSED SUBJECT	It didn't surprise us *that they refused*.
	iii		*I realise that you feel insulted.*
	iv	INTERNAL COMP OF VERB	*She informed me that she had been insulted.*
	v		*The problem is that we just can't afford it.*
	vi	COMP OF NOUN	You can't ignore the fact *that he was drunk*.
	vii	COMP OF ADJECTIVE	I'm glad *that you could come*.
	viii	COMP OF PREPOSITION	You can go provided *that you are careful*.

- In [i] the content clause is **subject**. It is licensed by *surprise*.
- In [ii] we see a much more frequent kind of case than [i], but synonymous with it: the subordinate clause is **extraposed** (see Ch. 15, §3.1).
- In the next three examples, the content clause is **internal complement** to the verb of a clause: in [iii], the sole complement of *realise*; in [iv], the second complement of *inform*; and in [v], the complement of *be* in its **specifying** sense.
- In the next two the content clause is complement to the noun *fact* ([vi]) and the adjective *glad* ([vii]).
- Finally in [viii] the content clause is complement of a preposition. As noted above, most prepositions disallow *that*, but *provided* (historically derived from the past participle of a verb) is one of the few that allow it.[1]

3.3   The mandative construction

One special construction with a declarative content clause as complement is the **mandative**. This term is based on the element *mand* that is found in *demand* and *mandatory*, two lexemes that license mandative complements. The meaning of

---

[1] The term 'content clause' is not used in traditional grammar. The clauses that function as complements are traditionally called 'noun clauses', but this is a highly misleading term. Content clauses aren't nouns, and it should be clear from the examples in [5] that they don't behave like nouns or NPs. Most importantly, nouns and NPs don't normally function as extraposed subject, or as complement to a noun or an adjective.

mandatives includes a component of meaning comparable to that expressed by the modal auxiliary *must* (see Ch. 3, §8.1 on **deontic modality**). The sentences in [6] illustrate; they are all similar in meaning to *He must be told immediately*.

[6] i SUBJUNCTIVE MANDATIVE   *It is essential <u>that he be told immediately</u>.*
      ii *Should* MANDATIVE   *It is essential <u>that he should be told immediately</u>.*
      iii COVERT MANDATIVE   *It is essential <u>that he is told immediately</u>.*

- Variant [i] involves the **subjunctive** use of the **plain form** of the verb *be*.
- In [ii] we have a special use of the modal auxiliary *should*; this *should* mandative is more common in BrE than in AmE, where the subjunctive mandative is generally preferred.
- With the covert variant [iii], nothing in the form of the content clause itself distinguishes the mandative use from ordinary non-mandative declaratives, as in *I hope <u>that he is told immediately</u>* (clearly non-mandative, since *hope* does not license a subjunctive complement).

With verbs other than *be*, and with subjects other than 3rd person singulars, the subjunctive and the covert mandative have the same form: *It is essential that they tell him immediately*.

Potential ambiguity

While content clause complements of ***demand***, *essential*, *mandatory*, *vital*, and the like are always mandative, there are some lexemes such as ***insist*** and *important* that license both mandative and non-mandative complements, and here we see ambiguities that show us the distinctness of the two constructions. These two examples make a sharp contrast:

[7] i *I insisted <u>that he meet her</u>.*   [not ambiguous: subjunctive mandative]
      ii *I insisted <u>that he met her</u>.*   [either non-mandative or covert mandative]

- Example [i] is unambiguously mandative by virtue of its subjunctive form. It carries the deontic meaning "I made it a requirement for him to meet her".
- Example [ii], by contrast, is ambiguous. It can be understood as either a covert mandative meaning "I made it a requirement that he meet her" or (more probably) a non-mandative with the meaning "I emphatically asserted that he met her".

The same sort of ambiguity is found with *important*: a doctor who says *It's important that he drinks a lot* might mean either "He should take plenty of fluids" or "The fact that he's a heavy drinker is significant"!

4   Interrogative content clauses

Main clause interrogatives are characteristically used to ASK questions; subordinate interrogatives EXPRESS questions, but do not themselves ask them. Usually (but not always) the construction can be glossed with the formula "the answer to the question":

[8]   i   *I know <u>where he is</u>.*   "I know the answer to the question 'Where is he?'"
     ii   *I told her <u>what it was</u>.*   "I told her the answer to the question 'What was it?'"

4.1   Closed interrogatives and the subordinators *whether* and *if*

Whereas **main clause closed interrogatives** are marked by **subject–auxiliary inversion**, their **subordinate** counterparts are normally introduced by one of the **interrogative subordinators** *whether* and *if*,[2] followed by basic subject–predicate order:

[9]   MAIN   SUBORDINATE
      i a. *Did he accept the offer?*   b. *I'm unsure <u>whether he accepted the offer</u>.*
     ii a. *Will you chair the meeting?*   b. *He asked me <u>if I'd chair the meeting</u>.*

Note that the inversion in [ia] requires the insertion of the dummy auxiliary **do**, but since there is no inversion in the subordinate version [ib], no **do** appears here.

4.2   Open interrogatives

Open interrogatives, whether main or subordinate, are marked by the presence of an **interrogative phrase** containing one of the **interrogative words** *who*, *what*, *which*, etc. In main clauses the interrogative phrase usually occupies initial position, and, if it is not subject, its placement in this position triggers subject–auxiliary inversion. In subordinate clauses, on the other hand, the interrogative phrase is initial and there is normally no inversion:

[10]   MAIN   SUBORDINATE
      i a. *Which candidate spoke first?*   b. *I can't say <u>which candidate spoke first</u>.*
     ii a. *Why did she resign?*   b. *It's obvious <u>why she resigned</u>.*

4.3   Interrogatives as complement

Like declaratives, interrogative content clauses usually function as complements, as illustrated in [11]:

[11]   i   SUBJECT   *<u>What caused the delay</u> remains unclear.*
      ii   EXTRAPOSED SUBJECT   *It remains unclear <u>what caused the delay</u>.*
     iii   ⎧ *I've discovered <u>where they keep the key</u>.*
      iv   INTERNAL COMP OF VERB   ⎨ *I asked them <u>what progress they had made</u>.*
       v   ⎩ *The only issue is <u>whether he was lying</u>.*
      vi   COMP OF NOUN   *The question <u>whether it's legal</u> was ignored.*
     vii   COMP OF ADJECTIVE   *I'm uncertain <u>what we can do about it</u>.*
    viii   COMP OF PREPOSITION   *That depends on <u>how much time we have</u>.*

---

[2] Recall that the interrogative subordinator *if* is to be distinguished from the preposition *if* that expresses conditional meaning: see Ch. 7, §2.1.

The range of functions is almost like that illustrated for declaratives in [5]. One difference from declaratives, however, is that prepositions are often optional; for example, we could add *of* after *question* in [vi], and we could omit *on* in [viii].

There is only partial overlap between the items that license declaratives and those that license interrogatives.

* **Know**, for example, accepts both: *I know she's right*; *I know what he did*.
* **Insist** accepts only declaratives: *I insist that she's right*; **I insist what he did*.
* **Inquire** accepts only interrogatives: **I inquire that he's ill*; *I inquired what he did*.

We have also noted that very few prepositions license declaratives, but there are more that accept interrogatives (like *on* in [viii]).

4.4   Interrogatives as adjunct

There is one construction where subordinate interrogatives appear in adjunct function:

[12]   i CLOSED   *He'll complain, whether we meet during the week or at the week-end.*
       ii OPEN   *He'll complain, whatever you ask him to do.*

* It follows from [i] that he'll complain if we meet during the week, and he'll complain if we meet at the week-end, and these two conditions exhaust the options. So we know he'll complain.
* Similarly in [ii], he'll complain if you ask him to peel the potatoes and he'll complain if you ask him to set the table and so on: he'll complain for every possible *x* where you ask him to do *x*, so again it follows that he'll complain.

We call this the **exhaustive conditional construction**. It uses an interrogative clause to express a set of conditions that exhaustively cover the possibilities.

Why would this exhaustive conditional meaning be expressed by an interrogative form? Because the interrogative expresses a question whose answers define an exhaustive set of conditions.

* For [i] the question is "Do we meet during the week or at the week-end?"; and this has a closed set of answers (just two of them).
* For [ii] it is "What do (or will) you ask him to do?", which has an open set of answers.

Each possible answer represents a 'case', and the examples say that he will complain no matter which of the possible cases turns out to be realised.

Note that the exhaustive element of meaning applies equally in an example like *He'll complain, whether we meet on Saturday or Sunday*. Although there are other days than these two, the sentence **presupposes**, or takes it for granted, that we will meet on one or other of the two days mentioned, so in this context there are in fact just these two possible 'cases'.

Variants of the exhaustive conditional construction

There are two variants of the exhaustive conditional construction, one where the interrogative clause itself realises the adjunct function, as in [12], and one where the adjunct has the form of a larger phrase headed by *independently*, *irrespective*, *regardless*, or *no matter*, as in [13].

[13]   i   *He'll complain,* [*regardless of <u>whether we meet during the week or at the week-end</u>*].
       ii *He'll complain,* [*no matter <u>what you ask him to do</u>*].

Here the interrogative clauses are complements, as they are in [11] (in the case of *independently*, *irrespective*, and *regardless*, complements of the preposition *of*).

In [12], where the interrogative clause is the adjunct, the internal form differs slightly from that of interrogatives in complement function. With open interrogatives, the interrogative word is compounded with ·*ever*, as in [12ii] – or *He'll complain, whenever the meeting is held*. With closed interrogatives the special feature is less obvious: an *or*-coordination is obligatory. Compare these:

[14]   i   *He'll complain, <u>whether we record the proceedings or not</u>.*
       ii *He'll complain, regardless of <u>whether we record the proceedings (or not)</u>.*

Or not is omissible from [ii], where the interrogative is complement, but not from [i], where it is adjunct.

5   Exclamative content clauses

Exclamative clauses, main or subordinate, are marked by an initial **exclamative phrase** containing *how* or *what*. In main but not subordinate clauses, subject–auxiliary inversion is PERMITTED if the exclamative phrase is in **non-subject** function, but it is rare. For the most part, therefore, there is no internal difference between subordinate and main exclamatives. Compare:

[15]   MAIN   SUBORDINATE
       i a. *How very kind you are!*   b. *I told them <u>how very kind you are</u>.*
       ii a. *What a shambles it was!*   b. *I remember <u>what a shambles it was</u>.*

Exclamatives as complement

Exclamative content clauses function exclusively as complements. They occur with much the same range of complement functions as other content clauses, though they are licensed by a far smaller set of lexemes. Examples are given in [16]:

[16]   i   SUBJECT   *<u>What a bargain it was</u> hadn't yet struck me.*
       ii EXTRAPOSED SUBJECT   *It's incredible <u>how much he wanted to charge</u>.*
       iii INTERNAL COMP OF VERB   *I'd forgotten <u>what a fine speaker she is</u>.*
       iv COMP OF PREPOSITION   *She was surprised at <u>how ill he looked</u>.*
       v   COMP OF ADJECTIVE   *She was surprised <u>how ill he looked</u>.*

Exclamatives vs open interrogatives

In main clauses, exclamatives may be distinguished from open interrogatives solely by the absence of subject–auxiliary inversion, but since such inversion doesn't normally occur in subordinate interrogatives there may be ambiguity between exclamative and interrogative content clause constructions:

[17]   *Do you remember <u>how big it was</u>?*   [ambiguous: exclamative or interrogative]

- The **exclamative** interpretation presupposes it was remarkably big and asks whether you have recollections of that.
- The **interrogative** content clause interpretation doesn't presuppose any size; it asks whether you remember the answer to the question "How big was it?". It may have been anywhere on the scale from extremely small to extremely big.

Exercises

1. Classify the following subordinate clauses (underlined) as **finite** or **non-finite**.
   i *They told us <u>not to start without them</u>.*
   ii *<u>Why people behave like that</u> is a mystery to me.*
   iii *They insisted <u>that everyone have equal voting rights</u>.*
   iv *We object to <u>their being given special privileges</u>.*
   v *Everyone knows <u>you cringe when she walks by</u>.*

2. In each of the following pairs, embed a **subordinate** counterpart of the main clause [a] in the position marked '[. . .]' in [b], and identify the **clause type** and **function** of the subordinate clause.
   i a. *Why did she resign?*
     b. *It's not clear to me [. . .].*
   ii a. *It was a hoax.*
     b. *Few people believe the rumour [. . .].*
   iii a. *Is it a serious threat?*
     b. *[. . .] remains to be seen.*
   iv a. *Who originated the idea?*
     b. *No one knows [. . .].*
   v a. *They moved to Boston.*
     b. *I met them several times before [. . .].*
   vi a. *What a bargain it was.*
     b. *She told me [. . .].*
   vii a. *You will get your money back.*
     b. *I'm determined [. . .].*
   viii a. *Can we rely on them?*
     b. *I'm not certain [. . .].*
   ix a. *It was a serious mistake.*
     b. *[. . .] is now indisputable.*
   x a. *Do you have any idea how much it cost?*
     b. *I'm not sure [. . .].*

3. For each of the lexemes below, say whether or not it can license the following types of content clause complement : (a) **mandative**; (b) other **declarative**; (c) **closed interrogative**; (d) **open interrogative**; (e) **exclamative**. (Note that closed interrogatives sometimes occur more readily in non-affirmative than in affirmative contexts: before giving a 'no' answer for (c), therefore, test with a negative matrix clause as well as a positive one.) Give an example to support each 'yes' answer.
   i *advise*   vi *idea*
   ii *ask*   vii *inquire*
   iii *convince*   viii *learn*
   iv *doubt* [verb]   ix *realise*
   v *forget*   x *sense* [verb]

4. Here is another selection of complement-taking lexemes; the instructions are the same as for the previous exercise, except that for the two adjectives the issue is whether they license the various kinds of content clause as subject (or as extraposed subject).

i   *amazing*   vi   *important*
ii   **belief**   vii **know**
iii **decision**   viii **question** [noun]
iv   **feel**   ix   **require**
v   **grasp** [verb]   x   **wonder**

5. For each of the underlined content clauses below say whether it is (a) an **open interrogative**; or (b) an **exclamative**; or (c) **ambiguous** between open interrogative and exclamative. If your answer is (a) or (b), explain what grammatical factors make the clause unambiguous. If your answer is (c), comment on the difference in meaning.

  i   *She didn't know <u>how valuable it was</u>.*
  ii   *I'd forgotten <u>what a difficult route it was</u>.*
  iii *He asked <u>how old I was</u>.*
  iv   *That depends on <u>how much we have to pay</u>.*
  v   *You won't believe <u>who they're planning to appoint</u>.*

6. Which of the following prepositions license a **declarative content clause** as complement? For each 'yes' answer give an example, and say whether or not the **subordinator** *that* is permitted in the content clause.

  i   *above*   vi   *in*
  ii   *as*   vii *on*
  iii *because*   viii *though*
  iv   *despite*   ix   *unless*
  v   *for*   x   *with*

7. Here is another selection of prepositions that may or may not license a declarative content clause complement; the instructions are the same as for the previous exercise.

  i   *after*   vi   *notwithstanding*
  ii   *at*   vii *since*
  iii *by*   viii *through*
  iv   *during*   ix   *until*
  v   *given*   x   *without*

11 Relative clauses

A **relative clause** is a special kind of subordinate clause whose primary function is as modifier to a noun or nominal. We examine the case of relative clause modifiers in NPs first, and then extend the description to cover less prototypical relative constructions.

1   Relative clauses as modifiers of nouns

Examples of the noun-modifying relative clause are given in [1]:

[1]   i   *The secretary wrote to* [*all the members <u>who were absent from the meeting</u>*].
     ii   [*The film <u>which I needed</u>*] *is unobtainable.*

- In [i] the underlined relative clause modifies *members* and combines with it to form the head nominal of the bracketed NP: *members who were absent from the meeting*.
- Similarly in [ii] the relative clause modifies *film*, and *film which I needed* forms the head nominal that is determined by *the*.

The relative clauses here are introduced by the **relative pronouns** *who* and *which*, whose interpretation is provided by their **antecedents**, *members* and *film* respectively. The relation between a pronoun and its antecedent is called **anaphora** (cf. Ch. 5, §8.1), and it is a crucial property of relative clauses that they always contains an element – actually present or understood – that is **anaphorically related** to an antecedent from which it derives its interpretation. This is the basis for the term **relative clause**, and likewise for **relative pronoun**, which applies to the *who* and *which* in [1]. In the construction we are dealing with in this section, the antecedent is always the head noun or nominal modified by the relative clause.

In order to draw attention to this essential feature of relative clauses, which distinguishes them from other kinds of finite subordinate clause, we will use the symbol 'R' for the element in them that is anaphorically related to an antecedent.

● For the relative clause in [1i] we thus have "R were absent from the meeting". R has *members* as antecedent, so we understand that some members were absent from the meeting, and it is to all of these that the secretary wrote.

● For [ii] we similarly have "I needed R". The antecedent is *film*, so I needed some film and this film is unobtainable.

The way this feature distinguishes relative clauses from content clauses is illustrated in [2]:

[2]   i   RELATIVE CLAUSE   *They rejected the suggestion <u>which your son made</u>.*
      ii CONTENT CLAUSE   *They rejected the suggestion <u>that your son was lying</u>.*

● For [i] we have "your son made R", with *suggestion* as the antecedent: we understand that your son made some suggestion, and they rejected it.

● In [ii], however, there is no such R element in the subordinate clause. The clause does not contain any anaphoric link to the head noun *suggestion*: it merely gives the content of the suggestion.[1]

Wh and non-*wh* relative clauses

Although it is an essential feature of the modifying relative clause that it contain an anaphoric link to the head noun, there doesn't have to be an overt pronoun to express that link, as there has been in each of the examples so far.

The relative clauses that do contain an overt anaphoric link like *who* or *which* are called **wh relatives**. There are others that don't, and they are the **non-wh relatives**. They come in two subtypes: one kind that is introduced by the clause subordinator *that* (which also occurs in declarative content clauses such as [2ii]) and another kind that doesn't. So we have this picture so far:

[3]   i   WH RELATIVE: *The film <u>which I needed</u> is not obtainable.*
      ii   ⎰ THAT RELATIVE   *The film <u>that I needed</u> __ is not obtainable.*
      iii NON-WH: ⎱ BARE RELATIVE   *The film <u>I needed</u> __ is not obtainable.*

● The non-*wh* relatives with the subordinator, as in [ii], are called **that relatives**.

● Those where the subordinator is omitted, as in [iii], are called **bare relatives**.

There is no relative pronoun in [ii] or [iii], but there is still an anaphoric relation to the head noun *film*; these, no less than [i], can be represented as "I needed R", with R functioning as object and interpreted as some film. The idea that *needed* in [ii–iii] has a covert object is evident from a very simple fact: although **need** is transitive, and has to have an object in canonical clauses, here we cannot add an overt object for it:

[4]   **The film that I needed <u>more time</u> was not obtainable.*

---

[1] There is also an important functional distinction between the two constructions. The content clause is a complement and is licensed by only a small proportion of nouns: we could not, for example, replace the relative clauses in [1] by content clauses. The relative clause is a modifier and hence not subject to such licensing restrictions.

Here the NP *more time* has been added as a direct object (and an appropriate one: *I needed more time* is fully grammatical as a main clause). But it makes the sentence ungrammatical. Why is that? Because *needed* has already got a direct object; it just isn't overt in this relative clause construction. The '__' notation in [ii/iii] thus indicates the covert presence of the R element.

The relativised element

The overt or covert element R that is anaphorically linked to the head noun is called the **relativised element**. It can have a range of functions within the relative clause, as illustrated in [5] (where we use *wh* relatives because the relativised element is overt):

[5]   i   SUBJECT   *some friends [who saw her]*
      ii   OBJECT   *a key [which she found]*
      iii COMP OF PREPOSITION   *those books [which I referred to]*
      iv   ADJUNCT OF TIME   *the day [when you were born]*
      v   ADJUNCT OF PLACE   *a place [where you can relax]*
      vi   ADJUNCT OF REASON   *the reason [why she got angry]*

Notice the different words beginning with *wh* that are used here: *who* for people, *which* for things, *when* for times, *where* for places, *why* for reasons.

Non-*wh* counterparts of the *wh* relatives in [5] are shown in [6], where the notation '__' again marks the position of the covert R element:

[6]   i   SUBJECT   *some friends [that __ saw her]*
      ii   OBJECT   *a key [(that) she found __]*
      iii COMP OF PREPOSITION   *those books [(that) I referred to __]*
      iv   ADJUNCT OF TIME   *the day [(that) you were born __]*
      v   ADJUNCT OF PLACE   *a place [(that) you can relax __]*
      vi   ADJUNCT OF REASON   *the reason [(that) she got angry __]*

- Parentheses around *that* indicate as usual that it is optional: in such cases both *that* and bare relatives are permitted.
- Where the gap is in subject position, *that* is not omissible. We can have, for example, *Anyone who wants this stuff can have it*, but ¹*Anyone wants this stuff can have it* is not Standard English.
- The non-*wh* construction is not always available when the relativised element is adjunct (or complement) of place; the example in [v], with the head noun *place*, is perfectly acceptable, but in sentences with head nouns less likely to suggest location, a *wh* relative would normally be required.[2]

R element within an embedded clause

It is possible for the R element to be located within a content clause embedded inside the relative clause:

---

[2] That is, we would say *This is the web page where the claim was first made*, not **This is the web page the claim was first made*.

[7]   i a. *a key [which he says she found]*   b. *a key [(that) he says she found___]*
       ii a. *some boys [who he says saw her]*   b. *some boys [(that) he says ___ saw her]*

- In [i] R is object of *found*, and the *found* clause is a content clause functioning as complement of *says*: "He says she found R". We understand that he says she found some key, and that's the key the whole NP refers to.
- In [ii] R is subject of the embedded *saw* clause: "He says R saw her". Note that the *that* is omissible in [iib]: this differs from [6i] above in that the R element is subject not of the relative clause itself but of the content clause embedded within it.

The relative phrase

We turn now to a more complex kind of relative construction found only in the *wh* type. It is illustrated in [8]:

[8]   i *She hasn't been able to contact [the people <u>whose house she's renting</u>].*
       ii *This is [the article <u>from which they were quoting</u>].*
      iii *He set us [a problem <u>the answer to which can be found in the textbook</u>].*

The doubly underlined expressions here contain not just the relative pronouns *whose* and *which*, but other material as well. We need therefore to distinguish between two concepts:

- the **relative phrase** – the constituent occupying initial position in the clause;
- the **relativised element** – the element that is anaphorically related to the head noun, the element we have been representing as R.

In earlier examples such as *some friends [who saw her]*, the relative phrase consists solely of the relativised element (i.e. *who*), but in [8] this is not so: the relative phrase is the one marked by double underlining, while the relativised element is just *whose* or *which*. It is just the latter, not the whole relative phrase, that is anaphorically related to the head noun.

- In [i], for example, it is just *whose*, not *whose house*, that has *people* as its antecedent. We can represent the clause as "she's renting R's house", with R anaphorically related to *people*. We understand that she's renting some people's house and she hasn't been able to contact these people.
- Similarly, in [ii–iii] the head nouns *article* and *problem* are antecedent just for the pronoun *which*. We have, for [ii], "they were quoting from R" – i.e. they were quoting from some article and this is it. And, for [iii], "the answer to R can be found in the textbook" – i.e. the answer to some problem can be found in the textbook and he set us this problem.

For [8ii–iii], but not for [8i], there are other versions in which less material is fronted, so that the relative phrase is a smaller constituent:

[9]   i **She hasn't been able to contact [the people <u>whose</u> she's renting house].*
       ii *This is [the article <u>which they were quoting from</u>].*
      iii *He set us [a problem <u>to which the answer can be found in the textbook</u>].*

- Example [i] is ungrammatical because *whose* requires that we front the whole of the NP in which it is determiner.
- In [9ii] the preposition *from* is left on its own – the term we use is **stranded** – instead of being fronted along with its complement, as in [8ii]. (The relation between preposition fronting and preposition stranding is discussed in Ch. 7, §5.)
- In [9iii] what is fronted is just the PP functioning as complement of *answer* instead of the whole NP, as in [8iii].

2   Integrated vs supplementary relatives

The relative clauses considered so far have all been tightly **integrated** into the structure of the NP containing them. As such, they contrast with another kind of relative clause that is more loosely attached. This second kind we call **supplementary** relative clauses. These examples illustrate the contrast:

[10]   i   INTEGRATED   *Politicians who make extravagant promises aren't trusted.*
         ii SUPPLEMENTARY   *Politicians, who make extravagant promises, aren't trusted.*

In this section we look in detail at the differences between integrated and supplementary relatives with respect to three things: (a) intonation and punctuation, (b) interpretation, and (c) syntax.

(a) Intonation and punctuation

Integrated relatives are integrated intonationally into the larger construction. Supplementary ones are set apart, spoken as a separate intonation unit. In writing, this difference is reflected in the punctuation, with supplementary relatives generally marked off by commas (or stronger punctuation, such as dashes or parentheses), as seen in [10ii]. Punctuation does not provide quite as reliable a criterion as intonation, however, because we do find relatives which are clearly supplementary but are written without being set apart by punctuation.

(b) Interpretation

The names we have given to the two types of relative clause directly reflect the difference in meaning.

- The information expressed in an integrated relative is presented as an integral part of the larger message.
- The information expressed in a supplementary relative is presented as supplementary to that expressed in the rest of the sentence: it is additional, often parenthetical, material.

The examples in [10] illustrate an important special case of this difference.

- In [i] the relative clause serves to restrict the **denotation** of the head noun *politicians* (i.e. the set of people to whom the term applies): the lack of trust doesn't apply to all politicians, but just the ones who make extravagant promises. The information given in the relative clause is an integral part of the larger message: it plays an essential role in defining who is being said to lack public trust.

- In [ii], by contrast, the property of not being trusted applies to politicians in general, not to a subset of them. Instead of picking out a subset of politicans it makes the claim that none of them are trusted. But it also adds an extra assertion about politicians in general, namely that they make extravagant promises.

On the basis of this kind of contrast, the two types of relative clause are traditionally called 'restrictive' (or sometimes 'defining') and 'non-restrictive' (or 'non-defining'), respectively. We don't use these terms. They are misleading: the integrated relative is NOT always restrictive, in the sense of picking out a subset of the set denoted by the head noun. Take these examples:

[11]   i *Martha has [two sons <u>who are still at school</u>] and [two <u>who are at university</u>].*
        ii *Martha has [two sons <u>she can rely on</u>] and hence is not unduly worried.*

- In [i] the relative clauses certainly are semantically restrictive: they distinguish two sets of sons (evidently Martha has at least four in all).
- In [ii], however, there is no restriction. There is no implication that Martha has more than two sons. The information given in the relative clause does NOT distinguish these two sons from any other sons that she might have. Nevertheless, it is presented as an integral part of the larger message. A natural reason for presenting it as such is that it is essential to explaining WHY she was not unduly worried. (Having two sons doesn't necessarily keep a mother from worrying; but being able to rely on them does.)

Here's another example, one that we found in a novel by Dick Francis, where the NP is definite rather than indefinite:

[12]   *[The father <u>who had planned my life to the point of my unsought arrival in Brighton</u>] took it for granted that in the last three weeks of his legal guardianship I would still act as he directed.*

Again the relative clause does not distinguish one father from another: the narrator here is talking about the only father he ever had. So the information given in the relative clause is NOT semantically restrictive. It is integrated, though. The reason for expressing it in an integrated relative is that it has crucial relevance to the rest of the message: it was because the father had planned the narrator's life hitherto that he assumed he would be able to continue to do so.

(c) Syntax

In addition to what we have just set out concerning the phonological (or punctuational) and semantic facts about integrated and supplementary relatives, there are also a number of syntactic differences. We will mention four.[3]

---

[3] We ignore in this chapter a special subtype of integrated relative found in what is called the 'cleft' construction, as in *It was Kim <u>who found the key</u>*; this construction is discussed in Ch. 15, §5.

Wh relatives vs non-*wh* relatives

Supplementary relatives are almost always of the *wh* type: the bare construction is not allowed at all as a supplementary relative, and supplementary *that* relatives are extremely rare and really only marginally present in Standard English.

Antecedents allowed for supplementary relatives

Supplementary relatives allow a wider range of antecedents than integrated ones. Most importantly, they accept **clauses**, and **proper nouns** without determiners, as in [13]:

[13]   i *Max arrived late, <u>which caused some delay</u>.*
      ii *Max, <u>who was usually very punctual,</u> was twenty minutes late.*

- In [i] the antecedent of *which* is the preceding clause. In our representation "R caused some delay", the R is interpreted as Max's arriving late.
- In [ii] the antecedent of *who* is *Max*: we understand that Max was usually very punctual. Proper nouns normally occur with integrated relatives only if there is a determiner, as in *He's not [the Max I was referring to]*.

Which as pronoun or determinative

Which occurs in integrated relatives only as a pronoun, but in supplementary relatives it can also be a determinative:

[14]   *This will keep us busy until Friday, <u>by which time the boss will be back</u>.*

Note that here the relativised element is *which time* (not *which* alone): it is this element that derives its interpretation from the antecedent *Friday*.

Function

Integrated relatives function as dependent – more specifically, modifier – within the construction containing them, but supplementary relatives are attached more loosely, and indeed may constitute a separate sentence, as in [15] (where, again, *which* has a clause as antecedent):

[15]   A: *Our rent is due next week.*
        B: *<u>Which is why we shouldn't be going out to dinner tonight.</u>*

3   Relative words in integrated and supplementary relative clauses

The major relative words in the constructions discussed above are listed in [16]:

[16]   *who   whom   whose   which   when   where   why*

When, where, and *why* indicate time, place, and reason respectively, as we illustrated in [5iv–vi].

Gender: personal vs non-personal

Normally the word 'gender' is associated with sexual characteristics or identity, but as a grammatical term it has a broader sense. The primary gender system in English, discussed in Ch. 5, §8.2 for the 3rd person singular personal pronouns, is indeed based on sex, but not all gender systems in language are, and even in English there is also a secondary gender system that is based on the contrast between **personal** and **non-personal**. This applies to interrogative and relative pronouns – but in the relative construction that we are currently considering the non-personal pronoun is different from the interrogative:

[17]		INTERROGATIVE	RELATIVE
i	PERSONAL	*Who did you see?*	*the person who annoys me most*
ii	NON-PERSONAL	*What did you see?*	*the thing which annoys me most*

Note also that while interrogative *whose* is personal, relative *whose* is neutral as to gender: compare personal *a guy whose car was stolen* and non-personal *a book whose pages were falling out*. (In interrogatives this doesn't happen: you can't ask about a collection of old books **Whose pages are falling out?*)

Who is used for humans primarily, but sometimes other entities, like robots, extraterrestrials, or animals, especially pets: *She was stroking the cat, who was looking extremely contented.*

Case: nominative vs accusative

Who is a variable lexeme. In addition to its nominative form *who* and its genitive form *whose*, it also has an accusative form *whom* (though this is vastly less common than *who*). The factors affecting the choice between *who* and *whom* are essentially the same as for interrogatives (see Ch. 9, §2.4):

- The **nominative** is required in **subject** or **predicative complement** function.
- The **complement of a fronted preposition** is normally **accusative** (*the woman to whom he was engaged*).
- Elsewhere BOTH cases are found, with the accusative being more formal in style.[4]

One difference from interrogative clauses, however, is that in integrated relatives the choice between the cases is very often avoided by use of the non-*wh* construction: [18iii] is used as a neutral way of sidestepping the choice between the distinctly formal [18ii] and the distinctly informal [18i].

[18]	i	*the applicants who we interviewed*	[nominative: informal]
	ii	*the applicants whom we interviewed*	[accusative: formal]
	iii	*the applicants (that) we interviewed*	[non-*wh*: neutral]

---

[4] Particularly in supplementary relatives, the PP may be complement within a fronted NP, as in *She hadn't yet informed her colleagues, most of whom were still on holiday.* The accusative in this construction (which has no interrogative counterpart) is not markedly formal in style.

> ### Prescriptive grammar note
>
> Some prescriptive usage books and style guides insist that integrated (or 'defining' or 'restrictive') relative clauses with non-personal heads should never be of the *wh* type – that is, that an integrated relative should not begin with *which*. We have paid no attention to this so far (the second example in this chapter, [1ii], is an integrated relative with *which*). Our reason is that the suggested restriction has no basis; no one who looked at the evidence could continue to believe in it. Integrated *wh* relatives with non-personal heads have been occurring in impeccable English for about 400 years. Among the most famous cases are sentences that everyone will recall hearing, such as *Render therefore unto Caesar the things which are Caesar's* (the King James Bible, 1611), and *a date which will live in infamy* (Franklin D. Roosevelt's often misquoted remark about the day of the 1941 Pearl Harbor attack). Those who recommend against integrated *which* often turn out to use it in their own writing (one usage expert said 'I recommend using *that* with defining clauses', but then wrote *a typical situation which a practiced writer corrects* on the very next page!). Integrated relatives with *which* are grammatical in all varieties of English, and the notion that there is something wrong with them is just an invention of prescriptivists.

4   Fused relatives

The final relative construction we consider in this chapter is the **fused relative**, illustrated in [19]:

[19]   i <u>*Whoever said that*</u> *was trying to mislead you.* ⎱
       ii *I've eaten* <u>*what you gave me*</u>.   ⎰   [fused relatives]

This is a more complex construction than those dealt with above. Here the antecedent and the relativised element are fused together instead of being expressed separately as in simpler constructions. The underlined expressions here are thus NPs whose head is fused with the first element in the relative clause.

- *Whoever* in [i] is simultaneously head of the NP and subject of the relative clause, and its gender indicates that we are talking about some person. The meaning is thus comparable to that of the non-fused *The <u>person</u> <u>who</u> said that was trying to mislead you.*
- *What* in [ii] is likewise head of the NP and object of *gave* in the relative clause, and the non-personal gender gives a meaning like that of the non-fused (and more formal) *I've eaten <u>that</u> <u>which</u> you gave me.*

Relative words in the fused construction

The major relative words that occur in this construction are as follows:

[20]   i *who*   *whom*   *what*   *which*   *where*   *when*
       ii *whoever* *whomever* *whatever* *whichever* *wherever* *whenever*

- The compound forms in [ii] do not occur in the other relative constructions, and nor, in Standard English, does *what*.
- On the other hand, *who, whom* and *which* occur in the fused construction only under very limited conditions (usually with verbs like **choose, want, like**, as in *I'll invite who I want*). For example, in Present-day English *who* could not replace *whoever* in [19i]: **Who said that was trying to mislead you*.

What as determinative

The *what* of [19ii] is a pronoun, but *what* can also occur as a determinative:

[21]   <u>*What mistakes she made*</u> *were very minor.*

The fusion here involves *what mistakes*. On the one hand, *what* is determiner and *mistakes* is head of the NP functioning as subject of *were very minor* – note that *were* agrees with plural *mistakes*. On the other hand, *what mistakes* is object of *made* in the relative clause. *Mistakes* thus has a role in both the subordinate clause and the matrix clause: we understand that she made some mistakes but those mistakes were very minor.

Determinative *what* also implies a relatively small number or amount: [21] implies that she made only a small number of mistakes.

Fused relatives and interrogative content clauses

There is a considerable amount of overlap between fused relatives and interrogative content clauses. Compare:

[22]   i   *I really liked <u>what she wrote</u>.*   [fused relative]
         ii   *I wonder <u>what she wrote</u>.*   [interrogative content clause]
        iii   <u>*What she wrote*</u> *is unclear.*   [ambiguous: relative or interrogative]

- The verb *like* does not license an interrogative complement, so *what she wrote* in [i] is unambiguously a fused relative. The sentence can again be glossed with non-fused *that which*: "I really liked that which she wrote".
- *Wonder*, by contrast, licenses an interrogative complement, but does not normally allow an NP object. *What she wrote* in [ii] is therefore unambiguously an interrogative clause: "I wonder about the answer to the question 'What did she write?'".
- *Unclear*, however, licenses both an interrogative and an NP subject, and [iii] can be interpreted in either way. The fused relative interpretation is "That which she wrote is unclear" – a letter or report, perhaps. In the interrogative interpretation, what is unclear is the answer to the question 'What did she write?'. On this interpretation the implication is that I'm not sure what it was that she wrote.

Exercises

1. Underline the **finite subordinate clauses** in the following examples and say whether they are (a) **relative clauses**; (b) **declarative content clauses**; or (c) **ambiguous** between the two. Give evidence in support of your answers.
    i   *She ridiculed the idea that he had proposed.*
    ii *The fact that it's illegal didn't seem to bother them.*
    iii *I've lost the map that you lent me.*
    iv *He was motivated by the conviction that he had been seriously wronged.*
    v   *They are spreading a rumour that is causing her great distress.*

2. All the following examples contain a finite subordinate clause: underline those that are **relative**, and for each of them identify the **antecedent** and the **function** of the (overt or covert) **relativised element**.
    i   *I wonder who they have in mind for the job.*
    ii   *I made a mistake I'll never forget.*
    iii *Go back the way you came.*
    iv   *The prize was awarded to the girl who spoke first.*
    v   *He's not the man he used to be.*
    vi   *It's the best movie I've seen all year.*
    vii *The fact that they are cousins is irrelevant.*
    viii *She started a shelter for women whose husbands beat them.*
    ix   *She goes to the same school that her mother went to.*
    x   *Which is the one you said you liked best?*

3. Convert any **non-*wh* relatives** in the following examples into their ***wh* relative** counterparts.
    i   *The reason he gave was that he wanted to spend more time with his family.*
    ii *The reason he resigned was that he wanted to spend more time with his family.*

    iii *The one that impressed me most was your sister.*
    iv   *Do you remember the time we first went out together?*
    v   *The concept that the agency came up with is really insulting.*
    vi   *The notion that he came up with was really ingenious.*
    vii *That's a person I wouldn't want to cross a river with.*
    viii *Do you have a socket wrench I could borrow?*
    ix   *They said that the one that I wanted was sold out.*
    x   *That car made the one that I was driving look crummy.*

4. The following examples are presented without the usual internal punctuation so as to avoid giving any clues as to whether the relative clauses are **integrated** or **supplementary**. Identify the **relative clauses**, and for each say whether it could be interpreted in either way (with corresponding differences in meaning and punctuation) or in only one way. In the latter case, specify which interpretation is required and explain why the other is excluded.
    i   *This year we're going to Majorca which is where we spent our honeymoon.*
    ii   *The necklace which Elvis gave her is in the safe.*
    iii *Lisa has just gone down with flu which means that the wedding will be postponed.*
    iv   *The only thing I can't understand is why you appointed him in the first place.*
    v   *They're interviewing the neighbours who saw her leave.*
    vi   *She was deeply offended by the letter which accused her of racism.*
    vii *No one who has studied the evidence could possibly doubt her innocence.*

viii *He's going to resign which is exactly the right course of action.*

ix *I took with me any files that I was responsible for.*

x *This is Pat who I am working with.*

5. Determine whether the underlined expressions below are: (a) **fused relatives**; (b) **open interrogative** content clauses; or (c) **ambiguous** between the two. Give evidence to support your answer.

i *I don't know who caused the accident.*

ii *You can do whatever you like.*

iii *What she wrote is completely illegible.*

iv *They've already spent what I gave them yesterday.*

v *I won't be resigning, whatever the report says.*

vi *I told them what you told me to tell them.*

vii *I asked what else I could do.*

viii *What Frankenstein has created will one day destroy him.*

ix *What Frankenstein has created is so far unknown.*

x *We must find whoever did this.*

12 Grade and comparison

1 Comparative and superlative grade

As we have seen in Ch. 6, §1.1, many **adjectives** inflect for **grade**: they have **plain**, **comparative** and **superlative** forms. This inflectional system applies also to a small number of other lexemes, most importantly certain **determinatives** and **adverbs**. Examples are given in [1]:

[1]		ADJECTIVE	DETERMINATIVE	ADVERB
i	PLAIN	*tall*	*many*	*soon*
ii	COMPARATIVE	*taller*	*more*	*sooner*
iii	SUPERLATIVE	*tallest*	*most*	*soonest*

The inflected forms of **tall** and **soon** are **regular** (i.e., they are formed by general rules). The forms for **many**, however, are irregular.

Although 'comparative' is the standard name for just one of the forms, the semantic concept of comparison is relevant to the whole system of grade. All the differences between the forms in the columns in [1] have to do with comparison.

The superlative and set comparison

In the case of the superlative we are concerned with **set comparison**. In these examples, it is comparison between the members of some set with respect to their position on the scale denoted by the lexeme: one member (or one subset) is located at a higher position on that scale than the others. Consider such examples as the following:

[2]   i *Max was the <u>tallest</u> boy in the class.*
     ii *A prize will be given to whoever scores the <u>most</u> points.*
     iii *I chose the life policy that will mature the <u>soonest</u>*

- In [i], the comparison is between the set of boys in the class with respect to height: Max occupies a higher position on this scale than all the others.
- In [ii], the set is not expressed in the sentence itself but it is implicit: it consists of those participating in some competition in which points are scored. The scale is the number of points scored. The prize will be given to the participant who ranks top on this scale.
- In [iii], the comparison is between a set of life insurance policies, ranked by date of maturing. I chose the one that matures before all the others.

The comparative and term comparison

The comparative form, by contrast, is predominantly used in **term comparison** – comparison between a **primary** term and a **secondary** term, as in [3]:

[3]   i *Max is <u>taller</u> than Tom.*
      ii *Sue scored <u>more</u> runs than I did.*
      iii *This policy will mature <u>sooner</u> than that one.*

In [i] the comparison is between Max's height and Tom's height. The sentence doesn't say how tall either of them is absolutely, but expresses the relation between them. We can describe the meaning by using variables, as in algebra: "Max is x tall; Tom is y tall; $x > y$ (i.e. x exceeds y)". This format enables us to handle the distinction between this type of term comparison and that illustrated in [4]:

[4]   *The aerial is taller than 100 feet.*

Here the comparison is between the height of the aerial and a specific height, 100 feet. In this case there is only one variable: "The aerial is x tall; $x > 100$ feet".

- The primary term in [3i] is "Max is x tall", and the secondary one is "Tom is y tall".
- In [ii], "Sue scored x many runs" is primary and "I scored y many runs" is secondary.
- In [iii], "this policy matures x soon" is primary and "that policy matures y soon" is secondary.

The secondary term can be left unexpressed if it is recoverable from the context, as for example in [5]:

[5]   i *Tim is quite tall, but* [*Max is <u>taller</u>*].
      ii *That's better.* [Imagine this being said after you have opened a window.]

- In [i], we understand "Max is taller than Tim", recovering "Tim" from the first clause.
- In [ii] (where *better* is an irregular form of **good**), we understand "That is better than it was before you opened the window"; the secondary term is recovered from the situation.

Set comparison with comparatives

Comparative grade is also used in set comparison when the set has just two members:

[6]   COMPARATIVE   SUPERLATIVE
        a. *Kim is the <u>taller</u> of the two.*   b. *Kim is the <u>tallest</u> of the three.*

The comparative form *taller* is inadmissible in [b].

> ### Prescriptive grammar note
>
> Usage manuals commonly say that the superlative is incorrect when the set has only two members (*the tallest of the twin towers*). However, the superlative is the default for set comparison, and it's fairly common as an informal variant of the comparative with two-member sets. It is relatively unlikely when the two-member status of the set is explicitly given in an *of* phrase, as in [6a], but sentences like *Kim and Pat were the only candidates, and Kim was clearly the best* are certainly grammatical.

Non-inflectional marking of grade

As we noted in Ch. 6, §1.1, comparative and superlative grade may be marked by a separate word, *more* or *most*, rather than by inflection. Examples are given in [7]:

[7]   ADJECTIVE   ADVERB
        i   PLAIN   *useful*   *rashly*
        ii COMPARATIVE   *more useful*   *more rashly*
        iii SUPERLATIVE   *most useful*   *most rashly*

The choice between the two ways of marking comparative and superlative grade – by inflection or by a separate word – is discussed in Ch. 16, §5.

2   *More* and *most*

The two words *more* and *most* figure in both the tables given as [1] and [7]: they can be either inflectional forms of the determinatives *many* and *much* or they can be adverbs marking non-inflectional comparatives and superlatives of adjectives and adverbs.

(a) *More* as determinative

[8]   PLAIN GRADE   COMPARATIVE GRADE
        i   a. *He didn't make <u>many</u> mistakes.*   b. *He made <u>more</u> mistakes than you did.*
        ii a. *We don't have <u>much</u> time.*   b. *We have <u>more</u> time than we need.*
        iii a. *I didn't enjoy it <u>much</u>.*   b. *I enjoyed it <u>more</u> than last time.*

The *more* of the [b] examples here is a **determinative**, the comparative counterpart of plain *many* and *much* in the corresponding [a] examples. The determinative is functioning as determiner in NP structure in [i] and [ii], and as an adjunct of degree in the clause in [iii].

Correspondence between the grades is complicated by the fact that the plain forms *much* (and to a lesser extent *many*) are **non-affirmative** items. This is why negative clauses are used in the [a] examples of [8]; it is not normal in present-day English to say, for example, *We have much time* or *We enjoyed it much* (see Ch. 8, §4).

(b) *More* as adverb

[9] i a. *It's expensive.* b. *It's more expensive than I expected.*
     ii a. *She behaved tactfully.* b. *She behaved more tactfully than her son.*

Here *more* is an **adverb**. In [i] it modifies the adjective *expensive*; in [ii] it modifies the adverb *tactfully*. It is a marker of the **comparative** grade. The crucial difference between [9] and [8] is that there is no *much* or *many* in the plain grade version in [9].

Most

The same distinction applies with *most*, though here we have an additional, non-superlative, sense of the adverb (shown in [10iiib]), where it means "extremely" or "very":

[10] i   a. *He didn't make many mistakes.* b. *He made the most mistakes.*
      ii a. *It's expensive.* b. *It's the most expensive of them all.*
      iii a. *I found her helpful.* b. *I found her most helpful.*

- In [ib], *most* is a **determinative** – the superlative form of *many*.
- In [iib], it is an **adverb**, marking the superlative grade of *expensive*.
- In [iiib], again it's an adverb, but it isn't a marker of superlative grade. There's no explicit comparison between members of a set: *most* just indicates a high degree.

3   *Less* and *least*

The words *less* and *least* similarly belong to both the determinative and adverb classes. As determinatives they are inflectional forms of *little*; as adverbs they function as degree modifiers. These examples illustrate for the comparative:

[11] i   a. *It has little value.* b. *It has less value than he claimed.*
      ii a. *It's expensive.* b. *It's less expensive than I expected.*
      iii a. *She behaved tactfully.* b. *She behaved less tactfully than her son.*

- In [ib] the determinative *less* has the same function, determiner, as *little* in [ia].
- In [iib–iiib] the degree adverb *less* is added as modifier to an adjective or adverb.

(a) The determinative *less*

As a determinative, *less* is syntactically quite similar to its opposite *more*, but there are also significant differences. *More* is the comparative form of both *many* and *much*, which occur with plural and non-count singular nouns respectively. The opposites of *many* and *much* are *few* and *little*, and these have distinct comparative forms *fewer* and *less*. Compare:

[12]   PLURAL   NON-COUNT SINGULAR
      i a. *He's had <u>more jobs</u> than me.*   b. *He's had <u>more experience</u> than me.*
     ii a. *He's had <u>fewer jobs</u> than me.*   b. *He's had <u>less experience</u> than me.*

Matters are complicated, however, by the fact that *less* (unlike *little*) is often used with plurals:

[13]   i *It costs <u>less</u> than twenty dollars.*
        ii *<u>Less/Fewer</u> than twenty people attended the meeting.*
       iii *He's had <u>fewer</u>/[%]<u>less</u> jobs than me.*

- In [i] *twenty dollars* is construed as a sum of money, rather than a set of individual dollars; *fewer than twenty dollars* would be unusual.
- In [ii], where we again have a numeral after *than*, both forms are possible, with *fewer* less common and somewhat formal.
- In [iii], the determinative is followed immediately by a plural noun. This use of *less* is informal; it is avoided by many speakers, and generally condemned by usage manuals.

(b) The adverb *less*

As an adverb, *less* also contrasts with *more* – the adverb *more* that marks comparative grade. *More* marks **superiority** (a higher degree on the relevant scale), while *less* marks **inferiority** (a lower degree). Superiority, however, can also be marked inflectionally, whereas there is no inflection corresponding to *less*. So we have this pattern:

[14]   COMPARISON OF SUPERIORITY   COMPARISON OF INFERIORITY
      i a. *Kim is <u>taller</u> than Pat.*   b. *Kim is <u>less tall</u> than Pat.*
     ii a. *Kim is <u>more energetic</u> than Pat.*   b. *Kim is <u>less energetic</u> than Pat.*

4   Comparison of equality

Superiority and inferiority represent two kinds of **inequality**, but there are also comparisons of **equality**. This, like inferiority, is always marked by a modifying adverb, rather than by inflection:

[15]   i *Kim is <u>as tall</u> as Pat.*
        ii *Kim is <u>as energetic</u> as Pat.*

We use the standard term 'equality' to contrast this construction with those in [14], but it is important to emphasise that it is not a matter of EXACT equality.

- Example [15i] says that Kim's height is AT LEAST equal to Pat's, not that it is identical. We can say, without contradiction: *Kim is as tall as Pat, in fact slightly taller.* And the negative *Kim isn't as tall as Pat* entails that Kim is SHORTER than Pat, not simply that Kim's height is different (either lower or higher on the height scale).

- Similarly in [15ii]: Kim is at least as high on the energetic scale as Pat. As normally understood, *energetic* does not denote a quality that can be precisely measured, as height can, so the issue of whether Kim and Pat are exactly equal on this scale doesn't really arise.

Each of the examples in [15] contains two occurrences of *as*.

- The first *as* is an adverb of degree, like *more* and *less* except that it can modify determinatives: *I had as much cash as you* (contrast **I had more much cash than you*).
- The second *as* is a preposition, like *than*. *As* is used for equality, and *than* for inequality.

In some contexts, primarily negatives, the adverb *as* is replaceable by *so*, and in some familiar phrases it is omitted altogether:

[16]   i   *It wasn't so straightforward as I'd been led to expect.*
       ii *The sea was flat as a pancake.*

5   Non-scalar comparison

All the comparisons considered so far have been concerned with relative positions on some scale – with relative degrees of some gradable property. There is also a type of comparison where the issue is not a matter of relative degree but simply of identity or similarity. We call this **non-scalar** comparison. The prepositions *as* and *than* are found here too, so we can generalise the contrast between equality (marked by *as*) and inequality (marked by *than*):

[17]   i   EQUALITY   *We went by the same route as we usually take.*
       ii INEQUALITY   *%We went by a different route than we usually take.*

The first expresses identity, the second non-identity, between the route we took (on the occasion in question) and the route we usually take.

The % annotation indicates, as usual, that not all speakers use this construction (it is somewhat more frequent in AmE). Some speakers would use a more complex construction with *from* and an NP here: *We went by a different route from the one we usually take.*

There are two items, however, that license a *than* complement for all speakers, namely *other* and *else*:

[18]   i   *There must be some other way of doing it than this.*
       ii *Anyone else than you would have complained.*

We only chose *different* in [17ii] because it permits a more direct contrast with *same*.

6   Comparative clauses

The prepositions *than* and *as* often take as complement a distinctive type of subordinate clause called a **comparative clause**:

[19] i *She did better in the exam than <u>we'd thought she would</u>.*   [superiority]
ii *The treatment was less painful than <u>it was last time</u>.*   [inferiority]
iii *The pool is nearly as wide as <u>it is long</u>.*   [scalar equality]
iv *They come from the same part of Britain as <u>I come from</u>.*   [non-scalar equality]

There are two points about the terminology used here that should be noted.

- First, 'comparative' has a broader sense in 'comparative clause' than elsewhere. Comparative **forms** are always associated with comparisons of superiority, whereas comparative **clauses** are found in all the types of comparison considered above, as indicated in the annotations on the right.
- Second, 'comparative clause' applies to the subordinate clause expressing the secondary term in the comparison, not to the matrix clause that expresses the comparison as a whole.

Comparative clauses constitute one of the three major kinds of **finite subordinate clause** that we introduced in Ch. 10, §1. What distinguishes them from **relative** and **content** clauses is that they are obligatorily **reduced** in certain ways relative to the structure of main clauses.

- In [19i] the complement of *would* is left understood. We could add *do*, but there would still be a missing adjunct. The meaning can be given as "She did x well in the exam; we'd thought she would do y well; $x > y$"; but the "y well" part cannot be syntactically overt.
- Similarly in [19ii] there is an obligatorily missing predicative complement; it's understood as "y painful".
- It is not so obvious that we have reduction in [19iii], since *it is long* can occur as an unreduced main clause. Nevertheless, in this comparative construction there is a missing degree modifier corresponding to the variable y: "The pool is nearly x wide; it is y long; $x = y$". The implicit presence of a degree modifier of *long* makes it impossible to add an overt one: **The pool is nearly as wide as it is very long.*
- Finally, in [19iv] the preposition *from* occurs without a complement. This can't happen in canonical clauses. Again, a complement is understood ("She comes from x part of the country; I come from y part of the country; $x = y$"), but it cannot be syntactically expressed. This represents a somewhat different case of preposition stranding from that discussed in Ch. 7, §5, since there is no corresponding construction in which the preposition is fronted.

A further case of *as* in non-scalar comparison of equality

In the examples of preposition *as* + comparative clause given so far, the *as* is in construction with the adverb *as* marking scalar equality (as in [19iii]) or with the adjective *same* marking non-scalar equality (as in [19iv] or [17i]). *As* can also occur in non-scalar comparison without any such preceding item to license it:

[20]   i   *As we'd expected, he refused to compromise.*
    ii   *He didn't behave as he usually does.*

- In [i] the comparison is between what we'd expected to happen and what did in fact happen. We can gloss as "We'd expected x; y (i.e. he refused to compromise); $x = y$". Here the y corresponds to a whole clause rather than to just a part of a clause.
- In [ii] we are comparing his behaviour on a particular occasion with his usual behaviour. We understand: "He didn't behave in x manner; he usually behaves in y manner; $x = y$".

Comparative clauses as complement to *like*

In non-scalar comparison of equality we also find comparative clauses after the preposition *like* – though *like* takes content clauses as well. Compare, then:

[21]   i   *They don't get on like <u>they used to</u>.*   [comparative clause]
    ii   *It looks like <u>it's going to rain</u>.*   [content clause]

- In [i] we have the familiar kind of comparison between the way they get on (now) and the way they used to get on.
- The content clause construction in [ii] most often occurs after **look** or **sound**, and the meaning is similar to that with **appear** + content clause: *It appears that it's going to rain*. Unlike *they used to* in [i], *it's going to rain* is not reduced.

Prescriptive grammar note

Conservative usage manuals tend to disapprove of both constructions in [21], where *like* takes a finite clause as complement. They would recommend replacing *like* by *as* in [i] and by *as if* (or *as though*) in [ii]. The versions with *like* are relatively informal, but they are very well established, especially in AmE.

1. Re-express the content of the following in a more natural way using **comparative** or **superlative** constructions.
   i *The extent to which my dad is big exceeds the extent to which yours is.*
   ii *Brian is the swimmer who is ranked top in the world as regards speed.*
   iii *That is a fish that is ugly beyond the ugliness of any fish I have ever seen.*
   iv *I wish I had a degree of intelligence that outstrips what I actually have.*
   v *The extent to which you are a good guitarist would increase if the time you practised were to increase.*

2. Underline all the **comparative clauses** (and nothing else) in the following examples (all from Lewis Carroll's Alice books, *Alice in Wonderland* and *Through the Looking Glass*).
   i *It was as much as she could do, lying down on one side, to look through into the garden with one eye.*
   ii *'But then,' thought Alice, 'shall I NEVER get any older than I am now?'*
   iii *'If everybody minded their own business,' the Duchess said in a hoarse growl, 'the world would go round a deal faster than it does.'*
   iv *This piece of rudeness was more than Alice could bear: she got up in great disgust, and walked off.*
   v *It was evidently more than he could manage by himself; however, she managed to shake him out of it at last.*

3. Using variables as appropriate, give the **primary** and **secondary** terms in the comparisons expressed in the examples below, following the model used in the commentary on [3–4] in the text. (For example, if we gave *The hotel felt more comfortable than my own home did*, you might write

"The hotel felt *x* comfortable [primary term]; my own home felt *y* comfortable [secondary term]".)
   i *Fido can run a lot faster than Rex.*
   ii *We're hoping to finish as early as tomorrow.*
   iii *More people came to the meeting than we had seats for.*
   iv *The meeting lasted longer than expected.*
   v *You can take as many copies as you need.*
   vi *More people believed that it was genuine than that it was a hoax.*
   vii *He had a more powerful motor-bike than I had had.*
   viii *Jill thinks Ed's better off than he is.*
   ix *Jill thinks Ed's better off than he does.*
   x *I got up later than usual this morning.*

4. Compare the following examples:
   i *She knows far more people than I know.*
   ii *She's the kindest person I know.*
   The underlined expression is a **comparative** clause in [i] but not in [ii]: what kind of a clause is it in [ii]? What grammatical evidence is there for assigning *I know* to different subcategories of subordinate clause in the two examples? Show how the difference ties in semantically with the distinction we have drawn between **term comparison** and **set comparison**.

5. *Same* occurs in (among others) the constructions illustrated in the following:
   i *She stayed in the same hotel as we stayed in.*
   ii *She stayed in the same hotel we stayed in.*
   Describe the syntactic difference between these constructions and explain why the examples have the same meaning even though they are syntactically different.

13 Non-finite clauses and clauses without verbs

1   Four kinds of non-finite clause

Clauses headed by a **gerund-participle** or a **past participle** are always non-finite, and clauses with a **plain form** verb are non-finite when they belong to the **infinitival** construction. Infinitival clauses come in two varieties: with and without the special marker *to*. This gives us four major kinds of non-finite clause:

[1]	CONSTRUCTION	EXAMPLE	VERB-FORM
i	*TO*-INFINITIVAL	*Liz wants <u>to write a novel.</u>* }	plain form
ii	BARE INFINITIVAL	*Liz might <u>write a novel</u>.* }	
iii	GERUND-PARTICIPIAL	*Liz dreams of <u>writing a novel</u>.*	gerund-participle
iv	PAST-PARTICIPIAL	*Liz has <u>written a novel</u>.*	past participle

Notice that we use the suffix ·*al* (or ·*ial*) to form names for kinds of clause, so that they aren't the same as the traditional terms for inflectional forms of the verb. *Writing* and *written* are verb-forms – the **gerund-participle** and the **past participle**. The underlined sequences in [iii–iv] are clauses that have those forms as their head verb – we call them **gerund-participial** and **past-participial** clauses, respectively.

There is no form in the English verb paradigm called 'the infinitive'. **Infinitival clauses** are non-finite clauses with the head verb in the **plain form**. There are also finite clauses with a plain form as head: **imperative** and **subjunctive** clauses (see Ch. 3, §2). The plain form serves as the form of the head verb in all these clause constructions. There is no special form for the infinitival ones.

2   The form of non-finite clauses

Non-finite clauses contain a predicate that has the form of a VP headed by a **secondary** form of the verb. This means that they do not have primary tense.

That in turn means that they can never contain a modal auxiliary (because, as you will remember from Ch. 3, §3.2, the modals have only primary verb-forms).

Non-finite clauses are normally embedded within a larger construction. There are likely to be aspects of the meaning that can be figured out from this larger construction, but that are not explicitly expressed in the non-finite clause itself the way they usually would be in main clauses. These two examples illustrate:

[2]   i *I remembered to talk to my doctor.*
      ii *I intended to talk to my doctor.*

- If [i] is true, then I actually did talk to my doctor. The preterite inflection on **remember** locates both the remembering and the talking to the doctor in past time.
- If [ii] is true, however, that does NOT necessarily mean that I talked to my doctor. Indeed, it rather suggests that I didn't. **Intend**, unlike **remember**, has a meaning that involves projection into the future, so the time of the intended action is always later than the time of the intention. There is no guarantee that intentions get carried out. Thus there is no guarantee that my planned conversation with the doctor ever happened.

If we look at the main clause *I talked to my doctor* we see a contrast. This clause is self-sufficient: the form of the clause itself indicates that the conversation took place in the past. That is what a non-finite clause such as *to talk to my doctor* can't do: it can't carry its own primary tense to convey the location in time of the action or situation it talks about.

Various other features, not related to the verb-form, further distinguish non-finite clauses from main clauses (see §§2.1–2.4 for more discussion):

- a non-finite clause can have special subordinators (*to* and *for*);
- a non-finite clause can lack overt subjects despite not being imperative;
- when a non-finite clause has a personal pronoun as subject, that pronoun generally does not have the nominative case-form; and
- under certain conditions a non-finite clause may have a non-subject NP left understood.

2.1   Subordinators in *to*-infinitivals: *to* and *for*

To-infinitivals are marked by the word *to*, which derives historically from the preposition *to* (notice the strong similarity in meaning between *I went to the doctor* and *I went to see the doctor*) but long ago lost its prepositional properties. It is now unique: no other item has exactly the same grammatical properties. We take it to be a member of the **subordinator** category – a special marker for VPs of infinitival clauses.

When a *to*-infinitival contains a subject, it also contains the clause subordinator *for*, which appears at the beginning of the clause, right before the subject:

[3]   i   [*For John to lose his temper like that*] *is highly unusual.*
        ii *We can't afford* [*for everyone to travel business class*].

Again, the history goes back to the preposition *for*, and we see a strong similarity in meaning between *I longed for your return* and *I longed for you to return*. But this *for* behaves as a clause subordinator. It does for infinitival clauses with subjects what the subordinator *that* does for declarative content clauses.

> **Prescriptive grammar note**
>
> There are still some prescriptive grammar books around that warn against what they call the 'split infinitive'. They mean the construction illustrated in *to really succeed*, where an adjunct (*really*) comes between *to* and the verb. (The term 'split infinitive' is misleading, since English doesn't have an infinitive form of the verb in the way that, say, French does.) *To succeed* is not a verb; it's two words, the subordinator *to* and the verb *succeed*. There is no rule of grammar requiring them to be adjacent. Phrases like *to really succeed* have been in use for hundreds of years. Most usage manuals now recognise this, and also recognise that in some cases placing the adjunct between *to* and the verb is stylistically preferable to other orderings.

2.2   Subjectless non-finites

Most non-finite clauses, including those in [1], have no overt subject. But in a sense we understand them as having subjects. For instance, the way we understand [1i], *Liz wants to write a novel*, Liz wants more than just for a novel to get written; Liz also wants to be the author – she wants "Liz has written a novel" to become true. So in a sense we take *Liz* as the subject not only of **want** but also of **write**. But *Liz* is not actually present in the **write** clause: we therefore speak of it as the **understood subject**.

Interpreting subjectless clauses

There are actually two different ways in which an understood subject is associated with a predicate: one way involves a grammatical linkage that we will refer to as **syntactic determination** and the other does not. These examples illustrate:

[4]   i   a. *Ed promised to resign from the board.*
            b. *They called on Ed to resign from the board.*   } [syntactic determination]
        ii a. *It is unwise to go swimming straight after a meal.*
            b. *It was unwise to invite Ed to the party.*   } [no syntactic determination]

(a)   Syntactic determination

In [i], there is syntactic determination, so we can immediately see what the understood subject must be, simply by looking at a linguistic antecedent that appears in some particular syntactic function in the matrix construction.

- In [ia], the matrix clause has the verb **promise** as its head verb, which means Ed did the promising, and this is enough to tell anyone (provided they know the grammar and meaning of the verb **promise**!) the understood subject of **resign**.

* In [ib], Ed was the one they called on, so again we know that Ed is the one whose resignation is being discussed.

In such cases the retrieval of the missing subject is said to be syntactically determined: it is determined by a rule referring to the syntactic structure. Notice that in [ia] that rule picks out a subject NP, while in [ib] the rule picks out an NP that is a complement in a PP. With different verbs, NPs in different functions are identified as the appropriate **antecedent**.

(b)   No syntactic determination

In [ii], by contrast, there is no syntactic determination. The meaning depends heavily on inference.

* The salient interpretation of [iia] is that it applies quite generally: "It is unwise for anyone to go swimming straight after a meal."
* In [iib], however, we are talking about a particular event of inviting at some time in the past, and someone issued the invitation to Ed to the party, so the missing subject is understood as referring to that person. It might have been explicitly stated earlier in the preceding discourse who issued the invitation, or it might not. It doesn't matter. There doesn't have to be any prior mention of the person (an accusing glance in your direction might be enough to suggest that it was you), and in any case the NP referring to the inviter certainly doesn't have to be located in some designated syntactic position in the matrix construction of the infinitival clause.

Non-finite clauses functioning as adjunct

One construction falls close to the boundary between the determined and non-determined constructions. That is the case of non-finite clauses functioning as, or within, certain kinds of supplementary adjunct:

[5]   *Having read the report, Mary was sure there had been a miscarriage of justice.*

Having read the report is an adjunct, and the missing subject of the non-finite is retrievable by looking at the subject of the matrix clause. It provides a plausible subject, and there is no other candidate, so we understand the sentence as saying that it was Mary who read the report.

Users of English don't always make it so clear what the intended understood subject might be. They leave it dangling, for the reader or hearer to guess. This issue is a celebrated topic discussed in prescriptive works on English usage, where it appears under the name **dangling modifiers** (or sometimes **dangling participles**).

In [5] the subject of the matrix clause is an appropriate basis for providing the clause with an understood subject, and that makes things easy. But we need to deal with two other cases:

* to some speakers a non-subject NP in the matrix clause seems just as good as a basis for figuring out what the understood subject in the adjunct should be (though speakers often don't agree on which ones);

- many sentences are found in which no NP in the sentence gives any clue as to the understood subject, so it must be filled in by guesswork from the context (and speakers don't all agree about when that is acceptable, either).

(a)   Understood subject given by non-subject NP

The examples in [6] appeared in print, with the double-underlined NP as the intended antecedent for the missing subject of the underlined clausal adjunct. (The symbol '%', it will be recalled, indicates that by no means every speaker of Standard English would find them acceptable.)

[6]   i %*Born and bred in Brisbane*, the Sunshine Coast was always <u>*my*</u> preferred destination to recharge and socialise from my teenage years.
       ii %*Jennifer Lopez stars as Marisa, a maid in a fancy New York City Hotel. While <u>trying on a wealthy woman's dress</u>, a handsome and rich politician mistakes <u>her</u> for a society woman.*

- In [i], the subject of the matrix clause is *the Sunshine Coast*, and that makes no sense as the subject of *born and bred*. We are forced to look for an alternative, and *my* provides one: we can assume that it is the speaker who was born and bred in Brisbane.
- In [ii] (from a description of the plot of *Maid in Manhattan* in a cinema's publicity leaflet), the second sentence is supposed to be saying that Marisa was trying on the dress. But the matrix clause subject, *a handsome and rich politician*, provides a distracting unintended meaning: that the handsome politician was trying on the dress. And there is nothing LINGUISTICALLY odd about *He was trying on a wealthy woman's dress*. So we only turn to the assumption that Marisa (referred to by the object pronoun *her*) was trying on the dress when we decide that this makes a more reasonable plot for the movie being described.

(b)   Understood subject not given by any NP

Sometimes no NP in the sentence gives us any clue about what we should take to be the understood subject. Here are two examples from print:

[7]   i %*Being desperately poor, paper was always scarce – as was ink.*
       ii %*Having failed once, is the fear of failure any less this time around?*

- In [i], the subject of *being desperately poor* is supposed to refer to the poet John Clare, son of an agricultural labourer; the example appeared in a review of a book about Clare's life. The matrix clause subject *paper* would make no sense as the understood subject (if *poor* denotes financial poverty), but Clare is not mentioned anywhere in the sentence. The surrounding sentences have to be read to see what the sentence is intended to mean.
- In [ii], the context makes it clear that the understood subject of *having failed* denotes the person addressed: the interviewer says, *You've just started up another company . . . Having failed once, is the fear of failure any less this time around?*

Examples of both the kinds illustrated in [6] and [7] are extremely common. Many speakers try to avoid them in careful writing (though it should be noted that the ones we have given appeared in carefully edited quality newspapers). And some expressions of the type seen in [7] have become more fully established, and would be allowed by any editor:

[8]   i   *In the long run, <u>taking everything into account</u>, which is the wisest choice?*
     ii   *<u>Turning to last week</u>, several numbers provided some reason for optimism.*
    iii   *<u>Speaking of heroes</u>, there's something kind of heroic about this show.*

Here no particular subject is intended for the underlined adjuncts: they could perhaps be paraphrased with indefinite *one* ("when one takes everything into account") or non-deictic *you* ("when you turn to last week") or *we* referring to the speaker and addressee in a collaboration ("given that we're speaking of heroes").

The situation with understood subjects of the above adjuncts is thus rather different from the situation illustrated in [4ia], where we illustrated **syntactic determination**: the subject of the infinitival in *Ed promised to resign from the board* MUST be interpreted with the subject of *promise* as its antecedent. No one understands it any other way. The adjunct construction shown in [5–8], on the other hand, is NOT syntactically determined.

The main clue to the understood subject in this construction is often given by the matrix clause subject (as in [5]), but there is a wide range of other possibilities for interpretation of differing degrees of acceptability.

> ### Prescriptive grammar note
>
> Many of the more conservative usage manuals, and many editors and writing teachers, disapprove of ambiguity about the understood subject of a non-finite clause, and regard 'dangling modifiers' as errors. What they are claiming is (putting it in our terms) that the missing subject of a non-finite clause in adjunct function MUST be under obligatory syntactic determination by the subject of the matrix clause. If that were true, it would be surprising if anyone understood sentences like those in [6] and [7]. But what we find is that such sentences are extremely common, and have been throughout the history of English literature. (In Shakespeare's *Hamlet* the ghost of Hamlet's father says *'Tis given out that, sleeping in mine orchard, a serpent stung me*; the **sleep** clause subject does not have the matrix subject – *a serpent* – as antecedent.) Moreover, far from being uninterpretable, they are generally understood by everyone. The few that have disruptive or hilarious unintended meanings are actually rather rare (though they tend to be cherished and much quoted by usage writers). Naturally, a careful writer will examine first drafts to remove unintended ambiguities that would damage intelligibility; but the danger from adjunct non-finite clauses with missing subjects that are not syntactically determined is often exaggerated.

2.3   Non-finites with an overt subject

When a subject is overtly present in the non-finite clause its form may differ from that of subjects in finite clauses.

Infinitival clauses

In *to*-infinitivals a personal pronoun with a nominative–accusative contrast always takes accusative form:[1]

[9]　　i　[*For them to refuse you a visa*] *was quite outrageous.*
　　　ii　*All I want is* [*for us to be reunited*].

Gerund-participials

Here the facts are more complex. There are various case possibilities for subjects of gerund-participles, but they differ depending on whether the clause is a complement or an adjunct.

Gerund-participial as complement

In the following examples the clause is complement of the preposition *on*:

[10]　　i　*She insisted on* [*my* / *me being present throughout the interview*].
　　　ii　*She insisted on* [*her father's* / *her father being present throughout the interview*].
　　　iii　*She insisted on* [*there being a counsellor present throughout the interview*].

Here, and in most other complement functions, we find both genitive and non-genitive subjects.

* If a personal pronoun subject is not in the genitive, then it takes accusative case, as with *me* in [i].
* The choice between genitive and non-genitive depends partly on style and partly on the type of NP. The genitive is characteristic of fairly formal style, and overall it is relatively infrequent. It is most likely with personal pronouns, and next most likely with short singular NPs denoting humans, like *her father's* in [ii].
* Some NPs, such as *there* in [iii], cannot take genitive case at all.[2]

Gerund-participial as adjunct

When a gerund-participial is in adjunct function, as in [11], genitive subjects are not permitted at all: the choice is between nominative and accusative:

[11]　　i　*She sought advice from Ed,* [*he being the most experienced of her colleagues*].
　　　ii　*She sought advice from Ed,* [*him being the most experienced of her colleagues*].

The accusative is markedly informal and somewhat unlikely: the construction itself is relatively formal, so the accusative tends to sound out of place here.

---

[1] However, when the pronoun does not form the whole subject, but is part of a coordination, some speakers have a nominative: *%They've arranged* [*for you and I to be picked up at six*] (see Ch. 5, §8.3).
[2] This *there* is a dummy (i.e. meaningless) pronoun discussed further in §4.2 below.

2.4   Hollow non-finite clauses

We have noted that most non-finite clauses have no overt subject, but there is also a type where some non-subject element is missing yet recoverable from an antecedent expression:

[12]   i   *The house will be ready [for you to inspect __] in a few days.*
    ii   *The new car took me quite a long time [to get used to __].*
    iii   *The report was far too long [to read __ in one evening].*
    iv   *They came up with a rather difficult argument [to refute __].*
    v   *Her new book is definitely worth [looking at __].*

The '__' marks the place where there is an element missing but understood, and underlining marks the antecedent that provides an interpretation for the missing NP. Thus what you will be inspecting in [i] is the house; what I was getting used to in [ii] was the new car; what would have taken too long to read in [iii] was the report; what was difficult to refute in [iv] was the argument; what is worth looking at in [v] is her new book.

The bracketed clauses here have incomplete structure – they have a hole somewhere inside them. We call them **hollow** non-finites. Their properties can be stated briefly as follows:

- Form: they are predominantly *to*-infinitivals.
- Function of missing element: this is normally direct object ([i], [iii–iv]) or object of a preposition ([ii], [v]).
- Antecedent: the antecedent is normally an NP (often the matrix subject, as in [i–iii], [v]), or a nominal (head of the NP in which the hollow clause is embedded, as in [iv]).
- Function of the hollow clause: the hollow clause can have a range of functions.
  - In [i] it's embedded within a predicative complement, licensed by *ready* (items like **good**, **bad**, and **nice** also allow this).
  - In [ii] it's a complement licensed by the VP **take** with a duration expression.
  - In [iii] it's an indirect complement licensed by *too* (*sufficient(ly)*) and *enough* also allow this).
  - In [iv] it's complement within an NP, licensed by the attributive modifier *difficult* (**easy**, **hard**, **simple**, and a few other adjectives also allow this).
  - In [v] it's a complement licensed by the adjective *worth*.

3   The functions of non-finite clauses

Non-finite clauses appear in a very wide range of functions, but there are major differences between the four types. We'll look at them separately in turn: first *to*-infinitivals, then bare infinitivals, then past-participials, then gerund-participials.

3.1   *To*-infinitivals

To-infinitivals function as complement or modifier/adjunct in a considerable number of constructions:

[13] i SUBJECT   *To turn back now* would be a mistake.
     ii EXTRAPOSED SUBJECT   It would be a mistake *to turn back now*.
    iii EXTRAPOSED OBJECT   We considered it sensible *to take legal advice*.
     iv INTERNAL COMP OF VERB   Her parents [intend *to buy her a car*].
      v COMP OF PREPOSITION   I go to the gym [in order *to keep fit*].
     vi ADJUNCT IN CLAUSE   I go to the gym *to keep fit*.
    vii COMP OF NOUN   It provides [an opportunity *to broaden the mind*].
   viii   { We found [a big box *in which to keep the CDs*].
     ix MODIFIER IN NP   { We found [a big box *to keep the CDs in*].
      x COMP OF ADJECTIVE   He was [anxious *to make a good impression*].
     xi INDIRECT COMP   He's still [too young *to be left alone*].

- As with content clauses, the construction with the infinitival as subject, as in [i], is much less common than the one where it is an extraposed subject, as in [ii].
- With objects, the extraposed construction, [iii], is virtually obligatory: the infinitival could not occur where *it* is (**We considered to take legal advice sensible*).
- In [iv] the infinitival is an internal complement of the verb – it's within the VP, not external like the subject.
- Leaving aside interrogatives (which we'll look at immediately below), infinitivals don't generally function as complement to a preposition. The major exception is with the compound preposition *in order* (which historically originates in a construction where *order* was a noun), illustrated in [v].
- Infinitivals occur as adjuncts of various kinds; the one in [vi] is a purpose adjunct, with the same meaning as the bracketed PP of [v].
- In [vii–ix] the infinitival is a dependent in NP structure, either a complement (licensed by the noun) or a modifier. Modifier infinitivals are a special case of relative clauses – of the *wh* type in [viii], and the non-*wh* type in [ix]. In the *wh* type the relative phrase in initial position must consist of preposition + NP, and no subject is permitted.
- Infinitival complements are licensed by numerous adjectives, such as *anxious* in [x].
- Finally, in [xi] the infinitival is an indirect complement in the structure of an AdjP. It is licensed by *too*, but it functions as a dependent in the phrase headed by *young* (see Ch. 5, §4).

Interrogative infinitivals

Infinitivals functioning as complement to verbs, prepositions, nouns and adjectives can be interrogative – if the head licenses one, of course. Some examples are given in [14], with the infinitival underlined and brackets round the phrase within which it has the complement function:

[14]	i	COMP OF VERB	*I don't [know <u>whether to accept their offer</u>].*
	ii	COMP OF ADJECTIVE	*I'm not [sure <u>how to proceed</u>].*
	iii	COMP OF PREPOSITION	*They can't agree [on <u>what to do about it</u>].*
	iv	COMP OF NOUN	*[A decision <u>whether to go ahead</u>] hasn't been made.*

Closed interrogatives are introduced by the subordinator *whether* and open ones by an interrogative phrase like *who* or *which one* or *how*. No overt subject is permitted in either kind of interrogative infinitival.

* In [i–iii] the understood subject is syntactically determined, with the matrix clause subject as the antecedent.
* In [iv] there is no syntactic determination, and no antecedent: the interpretation will be heavily dependent on the context.

The meaning of infinitival interrogatives is **deontic**, as if the modal auxiliary *should* were included. For example, [i] doesn't mean that I don't know whether I do accept their offer or did accept it, it means I don't know whether I should accept it.

3.2   Bare infinitivals

In contrast to *to*-infinitivals, with their wide range of uses, bare infinitival clauses occur in only a very limited set of functions. They hardly occur except as internal complements of certain verbs, with no subject permitted:

[15]	i	*You should <u>take legal advice</u>.*	[complement of modal auxiliary]
	ii	*I want you to help <u>clear up the garage</u>.*	[complement of **help**]
	iii	*The devil made me <u>do it</u>.*	[complement of **make**, **let**, **see**, etc.]
	iv	*All I did was <u>ask a simple question</u>.*	[complement of specifying **be**]

3.3   Gerund-participials

The range of functions in which gerund-participial clauses are found is broadly comparable to that of *to*-infinitivals, but there are some important differences.

[16]	i	SUBJECT	<u>*Bringing your dad in on the deal*</u> *was a great idea.*
	ii	EXTRAPOSED SUBJECT	*It's been a pleasure <u>talking to you both</u>.*
	iii	OBJECT	*I find <u>talking to Max</u> rather stressful.*
	iv	EXTRAPOSED OBJECT	*He considers it a waste of time <u>going to meetings</u>.*
	v	INTERNAL COMP OF VERB	*I remember <u>telling you about her visit</u>.*
	vi	COMP OF PREPOSITION	*He insists [on <u>checking everything himself</u>].*
	vii	ADJUNCT IN CLAUSE	<u>*Having read the paper*</u>, *I can't see why you care.*
	viii	MODIFIER IN NP	*Who was [the doctor <u>performing the operation</u>]?*

* We have seen that with *to*-infinitivals there is a strong preference for extraposed rather than subject or object positions, but the reverse is the case with gerund-participials; note that they can occur as object with a following predicative complement, as in [iii]. Infinitivals can't.

- Similarly, while prepositions generally don't accept *to*-infinitivals as complement, many can take gerund-participials, as *on* does in [vi].
- In NP structure, gerund-participials commonly function as modifier, but they are not found as complements, and they are virtually excluded from being complements to adjectives too.³

3.4   Past-participials

Past-participial clauses have a quite limited distribution. In the great majority of cases, they have one or other of the two functions shown in [17]:

[17] i   INTERNAL COMP OF VERB $\begin{cases} \textit{She [has \underline{written another novel}].} \\ \textit{I could [have you \underline{dismissed on the spot}].} \end{cases}$
    ii
    iii   MODIFIER IN NP   [*The guns* <u>stolen in the break-in</u>] *were recovered.*

- As complement of a verb the past-participial may have a perfect or passive interpretation – perfect as complement of the perfect auxiliary **have**, as in [i], and otherwise passive, as in [ii].
- As modifier, a past-participial clause is interpreted as passive: the underlined non-finite clause in [iii] is essentially equivalent to the finite relative clause *which were stolen in the break-in.*

4   The catenative construction

4.1   Introduction

One construction illustrated in the survey presented in §3 needs some further attention. This is the **catenative** construction.

Most cases where a non-finite clause is an internal complement of a verb illustrate the catenative construction, if we set aside the exceptions illustrated in [18]:

[18]   NON-CATENATIVE INTERNAL COMPLEMENTS
    i   *Our goal is* <u>to eliminate all these errors in the next version</u>.
    ii   *These rules are* <u>to protect the privacy of our clients</u>.
    iii   *This made* <u>working with them</u> *an unpleasant experience.*
    iv   *I'd call that* <u>shirking your responsibilities</u>.

- The non-finite clauses in [i] and [ii] are complements of **be** in its specifying and ascriptive senses respectively (recall Ch. 4, §4.3).
- In [iii] the non-finite clause is object, and is the predicand for the predicative complement *an unpleasant experience.*
- In [iv] the non-finite clause is a predicative complement of **call**, with the object *that* as its predicand.

---

³ In a sentence like *I felt anxious* <u>watching you up there</u>, the underlined clause is an adjunct in clause structure (it means "while I was watching you up there"); it's not a complement to *anxious*.

These can all be regarded as merely special cases of more general constructions in which the same function is filled by something other than a non-finite clause. For example, [i] has basically the same structure as *Our goal is an error-free version*, where the specifying *be* has an NP as complement; [ii] is like *These rules are for our clients' protection*, with a PP; [iii] is like *This made the job an unpleasant experience*, with an NP object; and [iv] is like *I'd call that laziness*, also with an NP.

In the catenative construction, substitutions by other categories in similar ways are not possible. The examples in [19] illustrate catenative complements:

[19]   i CATENATIVE COMP WITH *seem*:   *Kim seemed to understand it.*
      ii CATENATIVE COMP WITH *begin*:   *Kim began to understand it.*
     iii CATENATIVE COMP WITH *hope*:   *Kim hoped to understand it.*

Now, it is true that *seem*, *begin* and *hope* can take other categories of complement as well:

[20]   i NP (PREDICATIVE) WITH *seem*:   *Kim seemed a keen student.*
      ii NP (OBJECT) WITH *begin*:   *Kim began the journey.*
     iii PP WITH *hope*:   *Kim hoped for a successful outcome.*

But the function of the infinitival complement *to understand it* in [19] cannot be equated with any of these – it's not a predicative complement as in [20i], it's not an object like *the journey* in [20ii], and it's not like a PP complement in [20iii]. Instead, the examples in [19] illustrate a distinct construction.

The term 'catenative' is derived from the Latin word for "chain", for the construction is repeatable in a way that enables us to form chains of verbs in which all except the last have a non-finite complement:

[21]   *She seems to want to stop trying to avoid meeting him.*

Each of the underlined verbs here has a non-finite clause as complement:

[22]   HEAD VERB   COMPLEMENT
      i   *seems*   *to want to stop trying to avoid meeting him*
     ii   *want*   *to stop trying to avoid meeting him*
    iii   *stop*   *trying to avoid meeting him*
     iv   *trying*   *to avoid meeting him*
      v   *avoid*   *meeting him*

We'll apply the term 'catenative' to the complements, to the licensing verbs and to the construction. So all of the non-finite clauses in the complement column of [22] function as **catenative complements**; the matrix verbs in the first column of [22] are **catenative verbs**; and each verb + complement pair forms a **catenative construction**.

Simple and complex catenative constructions

We can distinguish two subtypes of the catenative construction depending on the absence or presence between the matrix and dependent verbs of **an intervening NP** – an NP that is interpreted semantically as subject of the non-finite clause:

[23]	SIMPLE CATENATIVE	COMPLEX CATENATIVE
i	a. *I promised to read the report.*	b. *We persuaded <u>Sue</u> to read the report.*
ii	a. *We daren't move the furniture.*	b. *We helped <u>Sue</u> move the furniture.*
iii	a. *Max regrets locking the door.*	b. *I remember <u>Sue</u> locking the door.*
iv	a. *Pat got nominated for treasurer.*	b. *He had <u>Sue</u> nominated for treasurer.*
v	a. *Ed seemed to me to cheer them up.*	b. *We rely on <u>Sue</u> to cheer them up.*

- There is never an intervening NP in the **simple** construction. Notice that *me* in [23va] is not an 'intervening NP' in the sense we have defined: it is not understood as the subject of *cheer*.
- There is always an intervening NP in the **complex** construction, except when it is passive (that is, we treat *Sue was persuaded to read the report* as a complex catenative like [23ib]).

4.2   The simple catenative construction

In the simple catenative construction the non-finite clause has no subject and there is no intervening NP that is understood as the subject. But as usual the interpretation requires that we supply an understood or implicit subject. In almost all cases this is syntactically determined by the subject of the matrix clause:[4] the promise in [23ia] is about my reading the report; [23iia] is about our moving the furniture; Max's regret in [23iiia] is about Max's having locked the door; the nominee for treasurer in [23iva] is Pat; and the cheerer-up in [23va] is Ed.

Ordinary subjects vs raised subjects

The subject of the catenative verb in the simple catenative construction may be an **ordinary** subject or a **raised** subject, depending on the particular catenative verb selected, and the difference is important.

[24]	ORDINARY SUBJECT	RAISED SUBJECT
	a. *<u>Sara</u> wanted to convince Ed.*	b. *<u>Sara</u> seemed to convince Ed.*

- An ordinary subject is semantically related to the verb (or VP). Thus in [a] the main clause subject *Sara* refers to the person who experienced the feeling of wanting to convince Ed.
- A raised subject, by contrast, doesn't have a direct semantic relation with the verb. Syntactically it is located in the matrix clause, but semantically it belongs solely in the embedded clause. The meaning of [24b] is very close to that of *Sara seemingly convinced Ed*, where we have the adverb *seemingly* instead of the catenative verb *seem*.

---

[4] The reason we say 'almost all cases' is that there are just one or two exceptional verbs like **say**, as in *Your mother said to meet her at two o'clock.* Here there is no syntactic determination: the understood subject is obtained from the context. You are to meet her, or we (you and I) are to meet her – it depends what the circumstances are.

■ Two ways of testing for ordinary or raised subjects in catenative constructions

This difference in the semantic status of the matrix subject is reflected in a number of ways. We'll consider just two: the effects of putting the non-finite clause into the **passive voice**, and the effects of considering clauses with **dummy pronouns** as subjects.

(a)   Using passive infinitivals

In a matrix clause with an ordinary subject, changing the subject changes the core meaning – the claims made about who did what. To test this, try making a transitive non-finite clause passive and switching the matrix clause subject with the infinitival clause object. The matrix has an ordinary subject if the new sentence has a clearly different core meaning from the old one; if it has a raised subject the core meaning will remain the same. This table illustrates:

[25]	ORDINARY SUBJECT	RAISED SUBJECT
Active non-finite clause	*Sara wanted to convince Ed.*	*Sara seemed to convince Ed.*
Passive non-finite clause	*Ed wanted to be convinced by Sara.*	*Ed seemed to be convinced by Sara.*
Same meaning in both?	No	Yes

What we mean by **core meaning** can be explained more precisely. This is the meaning which, in declarative clauses, determines the **truth conditions**, the conditions under which they can be used to make a true statement. When we ask whether the two declarative clauses have the same core meaning, we are asking whether they have the same truth conditions, whether it is impossible for there to be any situation where one is true and the other false.

- Can you imagine any situation in which Sara wanted to convince Ed while Ed didn't want to be convinced? Obviously, yes. That means that *want* takes an **ordinary** subject. The subject of *want* denotes the person whose desires are being talked about. If *Ed* is the subject, Ed felt the desire; if *Sara* is the subject, Sara felt it.
- Now, can you imagine circumstances in which Sara seemed to convince Ed but Ed didn't seem to be convinced? This time the answer must be no: if you think about what must be true if Sara seemed to convince Ed, and what must be true if Ed seemed to be convinced by Sara, then it is fairly clear that you simply can't invent a situation where one is true and the other simultaneously false. That is the sign of a **raised** subject. The subject of *seem* makes its meaning contribution in the subordinate clause, but is positioned in the matrix clause.

It's important not to be misled by the fact that the sentence with the passive infinitival might sound unnatural. Consider this pair, for example:

[26]   i *Max began to sweep the floor.*
    ii *?The floor began to be swept by Max.*

It's true that [26ii] doesn't sound like something anyone would say. You might therefore be tempted to think that *Max* in [26i] is an ordinary subject. But that would be a mistake. When you consider the conditions that would make the sentences in [26] true or false, you see that you cannot devise a context in which one is true while the other is false. The only difference is that [i] is a more natural way of describing the situation than [ii]. If we change the examples slightly to make both members equally natural, it becomes much easier to see that they are equivalent:

[27]   i *Max's off-colour jokes began to offend the audience.*
    ii *The audience began to be offended by Max's off-colour jokes.*

This experiment reveals that **begin** takes a raised subject: its subject belongs semantically in the subordinate clause, and the meaning of **begin** applies to the situation described in that clause (in [27], the process of Max's off-colour jokes offending the audience); *began* focuses on the initial, transitional phase of this process.

(b)   Using dummy pronouns

A **dummy** element is one that has no independent meaning of its own but occurs in certain constructions simply to satisfy some syntactic requirement.

An example we have referred to on quite a few occasions is the dummy auxiliary verb *do*. In interrogatives like *Do they want it?* and negatives like *They don't want it*, dummy *do* occurs because these constructions require the presence of an auxiliary verb even though there is no auxiliary in the corresponding canonical construction *They want it* (see Ch. 3, §3.1).

There are also two dummy elements belonging to the category of pronoun, namely *it* and *there*, as used, for example, in the following constructions:

[28]   i EXTRAPOSITION   *<u>It</u> is likely that she'll go.*
    ii EXISTENTIAL   *<u>There</u> is plenty of time.*

These are non-canonical constructions belonging in the information packaging domain. They are discussed in some detail in Ch. 15, though we have already had occasion to mention extraposition. *It* and *there* here are dummy elements inserted to satisfy the requirement that finite clauses (other than imperatives) must contain a subject.

● The canonical version of [i] is *That she'll go is likely*; extraposition places the subordinate clause at the end of the matrix and inserts dummy *it* to fill the vacated subject position.
● The existential clause [ii] has no canonical counterpart. You can't say **Plenty of time is* because the verb **be** normally requires an internal complement. *Plenty of time* is placed in internal complement function and the vacated subject position is again filled by a dummy, this time *there*.

The significance of these dummy pronouns for the concerns of this chapter is that they cannot function as an ordinary subject to a catenative verb. This can be seen from the following table:

[29]

	ORDINARY SUBJECT	RAISED SUBJECT
Extrapositional *it*	**It wants to be likely that she'll go.*	*It seems to be likely she'll go.*
Existental *there*	**There wants to be plenty of time.*	*There seems to be plenty of time.*
Dummy subject allowed?	No	Yes

An ordinary subject is semantically related to the catenative verb, and this is not possible with a meaningless dummy. But a dummy pronoun can occur as a raised subject provided the non-finite complement is of the appropriate kind, i.e. one corresponding to a main clause with a dummy subject, as those in the table correspond to the main clauses in [28].

Gerund-participials

The distinction between the two kinds of subject is also found with gerund-participials. ***Regret***, for example, takes an ordinary subject, while ***keep*** is a raising verb:

[30]

	ORDINARY SUBJECT		RAISED SUBJECT
i	a. *Ed regrets interrupting me.*	b.	*Ed keeps interrupting me.*
ii	a. *I regret being interrupted by Ed.*	b.	*I keep being interrupted by Ed.*
iii	a.**There regret being power black-outs.*	b.	*There keep being power black-outs.*

* The examples in [i–ii] involve the passive infinitival test. It's clear that [ia] and [iia] differ in truth conditions, for the first attributes regret to Ed, the second to me. But [ib] and [iib] are equivalent. Both say that the situation of Ed interrupting me occurred repeatedly: there is thus no direct semantic relation between ***keep*** and its subject.
* The dummy pronoun test gives the same results. ***Keep*** can take a dummy subject, but ***regret*** cannot.

Auxiliary verbs

Auxiliaries, when used as markers of tense, aspect, mood or voice, are catenative verbs, entering into the simple catenative construction. In general, they take **raised** subjects. ***Dare*** is exceptional. We can see that it takes an ordinary subject from examples such as the following:

[31]

i	a. *Kim daren't beat Sue.*	b.	*Kim may beat Sue.*
ii	a. *Sue daren't be beaten by Kim.*	b.	*Sue may be beaten by Kim.*
iii	a.**There daren't be a reporter present.*	b.	*There may be a reporter present.*

Example [iia] is not entirely natural-sounding, but it is certainly intelligible and different in meaning from [ia]; an authentic example of the construction with a passive infinitival is *I daren't be seen in public with him anymore.*

4.3   The complex catenative construction

This construction, in its basic form, contains an **intervening NP**, an NP located between the two verbs and interpreted as the subject of the dependent clause. Four subtypes can be distinguished:

[32] i   *We arranged <u>for them</u> to meet the manager.*
  ii *We resented <u>their</u> being given extra privileges.*
  iii *We counted on <u>them</u> to support us.*
  iv *We believed <u>them</u> to be conspiring against us.*

- In infinitival [i] the intervening NP is preceded by the subordinator *for*. This indicates clearly that the intervening NP belongs syntactically in the embedded clause, as subject.
- In [ii] the genitive case on *their* marks this NP as subject of the gerund-participial.
- In [iii] *them* is complement of the preposition *on*, with *on them* complement of the prepositional verb **count**; *them* thus clearly belongs in the matrix clause, not the infinitival, though it is also, of course, understood as subject of the latter.
- Less obvious is [iv], where there are no such overt indications of the syntactic status of *them*. This construction needs further consideration.

Although the syntactic status of the intervening NP in the infinitival construction [32iv] is not immediately obvious, there are several kinds of evidence showing that it belongs syntactically in the matrix clause. We illustrate here with three of them, contrasting the **believe** construction with the **arrange** construction containing the subordinator *for*, as in [32i]:

(a) Passives

[33] i   *They were believed to be conspiring against us.*
  ii *It was arranged for them to meet the manager.*

- With **believe** the intervening NP behaves like an object of the matrix clause in that it can be made subject of a passive, as in [i].
- In the **arrange** construction with *for*, by contrast, the passive has dummy *it* as subject, with the catenative complement occurring as extraposed subject, as in [ii].

(b) Insertion of adjuncts

[34] i   **We believed later them to be conspiring against us.*
  ii *We arranged later for them to meet the manager.*

- With **believe** the intervening NP also behaves like an object of the matrix clause in that it cannot be separated from the verb by an adjunct, such as *later*. The inadmissibility of [i] is like that of **We believed later their story.*

● In the *for* construction *for them to meet the manager* is, as a whole, a catenative complement and as such it can be separated from the matrix verb.

(c)   The 'pseudo-cleft' construction

[35]   i *What we believed was them to be conspiring against us.
       ii   What we arranged was for them to meet the manager.

The 'pseudo-cleft' is another construction belonging to the information packaging domain, and again the main discussion of it is in Ch. 15, §6. For present purposes it is sufficient to see in broad outline how [35ii] differs from the structurally more elementary [32i]. The latter has been divided into two parts (as reflected in the 'cleft' component of the name). One part (*for them to meet the manager*) is made complement of the verb *be*, while the other (*we arranged*) is contained within the subject, which begins with the relative pronoun *what*.

The examples in [35] show that the operation of forming a pseudo-cleft can be performed on [32i] but not on [32iv]. The reason is as follows:

● In [32i] *for them to meet the manager* is a syntactic constituent – a clause. As such, it can be placed in the position of complement to the verb *be*, as in [35ii].
● In [32iv] *them to be conspiring against us* is not a syntactic constituent and hence cannot function as complement to *be*, as shown in [35i]. It is not a syntactic constituent because it is a sequence of two complements of *believe*: *them* is object and *to be conspiring against us* is a non-finite clause functioning as catenative complement.

The distinction between ordinary and raised objects

In the simple catenative construction we have drawn a distinction between ordinary and raised SUBJECTS: in the complex construction there is a parallel distinction to be drawn between ordinary and raised OBJECTS. An ordinary object is semantically related to the matrix verb, while a raised object is not: it is located syntactically in the matrix clause but belongs semantically in the catenative complement.

The following examples show how the distinction between the two types of object matches that discussed earlier for the two types of subject:

[36]   ORDINARY OBJECT   RAISED OBJECT
    i a. We urged *a specialist* to   b. We wanted *a specialist* to
          examine Ed.   examine Ed.
   ii a. We urged *Ed* to be examined   b. We wanted *Ed* to be examined by
          by a specialist. (≠[ia])   a specialist. (=[ib])
  iii a.*We urged *there* to be   b. We wanted *there* to be
          an adult present.   an adult present.
   iv a.*We urged *it* to be clear   b. We wanted *it* to be clear
          to Ed that he was on probation.   to Ed that he was on probation.

- In [ia] the object *a specialist* is semantically related to the verb **urge**, indicating the person we spoke (or wrote) to with the aim of getting them to examine Ed.
- In [ib], however, there is no such direct semantic relation between *a specialist* and **want**. What we wanted was not a specialist, but the examination of Ed by a specialist.

This difference between the **urge** and **want** constructions can be brought out by the passive infinitival and dummy pronoun tests, modified to distinguish between different kinds of object rather than different kinds of subject.

- Example [iia] differs sharply in core meaning from [ia] because this time it is Ed, not a specialist, that we were trying to influence. But [iib] has the same truth conditions as [ib]: again, what we wanted was not Ed, but the examination of Ed by a specialist.
- While [iiib/ivb] are perfectly normal, [iiia/iva] are inadmissible, because the semantically empty *there* and *it* cannot enter into a semantic relation with **urge**: they cannot indicate who we tried to influence.[5]

5   Verbless clauses

Verbless clauses differ more radically in structure from canonical clauses than do non-finites: instead of merely failing to express primary tense or to allow for the marking of verbal mood, the predicator is missing altogether. They have a much more restricted distribution than non-finites, being associated primarily with the adjunct function.[6] Here they may function as complement to a preposition or else serve as adjunct directly.

(a) Verbless clauses as complement to a preposition

There is no preposition that licenses ONLY a verbless clause as complement, but *with* and *without* accept non-finite and verbless clauses, and a few others, such as *although*, *if*, *once*, and *while*, accept three kinds of clauses – finite, non-finite, and verbless:

[37] i a. *He'd been on the beach* [*without <u>anyone noticing him</u>*].   [non-finite]
      b. *He'd been on the beach* [*without <u>any sunscreen on</u>*].   [verbless]
     ii a. [*While <u>I was working in Boston</u>*] *I lived with my aunt.*   [finite]
      b. [*While <u>working in Boston</u>*] *I lived with my aunt.*   [non-finite]
      c. [*While <u>in Boston</u>*] *I lived with my aunt.*   [verbless]

---

[5] The verb **want** is somewhat exceptional in that the matrix clause in the complex catenative construction cannot be passivised, as seen in the ungrammaticality of **There was wanted to be an adult present*, etc. In other respects, however, it behaves like **believe** in [33], so that there is still evidence that the intervening NP is syntactically object of the matrix clause. Thus in the active it cannot be separated from the verb by an adjunct (cf. **We wanted desperately a specialist to examine Ed*), and we can't have a pseudo-cleft like **What we wanted was a specialist to examine Ed*.
[6] We leave aside in this chapter the construction where the absence of a verb is the result of 'gapping' in coordinative constructions, as in *Kim arrived on Tuesday <u>and everyone else the day after</u>* (see Ch. 14, §8.2).

- In [ib], *any sunscreen* is the subject and *on* is the predicate, consisting of the locative complement *on*. The relation is like that expressed in finite clauses by **be** (cf. *There wasn't any sunscreen on him*), though it would not be possible to insert **be** in [ib] itself.

- In [iic] the subject is missing as well as the predicator, but there is nevertheless a predicational relation understood: the adjunct can be expanded to *while I was in Boston*.

(b) Verbless clauses functioning directly as adjuncts

Verbless clauses with a subject + predicate structure can function as adjuncts, as illustrated in such examples as these:

[38]   i *The meeting finally over, they all adjourned to the local café.*
       ii *The passengers, many of them quite elderly, were forced to line up in the sun.*

The predicational relationship is again like the one expressed in finite clauses by **be**, as in examples like *The meeting was finally over*, or *Many of them were quite elderly*. The adjunct in [i] has a temporal interpretation (it means "when the meeting was finally over"). The one in [ii] is comparable to a supplementary relative clause ("many of whom were quite elderly").

Exercises

1. For each of the following examples, (a) say whether there is an NP in the matrix clause that is intended to be the antecedent for the **missing subject** of the underlined non-finite clause; (b) if there is, say which NP it is, or if there isn't, say what you would take to be the understood subject of the non-finite clause; and then (c) say whether you think a prescriptive grammarian would regard the example as an instance of the so-called **dangling modifier** construction.

   i From a 1987 opinion column by a British commentator:
   Having said all that, however, there is little doubt in my mind that Mrs. Thatcher is going to win and thoroughly deserves to do so.

   ii From a news story about causes of infantry battlefield deaths:
   Pinned down by gunfire and unreachable by medical evacuation teams, the main cause of death was loss of blood.

   iii In a restaurant review, describing a visit to a café:
   Meandering in at about 11:30 a.m. on a Sunday – somewhere between breakfast and brunch – the place was packed.

   iv In an editorial about a demonstration:
   Even allowing for the strong feelings on both sides, the behaviour of the demonstrators was indefensible.

   v From a journalist's description of a flight over the countryside:
   Flying low, a herd of cattle could be seen.

2. The verbs in the bracketed clauses below are all **plain forms**. Which of the clauses are **infinitival**, and hence **non-finite**?

   i *All I did was [give them your phone number].*

   ii *You can stay at our cabin, but [make sure you bring plenty of warm clothes].*

   iii *I recommend [that the proposal be approved without delay].*

   iv *They advised me [to reject your offer].*

v *Should we [give more money to charity than we do]?*

3. State the **function** of the underlined **non-finite clauses** in the following examples: subject in clause structure, complement of noun, etc.

   i *It gave us an opportunity to make a quick profit.*

   ii *This made obtaining a loan virtually impossible.*

   iii *We're looking forward to seeing you again.*

   iv *I can't decide what to do about it.*

   v *They are saving up to buy a washing-machine.*

   vi *They arrived home to find that the house had been burgled.*

   vii *Anyone knowing his whereabouts should contact the police.*

   viii *I'm afraid asking for special consideration won't do any good.*

   ix *The grid is to prevent cattle wandering off.*

   x *I'm determined to do better next time.*

4. For each adjective listed below, give an example of its predicative use licensing a **hollow infinitival clause** if that is possible; otherwise write 'none'. (The ones in bold italics have comparative and superlative forms, and of course your examples can involve those forms if you wish.)

   i *able*   vi *impossible*
   ii *bad*   vii *likely*
   iii *bright*   viii *nice*
   iv *difficult* ix *ready*
   v *eager*   x *suitable*

5. Classify the following **catenative** constructions as **simple** or **complex**.

   i *They invited me to join the board.*

   ii *I forgot to put the oven on.*

   iii *She intends at some stage to do a Ph.D.*

   iv *I appeal to you to give us a second chance.*

v *I promised them to be back by six.*

vi *Ed was told by his doctor to do exercises.*

vii *Max was advised to seek medical advice.*

viii *Get someone to help you.*

ix *Try to keep your eye on the ball.*

x *Not for nothing had I yearned to desist.*

6. Pick out the **catenative verbs** from the list of verbs given below, and for each of them answer the four questions:

   i *conjecture*   xi *lose*
   ii *continue*   xii *make*
   iii *convert*   xiii *pledge*
   iv *entertain*   xiv *proceed*
   v *expect*   xv *shower*
   vi *fail*   xvi *sink*
   vii *fall*   xvii *stop*
   viii *insist*   xviii *telephone*
   ix *instruct*   xix *tend*
   x *help*   xx *worry*

   (a) Which **catenative constructions** does it occur in: simple, complex, or both? Give examples.

   (b) Which of the four **types** of non-finite clause does it license as catenative complement? Give examples. (Bear in mind that many license more than one.)

   (c) If it occurs in the **simple** construction, does it take an **ordinary** or a **raised** subject? Cite relevant evidence.

   (d) If it takes an object in the complex construction, is it an **ordinary** or a **raised** object? Again, give evidence.

7. Think carefully about the syntax of these five verbs: [i] *allege*; [ii] *know*; [iii] *say*; [iv] *stand*; [v] *think*. Consider the full range of constructions in which each can appear. Are any of them catenative verbs in any of their uses? If so, what kind of **non-finite** subordinate clause do they take? Do they occur in **simple** or **complex** catenative constructions? With **ordinary** or **raised** subject or object? Are there any special syntactic or semantic restrictions on their catenative uses?

Coordination and more

1 Coordination as a non-headed construction

In a **coordination**, two or more elements of **equal status** are joined to make a larger unit. Special words called **coordinators** are used to mark this kind of joining. In [1], the joined elements are underlined, the larger unit formed is in brackets, and the coordinator is double-underlined.

[1]   i   [_Jane is a good teacher_ _and_ _her students really like her_].
     ii   _They offered us a choice of_ [_red wine, white wine_ _or_ _beer_].
    iii   _Her assistant is_ [_very young_ _but_ _a quick learner_].

The underlined constituents that are joined are called the **coordinates**. The coordinators illustrated are the most common ones in English: _and_, _or_ and _but_.

Internal syntax: the composition of coordinate structures

The coordinates of the examples in [1] are equal in status: each makes the same sort of contribution to the whole thing. They cannot be distinguished as head vs dependent(s). The constructions dealt with earlier (clauses, NPs, VPs, PPs, etc.) have all had heads. Coordination is different: it is a **non-headed** construction.

The coordinator indicates the particular relation holding between the coordinates. But there is a difference between the RELATION holding between the coordinates and the POSITION of the coordinator in the structure. The coordinator is not one of the coordinates; it forms a constituent with the coordinate following it.

For example, [1i] is not in three parts; it has two parts. The first immediate constituent is the clause _Jane is a good teacher_. The second, _and her students really like her_, is also a clause, but it is marked with a coordinator.

A simple piece of evidence for this is that a sentence division can occur between the two clauses. The two sentences might even be spoken by two different people, one adding to what the other said. And when we separate the two clauses like this, the coordinator goes with the second:

[2]   A: *She's a good teacher.*   B: *And her students really like her.*

We therefore use the term 'coordinate' not only for *her students really like her*, but also for *and her students really like her*. We distinguish them, when we need to, by calling the first a **bare coordinate** and the second an **expanded coordinate**. Here are simplified diagrams representing the structure for [1i] and [1iii]:

[3]

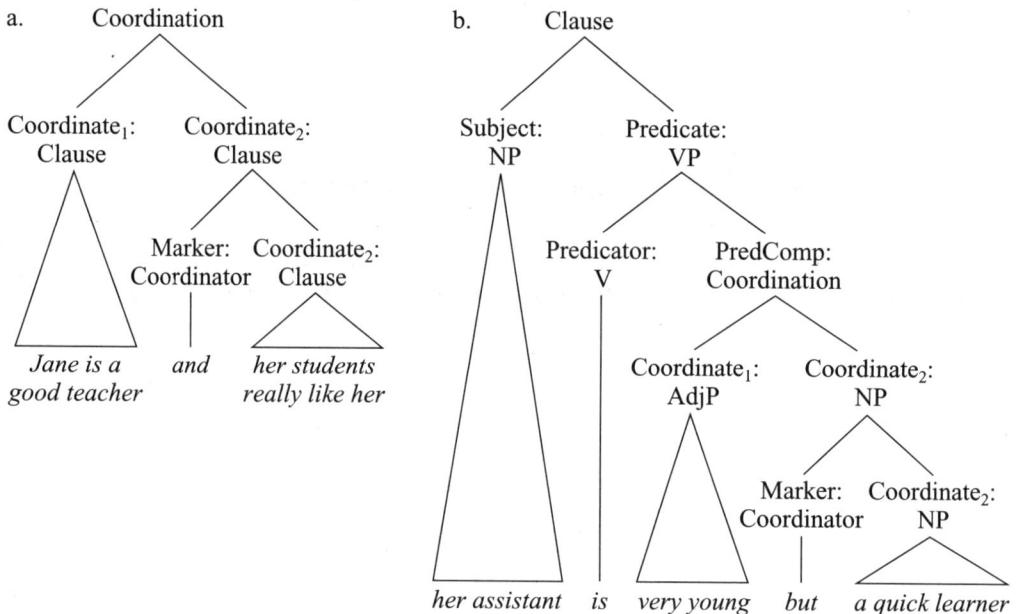

External syntax: where coordinate constituents can occur

Whether a coordination is admissible in a certain position depends primarily on the individual coordinates. In the default case, if each of the bare coordinates can occur on its own in some position, the coordination can occur there. Thus the admissibility of [1iii] is predictable from that of the separate clauses *Her assistant is very young* and *Her assistant is a quick learner*.

The fact that it is usually possible to replace a coordination by any one of the coordinates is the key reason for saying that coordination is a non-headed construction. This kind of replacement distinguishes coordination very sharply from head + dependent constructions, as illustrated in the following examples:

[4]   HEAD + DEPENDENT   COORDINATION

    i   a. *Pat is* [*very young*].   b. *Ed is* [*fond of kids*].   c. *I* [*went in and sat down*].

   ii   a. *Pat is* [*young*].   b. **Ed is* [*fond*].   c. *I went in*.

  iii   a. **Pat is* [*very*].   b. **Ed is* [*of kids*].   c. *I sat down*.

- In the [a] and [b] examples the bracketed expression consists of a head (doubly underlined) and a dependent. The dependent, *very*, is optional in [ia]; the phrase can be replaced by the head alone ([iia]), but not by the dependent ([iiia]). In [ib] the dependent *of kids* is obligatory, and the phrase can't be replaced by either the head ([iib]) or the dependent ([iiib]).

- But in [ic] the bracketed expression is a coordination, with the bare coordinates underlined. And in this case each coordinate can replace the whole coordination.

2   Distinctive syntactic properties of coordination

Prototypical coordination has three properties which we summarise in [5] and then explain in the following subsections.

[5]   i   The grammar sets no limit on how many coordinates a coordination can have.

      ii   The bare coordinates are required to be syntactically similar in certain ways.

    iii   An expanded coordinate can never be preposed.

2.1   Unlimited number of coordinates

A coordinate construction can have any number of coordinates from two up. Examples [1i] and [1iii] have two each, and [1ii] has three, while the following have four, five and six respectively, and there is clearly no grammatical limit on how many there can be:[1]

[6]   i   [*Free sexual expression, anarchism, mining of the irrational unconscious and giving it free rein*] *are what they have in common.*

     ii   . . .[*the caste system, witch-burning, harems, cannibalism, and gladiatorial combats*]. . .

    iii   *Nothing* [*noble, sublime, profound, delicate, tasteful or even decent*] *can find a place in such tableaux.*

2.2   Bare coordinates must be syntactically similar

In an acceptable coordination the coordinates are syntactically similar. The examples given so far contrast with the ungrammatical combinations shown in [7], where the underlined elements are manifestly quite different in kind:

---

[1] The examples in [6] are all from pages 74–8 of Allan Bloom's polemic against rock music in *The Closing of the American Mind* (New York: Simon and Schuster, 1987).

[7] i *We invited [*the Smiths* and *because they can speak Italian*].
     ii *She argued [*persuasively* or *that their offer should be rejected*].

Function rather than category is the crucial factor

In a large majority of the coordinate structures found in texts, the coordinates belong to the same CATEGORY. Thus in [1i] both coordinates are declarative main clauses, and in [1ii] all are NPs. But coordinates do not have to be of the same category. We saw this in [1iii], where *very young* is an AdjP and *a quick learner* an NP. Other examples are given in [8]:

[8] i   *He won't reveal* [*the nature of the threat* or *where it came from*].   [NP + clause]
     ii *I'll be back* [*next week* or *at the end of the month*].   [NP + PP]
     iii *He acted* [*selfishly* and *with no thought for the consequences*].   [AdvP + PP]
     iv *They rejected the* [*United States* and *British*] *objections*.   [Nom + Adj]

The coordinates here belong to the categories shown on the right; *where it came from* in [i] is, more specifically, a subordinate interrogative clause, while *United States* in [iv] is a nominal, the name we use for the unit intermediate between noun and noun phrase (Ch. 5, §1).

FUNCTION is more important than category in determining the permissibility of coordination. What makes the coordinations in [8] acceptable despite the differences of category is that each coordinate could occur alone with the same function.

[9] i a. *He won't reveal* *the nature of the*   b. *He won't reveal* *where it came from*.
           threat.
     ii a. *I'll be back* *next week*.   b. *I'll be back* *at the end of the month*.
     iii a. *He acted* *selfishly*.   b. *He acted* *with no thought for the*
                                                          consequences.
     iv a. *They rejected the* *United States*   b. *They rejected the* *British* *objections*.
           objections.

In each pair here the underlined element in [b] has the same function as that in [a]: complement of the verb in [i], time adjunct in [ii], manner adjunct in [iii], attributive modifier in [iv]. Contrast these examples with those in [10]:

[10] i *We're leaving* [*Rome* and *next week*].   [NP + NP]
     ii *I ran* [*to the park* and *for health reasons*]. [PP + PP]

Here the coordinates belong to the same category, but don't satisfy the requirement of functional likeness. Each could appear in place of the whole coordination, but the functions would be different:

[11] i a. *We're leaving* *Rome*.   b. *We're leaving* *next week*.
     ii a. *I ran* *to the park*.   b. *I ran* *for health reasons*.

● Example [ia] has *Rome* as direct object, but *next week* in [ib] is an adjunct of time.
● In example [iia], *to the park* is a goal complement, but *for health reasons* in [iib] is an adjunct of reason.

In [12] we state the likeness requirement a bit more precisely in the light of these observations.

[12]   A coordination of *X* and *Y* is admissible at a given place in sentence structure if and only if each of *X* and *Y* is individually admissible at that place with the same function.

To see how this works, consider the examples given in [13]:

[13]   i   a.   *We invited [Kim and Pat].*   b.   *She is [very young but a quick learner].*
   ii   a.   *We invited Kim.*   b.   *She is very young.*
  iii   a.   *We invited Pat.*   b.   *She is a quick learner.*

- In the [a] set, let *X* be *Kim* and let *Y* be *Pat*: we can replace *Kim and Pat* by *Kim*, and we can replace it by *Pat*, without change of function, so the coordination is admissible.
- The same holds in the [b] examples, where the coordinates are of different categories: *very young* and *a quick learner* can both stand in place of the coordination with the same function (predicative complement), so again this is an admissible coordination.

But [10i–ii] are not permitted by condition [12]. Although we can replace the coordination by each of the coordinates *Rome* and *next week* or *to the park* and *for health reasons*, the functions are not the same, as explained in the discussion of [11]. So condition [12] is not satisfied in these cases.

A number of qualifications and refinements to [12] are needed to cover various additional facts,[2] but [12] does represent the basic generalisation. And of course, [12] does not have any application to the combination of *X* and *Y* in a head + dependent construction.

Relativisation across the board

A special case of the syntactic likeness requirement applies in various constructions such as relative clauses. Compare the following examples:

[14]   i   *They attended the dinner but they are not members.*
  ii   *The people [who attended the dinner but who are not members] owe $20.*
  iii   **The people [who attended the dinner but they are not members] owe $20.*

In [i] we have a coordination of main clauses. If we embed this to make it a modifier in NP structure, we have to relativise BOTH clauses, not just one.

- In [ii] both coordinates are relative clauses (marked by *who*): *who attended the dinner* is a relative clause and so is *who are not members*. That makes the coordination admissible.

---

[2] One obvious case involves agreement features. *Kim and Pat like it*, for example, is sanctioned by the admissibility of *Kim likes it* and *Pat likes it*, not **Kim like it* and **Pat like it*. See also §7 below.

● In [iii], by contrast, just the first embedded clause is relativised: *who attended the dinner* is a relative clause but *they are not members* isn't, so the coordination is ungrammatical.

Relativisation is thus said to work **across the board**, i.e. to all coordinates. Example [14iii] clearly doesn't satisfy condition [12]: the second underlined clause cannot occur alone in this context (**The people <u>they are not members</u> owe $20* is ungrammatical), so the coordination of the two underlined clauses is inadmissible.

We find a sharp contrast here with head + dependent constructions:

[15]   i   <u>*They attended the dinner*</u> although <u>*they are not members*</u>.
    ii   *The people [<u>*who attended the dinner*</u> although <u>*who are not members*</u>] owe $20.
    iii   The people [<u>*who attended the dinner*</u> although <u>*they are not members*</u>] owe $20.

But in [14] is a coordinator. *Although* in [15] is not: it's a preposition with a content clause complement. When we relativise here, then, it is just the ***attend*** clause that is affected, as in [15iii] (the clause *they are not members* is the complement of a preposition inside the ***attend*** clause). Version [15ii] is ungrammatical, because the relative clause *who are not members* is complement of a preposition. This is not a permitted function for relative clauses.

2.3   Impossibility of preposing an expanded coordinate

It is completely inadmissible to prepose an expanded coordinate. There is a sharp contrast between the coordinator *but* and the preposition *although* when we apply preposing to [14i] and [15i]:

[16]   i   **But they are not members, they attended the dinner.*
    ii   *Although they are not members, they attended the dinner.*

The adjunct in [16ii] is placed at the beginning of the clause (instead of the end, as in [15i]), and this is fully acceptable. But an expanded coordinate behaves quite differently: changing the structure of [14i] in a comparable way makes [16i], which is completely unacceptable.

3   The order of coordinates

In the simplest and most straightforward cases, the order of the coordinates can be changed without perceptible effect on the acceptability or interpretation of the coordination:

[17]   i a. *We can have [<u>beans</u> or <u>broccoli</u>].*   b. *We can have [<u>broccoli</u> or <u>beans</u>].*
    ii a. *I was [<u>hungry</u> and <u>tired</u>].*   b. *I was [<u>tired</u> and <u>hungry</u>].*

Coordination of this kind is called **symmetric** – and contrasts with **asymmetric** coordination, such as we find in [18]:

[18] i a. *We were left [high and dry].*   b. **We were left [dry and high].*
     ii a. *I [got up and had breakfast].*   b. *I [had breakfast and got up].*

High and dry ("above the tide line, abandoned") is fossilised, so that the order is fixed. There are a good number of expressions of this kind: *aid and abet, betwixt and between, common or garden, hem and haw*, and so on.[3]

In [ii] the [a] and [b] versions are both fully acceptable, but they differ in their natural interpretations. This is because there is an implication that the events took place in the order described: in [iia] you understand that I got up and then had breakfast, while in [iib] I had breakfast first (in bed) and then got up.

There are a good many cases of *and* and *or* coordinations carrying implications beyond the basic additive or alternative meaning of the coordinator, and making the coordination asymmetric. A few examples are given in [19]:

[19] i   *He [parked his car at a bus-stop and was fined $100].*
     ii *[Pay within a week and you'll get a 10% discount].*
     iii *[We need to pay the bill today or we won't get the discount].*

- In [i] there is again an implication that the parking took place before the fining, but also a further implication that the fining was the CONSEQUENCE of the parking.
- In [ii] there is a conditional implication: "IF you pay within a week you get the discount".
- There is also a conditional implication in [iii], but with *or* the implicit condition is negative: "IF WE DON'T pay the bill today we won't get the discount".

4   The marking of coordination

In all the examples so far the coordination construction has been marked by a coordinator introducing the final coordinate. This is the most common pattern, but not the only one. There are three other possibilities.

(a) Unmarked coordination

Sometimes no coordinator is used, so the coordination is just a list. Commas are used to separate the items in writing.

[20] i *He felt [tired, depressed, listless].*   [*and* understood]
     ii *Did they ever offer you [red wine, white wine, beer]?*   [*or* understood]

(b) Repetition of coordinator

The coordinator can introduce all except the first of a series of coordinates. The repetition of the coordinator gives added emphasis to the relation it expresses:

---

[3] There are also numerous expressions where the order is not rigidly fixed but one order is usual and familiar, so that reversal sounds a bit strange: *knife and fork, hope and pray, men and women*. Fossilised expressions are another example of something that condition [12] doesn't cover: *hem and haw*, for example, cannot be replaced by either of its coordinates.

[21]   i   *He felt [tired, and depressed, and listless].*
       ii *They offered us a choice of [red wine or white wine or beer].*

(c) Correlative coordination

Although the first coordinate is never introduced by a coordinator, it can be marked by one of the determinatives *both*, *either*, and *neither*, paired respectively with the coordinators *and*, *or*, and *nor*, yielding **correlative coordination**:

[22]   i   *[Both the managing director and the company secretary] have been arrested.*
       ii *It's one of those movies that you'll [either love or hate].*
       iii *[Neither Sue nor her husband] supported the plan.*[4]

Two prescriptive grammar notes

1. *Both* is restricted to two-coordinate constructions. Around 1900, usage books began to claim that this was also true of *either* and *neither*, but the evidence does not support them.
2. *Both*, *either*, and *neither* are often found **displaced** from their basic position in one direction or the other. Thus we find phrases like *both* to [*the men and their employers*], where *both* is displaced to the left: the more basic order would be *to* [*both the men and their employers*], with *both* immediately before the first coordinate. We also find phrases like *rapid changes* [*in either the mixed liquor or in the effluent*], with *either* displaced to the right: the basic order would be *rapid changes either* [*in the mixed liquor or in the effluent*]. Most people accept the displaced versions without noticing them, but some prescriptive grammarians insist that all displacements are errors.

5   Layered coordination

Subject to a suitably refined condition along the lines of [12], a coordinate can belong to virtually any syntactic category. And that means a coordinate can itself be a coordination:

[23]   i   *[[Kim works in a bank and Pat is a teacher], but [Sam is still unemployed]].*
       ii *You can have [[pancakes] or [egg and bacon]].*
       iii *[[Laurel and Hardy] and [Fred and Ginger]] are my favorite movie duos.*

Here we have **layered coordination**: one coordinate structure functioning as a coordinate within a larger one. The outer square brackets enclose the larger coordination, with the inner brackets enclosing the coordinates within it; underlining then marks the coordinates at the lower level.

- In [i] the larger coordination has the form *X but Y*; the *Y* is just a clause, *Sam is still unemployed*, but the *X* is a coordination of the two underlined clauses. At the

---

[4] This illustrates the usual pattern for *neither*, but sometimes *or* rather than *nor* is found paired with it, as in *She was constrained by neither fashion or conformity.*

top level we contrast *employed* with *unemployed*; at the lower level we distinguish two jobs.

- In [ii] we have *X or Y* expressing a choice, where X is an NP and Y is a coordination.
- In [iii] we have *X and Y* at the top level, and at the lower level each of X and Y has the form of a coordination.

In the first two examples we have contrasting coordinators: *and* and *but* in [i], *or* and *and* in [ii]. This itself is sufficient to indicate that there is layered coordination. A single coordination with more than two coordinates may have just one coordinator or multiple occurrences of the same coordinator (as in [21]), but not two different coordinators.

6   Main-clause and lower-level coordination

Coordinations can occur at almost any place in constituent structure, from large constituents down to small ones like individual words. We make a general distinction between **main-clause coordination** and **lower-level coordination**:

[24] i   MAIN-CLAUSE COORDINATION
          [*It was a perfect day* and *everyone was in good spirits*.]   [main clauses]
     ii   LOWER-LEVEL COORDINATION
          a. He [*made a mistake* or *changed his mind*].   [VPs]
          b. We met [*my bank manager* and *her husband*] at the airport.   [NPs]
          c. She introduced me to her [*mother* and *father*].   [nouns]

Equivalent main-clause and lower-level coordinations

In many cases a lower-level coordination can be expanded into a logically equivalent main-clause one. This is so with all of the examples in [24ii], which can be expanded as follows:

[25] i   *He made a mistake* or *he changed his mind*.
     ii   *We met my bank manager at the airport* and *we met her husband at the airport*.
    iii   *She introduced me to her mother* and *she introduced me to her father*.

These are logically equivalent to [24iia–c]. There may be subtle meaning differences: the versions in [25ii–iii] do seem to separate the events more, so that you would be more likely to infer from [24iic] that she introduced me to her parents together, and from [25iii] that the introductions were on different occasions. But if [24iic] is true, then [25iii] is, and vice versa. That's what is meant by logical equivalence.

Non-equivalent main-clause and lower-level coordinations

There are some cases where pairs with lower-level and main-clause coordination are NOT logically equivalent:

[26] i a. *One teacher was [popular and patient].*
      b. *One teacher was popular and one teacher was patient.*
   ii a. *No one [stood up and complained].*
      b. *No one stood up and no one complained.*
   iii a. *She didn't have any [tea or coffee].*
      b. *She didn't have any tea or she didn't have any coffee.*

- In [ia] we have a single teacher with two properties; [ib] talks about two teachers.
- In [iia] no one both stood up and complained. But standing without complaining and complaining while seated are both excluded by [iib].
- In [iii], suppose she had tea but not coffee. Then [b] is true but [a] is false. (Compare with *She didn't have any tea **and** she didn't have any coffee*.)

7   Joint vs distributive coordination

One special case where a lower-level coordination is not equivalent to a corresponding main-clause coordination is in **joint coordination**, as opposed to the default **distributive coordination**:

[27] DISTRIBUTIVE COORDINATION   JOINT COORDINATION
   i a. *[Kim and Pat] are fine players.*   b. *[Kim and Pat] are a good pair.*
   ii a. *[Lee, Robin and Sam] like you.*   b. *[Lee, Robin and Sam] like each other.*

- In [i] the property of being a fine player applies to Kim and Pat separately – it's distributed between them; whereas that of making a good pair applies to the two of them jointly.
- In [ii] the property of liking you applies to Lee, Robin and Sam individually, but the property of liking each other can only apply to them jointly, as a group.

Joint coordination is almost always marked by the coordinator *and*. The central cases are NP coordinations. In cases like [ib] and [iib] it is not possible to replace the coordination by either coordinate alone: it is incoherent to say **Kim is a good pair* or **Lee likes each other*. Condition [12], therefore, doesn't cover joint coordination. Joint coordination has the following properties:

- It requires that each coordinate denote a member of a set.
- It requires that the coordinates belong to the same syntactic category.
- It disallows correlative coordination (**Both Kim and Pat are a good pair*).

8   Non-basic coordination

So far we have focused on what can be called **basic coordination** constructions, the ones where all the following properties hold:

[28] i The coordination consists of a **continuous sequence** of coordinates.
   ii The coordinates are either **bare** or **expanded** (by a coordinator or determinative).
   iii The coordinates can occur as **constituents** in non-coordination constructions.

In this final section we very briefly discuss various kinds of **non-basic coordination**, which depart from that elementary pattern.

8.1 Expansion of coordinates by modifiers

An expanded coordinate can contain a modifier as well as (or instead of) a marker:

[29]   i   *She comes home [every Christmas and <u>sometimes</u> at Easter <u>as well</u>].*
    ii *We could meet [on Friday or <u>alternatively</u> at the week-end <u>if you prefer</u>].*
    iii *She can speak [French but <u>not</u> German].*
    iv *He felt [<u>not</u> angry but <u>rather</u> deeply disappointed].*

The underlined expressions here are neither markers of the relation holding between the coordinates nor part of the bare coordinates. They are **modifiers** of the coordinate in which they are located. Sometimes they reinforce the relation expressed (*as well* or *too* reinforce the sense of *and*; *alternatively* or *else* reinforce *or*), and sometimes (as with *but not*) they indicate a contrast.

8.2 Gapped coordination

The middle part of a non-initial coordinate can be omitted if it is recoverable from the corresponding part of the initial coordinate:

[30]   i   *Her son lives in Boston and her daughter ___ in Chicago.*
    ii *Kim joined the company in 1988, and Pat ___ the following year.*
    iii *Sue wants to be a doctor, Max ___ a dentist.*

The gap marked '___' is understood by reference to the first coordinate: in these cases "lives", "joined the company", and "wants to be". The gap normally includes the verb, but can include other material too (as in [ii]). The antecedent needn't be a syntactic constituent; it isn't in [iii] (*wants to be a doctor* is made up of *wants* plus *to be a doctor*, so *wants to be* isn't a phrase).

8.3 Right nonce-constituent coordination

A third non-basic coordination construction is illustrated in [31]:

[31]   i   *We gave [<u>Kim a book</u> and <u>Pat a CD</u>].*
    ii *They stay [<u>in Boston during the week</u> and <u>with their parents at week-ends</u>].*
    iii *I could lend you [<u>$30 now</u> or <u>$50 at the end of the week</u>].*

There are two distinctive properties here.

• First, the coordinates do not form constituents in corresponding non-coordination constructions. In *We gave <u>Kim a book</u>,* for example, the underlined part does not form a single constituent: it is a sequence of two NPs.

- Second, the coordinates are required to be syntactically parallel: the separate elements of each coordinate must have the same functions in corresponding non-coordination constructions. In the clauses *We gave Kim a book* and *We gave Pat a CD*, both the first elements (*Kim* and *Pat*) are indirect objects and both second elements (*a book* and *a CD*) are direct objects, so [31i] is acceptable. The coordination is ungrammatical if the functions don't match in this way, as in *We gave [Kim $1,000 and generously to charity]*, with two objects in the first coordinate and a manner adjunct plus PP complement in the second.[5]

8.4   Delayed right constituent coordination

Another odd coordination construction is illustrated in the [a] members of the pairs in [32], where the [b] members are the corresponding basic coordinations:

[32]   i   a.   *She [noticed but didn't comment on] his inconsistencies.*
            b.   *She [noticed his inconsistencies but didn't comment on them].*
        ii a.   *[Two perfect and four slightly damaged] copies were found.*
            b.   *[Two perfect copies and four slightly damaged ones] were found.*

The delayed right constituent coordination construction has the following distinctive properties:

- At least one of the coordinates does not form a constituent in a corresponding non-coordination construction. In *She didn't comment on his inconsistencies*, for example, the underlined sequence is not a constituent, since *on* is head of the PP *on his inconsistencies*. Similarly *two perfect* does not form a constituent *two perfect copies*, which consists of the determiner *two* plus the head nominal *perfect copies*.
- The element on the right of the coordination (doubly underlined) is understood as related to each coordinate. In [i], for example, *his inconsistencies* is understood both as object of the verb *noticed* and as object of the preposition *on*.

The term **delayed right constituent coordination** reflects the salient difference between this construction and basic coordination. In the latter the doubly underlined expression occurs earlier, as the rightmost constituent of the first coordinate (and then is repeated, normally in reduced form, at the end of the second): *She noticed his inconsistencies but didn't comment on them*. In the non-basic version, therefore, this element appears to be held back, delayed.

8.5   End-attachment coordination

One more non-basic coordination construction we should mention is seen in the [a] members of the following pairs:

---

[5] Nonce constituents have constituent status only for one special occasion, by courtesy of the coordination relation. We call this construction **right nonce-constituent coordination** because the coordinations occur to the right of the head (predicator) of the clause – *gave*, *stay* and *lend* in our examples.

[33]   i a. *Kim was included on the shortlist, but not Pat.*
         b. *[Kim but not Pat] was included on the shortlist.*
       ii a. *They've charged the boss with perjury – and her secretary.*
         b. *They've charged [the boss and her secretary] with perjury.*

They differ from the more elementary [b] versions in that the second coordinate (including the coordinator) is not adjacent to the first but is attached at the end of the clause. The relation marked by the coordinators *but* and *and* is still expressed, but in the [a] examples the constituents related by the coordinators don't make up a constituent.

Exercises

1. Consider the **determinatives** *both, either,* and *neither* that occur in **correlative** coordinations. Which, if any, can occur introducing **main clause coordinations**? Give grammatical and ungrammatical examples to support your answer.

2. In Ch. 7 we referred to cases like *What are you looking at?* as illustrating **preposition stranding**. Consider the question of whether **coordinators** can be stranded, illustrating your discussion with grammatical and ungrammatical sequences of words as appropriate.

3. Some prescriptive manuals and English teachers advise against beginning a sentence with a **coordinator**. Choose a published work that you think is a good example of written Standard English, preferably one that you enjoy and admire, and read from the beginning looking for a sentence that begins with a coordinator (*And, Or, But*). How many sentences did you have to read before you found one?

4. Choose a published work that you think is a good example of written Standard English, preferably one that you enjoy and admire, and read it from the beginning, keeping count of each **coordinate structure** you encounter. At what point do you find the first one that has coordinates of different categories? How many sentences did you have to read before you found one?

5. Explain why the following coordinations are asymmetric.

   i *He lost control of the car and crashed into a tree.*
   ii *Talk to me like that again and you'll be fired.*
   iii *Don't tell anyone or we'll be in heaps of trouble.*
   iv *You can't work 18 hours a day and not endanger your health.*
   v *You can eat as much of this as you like and not put on any weight.*

6. Explain why the following lower-level coordinations are not equivalent to main-clause coordination.

   i *Who went to the movies and left the house unlocked?*
   ii *Did she take the car and go to the beach?*
   iii *The last and most telling objection concerned the cost.*
   iv *They could find nothing wrong with the battery or with the thermostat.*
   v *One guy was drunk and abusive.*

7. For each of the following examples, say which kind of non-basic coordination construction it exemplifies.

   i *I'd expected Jill to back us, but not her father.*
   ii *It was criticised by some for being too long and by others for being too short.*
   iii *Both the British and the French delegates supported the proposal.*
   iv *You can have a banana or else an apple instead.*
   v *Max left the country in May and the rest of the family in June.*

15 Information packaging in the clause

1 Introduction

The bulk of this chapter is concerned with a family of constructions which we illustrate initially in the [a] members of the following pairs:

[1]
  i   a. *Her son was arrested by the police.* b. *The police arrested her son.*
  ii a. *It's unusual for her to be this late.* b. *For her to be this late is unusual.*
  iii a. *There were two doctors on the plane.* b. *Two doctors were on the plane.*

Example [ia] belongs to the **passive** construction, [iia] to the **extraposition** construction, and [iiia] to the **existential** construction. These constructions have the following properties in common:

[2]
  i They are non-canonical constructions; characteristically, they have a syntactically more elementary or basic counterpart, given here in the [b] examples.
  ii They generally have the same core meaning as their basic counterpart, but they present – or 'package' – the information differently.

The basic counterpart

The [b] examples in [1] are all structurally simpler than those in [a], as is evident from the fact that the latter contain extra words – the auxiliary *be* and the preposition *by* in [ia], the dummy pronouns *it* and *there* in [iia/iiia]. In the examples chosen, the [b] versions are all canonical clauses, but there are similar pairs where both members are non-canonical, as in the negatives *Her son wasn't arrested by the police* and *The police didn't arrest her son.*

238

For the passive, there is an established name for the basic counterpart: [1ib] is an **active** clause. But there is no established name for [iib]: this is simply the non-extraposition counterpart of [iia]. Similarly, [iiib] is just the non-existential counterpart of [iiia]. And this will be the case with the other constructions we deal with in this chapter: we have special names for the non-basic constructions, but not for their basic counterparts.

Exceptional cases without a grammatically well-formed basic counterpart

We said that the non-canonical clauses CHARACTERISTICALLY have syntactically more basic counterparts. There are exceptions. In some cases the basic counterpart is in fact ungrammatical. This can arise, for example, with the existential construction:

[3]   EXISTENTIAL   NON-EXISTENTIAL
     i   a. *There was a bottle of wine on the table.*   b. *A bottle of wine was on the table.*
     ii a. *There is plenty of time.*   b. **Plenty of time is.*

Both versions are permitted in [3i] (or in our original pair [1iii]), but only the existential version is grammatical in [3ii]. The verb *be* can't normally occur without an internal complement, so [3iib] is ungrammatical. There are other cases of this sort, as we'll see later.

▨ Core meaning and information packaging

The pairs in [1] have the same core meaning in the sense explained in Ch. 13, §4.2: since they are declarative clauses, having the same core meaning is a matter of having the same truth conditions. With pair [i], for example, if it's true that her son was arrested by the police it must be true that the police arrested her son, and vice versa And likewise if [ia] is false, [ib] must be false too. The differences have to do not with the information presented but how it is organised and presented: the two clauses in each pair PACKAGE THE INFORMATION DIFFERENTLY. We refer collectively to the passive, extraposition and existential constructions – and others to be introduced below – as **information-packaging constructions**: they depart from the most elementary syntactic structure in order to package the information in special ways. Our major concern in this chapter will therefore be to describe the syntactic differences between these constructions and their basic counterparts and to investigate the factors which favour or disfavour the use of one of these constructions rather than the more basic counterpart.

Exceptional cases where the core meanings are different

We have said that clauses belonging to one of the information-packaging constructions GENERALLY have the same core meaning as their basic counterpart: the qualification is needed because there are special factors that can cause a difference in the core meanings. Consider the following existential/non-existential pair:

[4]	EXISTENTIAL	NON-EXISTENTIAL
	a. *There weren't many members present.*	b. *Many members weren't present.*

Suppose we are talking about the annual general meeting of a large organisation. It's perfectly possible for [b] to be true while [a] is false: thousands of members were not present, so [b] is true, yet thousands of others were present, making [a] false. These sentences are not saying the same thing in different ways: they're saying different things.

The reason has to do with the fact that the clauses contain a quantifier (*many*) and a negative word (*weren't*). The negative comes first in [a] but the quantifier is first in [b]. The relative order affects the scope of the negative, as explained in Ch. 8, §5. This isn't a fact about existential clauses: any clause in which a negative word precedes a quantifier tends to be interpreted with the negative including the quantifier in its scope.

Setting aside the special factor of scope, corresponding existential and non-existential clauses do have the same truth conditions, as illustrated in [3i]. And that is also true for the other constructions considered. In the remainder of this chapter we will set aside such special factors as scope.

2   Passive clauses

The first information-packaging construction we consider is the **passive** clause. Passive clauses contrast with **active** clauses in a system called **voice**, so we consider that first.

2.1   The system of voice

A system of voice is one where the terms differ as to how the SYNTACTIC FUNCTIONS are aligned with SEMANTIC ROLES. Usually there are also formal differences either associated with the verb (e.g. special inflection or auxiliaries) or associated with the NPs (e.g. special case marking or prepositions).

The general terms **active** and **passive** are based on the semantic role of the subject in clauses expressing actions:

[5]   In clauses describing some deliberate action, the subject is normally aligned with the active participant (the actor) in the active voice, but with the passive participant (the patient) in the passive voice.

- In [1ib], for example, *the police* refers to the actor and is subject; *her son* refers to the patient, yet is subject in [1ia].
- There are also differences associated with the verb and one of the NPs: [1ia] contains the passive auxiliary verb *be*, and the second NP is complement of the preposition *by*.

Many clauses, of course, do not describe actions, but they can be assigned to the active and passive categories on the basis of their syntactic likeness to clauses like those in [1i]:

[6]   ACTIVE VOICE   PASSIVE VOICE
     i   a. *Everyone saw the accident.*   b. *The accident was seen by everyone.*
     ii   a. *His colleagues dislike him.*   b. *He is disliked by his colleagues.*

Seeing and disliking aren't actions, but the syntactic relation between the members of these pairs is the same as that between [1ib] and [1ia], so they can be classified as active and passive pairs.

2.2   Differences between active and passive clauses

Examples like [1ia], and the [b] examples in [6], illustrate the most straightforward kind of passive clause. We'll look first at how they differ from their active counterparts, and then extend the account to cover other passive constructions.

Structural diagrams for the examples in [6i] are shown in [7]. The syntactic differences are summarised in [8]:

[7]   a.   Clause / Subject: NP (*everyone*) — Predicate: VP / Predicator: V (*saw*) — Object: NP (*the accident*)
    b.   Clause / Subject: NP (*the accident*) — Predicate: VP / Predicator: V (*was*) — Comp: Clause / Predicate: VP / Predicator: V (*seen*) — Internalised Comp: PP / Head: Prep (*by*) — Comp: NP (*everyone*)

[8]   i   The subject of the active (*everyone*) appears in the passive as complement of the preposition *by* in a PP functioning as complement.
    ii   The direct object of the active appears as subject of the passive.
    iii   The passive has auxiliary **be** carrying the tense inflection and taking as complement a subjectless non-finite clause with a head (*seen*) in past participle form.

We use the term **internalised complement** to label the function of *by everyone*,[1] because when we replace an active clause by its corresponding passive, the active

---

[1] It is more usually referred to as the agent, but we're avoiding that term because it is also in widespread use as the name of a semantic role, equivalent to 'actor'. As we just argued in discussing [6], the complement of *by* very often does not have that semantic role.

clause subject appears internal to the passive VP, like internal complements (see Ch. 4, §1).

The auxiliary *be* of passive clauses takes on the inflectional properties of the verb of the corresponding active, except that any person and number features are determined by AGREEMENT WITH THE PASSIVE SUBJECT (compare *was* above with *were* in *The accidents were seen by everyone*).

Voice and information packaging

The voice system provides different ways of aligning the two major NPs in a clause with the syntactic functions and hence of selecting their order of appearance. Generally the subject comes first in the clause and the object or internalised complement later. A major factor influencing the choice between these orders of presentation has to do with the **familiarity** status of the NPs. This involves the contrast between **old** (familiar) and **new** (unfamiliar) information.

To illustrate the contrast between old and new, suppose a conversation began with one of the following sentences:

[9]   i *The plumber says the dishwasher can't be repaired*, but I don't think *that's* true.
      ii *My neighbour* came over this morning; *she* asked *me* if *I*'d seen *her cat*.

- In [i] the first underlined sequence represents new information: I'm telling you this, not treating it as something you are already familiar with. The word *that* is interpreted as "the dishwasher can't be repaired", which is old – it's part of the information that has already been introduced.
- But information is to be understood in a broad sense that covers entities as well as facts or propositions. *My neighbour* and *her cat* in [ii] refer to entities that haven't been mentioned previously, so they represent new information. *She* is old information, since it makes a second reference to my neighbour. *Me* and *I* count as old because the deictic 1st and 2nd person pronouns refer to participants in the discourse who can always be regarded as familiar (if I'm telling you something, then there are at least two people in the world that we can both agree that we already know about: me and you).

In English there is a broad preference for packaging information so that SUBJECTS REPRESENT OLD INFORMATION. It's only a preference, of course: there's no question of a ban on subjects being new (that's obvious from [9], where both *the plumber* and *my neighbour* are new). But the preference is strong enough to be a clear influence on the choice between equivalent active and passive clauses. Compare these:

[10]   i a. *A dog attacked me in the park.*   b. *I was attacked by a dog in the park.*
      ii a. *I bought a tie.*   b. *?A tie was bought by me.*

- In [i], the active example [a] has a new-information subject, and [b], the passive, has an old-information subject. The passive version will often be preferred in such pairs (though [ia] is nonetheless perfectly grammatical and acceptable).

- Things are different in [ii], however. Suppose the context is one where I've just said that I've been shopping: *a tie* is new, while *I* (or *me*) is old information. Here only the active version will normally be acceptable.

Active is the **default** in the voice system. The use of actives is not restricted by actual **constraints** relating to the combination of old and new information, but the passive is. This is the generalisation that holds:

[11]   In a passive clause it is not normally possible for the **subject** to be **new** when the **internalised complement** is **old**.

There is far more to the choice between active and passive clauses than there is space to discuss here. But all we want to point out is that while they normally have the same core meaning, they are NOT FREELY INTERCHANGEABLE. They differ in how the information is presented, and one important factor in the choice between them concerns the status of the two major NPs as representing old or new information.

2.3   Short passives

In almost all cases the internalised complement is OPTIONAL. The passive clauses with no internalised complement are called **short passives**; the ones discussed so far are called **long passives**. Short passives are actually much more frequent than long passives. They have an important function: they enable us to LEAVE OUT something that would be obligatory in the active, namely a main clause subject. In [12] the active versions are not grammatical, but the passive ones are fine:

[12]   ACTIVE VOICE   PASSIVE VOICE
   i a. *Built the house in 1960.   b. *The house was built in 1960.*
  ii a. *Damaged your car.*   b. *Your car was damaged.*
 iii a. *Know little about the cause of ALS.* b. *Little is known about the cause of ALS.*
  iv a. *Made mistakes.*   b. *Mistakes were made.*

The passive versions enable us to avoid saying anything about

- who built the house (we may have no idea who it was, or it may not be relevant);
- which employee of ours accidentally damaged your car (there are liability issues!);
- who exactly is ignorant (nobody knows the cause of amyotrophic lateral sclerosis); or
- who blundered (people don't always want to directly admit error).

2.4   Lexical restrictions

Most transitive active clauses have passive counterparts, but not all. Some exceptional verbs are (either generally or in certain uses) inadmissible in passives:

[13] i a. *The town <u>boasts</u> a great beach.*   b. **A great beach is <u>boasted</u> by the town.*
      ii a. *Max <u>lacks</u> tact.*   b. **Tact is <u>lacked</u> by Max.*
     iii a. *Jill <u>has</u> three wonderful kids.*   b. **Three wonderful kids are <u>had</u> by Jill.*
      iv a. *The jug <u>holds</u> three litres.*   b. **Three litres are <u>held</u> by the jug.*

Boast and ***lack*** occur only in active clauses. ***Have*** occurs in passive constructions, in its dynamic sense, as in *She was happy to find there was both water and gas <u>to be had</u>*. ***Hold*** occurs in passives like *It was held in place by duct tape*, but not where it means "contain".

2.5   Passives of ditransitive actives

Ditransitive clauses have two objects. Usually the passive of a ditransitive has a subject corresponding to the first one, the **indirect** object. However, some speakers (BrE rather than AmE) have an alternative passive construction, illustrated by [14iib], in which the subject corresponds to the **direct** object of the active ditransitive, but the passive of the construction with one object and a PP complement, as in [14iiib], is widely preferred over it:

[14] i a. *The boss gave <u>me</u> the key.*   b. *<u>I</u> was given the key by the boss.*
      ii a. *The boss gave me <u>the key</u>.*   b. [%]*<u>The key</u> was given me by the boss.*
     iii a. *The boss gave <u>the key to me</u>.*   b. *<u>The key</u> was given <u>to me</u> by the boss.*

2.6   Prepositional passives

The subject of a passive may correspond to an object of a preposition rather than of the verb (we cite short passives in [15] for greater naturalness; the [b] examples are not exactly equivalent to the actives shown in [a]):

[15] i a. *People are looking <u>into</u> the matter.*   b. *<u>The matter</u> is being looked <u>into</u>.*
      ii a. *They took advantage <u>of</u> us.*   b. *<u>We</u> were taken advantage <u>of</u>.*
     iii a. *Someone has slept <u>in</u> this bed.*   b. *<u>This bed</u> has been slept <u>in</u>.*

In the [b] examples the doubly underlined preposition is stranded: no actual complement follows it, but an understood complement is retrievable from the subject. Clauses of this kind are called **prepositional passives**. Two subtypes can be distinguished.

(a) Specified preposition

In [15i–ii] the preposition is **specified** by the preceding verb or verbal idiom. ***Look*** is a prepositional verb (see Ch. 7, §7.2) specifying *into* as preposition for the meaning "investigate", and the idiom ***take*** *advantage* specifies *of*. This type of passive has **lexical** restrictions on its availability: some verbs or verbal idioms permit the prepositional passive and some don't. ***Come*** *across* (meaning "encounter") and ***lose patience with*** don't permit it:

[16]   i   a. *We came across some old letters.*   b. **Some old letters were come across.*
       ii a. *He lost patience with the children.*   b. **The children were lost patience with.*

(b) Unspecified preposition

In [15iii] the preposition is not specified; it has its ordinary meaning and in the active can be replaced by other prepositions: *Someone has slept under / on / near this bed.* Passives of this type are admissible only if the clause describes some significant EFFECT on the subject referent or some significant PROPERTY of it. Example [15iiib] is acceptable because sleeping in a bed affects it (that's why we change the sheets). And *Nauru can be driven around in about half an hour* is acceptable because if you can drive around a country in two hours, it is very small, and that's a significant property. On the other hand, **The bed was sat near* is not acceptable: sitting near the bed wouldn't affect it, and doesn't suggest any significant property of it.

2.7   *Get*-passives

The passive clauses considered so far have the auxiliary *be*; we can call them ***be*-passives**. There is also a passive with ***get*** instead of ***be***:

[17]   BE-PASSIVE   GET-PASSIVE
       i   a. *Pat was bitten by a snake.*   b. *Pat got bitten by a snake.*
       ii a. *They weren't charged until later.*   b. *They didn't get charged until later.*
       iii a. *She was elected mayor in 1990.*   b. *She got elected mayor in 1990.*
       iv a. *Several shots were heard.*   b. **Several shots got heard.*

Be is an auxiliary verb, but ***get*** isn't. In the negative and interrogative, therefore, ***get***-passives require the dummy auxiliary ***do***, as seen in [iib].

The ***be***-passive is stylistically neutral, but ***get***-passives are a mark of **informal style**. They are used for describing situations where the subject-referent is involved in bringing the situation about, or where there is an adverse or beneficial effect on the subject-referent, as in [i–iii]. If no such factor is present, as with the inanimate subject in [iv], only the ***be***-passive is acceptable.

2.8   Bare passives

Be*-passives** and ***get*-passives** have ***be and ***get*** as catenative verbs with past-participial complements. Past-participial clauses also occur elsewhere with passive interpretation, and we call these **bare passives** because they lack the ***be*** and ***get*** markers. They can be either **complements** or **modifiers**.

▓ (a) Bare passives as complement in complex catenatives

A few verbs that occur in the complex catenative construction – the one with an 'intervening NP' (Ch. 13, §4.3) – license bare passives as complement. They include *have*, *get* (in a different use from that of *get*-passives), *order*, and certain sense verbs, such as *see*:

[18]   i   *We had the documents checked by a lawyer.*
       ii   *You should get yourself vaccinated against measles.*
       iii   *She ordered the records destroyed.*
       iv   *He saw his son knocked down by a bus.*

▓ (b) Bare passives as modifier

As modifiers, bare passives function in the structure of NPs:

[19]   i   *We want [a house built after 1990].*
       ii   *[The complaint made by her lawyer] is being investigated.*

These are comparable to relative clauses in *be*-passive form: *a house which was built after 1990*; *the complaint that was made by her lawyer*.

2.9   Adjectival passives

Be can be followed by an adjective, and sometimes an adjective is formed from the past participle of a verb. This case must be distinguished from the *be*-passive. We can see this from the ambiguity of examples like [20], which can be either:

[20]   a. *Her leg was broken.*   b. *They were married.*

- As a passive clause, [a] describes an event, as in *Her leg was broken in a hockey accident*. But it can also be a **complex-intransitive** clause – an intransitive clause containing a predicative complement, as in *Her leg was sore*. In this interpretation, [a] describes a state resulting from an earlier event: *She was using crutches because her leg was broken*. Here we say that *broken* (not the whole clause) is an **adjectival passive**.
- The *be*-passive reading of [b] also involves an event, as in *They were married in the College Chapel*, but the complex-intransitive interpretation describes a state resulting from a prior event, as in *They were still happily married*.

The key syntactic difference between the constructions is that THE ADJECTIVAL PASSIVE CAN OCCUR WITH COMPLEX-INTRANSITIVE VERBS OTHER THAN *BE*:

[21]   a. *Her leg felt broken.*   b. *They stayed married.*

Here *broken* and *married* have only their adjectival, state interpretation.

Some writers on scientific topics appear to think that passives are required for objectivity (*The mice were anaesthetised* rather than *We anaesthetised the mice*). At the other extreme, some usage books and style guides insist that the passive is better avoided altogether. Both policies are excessive: passives are fully grammatical and acceptable, and a passive is often the right stylistic choice.

Short passives are sometimes criticised for a lack of frankness: they conceal the identity of the agent. In *Mistakes were made* we are not told who made the mistakes. But that is not an objection to passive clauses; there are many ways of avoiding identifying the responsible agent. For example, *Mistakes occurred* does not specify who made the mistakes either, but that is not a passive clause.

3   Extraposition

There are actually two **extraposition** constructions: **subject** extraposition and **internal complement** extraposition. Subject extraposition (the one illustrated in our original example [1iia]) is more commonly encountered, so we'll deal with it first.

3.1   Subject extraposition

Clauses with a subordinate clause subject generally have variants with the subordinate clause at the end and dummy *it* as subject:

[22]	BASIC VERSION		VERSION WITH EXTRAPOSITION
i	a. *That he was acquitted disturbs her.*	b.	*It disturbs her that he was acquitted.*
ii	a. *How she escaped remains a mystery.*	b.	*It remains a mystery how she escaped.*
iii	a. *To give up now would be a mistake.*	b.	*It would be a mistake to give up now.*

At least two distinctive properties of the subject outlined in Ch. 4, §2.1 show that the dummy *it* must be the subject: it occurs before the VP, in the basic subject position, and it occurs after the auxiliary when there is subject–auxiliary inversion (the closed interrogative counterpart of [ib], for example, is *Does it disturb her that he was acquitted?*).

We call the subordinate clause in the [b] version an **extraposed subject**, but that doesn't mean it's a kind of subject; it's an element in extraposed position, outside the VP, that CORRESPONDS to the subject of the basic version.

With minor exceptions, extraposition is admissible only with subordinate clauses. Note, for example, the contrast between [22i] and [23]:

[23]   a. *His letters disturb her.*   b. **It disturbs her his letters.*

The subject in [a] is an NP and cannot be extraposed. The subordinate clauses concerned are predominantly declarative and interrogative content clauses and infinitivals, as in [22i–iii] respectively. (Gerund-participials are also found extraposed under sharply limited conditions; *It's been a pleasure talking to you* is an example.)

▨ Extraposition: more frequent and less constrained than the alternative

In [22] we have labelled the version on the left as the syntactically basic one: the one on the right has the extra pronoun *it*, and has a structure not found in any canonical clause. However, in pairs like these there are good reasons for regarding the version with extraposition as the default, as far as information packaging is concerned.

In the first place, it is much more common. This is because subordinate clauses tend to be **heavier** (longer and structurally more complex) than NPs, and there is in general a preference for placing heavy material at the end of the matrix clause, where it's easier to process.

Secondly, there are informational constraints applying to the version without extraposition but not to the one with extraposition, so extraposition is acceptable in a wider range of contexts. The context for a non-extraposed subject must permit its content to be taken as old information – familiar to the addressee, either through previous mention or the addressee's current knowledge. Take the following two passages, from a science article on human skin:

[24]   i *It is not easy to see, however, what positive advantages may have been responsible for human evolution toward nakedness, as compared with other primates. [It has been suggested <u>that lack of a heavy fur may have had some adaptive value for running and hunting in the open savannas</u>], but this is conjectural.*

       ii *In the effort to enhance its attractiveness, men and women submit their skin to systematic stretching, scraping, gouging, soaking and burning . . . To give it a 'healthy' tan, the skin is ritualistically exposed to excessive and injurious doses of sunlight and wind.*
            [<u>That the skin survives these daily torments</u> is a remarkable tribute to its toughness.]

- The non-extraposed version of the bracketed clause in [i] would be completely unacceptable in that context. The content of the underlined clause can't be construed as old. The writer is introducing a new idea that might represent a positive advantage of nakedness: the content clause expresses the main informational content of the bracketed clause, and has to be extraposed.

- In [ii] the first paragraph lists a number of 'torments' inflicted on the skin, and then we get a non-extraposed subject clause (underlined) that does represent old information: the reader of course knows already that our skin survives. What is new in this sentence is that our skin's durability indicates how tough it is. That means the constraint on using the non-extraposed version is satisfied. It doesn't mean, though, that we MUST use the extraposed version. It would also be acceptable to use the default version, with extraposition: *It is a remarkable tribute to its toughness that the skin survives these daily torments.*

3.2   Internal complement extraposition

Extraposition of an internal complement is found predominantly in complex-transitive constructions, where it is just about obligatory:

[25] i a. *I find *that he gave up* disappointing.   b. *I find* it *disappointing* that he gave up.
      ii a. *She considers *that I didn't consult*   b. *She considers* it *quite outrageous*
             her *quite outrageous.*   *that I didn't consult her.*

- In [b] dummy *it* appears as object and the subordinate clause as extraposed object.
- The [a] versions are inadmissible by virtue of having the subordinate clause located between the verb and another complement.

4 Existential clauses

The pronoun *it* is not the only pronoun used as a dummy in English. The spelling *there* is today used for two different words, one a locative rhyming with *dare* and meaning "in or at that place" (as in *Put it there*), and the other a dummy pronoun pronounced unstressed with a reduced vowel. The primary role of the dummy *there* is to fill the syntactic subject position in clauses like the [b] examples in [26], which are called **existential clauses**:

[26]   BASIC VERSION   EXISTENTIAL CLAUSE
      i a. *Some keys were near the safe.*   b. *There were some keys near the safe.*
      ii a. *A nurse was present.*   b. *There was a nurse present.*

There is the subject of the existential clauses in [26], just as *it* is subject in the extraposed subject construction, and similar arguments support this conclusion:

- *there* occupies the basic subject position before the VP;
- in subject–auxiliary inversion constructions it occurs after the auxiliary, as in *Was there a nurse present?*

It is significant that *there* also occurs as subject in interrogative tags, as in:

[27]   *There was a nurse present, wasn't there?*

Only pronouns are admissible in a tag like the one here, as we noted in Ch. 9, §2.3. That means we not only know dummy *there* is a subject, we know it is a pronoun.

We will refer to *some keys* and *a nurse* in [26ib] and [26iib] as **displaced subjects**. A displaced subject (like an extraposed subject) is not a kind of subject; it's the phrase that corresponds to the subject of the syntactically more basic construction.[2]

Bare existentials

One common kind of existential clause contains just dummy *there*, the verb **be**, and a displaced subject (possibly with optional adjuncts that have no bearing on the

---

[2] *There* is an unusual kind of subject: it has no inherent number but takes on the number of the displaced subject – plural in [26ib], with *were* as the verb, and singular in [iib], with *was*. It's comparable to the relative pronouns *which* and *who*, which take on the number of their antecedent (*the guys who were talking* vs *the guy who was talking*). Note, however, that in informal style, especially in present tense declaratives with reduced *is*, many speakers treat *there* as always singular: they say %*There's a few problems* instead of *There are a few problems*. Prescriptivists disapprove, but the usage is too well established to be treated as an occasional slip.

structure or acceptability). We call these **bare existentials**. They have NO CORRE-
SPONDING BASIC VERSION. The verb *be* normally requires an internal complement,
so the basic versions that would have corresponded to bare existentials are all
ungrammatical:

[28]   BARE EXISTENTIAL CLAUSE   UNGRAMMATICAL BASIC VERSION
    i a. *There is a god.*   b. **A god is.*
    ii a. *There are many species of spiders.*   b. **Many species of spiders are.*
    iii a. *There has been no news of them.*   b. **No news of them has been.*
    iv a. *There was a serious accident.*   b. **A serious accident was.*

The general term 'existential' is based on examples like [ia] and [iia] in [28], which
are used to assert the existence of various things. But the existential construction
described in this section covers other uses than merely talking about existence.

Extended existentials

There are also **extended existentials**, which contain an additional element, the **extension**, within the VP. Some examples are given in [29], with the extension underlined.

[29]   i   LOCATIVE   *There's a snake <u>in the grass</u>.*
       ii TEMPORAL   *There's another meeting <u>this afternoon</u>.*
       iii PREDICATIVE ADJECTIVE   *There are still some seats <u>available</u>.*
       iv HOLLOW INFINITIVAL   *There is poor old Albert <u>to consider</u>.*

- **Locative** complements as in [i] are particularly common extensions.
- **Temporal** extensions occur with displaced subjects that denote events, e.g.
  another meeting in [ii].
- **Predicative** complement extensions are restricted to a range of adjectives denoting temporary states as in [iii], e.g. *absent, available, missing, present, vacant*,
  and *wrong* (as in *There's something wrong*). Most adjectives don't occur as
  extensions like this: a sentence like *Some politicians are honest* doesn't have a
  corresponding bare existential **There are some politicians honest*.
- **Infinitival** extensions are hollow clauses in the sense of Ch. 13, §2.4: they have a gap
  in internal complement function, usually object, as in [iv], where there is a missing
  object for *consider*: we interpret [iv] as being about consideration for poor old Albert.

Constraints on the use of basic and existential constructions

We showed in [28] that bare existential clauses don't have non-existential counterparts. The same is true of existentials extended by a hollow infinitival: [29iv] cannot
be reformulated as **Poor old Albert is to consider*. With other kinds of extended
existential we cannot make a general statement about either the existential or the
non-existential version being the default: there are constraints applying to both versions. We'll briefly mention two that apply to both bare and extended existentials.

(a)   Indefinite NPs

With **indefinite NPs** there is a PREFERENCE FOR THE EXISTENTIAL CONSTRUCTION.
In fact sometimes only the existential is acceptable:

[30]   i a. *A policeman is here.*   b. *There's a policeman here.*
        ii a. **Two holes* were in my sock.*   b. *There were two holes in my sock.*

- In [i] both versions are possible, but the second is considerably more likely.
- In [ii] the basic version is unacceptable (this is generally the case with NPs denoting abstract entities).

(b)   Definite NPs

With **definite NPs** the preference is reversed, with the NON-EXISTENTIAL MORE LIKELY:

[31]   a. *Your mother is here.*   b. *?There's your mother here.*

Displaced subjects are presented as information that is **new to the addressee**. Definite NPs tend to be associated with **old** information, but they don't have to be. Consider this example:

[32]   A: *Who could we get to give a lecture on intonation?*
        B: *Well, [there's Sue Jones,] I suppose.*

The underlined definite NP represents **new** information – the name is offered as a suggestion.

▪ Presentationals

A construction similar to the existential, known as the **presentational** clause, has dummy *there* as subject not of *be* but of an intransitive verb such as *appear*, *emerge*, *follow*, or *remain*:

[33]   a. *Many problems remain.*   b. *There remain many problems.*

5   The *it*-cleft construction

We turn now to a number of information-packaging constructions not illustrated in the introduction to the chapter, beginning with the *it*-**cleft construction.** This generally provides more than one variant of the corresponding non-cleft clause – at least one for each NP, in fact:

[34]   NON-CLEFT   *IT*-CLEFT
                                         b. *It was Sue who introduced Jim to Pat.*
        a. *Sue introduced Jim to Pat.* c. *It was Jim who Sue introduced to Pat.*
                                         d. *It was Pat who Sue introduced Jim to.*

To form an *it*-cleft clause from a syntactically more basic non-cleft we divide it into two parts – hence the 'cleft' component of the name. One part (marked here by double underlining) is **foregrounded**, while the other (single underlining) is **backgrounded**. A considerable range of elements can be selected as the foregrounded element: for example, in [b] it is the subject, in [c] the object, in [d] the complement of the preposition *to*.

Syntactic structure of the *it*-cleft

The foregrounded element functions as complement to **be**. The subject is invariably *it*, a meaningless dummy pronoun. The backgrounded part is expressed as a relative clause, with the foregrounded element as antecedent for the relativised element, here *who* (see Ch. 11, §1). So the structure of [b] is as follows:

[35]

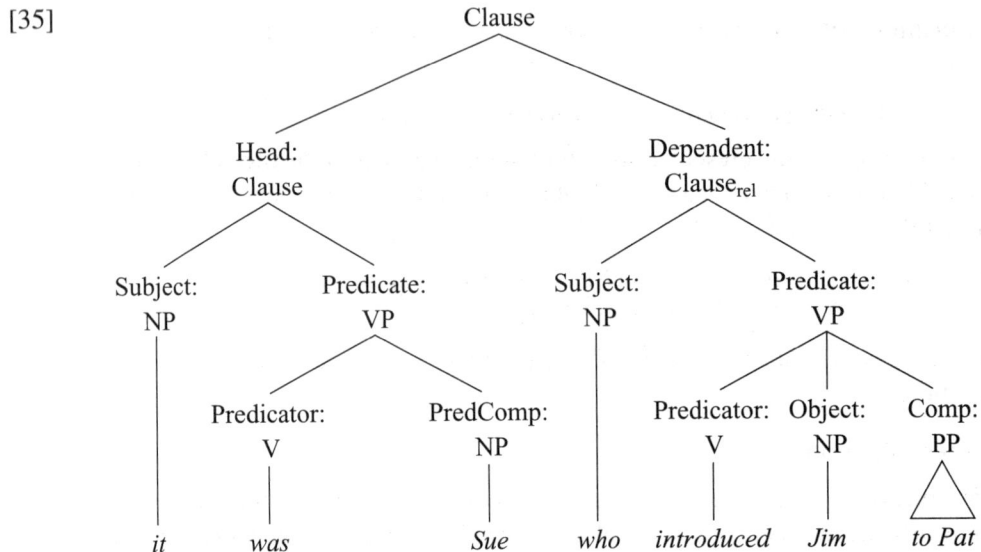

The relative clause is of the integrated type (cf. Ch. 11, §2), but it's not a dependent of *Sue*: the words *Sue who introduced Jim to Pat* do not form a syntactic constituent. In an ordinary integrated relative like *They were [people who needed help]*, the bracketed sequence *people who needed help* is a constituent, an NP. This means there may be ambiguity between *it*-clefts and ordinary integrated relatives:

[36]   *It was the song that impressed them.*

- As an *it*-cleft, this means *The song impressed them*, and the *it* is a dummy. It might be used to answer the question *What impressed the record company?*
- As a non-cleft, you can imagine [36] as an answer to *Why did they choose that song to release as a single?* Here *it* is an ordinary pronoun referring to the song, and *the song that impressed them* does form a constituent.

The foregrounded element

In our initial example, [34b–d], the foregrounded element was an NP whose function in the corresponding non-cleft clause was subject, object, and complement of a preposition. There are many other possibilities, a few of which are illustrated in [37] (where the relative clauses are of the non-*wh* type):

[37]	NON-CLEFT	*IT*-CLEFT
i	a. *They think <u>you</u> should leave.*	b. *It's <u>you</u> they think should leave.*
ii	a. *Sue introduced Jim <u>to Pat</u>.*	b. *It was <u>to Pat</u> that Sue introduced Jim.*
iii	a. *He signed the bill <u>with this pen</u>.*	b. *It was <u>with this pen</u> that he signed the bill.*
iv	a. *She doesn't <u>often</u> miss a class.*	b. *It isn't <u>often</u> that she misses a class.*
v	a. *I resigned <u>to avoid being fired</u>.*	b. *It was <u>to avoid being fired</u> that I resigned.*

- In [ia] *you* is **subject of an embedded content clause** (*you should leave* is complement of *think*).
- In [iia] *to Pat* is a **PP** in **complement** function; note that [iib] is a variant of [34d], more formal in style, avoiding the stranded preposition; see Ch. 7, §5.
- The underlined elements in the other [a] examples – a **PP**, an **adverb**, and a **nonfinite clause** respectively – are all **adjuncts** of various kinds.

This wide range of possibilities further distinguishes this type of relative clause from the prototypical type that modifies a noun. For example, *that he signed the bill* in [iiib] couldn't occur as modifier to *pen*: we couldn't say *This is [*the pen <u>that he signed the bill</u>*] (we'd need to include the preposition: *This is* [*the pen <u>that he signed the bill with</u>*]).

Backgrounded element as presupposition

The effect of backgrounding is to present the information in question as a **presupposition** – information that is taken for granted, its truth not being at issue. In [37ib] I take it for granted that they think someone should leave, and assert that you're the one they have in mind. And in [37iib] it is not at issue whether Sue introduced Jim to someone: the question is who.

Presuppositions are normally not affected when we negate the containing construction, and this is the source of a sharp difference between clefts and their non-cleft counterparts:

[38]   a. *Sue didn't introduce Jim to Pat.*   b. *It wasn't to Pat that Sue introduced Jim.*

The non-cleft [a] simply denies that Sue introduced Jim to Pat: it doesn't convey that she introduced Jim to someone else. The cleft [b] is different: the presupposition that Sue introduced Jim to someone stands, and what's denied is that Pat was that person.

In likely uses of all the examples considered so far, the presupposition will be **old** information, introduced into the prior discourse or inferrable from it. The natural context for [37iib] and [38b], for example, is one where Sue is introducing Jim to someone who has already been mentioned. But this is not a necessary feature of *it*-clefts. The backgrounded material may introduce **new** information into the discourse. This happens in [39]:

[39]   *The Indians were helpful in many ways.* [*It was they <u>who taught the settlers how to plant and harvest crops successfully in the New World</u>.*]

6   Pseudo-clefts

The **pseudo-cleft** is quite similar to the *it*-cleft in some ways: again we have a division between foregrounded and backgrounded elements, with the backgrounded material representing presupposed information. But in the case of pseudocleft, the backgrounded material is placed in a **fused relative** construction:

[40]   NON-CLEFT   PSEUDO-CLEFT
  i a. *We need more time.*   b. *What we need is more time.*
 ii a. *He claims he was insulted.* b. *What he claims is that he was insulted.*
iii a. *I'll postpone the meeting.* b. *What I'll do is postpone the meeting.*

Again we use single underlining for the backgrounded element and double underlining for the foregrounded one. The backgrounded material forms a fused relative construction in the sense explained in Ch. 11, §4 (compare *what we need* with the non-fused relative *that which we need*). In [ib], for example, I take it for granted that we need something and assert that that something is more time. As before, the presupposition normally survives negation: if I say *What we need is not more time, it's some fresh ideas*, I'm still taking it for granted that we need something.

The foregrounded element

There is only partial overlap between the elements that can be foregrounded in the pseudo-cleft and those that can be in the *it*-cleft. Thus we could have an *it*-cleft instead of [40ib] (*It's more time that we need*), but not the others (**It is that he was insulted that he claims*, **It's postpone the meeting that I'll do*). Pseudoclefts accept subordinate clauses as foregrounded element much more readily than *it*-clefts do.

Who is not normally found in fused relatives in present-day usage, so pseudo-clefts don't allow foregrounding of personal NPs: we don't find **Who introduced Jim to Pat was Sue*. Instead we use an *it*-cleft or a non-fused relative construction such as *The one who introduced Jim to Pat was Sue*.

Pseudo-clefts and the specifying *be* construction

The pseudo-cleft is really just a particular case of the specifying *be* construction discussed in Ch. 4, §4.3. As usual, subject and complement can be reversed, giving *More time is what we need*, and so on.

Note also that the pseudo-cleft is less systematically related to non-clefts than the *it*-cleft. There are cases of pseudo-clefts with no non-cleft counterparts:

[41]   PSEUDO-CLEFT   NON-CLEFT
  i a. *What I object to is that he lied.*   b. **I object to that he lied.*
 ii a. *What I like about her is that she*   b. **I like about her that she*
        always means what she says.   *always means what she says.*

7   Dislocation

The prototypical **dislocation** construction has an extra NP located to the left or right of the main part of the clause, consisting of subject and predicate, which we call the **nucleus**. The extra NP serves as antecedent for a **personal pronoun** within the nucleus:

[42]   NON-DISLOCATED CLAUSE   DISLOCATED CLAUSE
   i a. _One of my cousins_ has triplets.   b. _One of my cousins_, _she has_ triplets.
  ii a. I think _the man next door's_   b. _The man next door_, I think _his_ car
         car was stolen.   was stolen.
 iii a. _Her father_ can be very judgemental.   b. _He_ can be very judgemental, _her father_.

Examples [ib/iib] illustrate **left dislocation** (the NP in question is positioned to the left of the clause nucleus), while [iiib] has **right dislocation**. Both are characteristic of relatively informal style, such as conversation, especially oral personal narrative.

The pronoun may be the subject within the nucleus, as in [ib] and [iiib]. It can also be direct or indirect object, complement of a preposition, and so on. In [iib] it is subject-determiner within the subject of an embedded clause.

Dislocated constructions can be easier to understand than their basic counterpart.

- Left dislocation may put a complex NP early in the sentence, replacing it with a pronoun in the nucleus, so the nucleus is structurally simpler. (Note that in [42iib] the subject-determiner in the dislocated version is simply _his_, whereas in [42iia] it is the more complex genitive _the man next door's_.)
- Right dislocation often has an NP that clarifies the reference of the pronoun. (Imagine that [42iiib] was uttered following _Tom didn't dare tell her father_: the NP _her father_ would make clear that _he_ means her father, not Tom.)

Extraposition is not right dislocation

The extraposition construction discussed in §3 above looks superficially like a special case of right dislocation, but in fact it isn't. The differences are as follows:

- In dislocation the NP placed to the left or right of the nucleus is set apart prosodically from the rest of the clause, but extraposition clauses usually have unbroken intonation.
- The _it_ of extraposition is a dummy, not a referential pronoun like the _he_ of [42iiib]. Thus the extraposed clause doesn't 'clarify the reference' of _it_: the _it_ has no reference. If the extraposed clause were omitted, the speaker's intended meaning would normally be lost. The right dislocation [42iiib], by contrast, would make sense even without the final NP.
- Extraposition is stylistically quite neutral, whereas right dislocation, as noted above, belongs mainly to informal style.

8   Preposing and postposing

All the information-packaging constructions considered so far in this chapter differ structurally from their syntactically more elementary counterpart in a way which involves one or more functions:

- a passive clause has a different subject from the corresponding active;
- a cleft clause has as complement of *be* a foregrounded element that can have a range of functions within the non-cleft counterpart;
- extraposition and existentials have dummy subjects;
- dislocation involves pronouns substituting for dislocated NPs.

In this section we review some constructions where there are no such changes to the syntactic functions in the clause; rather, constituents with given functions appear in an unexpected position in the sentence. We look in turn at **preposing**, **postposing** and two kinds of **inversion**.

[43] i   PREPOSING   *Some of them he hadn't even read.*
      ii POSTPOSING   *I understood eventually the reason for their antagonism.*
      iii INVERSION   { a. *Never had I felt so alone.*   [subject–auxiliary inversion]
                           { b. *In the drawer was a gun.*   [subject–dependent inversion]

- **Preposing** involves putting an element before the subject of a clause when its basic position would be after the verb.
- **Postposing** involves putting an element at or near the end of the clause rather than in the earlier position that would be its default place.
- In [iiia] there is **inversion** of subject and auxiliary verb following preposed *never*.
- The inversion in [iiib] combines preposing (of a PP) and postposing (of the subject NP).

(a) Preposing

The contrast between basic order and preposing is seen in such pairs as the following:

[44]   BASIC ORDER   PREPOSING
      i   a. *I wasn't allowed to watch TV when*   b. *When I was at school I wasn't*
             I was at school.   *allowed to watch TV.*
      ii a. *I said he could have the others.*   b. *The others I said he could have.*
      iii a. *They made costume jewellery.*   b. *Costume jewellery, they made.*
      iv a. *Mr Brown is not humble.*   b. *Humble, Mr Brown is not.*
      v   a. *I said I'd pay for it, [and I will*   b. *I said I'd pay for it, [and*
             pay for it].   *pay for it I will].*

The preposed element in [ib] is an **adjunct**. Preposing of adjuncts occurs relatively freely. In the other examples it is a **complement** that is preposed. This is more constrained; a preposed complement serves as a link to the preceding discourse, and must be closely related to information previously introduced into the discourse:

- In [iib], *the others* refers to a subset of some set of things already mentioned.
- The original preceding context for [iiib] was this: *So when I left school I took some of those things to show to a jewellery manufacturer and asked for a job.* There is previous mention of jewellery, and the preposed element denotes a kind of jewellery.
- The original full version of [ivb] was this: *His humility must have been invented by the adman, for humble, Mr Brown is not.* So *humble* relates to the earlier mention of humility.
- In [vb] we see a special case of complement preposing that occurs with complements of auxiliary verbs and typically serves to emphasise the truth of what is being asserted.

(b) Postposing

Further examples of postposing are given in [45], along with their default order counterparts:

[45] BASIC ORDER | POSTPOSING
| |
i a. *They brought <u>an extraordinarily lavish lunch</u> with them.* | b. *They brought with them <u>an extraordinarily lavish lunch</u>.*
ii a. *A man <u>whom I'd never seen before</u> came in.* | b. *A man came in <u>whom I'd never seen before</u>.*

The postposed element is an object in [ib] (as in [43ii]), and a dependent (modifier) within the subject NP in [iib].

The major factor leading to the choice of a postposing construction is relative **weight**. Weight of constituents is primarily a matter of length and complexity. In [45i] the object NP is quite heavy in comparison with the PP complement *with them*, and for this reason can readily be put at the end of the clause instead of in the default object position immediately after the verb. Note two things:

- If the object were simply *lunch* then the basic order would normally be required.
- If we lengthened it to something like *an extraordinarily lavish lunch that their daughter had helped them prepare*, then postposing would be more or less obligatory.

A postposed element occurs in a position that tends to receive greater phonological prominence and where complex material is easier to process. Extraposition is syntactically distinct from postposing in that it introduces the dummy pronoun *it* into the structure, but it shares with postposing the effect of positioning heavy material (a subordinate clause) at the end of the matrix clause.

(c) Subject–auxiliary inversion

[46] BASIC ORDER | SUBJECT–AUXILIARY INVERSION
| |
i a. *<u>The pain</u> <u>was</u> <u>so bad</u> that I fainted.* | b. *<u>So bad</u> <u>was</u> <u>the pain</u> that I fainted.*
ii a. *<u>I</u> <u>realised</u> my mistake <u>only later</u>.* | b. *<u>Only later</u> <u>did</u> <u>I</u> realise my mistake.*

This type of inversion, as the name implies, requires the presence of an auxiliary verb. If there is no auxiliary in the basic order version, then dummy *do* is inserted, as in [iib] (cf. Ch. 3, §3.1).

Subject–auxiliary inversion is found in a considerable range of constructions, some of which have nothing to do with information packaging; most obvious among the latter is the closed interrogative construction, with inversion distinguishing interrogative *Is it ready?*, say, from declarative *It is ready* (Ch. 9, §2.1). Here, though, we're concerned with subject–auxiliary inversion as an accompaniment of preposing. In the examples given, subject–auxiliary inversion is triggered by the preposing of *so bad* and *only later*. The main elements that trigger inversion like this include:

- negatives, as in [43iiia];
- expressions containing *so* or *only*, as in [46] – or *Sue is going, and <u>so am I</u>.
- similar forms with *such*: *<u>Such a fuss</u> <u>did</u> <u>they</u> make that we abandoned the idea.*

(d) Subject–dependent inversion

[47]

	BASIC ORDER	SUBJECT–DEPENDENT INVERSION
i a.	*<u>A bowl of fruit</u> was <u>on her desk</u>.*	b. *<u>On her desk</u> was <u>a bowl of fruit</u>.*
ii a.	*<u>The view from the top</u> is <u>even better</u>.*	b. *<u>Even better</u> is <u>the view from the top</u>.*

This time the elements inverted are the subject and another dependent of the verb. The latter is usually a complement – most commonly a locative or an adjectival predicative complement, as in [47]. The verb is most often *be*, but other verbs of relatively little informational content, such as ***appear, lie, sit,*** etc., are also found.

This type of inversion puts the subject in final position, where it typically receives greater phonological prominence than in its basic position. It very often represents new information, and we will not normally have inversion if the subject is old and the dependent new. Compare [a] and [b] in [48], where the version with old + new is completely natural while the one with new + old is highly unnatural:

[48]

	OLD		NEW		NEW		OLD
a.	*In the drawer*	*was*	*a gun.*	b.	*?In a drawer*	*was*	*the gun.*

9   Reduction

In this final section of the chapter we review summarily a number of constructions where a constituent representing old information is reduced to a pronoun or similar form or else omitted altogether. We use **ellipsis** for the omission of old information and introduce the modern term **pro-form** in place of 'pronoun or similar form':

[49]

i	*I'd like to go with you but I can't ___.*	[reduction by ellipsis]
ii	*My father said <u>he</u> would help you.*	[reduction by pro-form]

- In [i] the VP *can't* is understood as "can't go with you", the missing infinitival complement being recoverable from the preceding clause. We can generalise the concepts of **anaphora** and **antecedent** to cover such cases of ellipsis (cf. Ch. 5, §8.1): the ellipted complement is thus anaphorically related to the antecedent *go with you* in the first clause.
- In the salient interpretation of [ii] it is a matter of my father helping you: the pronoun *he* is anaphoric to the antecedent *my father*.

Pro-form VS pronoun

The reason why we need the term 'pro-form' as well as 'pronoun' can be seen from such examples as the following:

[50]		PRONOUN?	PRO-FORM?
i	A: *Was she arrested?* B: *I'm afraid <u>so</u>.*	No	Yes
ii	*<u>It</u>'s time to go.* *<u>Who</u> broke the vase?*	<u>Yes</u>	<u>No</u>

- In [i], *so* is a pro-form (interpreted anaphorically as "she was arrested"), but it isn't a pronoun. It couldn't be: *afraid* takes a clause as complement (*I'm afraid she was arrested*) but not any kind of NP (**I'm afraid her fate*; **I'm afraid it*).
- In [ii], *it* and *who* are pronouns: they head NPs in subject position and do not permit determiners. But they are not pro-forms: they do not represent old information retrievable in full from the context.

9.1   Reduction of NPs

There are three main types of reduction to consider under this heading.

(a) Personal pronouns

This is the central case illustrated in [49ii]; it was discussed in Ch. 5, §8.1 and needs no further commentary here.

(b) The pro-forms *one* and *other*

[51]   *She left us six pears; this <u>one</u> is riper than the <u>others</u> / the other <u>ones</u>.*

These forms always have a count interpretation, and unlike pronouns they have an antecedent that is not a full NP: in this example it is *pears*, not *six pears*. Syntactically they are common nouns, not pronouns.

- They differ from pronouns in that they take determiners, such as *this* and *the* in [51].
- They are like prototypical common nouns in having an inflectional contrast between singular *one/other* and plural *ones/others*.

(c) The fused head construction

What we have called the **simple** and **implicit partitive** uses of the fused head construction (Ch. 5, §7.1) are generally interpreted anaphorically:

[52]   i *I need some ink, but I can't find <u>any</u>.*
    ii *I had put some mangoes on the table and as usual Max took the <u>largest</u>.*

The fused determiner-head *any* is interpreted anaphorically as "any ink" and the fused modifier-head *largest* as "largest of them", i.e., "largest of the mangoes".

9.2   Reduction of clauses, VPs and other phrases

(a) Clause reduction

[53]   i *He says Jill informed the press, but <u>that</u> can't be true.*
    ii *She may change her mind, but I doubt <u>it</u>.*
    iii *I'm not sure I'll finish today, but I hope <u>so</u>.*
    iv *She's coming round to see us, but she didn't say when __.*

- NPs such as *that*, *this* and *it* can have clauses rather than NPs as antecedent, as in [i–ii].
- *So* can serve as a kind of 'pro-clause', as in [iii] and [50i] above. It functions mainly as internal complement to such verbs as **believe**, **think**, **seem** (as in *It seems so*), etc.
- In [iv] we see ellipsis of everything but the initial phrase of an interrogative content clause.

(b) VP reduction

[54]   i *He suggested we put the house on the market, but I don't want to <u>do that</u> yet.*
    ii *She drove us to the station, but she <u>did so</u> reluctantly.*
    iii *Ed isn't ready, but I am __.   Come if you can __.   I saw it and Pat did __ too.*
    iv *You can come with us if you want to __.*
    v *I don't promise to get it finished today, but I'll try __.*
    vi *They asked me who informed the press, but I don't know __.*

- The NPs *this, that* and *it* can combine with the lexical verb **do** to form a 'pro-VP'; *do that* in [i] is interpreted anaphorically as "put the house on the market".
- *So* combines with **do** in a similar way: *did so* in [ii] is understood as "drove us to the station".
- The examples in [iii] involve the ellipsis of the complement of an auxiliary verb. This is another construction where the dummy auxiliary verb **do** is used if there would not otherwise be an auxiliary verb present, as in the third example ("Pat saw it too").[3]
- Quite similar is the ellipsis of a VP following the infinitival marker *to*, as in [iv].
- A relatively small number of lexical catenative verbs allow ellipsis of their non-finite complement: *try* in [v] is understood as "try to get it finished today".
- Similarly, some verbs, such as **know** in [vi], permit ellipsis of a content clause complement: "I don't know who informed the press".

[3] A further construction of this kind is the one where stress is used to emphasise that a clause is positive, not negative: *I HAVE told you.* Dummy *do* is needed if there is no other auxiliary to carry the stress: *I DID tell you* (contrasting with non-emphatic *I told you*).

(c) Pro-forms for predicative complements and locative PPs

[55] i *She was extremely bright / an excellent manager, or at least she seemed <u>so</u>.*
     ii *He was born in Boston and lived <u>there</u> all his life.*

- *So* has other anaphoric uses than those mentioned above; in particular, it can function as predicative complement, allowing a variety of categories of antecedent, such as the AdjP *extremely bright* or the NP *an excellent manager* in [i].
- The preposition *there* is commonly used anaphorically with a locative expression as antecedent, as in [ii]. It can also be used deictically, as in *Just put it over there*.

Exercises

1. For each of the main clauses below say whether it is **canonical** or **non-canonical**. If it's non-canonical, say which non-canonical construction it belongs to.
     i *It doesn't matter any more.*
     ii *That'll be the day.*
     iii *I'm looking for someone to love.*
     iv *It's so lucky that you found me.*
     v *I want money.*
     vi *Do you love me?*
     vii *What a time we had.*
     viii *What's wrong with me?*
     ix *I feel so bad.*
     x *This sort of thing I have no patience with.*

2. Classify the **main** clauses of the following examples with respect to **voice**, saying whether each is **active** or **passive**.
     i *A bus blew up in Jerusalem today.*
     ii *Buses often get blown up in Jerusalem.*
     iii *Someone blew up a bus in Jerusalem.*
     iv *A bus was blown up in Jerusalem.*
     v *They blew up a bus in Jerusalem.*
     vi *Was a bus blown up in Jerusalem today?*
     vii *The attack was planned by an unknown terrorist group.*
     viii *An unknown terrorist group is responsible.*
     ix *An unknown terrorist group is thought to be responsible.*
     x *An unknown terrorist group is thought by intelligence specialists to be responsible.*

3. For each of the following **active** clauses, if it has a **passive** counterpart, supply it; if not, do your best to give a general statement of why this sort of clause doesn't have a passive. (For example, if given *Jim remains chairman* you might say that *chairman* is a predicative complement and as such could never become the subject of a corresponding passive clause, as seen by **Chairman is remained by Jim*.)
     i *The weather ruined our holiday.*
     ii *The secretary gave a copy of the report to all board members.*
     iii *Both her children have malaria.*
     iv *One of the guests sat on my glasses.*
     v *My sister lives just around the corner.*
     vi *Your letter arrived this morning.*
     vii *Most people believe them to be genuine.*
     viii *Your new proposal looks a real improvement on the last one.*
     ix *The college awarded her a prize.*
     x *My schoolmates often made fun of me because of my accent.*

4. Express each of these examples with all clauses entirely in the **active voice**.
     i *I'm afraid I was robbed by bandits on the way to class and my homework was stolen.*
     ii *It is clear that your goldfish has been killed by an evildoer.*
     iii *'You should have that looked at by an expert,' I was told by all my friends.*
     iv *On Thursday I was hit by the bad news that we were being shut down by the police.*

   v *She went swimming and was attacked by a crocodile.*

5. For each of the following, say whether it is (a) a **passive** clause (a ***be***-passive or a ***get***-passive); (b) a **complex-intransitive** clause with an **adjectival passive** as complement; or (c) **ambiguous** between the two. For the ambiguous cases, describe the difference in meaning.
   i *The motion was carried unanimously.*
   ii *The rod was magnetised.*
   iii *The farm was surrounded by troops.*
   iv *One of the letters wasn't signed.*
   v *Several people were injured during the demonstration.*
   vi *I got bitten by the neighbours' dog.*
   vii *They got reprimanded for it.*
   viii *They were lost.*
   ix *They got dressed.*
   x *One of the letters didn't get signed.*

6. For each underlined clause, give an **extraposed** counterpart if one is available, or if none is available, explain why.
   i *<u>Why you put up with it</u> is incomprehensible.*
   ii *It isn't clear to me <u>whether he was even listening</u>.*
   iii *The fact <u>that they are married</u> should make no difference.*
   iv *It feels good <u>to be back in my home town</u>.*
   v *<u>For you to do that</u> would be deeply unethical.*
   vi *I appreciate <u>that you returned it</u> sincerely.*
   vii *<u>That I should have to clean it all up</u> seems a bit unfair.*
   viii *I'm afraid <u>whining about the pain</u> is no use.*
   ix *<u>Why she had to do that</u> will always be a mystery.*
   x *<u>Meeting you and your family</u> has been a great pleasure.*

7. Give **existential** or **presentational** counterparts of the following clauses if they are available. If none is available explain why.
   i *Carpentry tools are available for your use.*

   ii *A friend of yours is on the phone.*
   iii *His wife was very rich.*
   iv *Only one doctor was present.*
   v *Several important points emerged.*
   vi *A beggar followed her home.*
   vii *One key was missing.*
   viii *His father died on the plane.*
   ix *Something is wrong with the battery.*
   x *Is your job available?*

8. Give **non-existential** counterparts of the following clauses if one is available, and where none is available explain why.
   i *There's a serious mistake in your argument.*
   ii *There were two students on the committee.*
   iii *There's nothing to worry about.*
   iv *There had been a violent demonstration against the new bill.*
   v *There's no doubt that he's the main culprit.*

9. For each of the following, give an ***it*-cleft** counterpart with the same truth conditions, with the underlined constituent as the foregrounded element.
   i *I blame <u>you</u>.*
   ii *Most of the leaf growth occurs <u>in the spring</u>.*
   iii *They left the campground <u>only reluctantly</u>.*
   iv *<u>George</u> took the Volvo.*
   v *I liked <u>the other one</u> most.*

10. For each of the following, give a **pseudo-cleft** with the same truth conditions, with the underlined constituent as the foregrounded element.
    i *<u>The absurd waste of it all</u> bothers me.*
    ii *<u>Most of the leaf growth</u> occurs in the spring.*
    iii *<u>The backgrounded material</u> gets put in the fused relative construction.*
    iv *George took <u>the Volvo</u>.*
    v *I liked <u>the music</u> most.*

11. Classify the following examples as (a) **left dislocation**; (b) **right dislocation**; (c) **preposing**; or (d) **postposing**. Underline the dislocated or reordered constituent. In cases of dislocation, also underline the

personal pronoun in the nucleus that has the dislocated phrase as its antecedent.

 i *To my son Ben I leave my collection of antique chess pieces.*

 ii *They said he was a professional, the guy that stole your stuff.*

 iii *Richard, who built this wall, he's my brother, and he lives in England.*

 iv *The garage, I don't really use it except for storing junk.*

 v *We explained to the police everything they asked us to explain.*

 vi *People like that you can never really trust.*

 vii *Was she just crazy, that teacher who had an affair with that boy?*

 viii *Surprise everyone you certainly did!*

 ix *You should get it checked out, soon, that rattling sound in the transmission.*

 x *The Monkey Club is proud to present for the first time in Grenville this coming Saturday at eight p.m. the fabulous Rockmonsters.*

Morphology: words and lexemes

1 Inflectional morphology and lexical morphology

Morphology deals with the composition and internal structure of words, and the way that structure determines the word meaning, rather than the way they combine to make larger units like phrases and clauses. We divide the topic into **inflectional** and **lexical** morphology.

Inflectional morphology deals with the differences between the shapes of the inflectional forms of variable lexemes; for example, the formation of the verb-forms *endangers*, *endangered* and *endangering* from the **lexical base** *endanger*.

Lexical morphology deals with the formation of lexical bases – with the formation of *endanger*, for example, from *en·* and *danger*. This includes the formation of the lexical bases of invariable lexemes, such as *cleverly*. This doesn't inflect (there are no forms **cleverlier* or **cleverliest*), but the fact that it is made up out of *clever* and *·ly* is a fact of lexical morphology.

The motivation for dividing morphology into these two branches can be illustrated by means of an example such as the following:

[1]   LEXEME   INFLECTIONAL FORMS
   i *friend* (N):   *friend*   *friends*   *friend's*   *friends'*
  ii *friendly* (Adj): *friendly*   *friendlier* *friendliest*

Within each of the two rows, the different words are inflectional forms of the same lexeme. But row [i] lists forms of a different lexeme from row [ii]. Most ordinary dictionaries would have just two entries to cover these words: one for the noun *friend* and one for the adjective *friendly*.

Inflectional morphology deals with the horizontal relationships in [1]: the different shapes that share the **lexical base** of a lexeme. In [i] the shapes are based on *friend*; in [ii] the shapes are based on *friendly*.

Lexical morphology deals with the vertical dimension in [1]: the structure of, and relation between, the different lexical bases. In this example, the noun base *friend* is morphologically simple, while the adjective base *friendly* is formed from it by the addition of ·*ly*.

The reason we treat the relation between the forms *friendly*, *friendlier*, *friendliest* differently from that between *friendly* and *friend* is that there are **rules of syntax** that determine where the various inflectional forms of a lexeme may or must appear. Suppose, for example, that we want to insert the noun lexeme *friend* in the contexts shown in [2i] and the adjective lexeme *friendly* in those shown in [2ii]:

[2]   i a. *She's been a good _____ .*   b. *Their _____ own car was a VW.*
       ii a. *He's _____ than his brother.*   b. *He's the _____ of them all.*

If you want to use *friend* to fill the gaps in [i], you must use the plain singular form *friend* in [ia], and you must use a genitive form in [ib] – either singular (*their friend's own car*) or plural (*their friends' own car*). And if you want to fill the blanks in [ii] with *friendly*, you need the comparative form *friendlier* in [a] and the superlative form *friendliest* in [b] – no other choices are allowed.

These rules apply quite generally: context [ia] requires the plain singular form of any noun you might want to substitute for the blank; [ib] needs a genitive, [iia] needs a comparative, and [iib] needs a superlative.

But there is no rule of syntax saying that an adjective appearing in [ii] must be formed from a noun, in the way that the base *friendly* is formed from *friend*. The blanks in [iia–b] could just as well be filled by *older* and *oldest*, respectively, forms whose lexical base is morphologically simple, not formed from anything else.

Nor is there a rule saying that the lexical base of nouns filling the blanks in [i] must be morphologically simple, like *friend*. We could fill the blank in [ia], for example, with *teacher* (which is derived from the verb *teach* by adding ·*er*). It doesn't matter how the lexical base of the lexeme is made up internally. All that matters is whether you have picked a syntactically admissible inflectional form of the lexeme you decide on.

So, to summarise, **inflectional** morphology ties in mainly with **syntax**, while **lexical** morphology is mainly relevant to the content of the dictionary. Inflectional forms matter for rules of syntax, whereas lexical morphology relates only to the structure of the words in the dictionary and the formation of new words added to it.

Most of this chapter will concern inflection, in keeping with the focus throughout the book. Our main concern is with the syntax of English, not the dictionary – explaining how sentences are built rather than how lexemes are constructed or related to each other.

2   Basic concepts in inflectional morphology

In this section we introduce the basic concepts and terminology needed in the description of English inflection.

(a) Lexical base

The **lexical base** of a lexeme is the starting-point for describing the inflectional forms. In English, the lexical base is almost always identical with one of the inflectional forms. For example, the noun lexeme *friend* has the lexical base *friend*, and the plain (i.e. non-genitive) singular form is identical with the lexical base. Likewise, the adjective lexeme *friendly* has the lexical base *friendly*, and the plain form is identical with this. The other forms – the plural and genitive forms of the noun, the comparative and superlative forms of the adjective – consist of the lexical base with various suffixes added.

There are a few exceptional lexemes whose lexical base is not identical with any of the inflectional forms. They are lexemes that don't have the full set of inflectional forms normally associated with their category. Specifically, there are **plural-only** nouns: examples include *auspices*, *binoculars*, *clothes*, *condolences*, *credentials*, and *scissors*. These plurals are formed in the usual way by adding a suffix to the lexical base (*auspice*, *binocular*, *clothe*, etc.), but the lexical base is not normally found standing alone as a form of the noun lexeme.

(b) Morphological operations

Inflectional forms of a lexeme are formed in various ways, by different **operations** on lexical bases; an example would be the operation of **suffixation** of ·*s*, i.e., adding ·*s* to the end of the base. In English, suffixation is the main operation in the inflectional system, but **modification** of the base also plays an important role. Examples from plural nouns and preterite verbs are shown in [3]:

[3]		PLURAL NOUN FORMATION	PRETERITE VERB FORMATION
i	SUFFIXATION	*dog* + ·*s* = *dogs*	*want* + ·*ed* = *wanted*
ii	MODIFICATION	*goose* modified = *geese*	*take* modified = *took*

The two operations may combine: the plural *wive·s* is formed from *wife* by suffixation of ·*s* and changing the final consonant of the base from *f* to *v*. A few other (relatively minor) operations will be introduced below.

(c) Shape sharing

As we saw in our discussion of verb inflection in Ch. 3, §1, the various inflectional forms of a lexeme are not always overtly distinct: two (or more) of them may share the same shape. With **want**, for example, not only the preterite but also the past participle has the shape *wanted*. The same phenomenon is found with nouns. The plurals of some nouns are identical with the lexical base and hence share the same shape as the singular. With **bison**, for example, the singular and plural forms share the same shape, *bison*; similarly for **series**, and others listed in §5.1 below.

(d) Alternation

Very often a given inflectional form is formed in different ways for different subsets of lexemes. For example, while many nouns form their written plural by adding the suffix ·*s*, there are others that add ·*es*: compare *dog·s* and *fox·es*. This use of the suffixes ·*s* and ·*es* for the same purpose in different contexts is called an **alternation**. The two shapes are called **alternants**, and the rules of inflectional morphology need to specify the conditions under which one alternant or the other is required.

(e) The priority of speech

So far in this book we haven't had to talk much about how words or sentences are pronounced. We've just shown them in written form. But when we deal with the internal structure of words, we have to pay some attention to speech, for at least two reasons.

- In the first place, there are alternations in speech that don't show up in writing. The plural suffixes in *cats* and *dogs*, for example, are written the same way but they sound different. Try saying this aloud: *Let the cats in.* The last part sounds like *sin.* Now say: *Let the dogs in.* The last part sounds like *zin.* That difference is never shown in English spelling.
- Secondly, and more importantly for our purposes, the choice between alternants in writing often depends on features of the pronunciation. Consider these two plural nouns:

[4]	LEXEME	SINGULAR	PLURAL
i	***stomach***	*stomach*	*stomach·s*
ii	***coach***	*coach*	*coach·es*

The reason why we have the ·*s* alternant in *stomachs* but ·*es* in *coaches* can't be explained by looking at the spelling of the lexical base: both bases end in *ch* (with *a* before that). Rather, the alternation reflects the fact that in speech the suffix in *stomachs* is simply a consonant sound, whereas in *coaches* it is made up of a vowel sound plus a consonant sound. And in speech the reason we select the vowel-plus-consonant alternant spelled as ·*es* has to do with the phonetic properties of the lexical base. This suffix is added to a lexical base that ends in a **sibilant**, a 'hissing sound' like the sounds at the ends of bases like *kiss, quiz, bush, rouge, bench, judge*.

Despite the frequent relevance of pronunciation, we don't attempt a full description of inflection in spoken English here. There are several reasons for focusing on writing in a short introductory book like this.

- One is that writing is much more uniform than speech. There are extensive differences in pronunciation between British English and American English, and between these and other regional varieties, whereas differences in spelling are few in number, small in scale, and easy to describe in full.
- A second reason is that the writing system has the advantage of familiarity. Examples in written English can just be shown in their usual written form, whereas exhibiting spoken forms would call for a phonetic alphabet. There is an International Phonetic Alphabet which would serve this purpose, but although it is being used in an increasing number of dictionaries, not everyone knows it, and it would take some space to explain.

So what we do here is to continue presenting words and parts of words in ordinary spelling, making reference informally to how they're pronounced when we need to explain spelling rules.

(f) Letters and symbols

In describing spelling alternations we need to distinguish between **letters** of the alphabet and **symbols** for sounds. These aren't the same.

- In very simple cases like *hit*, letters and symbols coincide, because each letter happens to be a symbol for a single sound.
- In *heat* there are four letters, though still only three sounds: *ea* is a **composite symbol** representing a single vowel sound.
- In *heath* there are two composite symbols: *ea* again, and *th* standing for a single consonant sound.
- In *sheath* we have six letters, but again only three sounds: *sh*, *ea* and *th* are composite symbols.

Vowel and **consonant** are terms that by themselves apply purely to speech sounds. Vowels have unimpeded smooth continuing airflow through the mouth, whereas with consonants there is some kind of audible constriction that makes a difference to the sound. When we talk about **vowel symbols** and **consonant symbols**, all we'll mean is symbols representing vowel sounds and symbols representing consonant sounds.

We will have no use at all for the traditional classification of letters into five vowels (*a, e, i, o, u*) and twenty-one consonants (all the rest). Take *y*, for example: it's a consonant symbol in *you* and *yacht*; it's a vowel symbol in *by* and *pity*; and in *boy* and *guy* it's neither – it's simply part of a composite symbol.

(g) Regular and irregular forms

An inflectional form is **regular** if it is formed by a general rule and **irregular** if it is formed by a rule applying only to some fixed number of particular lexemes.

- Take the preterite verb-form *killed*, for example. We say it's a regular form because it is formed by adding ·*ed* to the lexical base, like the preterite of nearly all verbs, with only a limited number of special exceptional ones (there are only about 200 of them, compared with an essentially unlimited number of regular verbs).
- We say that the preterite *drank*, on the other hand, is irregular: the modification of the base vowel here (replacing the vowel heard in *ring* by the vowel heard in *gang*) is found with only a handful of lexemes including **drink**, **begin**, **ring**, **swim**, etc.
- In a few cases, regular and irregular forms co-exist as variants for the same inflectional form. The verb **burn**, for example, has regular *burned* and irregular *burnt* as variants of the preterite and past participle forms, and a number of other verbs behave similarly (*spelled* ~ *spelt*, *dreamed* ~ *dreamt*, etc.).

We call an entire lexeme regular only if ALL its inflectional forms are regular: the general rules must correctly account for every single one of its forms for it to be a regular lexeme.

For the most part, forms that are regular in speech are regular in writing, and vice versa. But there are some exceptions in most people's speech, such as those in [5]:

[5]			SPEECH	WRITING
i	*says*	3rd sing present tense of *say*	irregular	regular
ii	*paid*	preterite / past participle of *pay*	regular	irregular

Says is perfectly regular in writing, but for most speakers, it is irregular in speech because it has a different vowel from the lexical base (it rhymes with *fez*, not *faze*). Conversely, *paid* is regular in speech but irregular in writing: the regular form would be **payed* (compare *pray ~ prayed*), but the spelling actually used is different from that.

3   Some general spelling rules

In this section we introduce four spelling rules that apply in the formation of more than one inflectional form. The first three actually apply in lexical as well as inflectional morphology. In all of them we need to take account of the pronunciation of bases and suffixes in accordance with the point made above concerning the priority of speech over writing. Keep in mind, though, that relevant features of the spelling system were established several centuries ago, and may reflect pronunciations that are no longer current for all or some varieties of English. There are two cases of this kind we should mention here:

- The suffix used to form regular preterites and past participles is now pronounced with a vowel only after bases ending in a *t* or *d* sound, as in *waited* or *landed*: elsewhere it is pronounced as a consonant, as in *scoffed* (which rhymes with *soft*), *feared* (which rhymes with *beard*), etc. In earlier centuries the ·*ed* ending was pronounced with a vowel in all cases, and as far as the writing system is concerned it still behaves in all cases as if it were a suffix beginning with a vowel sound.
- In some varieties of English, the sound represented by the letter *r* now occurs only before a vowel: it occurs, for example, in *ram* but not in *mar*, which is pronounced just like *ma*. Most varieties of British English are of this kind, whereas most American varieties still have this sound both before and after vowels. This variation is irrelevant to the writing system, however: bases like *mar* are treated as ending in a consonant sound in all varieties.

3.1   Consonant doubling

Consonant doubling is illustrated in sets of forms like the ones in [6], where *stop* has one *p* but *stopped* has two, and so on:

[6]	i	VERB	stop	stopped	stopping	stops
	ii	ADJECTIVE	fat	fatter	fattest	
	iii	NOUN	quiz	quizzes		

There is a rule that describes where you get this doubling and where you don't. It can be stated like this:

[7]   The final consonant letter of the base is doubled if all of the following conditions are satisfied:
    (a) it occurs before a suffix beginning with a vowel sound;
    (b) the base ends in a single consonant sound represented by a single letter;
    (c) the consonant letter follows a single-letter vowel symbol;
    (d) the base is stressed on the final (or only) syllable.

(a) Doubling occurs before suffixes beginning with a vowel

As we noted above, the suffix·ed is treated as beginning with a vowel whether or not it is still pronounced with a vowel in Present-day English (stopped used to be pronounced more like stop Ed, and the spelling rules have largely remained the same since then). So in [6i] we get doubling in stopped as well as stopping. But there is no doubling in stops, where the suffix consists of a consonant. In plural nouns we have doubling in quizzes, where the suffix begins with a vowel, but not in hats, where again it consists of a consonant.

(b) Base ends in single consonant

There is no doubling in forms like grasping, where the base ends in a sequence of two consonants. Nor is there doubling in sawing, boxing and the like. The base saw ends in a vowel, not a consonant, while box again ends in a sequence of two consonants (x represents the two sounds that in the word phonetics are represented separately by c and s). Note that we do have doubling in marring: as noted in above, mar is treated as ending in a consonant even in those varieties where the final 'r' sound has been lost.

(c) Consonant letter follows single-letter vowel symbol

The consonants doubled in [6] are preceded by the vowel symbols o, a and i respectively – note that the u in quiz represents a consonant. There is no doubling in forms like beating, roaring, cooler, etc., where the vowel is represented by the complex symbols ea, oa, oo.

(d) Stress on final (or only) syllable

This condition accounts for the difference in such verbs as **prefer** and **offer**:

[8]   a. prefer preferred preferring   b. offer offered offering

The base prefer has the stress on the second syllable, so doubling applies, but offer has the stress on the first syllable, which prevents doubling.

The rule does most of the work, but English spelling is always quite difficult and, sure enough, there are some exceptions to this last condition.

- Firstly, non-final stress does not prevent doubling of final *l* in British English, as in *travelling* or *crueller* (American English spelling has *traveling* and *crueler*, in keeping with the rule).
- Secondly, there are a number of other verbs with non-final stress where doubling is found, either obligatorily (e.g. *formatted*, *leapfrogged*) or optionally (*benefitted/ benefited*, *worshipped/worshiped*), and those you just have to learn by acquaintance.

3.2   Final *e* deletion

Bases ending in *e* often lose this *e* when a suffix beginning with a vowel is added. There are two different cases, though. The first is where the *e* is what some children are taught to call the 'magic *e*', which we will call '**mute *e***'. The second case is where the *e* is part of a composite symbol.

[9]	i MUTE *e*	*hope*	*hoping*	*hoped*
	ii PART OF COMPOSITE SYMBOL	*subdue*	*subduing*	*subdued*

(a) Mute *e*

The term **mute *e*** applies to a base-final *e* that is preceded by a consonant symbol and does not itself represent a sound. In speech, for example, the base *hope* ends in a consonant, so the written *e* is mute.

Mute *e* always drops before a suffix beginning with *e*, and normally does so before the ·*ing* suffix of gerund-participles. The few verbs where *e* is retained before ·*ing* include a number whose base ends in *inge*; the *e* is obligatory in *singeing* (keeping the *e* distinguishes the gerund-participles of **singe** and **sing**). In the British and Australian word **whinge** ("complain passively"), the *e* remains optionally: both *whingeing* and *whinging* are found.

(b) Composite vowel symbols ending in *e*

The *e* at the end of *subdue* is part of a composite symbol, *ue*. A final *e* of this kind always drops (like mute *e*) before a suffix beginning with *e*, and sometimes also before ·*ing*. It generally drops when the composite symbol is *ue*, but not when it is *ee* (*freeing*), *oe* (*hoeing*) or *ye* (*dyeing*). The composite symbol *ie* is usually replaced by *y* before ·*ing*, as in *lying*. Note the contrast between *dying*, a form of **die** ("cease living"), and *dyeing*, a form of **dye** ("colour with chemicals").

3.3   Final *y* replacement

The third rule applies with bases ending in *y* as a single-letter vowel symbol. Before a suffix we have the alternation shown in [10]:

[10]	TREATMENT OF *y*	CONTEXT		EXAMPLES		
i	*y* is retained	before ·*ing* or ·*'s*	*deny*	*deny·ing*	*baby*	*baby·'s*
ii	replaced by *ie*	before ·*s*	*deny*	*denie·s*	*baby*	*babie·s*
iii	replaced by *i*	elsewhere	*deny*	*deni·ed*	*pretty*	*pretti·er*

The replacement of *y* by *ie* occurs in verbs before 3rd person singular present tense ·*s* (*denies*), and in nouns before plural ·*s* (*babies*), but never before genitive ·*'s* (*baby's*). Replacement by *i* is found in verbs before ·*ed* (*denied*) and in adjectives before comparative ·*er* and superlative ·*est* (*prettier*, *prettiest*).[1] It also occurs before various suffixes in lexical morphology (as in *denial*, *embodiment*, etc.).

As we said earlier, all of this applies only when *y* represents a vowel by itself; when *y* is part of a composite symbol, it is retained in all contexts, as in *buys*, *boys*, *played*, *coyer*, etc.

3.4   Alternation between ·*s* and ·*es*

This alternation occurs with the 3rd person singular present tense suffix in verbs and the plural suffix in nouns. In speech, the corresponding alternation is also found with the genitive suffix in singular nouns but in writing this is invariably ·*'s* (in regular forms). Thus in speech it is found not only in plural *cats* and *foxes* but also in genitive singular *cat's* and *fox's*, which sound exactly the same as the plurals. In writing things are quite different: the genitives have the same suffix, and it is different from the plural one.

The alternation between ·*s* and ·*es* can best be described by taking ·*s* as the default form of the suffix and stating where it is that you have to use ·*es* instead. There are two cases to consider.

(a) The ·*es* alternant represents spoken vowel + consonant

The ·*es* alternant is added to bases which in speech take a suffix with the form of vowel + consonant. As noted above, these are bases that end in a sibilant, or hissing sound:

[11]	i	*kiss*	*rose*	*bush*	*rouge*	*bench*	*judge*
	ii	*kiss·es*	*ros·es*	*bush·es*	*roug·es*	*bench·es*	*judg·es*

A good number of bases which in speech end in a sibilant end in writing with mute *e*: in the examples in [11] this applies to *rose*, *rouge* and *judge*. However, this mute *e* drops by the general rule of *e* deletion described in §3.2 above, and the suffixed forms in [ii] can be treated in a uniform way.

(b) The ·*es* alternant is commonly required after bases ending in consonant + *o*

Bases ending in *o* commonly take ·*es* if the *o* follows a consonant symbol; otherwise they take the default ·*s* alternant. This rule is illustrated in [12]:

---

[1] **Dry** and **shy** are exceptions, having *dryer/dryest* and *shyer/shyest* as optional variants of regular *drier/driest* and *shier/shiest*.

[12] i When the *o* follows a consonant symbol, we typically get ·*es*:

      go·es   hero·es   potato·es   tomato·es   torpedo·es   veto·es

  ii When the *o* does not follow a consonant symbol, we invariably get ·*s*:

      boo·s   embryo·s   folio·s   radio·s   video·s   zoo·s

There is some difference between verbs and nouns here. With verbs, the ·*es* alternant is almost invariably used when *o* follows a consonant – as in the verb uses of *goes*, *torpedoes* and *vetoes*. The same applies to nouns which are identical in form to verbs (*goes*, *torpedoes*, *vetoes*, *echoes* and *embargoes* can be either 3rd singular present tense verbs or plural nouns). But a good number of other nouns with *o* following a consonant take the default ·*s* instead: this is obligatory for *dynamo*, *kilo*, *piano*, *Eskimo*, and optional with *bongo*, *buffalo*, *halo*, *motto*, *volcano*, and some others.

4   Verb inflection

     The inflectional categories of verbs were introduced in Ch. 3, §1, where we discussed their meaning and syntactic distribution. In this chapter we're concerned solely with their morphological formation – which forms have which suffixes, and how the results are spelled. Our main focus will be on lexical verbs (i.e. verbs other than auxiliaries).

    Almost all lexical verbs have six inflectional forms. The plain form and the plain present tense are identical with the lexical base, so we don't need to say any more about them. Of the others, the gerund-participle and the 3rd person singular present tense are very straightforward, so we'll deal with them first. Then we'll turn to the preterite and past participle forms, where we find virtually all of the considerable complexity in English verb inflection.

4.1   The gerund-participle

     The gerund-participle is invariably formed by adding the suffix ·*ing* to the lexical base. In speech, that is all there is to it; even *be·ing* is completely regular. In writing, addition of the suffix may lead to modification of the base involving consonant doubling, *e* deletion and replacement of *ie* by *y*, as described in §§3.1–3.3:

[13] i LEXICAL BASE   *see   stop   hope   subdue   hoe   lie*

  ii GERUND-PARTICIPLE   *see·ing stopp·ing hop·ing subdu·ing hoe·ing ly·ing*

4.2   The 3rd person singular present tense

     This is normally formed by adding ·*s* or ·*es* to the base. But in this case *be* is irregular: we get *is*, not *bes. *Have* is also irregular, losing the *ve* of the base: *has*, not *haves. In speech, *does* is also irregular in that the vowel differs from that of the base (it rhymes with *buzz*, not *booze*). The same applies to *says* (as we noted in connection with [5i], for most speakers it rhymes with *fez*, not *faze*).

The choice between ·*es* and the default alternant ·*s* has been described in §3.4. A sample of forms is given in [14]:

[14]	i LEXICAL BASE	*miss*	*lose*	*touch*	*go*	*boo*	*stop*
	ii 3RD SING PRESENT	*miss·es*	*los·es*	*touch·es*	*go·es*	*boo·s*	*stop·s*

4.3   The preterite and past participle

We take these two forms together, since for all regular verbs and a high proportion of irregular ones they are morphologically identical – they share exactly the same shape. Where they share shape we'll simplify tabular presentations by giving only the preterite form, but when the past participle is different we'll show it separately.

Regular forms

We begin with verbs whose preterite and past participle are regular in speech. In writing, these are formed by the addition of the suffix ·*ed*, with consonant doubling, *e* deletion and replacement of *y* by *i* applying as described in §§3.1–3.3. Examples are given in [15]:

[15]	i LEXICAL BASE	*laugh*	*stop*	*prefer*	*hope*	*subdue*	*deny*
	ii PRETERITE	*laugh·ed*	*stopp·ed*	*preferr·ed*	*hop·ed*	*subdu·ed*	*deni·ed*

Irregular forms with preterite and past participle identical

Many irregular verbs are like regular ones in having shape sharing between preterite and past participle. There are a dozen or so where there is variation between a regular form and a mildly irregular one, as with **spell**, whose preterite can be *spelled* or *spelt*.

We find a considerable range of morphological relations between the preterite / past participle and the lexical base. A sample of these are illustrated in [16], with commentary given below:

[16]		A	B	C	D	E	F	G	H
	i BASE	*hit*	*bend*	*burn*	*keep*	*flee*	*think*	*dig*	*stand*
	ii PRETERITE	*hit*	*bent*	*burnt*	*kept*	*fled*	*thought*	*dug*	*stood*

Type A.   Preterite identical with base

There are over twenty verbs where the preterite is identical with the lexical base. Most of them have bases ending in *t*, but there are also a few in *d*, such as *shed*. Some lexemes, such as **quit**, have variant regular forms: *He quit* or *He quitted*.

Type B.   Base-final *d* replaced by *t*

Similar to Type A are those where the preterite is not identical to the base but differs simply in the replacement of final *d* by *t*. They include **build**, **send**, **spend**, etc.

Type C.   Preterite formed by addition of *·t*

This is a small class with all members having regular variants too: *burnt* or *burned*. Bases ending in *ll* lose one *l* before *·t*: *smell ~ smelt*. Other examples include **dwell**, **learn**, **spoil**.

Type D.   Addition of *·t* with modification of the base

These are similar to Type C, but the addition of *·t* is accompanied by modification of the base. The modification is usually just a change in the vowel, but a more extensive modification is found in *leave ~ left*. Other members of the class include **feel**, **mean**, **sleep**. **Leap** is Type D in speech, but Type C in writing.

Type E.   Addition of *·d* with modification of the base

A small number of verbs add *·d* rather than *·t*, in all cases with modification of the base. Others include **hear**, **say**, **sell**.

Type F.   Preterites in *ought* or *aught*

A handful of verbs have highly irregular preterites with *ought* or *aught* (which are pronounced alike) replacing vowel + any following consonants in the base. Others include **buy**, **catch**, **seek**. They might be subsumed under Type D, but the final *t* can hardly be analysed as a suffix.

Type G.   Preterite formed by vowel change

In a fair number of verbs the preterite differs from the base just in respect of the vowel. A variety of different vowel pairs are found: compare *hang ~ hung*, *find ~ found*, *shine ~ shone*, etc.

Type H.   Miscellaneous

There are a few verbs that don't fit into any of the above patterns, and have a unique difference between preterite and base. *Stood* differs from *stand* in the vowel and loss of *n*; *had* and *made* differ from *have* and *make* in the second consonant.

▨ Irregular forms with preterite and past participle distinct

We turn finally to verbs where the preterite and past participle are different in form. In most cases the past participle contains a distinctive suffix spelled in three alternant ways shown in [17]:

[17]	i	*n*	after vowel symbol or *re*:	*grown*	*lain*	*seen*	*sewn*	*torn*
	ii	*ne*	for **bear**, **do**, and **go**:	*borne*	*done*	*gone*		
	iii	*en*	elsewhere:	*broken*	*chosen*	*fallen*	*swollen*	*taken*

- *Grow*, *see* and *sew* end in complex vowel symbols, and ·*n* is added directly to them. With *lay* we have a special case of *y* replacement. When the suffix is added to *tore* and *wore*, the mute *e* following *r* is deleted.

- The items in [ii] are simply exceptions; there is no general rule that assigns them the *ne* spelling.

- The ·*en* alternant is found in all other cases. When it is added to a form ending in mute *e*, the ordinary rule of *e* deletion applies, as we see in *broken*, *chosen*, and *taken*.

Again we find a variety of morphological relations between lexical base, preterite and past participle. Here's a sample of examples, with discussion following.

[18]		A	B	C	D	E	F
i	BASE	*show*	*take*	*ride*	*lie*	*drink*	*fly*
ii	PRETERITE	*showed*	*took*	*rode*	*lay*	*drank*	*flew*
iii	PAST PARTICIPLE	*shown*	*taken*	*ridden*	*lain*	*drunk*	*flown*

Type A.   Preterite: regular; past participle: base + suffix

Showed is a regular preterite, while *shown* consists of the base and the distinctive past participle suffix. Other such verbs include ***mow***, ***prove***, ***sew***. All have a regular past participle as a variant of the irregular one.

Type B.   Preterite: vowel change; past participle: base + suffix

Here the past participle is formed in the same way as in Type A, but the preterite is irregular, formed by vowel change. Other examples: ***blow***, ***eat***, ***give***.

Type C. Preterite: vowel change; past participle: modified base + suffix

These verbs differ from those of Type B in that the base to which the past participle suffix is added is modified. In speech the base vowel is changed; in writing mute *e* is dropped and *d* or *t* is doubled. Other examples: ***smite***, ***stride***, ***write***. Such verbs as ***drive*** and ***rise*** belong here in speech but in Type B in writing.

Type D.   Preterite: vowel change; past participle: preterite form + suffix

In this type the past participle suffix is added not to the lexical base but to the preterite form. Other examples: ***break***, ***choose***, ***tread*** (with the general rule of consonant doubling applying with the last to give *trodden* for the past participle).[2]

Type E.   Three different vowels; no suffix

With a few verbs the three forms are distinguished solely by their vowels. Other examples include ***begin***, ***ring***, ***swim***. All have the same pattern of vowel change: *i ~ a ~ u*.

---

[2] There are a few differences in verb inflection between AmE and BrE. One of the most striking is that ***get*** belongs in this class in AmE (with the three forms *get*, *got*, *gotten*), whereas in BrE the past participle has the same shape as the preterite, *got*, with ***get*** thus belonging in Type G of [16].

Type F.   Miscellaneous

There are a few verbs which don't fit into any of the above patterns. With *fly*, the three forms have different vowels but the past participle also contains the suffix; similarly with *do*.

With *be* and *go* the preterite bears no resemblance at all to the lexical base, while the past participle consists of base + suffix. With *come* and *run* the past participle is identical with the lexical base but the preterite is formed by vowel change.

5   Noun inflection

Nouns inflect for **number** and for **case**. The non-genitive singular, or **plain singular**, is identical with the lexical base. What we need to consider here is the marking of **plural** number and **genitive** case. We do not cover the inflection of pronouns in this chapter; the forms are listed in Ch. 5, and there is nothing interesting we can add here about how they are formed.[3]

5.1   Plural formation

Plurals which are regular in speech are formed in writing by adding ·*es* or the default ·*s* to the lexical base. The choice between these alternants has been discussed in §3.4 and is illustrated again in [19]:

[19]	i LEXICAL BASE	cross	horse	edge	echo	book	studio
	ii PLURAL	cross·es	hors·es	edg·es	echo·es	book·s	studio·s

Plurals that are irregular in speech we discuss under four headings.

(a) Modification of the base-final consonant

With a good number of nouns, addition of the plural suffix is accompanied by a modification of the consonant at the end of the base. When the consonant in question is represented in writing by *f*, the modification is reflected in the spelling, as in:

[20]	i BASE	calf	knife	leaf	loaf	thief	wife	wolf
	ii PLURAL	calve·s	knive·s	leave·s	loave·s	thieve·s	wive·s	wolve·s

The consonant symbol *f* is changed to *v*, and mute *e* is added if not already present. The default is for noun bases not to undergo such modification: words such as *belief, chief, proof, safe* don't, and when an invented word ending in *f* is added to the lexicon, its plural does not show the modification (the noun *Smurf* appeared in English with a TV cartoon series in the 1980s, and the plural is of course *Smurfs*).

Some words, such as *dwarf* and *hoof*, have both regular and irregular plurals: *dwarfs* and *hoofs* or *dwarves* and *hooves*.

---

[3] For the same reason we omit consideration of the inflectional number contrast in the demonstratives *this* and *that*; see again Ch. 5, §3.1.

In speech the noun *house* undergoes a similar modification, and so do some nouns ending in the consonant represented as *th* (e.g. *mouth*), but this is not reflected in the spelling.

(b) Vowel change and the suffix ·en/·ren

With a small number of nouns the plural is formed by changing the vowel and/or adding the suffix ·en or ·ren. Examples are given in [21]:

[21]	i BASE	man	woman	foot	tooth	mouse	ox	child
	ii PLURAL	men	women	feet	teeth	mice	ox·en	child·ren

With *woman*, both vowels are changed in speech (*women* rhymes with *him in*), but only the second in writing. With *mouse* (and also *louse*) the vowel change is accompanied by a change in the consonant symbol. In speech, *children* shows both a suffix and a vowel change in the base (notice that *child* rhymes with *filed*, but the beginning of *children* sounds like *chill*).

(c) Base plurals

A fair number of nouns have plurals that are, like the singular, identical with the base:

[22]	BASE = PLURAL	*sheep*	*cod*	*bison*	*barracks*	*series*	*Chinese*	*Roma*

Most of these nouns belong to one or other of the following categories:

- Nouns denoting edible fish and game animals – creatures that are traditionally hunted. *Cod* and *bison* from [22] belong here; others include *salmon, trout, deer, grouse, reindeer*. Some (such as *elk*) have a regular plural alternant. For animals that have never been the target of hunting or fishing, the base plural is impossible: **three cockroach, *several spider, *two large dog*.
- Nouns with bases ending in *s* (a single *s*, not double): *barracks, headquarters, means, series, species*, etc. (we never find **three different barrackses*).
- Nationality nouns in ·*ese*: *Chinese, Japanese, Vietnamese*, etc. (we never find **millions of Chineses*).
- Many names of tribes and ethnic groups: *Apache, Bedouin, Inuit, Kikuyu, Navajo, Roma*, etc. With most of these a regular plural alternant is sometimes used, but not as commonly as the base plural.

(d) Foreign plurals

A considerable number of nouns of Latin, Greek and various other origins have plurals taken from those languages. Many belong to scientific or otherwise relatively learned vocabulary. A good proportion have regular plurals as variants, and these tend to be preferred in informal contexts. Some examples are given in [23]:

[23]	i BASE	*formula*	*larva*	*stimulus*	*syllabus*	*phenomenon*	*chassis*
	ii FOREIGN PLURAL	*formulae*	*larvae*	*stimuli*	*syllabi*	*phenomena*	*chassis*
	iii REGULAR PLURAL	*formulas*	–	–	*syllabuses*	–	–

With some of these nouns the foreign plural is much more common than the singular, and for some speakers has been learned as a singular. Examples include *data* (from *datum*), *media* (*medium*), *algae* (*alga*), *bacteria* (*bacterium*), *criteria* (*criterion*) and *phenomena* (*phenomenon*). There is considerable variation, however, with respect to how far this singular usage has become established as a variant of the plural. Singular *data* and *media* are firmly established in Standard English (examples like *The data is reliable* or *The media keeps hounding her* are widely used and considered acceptable); but singular *criteria* and *phenomena* definitely are not (expressions like ¹*this criteria* or ¹*a new phenomena* are regarded as non-standard). Various other items, such as *algae* and *bacteria*, belong in the middle ground.

5.2   Genitive formation

The genitive forms of the personal pronouns and the interrogative/relative genitive pronoun *whose* have been described in Ch. 5, §8.3, and Ch. 11, §3: in this chapter we confine our attention to other genitive forms.

From a morphological point of view, there are two kinds of genitive, the **'s genitive** and the **bare genitive**:

[24] i 's GENITIVE   *girl ~ girl's*   *woman ~ woman's*   *women ~ women's* *James ~ James's*
      ii BARE GENITIVE   *girls ~ girls'*   *barracks ~ barracks'*   *James ~ James'*

The *'s* genitive is the default form: we need only give the particular conditions under which the bare genitive must or may occur, and can then say that the *'s* genitive is used for the remainder.

(a) The bare genitive

In speech, the bare genitive is not overtly marked at all, being identical in form with its non-genitive counterpart. In writing, it is marked by a final apostrophe.

The bare genitive is virtually restricted to nouns ending in *s*. It is usually obligatory, but it may also be optional, alternating with the *'s* genitive:

[25] i   PLURALS FORMED WITH THE ·s/·es SUFFIX   obligatory   *girls'*   *foxes'*
      ii NOUNS IN *s* WITH BASE PLURALS   obligatory   *barracks'* *series'*
      iii CERTAIN PROPER NOUNS IN *s*   optional   *James'*   *Socrates'*

- The obligatory bare genitives are found with plural nouns marked as such by the ·s or ·es suffix (including those with modification of the lexical base, as in *wives'*), and with nouns ending in *s* that have base plurals, as described in §5.1 above. Note that *barracks'* and *series'*, like the non-genitive counterparts, can be either singular or plural.

- The optional bare genitive is found in proper nouns ending in a single *s*, especially classical ones. It is more likely in writing than in speech, and more formal than the variant with *'s*.

(b) The 's genitive

In writing, the 's genitive is invariably formed by adding 's to the non-genitive counterpart – which may be a singular (*woman's*) or a plural that is not marked by the ·*s*/·*es* suffix (*women's*). In speech it has the same form and alternation as the regular plural suffix: *fox's*, for example, is pronounced the same as *foxes*.

The genitive 's sounds exactly like the plural suffix ·*s*/·*es*, but there is an interesting difference: the genitive does not trigger any modification of the base. The genitive of *wife* is *wife's*, not **wive's* – and in speech *mouth's* is pronounced differently from *mouths*.

6   Grade

The last of the three inflectional systems of English to consider is that of **grade**, with three contrasting terms: plain, comparative and superlative. It applies primarily to adjectives, but is found also with a few lexemes from other categories, most clearly adverbs and determinatives. Regular forms are illustrated in [26]:

[26]		ADJECTIVE				ADVERB	DETERMINATIVE
i	PLAIN	cold	hot	rare	easy	soon	few
ii	COMPARATIVE	cold·er	hott·er	rar·er	easi·er	soon·er	few·er
iii	SUPERLATIVE	cold·est	hott·est	rar·est	easi·est	soon·est	few·est

The plain form is identical with the lexical base while the comparative and superlative forms are marked by the suffixes ·*er* and ·*est*. These begin with a vowel, which triggers the modification of the base by the general spelling rules given in §§3.1–3.3 above: consonant doubling with *hot*, *e* deletion with *rare*, *y* replacement with *easy*.

There are a few lexemes where the comparative and superlative forms are highly irregular, bearing little if any resemblance to the plain form. These include the following:

[27]	i PLAIN	good / well	bad / badly	much / many	little
	ii COMPARATIVE	better	worse	more	less
	iii SUPERLATIVE	best	worst	most	least

- **Good** and **bad** are adjectives, while **well** and **badly** can be either adjectives (as in *I'm feeling well/badly*) or adverbs (*He behaved well/badly*).
- **Much**, **many** and **little** are determinatives. The determinative **little** (as in *It has little merit*) is a different word from the adjective **little** (as in *a little creature*), which we're not referring to here: the adjective has regular inflection.[4]

---

[4] The inflected forms, however, are now rare, *smaller* and *smallest* being usually preferred.

Inflectional and non-inflectional marking of grade

The comparative and superlative categories differ from those discussed in §§4–5 above in that they can be marked by the separate words *more* and *most* as well as by means of inflection. Some lexemes have only inflectional comparatives and superlatives, others have only the non-inflectional type, while others accept both. These comparative examples illustrate:

[28]		INFLECTIONAL COMPARATIVE	NON-INFLECTIONAL COMPARATIVE
i	INFLECTIONAL ONLY	*This is better than that.*	**This is more good than that.*
ii	NON-INFLECTIONAL ONLY	**This is usefuller than that.*	*This is more useful than that.*
iii	EITHER TYPE	*This is gentler than that.*	*This is more gentle than that.*

- Very few lexemes accept only the inflectional type. The clearest examples are the determinative *few* from [26] and the irregular lexemes given in [27].
- The *·ly* suffix is never compatible with grade inflection: neither **clearlier* nor **clearerly* is possible. That means grade for *·ly* adverbs must always be expressed in the non-inflectional way (*You should speak more clearly*).
- Lexemes with monosyllabic bases nearly always prefer the inflectional type, but with some such as *fake*, *ill*, *right*, and *wrong* the inflected forms are very rare.
- Adjectives with two-syllable bases accept non-inflectional grade marking, but inflected forms are often not available, especially for the ones that do not have final stress. Bases of this kind formed with *·y* do take inflection (*sticky, stickier, stickiest*), but examples of adjectives that do not accept inflection include *brutish, careful, legal, jealous, public*, and others formed with the suffixes *·ish, ·ful, ·al, ·ous*, and *·ic*.

7   Lexical morphology

Lexical morphology is concerned with the formation and structure of the lexical bases of lexemes. It is **complementary** with inflectional morphology: it deals with those aspects of the formation and structure of words that are NOT a matter of inflection.

7.1   The structure of words

Words may be morphologically **complex** or **simple**:

[29]	i	COMPLEX WORD:	a word that can be analysed into a sequence of smaller morphological units, such as *un·usual, gentle·man·ly, luck·y*
	ii	SIMPLE WORD:	a word that is not complex, such as *usual, gentle, man, luck*

Bases and affixes

The two main kinds of morphological unit are **bases** and **affixes**. Of the units appearing in the examples in [29], *luck, usual, gentle, man* are bases, while *un·, ·ly,* and *·y* are affixes. As a starting-point we can distinguish between bases and affixes as follows:

[30]   i BASE: usually a **free** element, one able to stand alone as a word
       ii AFFIX: a **bound** element, one unable to stand alone as a word

This covers the examples given so far. But there is a complication: not all bases are free. Two kinds of **bound base** are illustrated in *dur·able* and *scissor·like*.

- The *dur·* in *durable* is a base in another language (it comes from Latin via Old French), and the word *durable* was borrowed as a whole, not created by the operations of word formation in English. The other component of the word, *·able*, is recognisable as the suffix that combines with free bases in innumerable words like *enjoyable, perishable, readable, retrievable*. Thus although it is bound, *dur·* occupies the same place in word structure as free bases like *enjoy, perish, read, retrieve*, etc.
- As we noted in §2, there are a number of plural-only nouns which have no singulars. A base like *scissor·* is bound, occurring in *scissors* and certain derived words, but not on its own.

Once we allow for bound bases, the following two claims hold without exception:

- ALL complex words contain at least one base.
- ALL affixes attach to bases.

Individual affixes typically attach to a good number of bases, whereas bases typically combine with just a small number of affixes. Of the affixes mentioned above, for example, *un·, ·ly* and *·able* occur with innumerable bases, and *·y* with a considerable number, whereas the base *luck* combines with just *·y* and *·less* (*lucky, luckless*), *usual* with *un·, ·ly, ·ness* (*unusual, usually, usualness*), and so on.

The layered structure of words

Bases containing more than two elements almost always have a layered structure defining a hierarchy, very similar to the hierarchical structure we see in syntax. For example:

- In the adjective *gentle·man·ly* the bases *gentle* and *man* combine to form *gentleman*, and the suffix *·ly* is added to that: it's not *gentle + manly*, it's *gentleman + ·ly*.
- In *whistle·blow·er* the suffix *·er* is added to *blow* to form the base *blower*, and *whistle* combines with this: it's not *whistleblow + ·er*, it's *whistle + blower*.

A similar difference in the hierarchical structure is seen in such a pair as *un·couth·ness* (with *un·* added to *couth*, and *·ness* to *uncouth*) and *un·luck·y* (with *·y* added to *luck*, and *un·* to *lucky*). Structural diagrams for the four examples are shown in [31]:

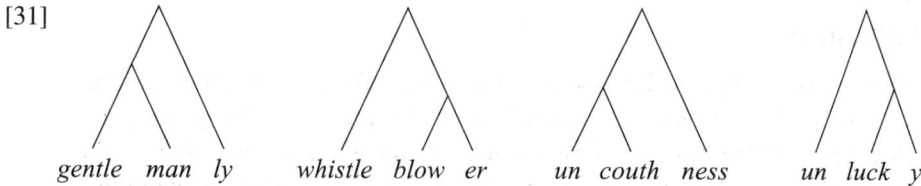

[31]

gentle man ly   whistle blow er   un couth ness   un luck y

7.2 Morphological operations

A wide range of morphological operations are involved in the formation of lexical bases – considerably more than are used in inflectional morphology. In the following brief survey, the first three are the most important operations, the others being relatively minor and small-scale.

(a) Compounding

Compounding forms a complex base from a combination of smaller bases – almost always two. We illustrate here with compound nouns, adjectives and verbs:

[32]

i NOUNS	*birdcage*	*gentleman*	*hangman*	*loudmouth*	*outpatient*	*stage-manager*
ii ADJECTIVES	*dirt-cheap*	*heart-breaking*	*heart-broken*	*skin-deep*	*snow-white*	*stress-free*
iii VERBS	*baby-sit*	*blow-dry*	*handwash*	*over-react*	*sleepwalk*	*underachieve*

- Compound nouns constitute by far the largest and most varied category. Most denote a subset of what is denoted by the second component: a birdcage is a kind of cage, a gentleman is a kind of man, and so on. But there are certainly a good number that do not have this interpretation: a loudmouth is not a kind of mouth (but a person with a loud mouth – one who talks a lot, typically in an offensive way). The second base is most often a noun, while the first can belong to a range of categories: *bird* is a noun, *gentle* an adjective, *hang* a verb, *out* a preposition.

- Compound adjectives often similarly have a denotation included in that of the second element: if something is dirt-cheap, then it must be cheap, and if it's snow-white, it's white. But there are numerous cases where this is not so. A stress-free job is not a free job (it's free of stress), and something that is only skin-deep is not deep. *Heart-breaking* and *heart-broken* illustrate a frequent type where the first base is a noun and the second a gerund-participle or past participle form of a verb.

- There are many compound verbs with a preposition such as *over*, *under*, *out* as first base, but for the rest compound verbs are far less numerous than compound nouns and adjectives.

- One distinctive type of compound noun combines two normally bound bases taken from Greek or Latin, as in: *osteometry*, *osteopath*, *psychopath*, *pathology*, *psychology*, etc. Such 'neo-classical' compounds figure very prominently in the learned and scientific vocabulary of the language.

(b) Affixation

In affixation a base is expanded by the addition of a **prefix** at the beginning of the base or a **suffix** at the end. Very often the effect of affixation is to change the part-of-speech category of the base – to form a noun from an adjective or verb, to form a verb from a noun or adjective, and so on. We speak here of **category-changing** affixes, as opposed to **category-preserving** affixes:

[33]

		CATEGORY-CHANGING		CATEGORY-PRESERVING	
i	PREFIX	*be·friend*	*en·danger*	*un·happy*	*re·open*
ii	SUFFIX	*wet·ness*	*achiev·able*	*green·ish*	*lion·ess*

Befriend and *endanger* are verbs formed from nouns, while *wetness* is a noun formed from an adjective, and *achievable* is an adjective formed from a verb. Most category-changing affixes are **suffixes**.

Some affixes can be used in EITHER a category-changing OR a category-preserving way.

● The suffix *·ly*, for example, often derives adverbs from adjectives (*rapid·ly*) and, much less often, derives adjectives from nouns (*friend·ly*, *gentleman·ly*, *prince·ly*), so it can be category-changing.
● In a few cases, however, it derives adjectives from more elementary adjectives. These are not that common in the contemporary language, but examples include *good·ly* "considerable", *kind·ly* "benevolent", and *poor·ly* "not in good health".[5]

Affixation is commonly accompanied by **modification** of the base, sometimes just in spelling, and sometimes in pronunciation as well. In *achievable*, for example, the mute *e* of *achieve* is dropped, while in *persuasion* we have a change in the consonant at the end of *persuade*.

(c) Conversion

Whereas the verb *hospitalise* is formed from *hospital* by adding the suffix *·ise*, the verb *bottle* (as in *Where do they bottle Coca-Cola?*) is formed from the noun *bottle* without any change of shape at all. This is called **conversion**: a base of one category is formed by extending the use of a base of another category. The main types are illustrated in [34]:

[34]

		PRIMARY USE	CONVERSION
i	NOUN TO VERB	*The plants need water_N.*	*I'll water_V the plants.*
ii	VERB TO NOUN	*I'll try_V to persuade her.*	*It was a good try_N.*

---

[5] *Kindly* and *poorly* also exist as adverbs, of course. But notice that grade inflection distinguishes them: grade inflection never occurs with *·ly* adverbs, but for the adjective **kindly** we have comparative *kindlier* and superlative *kindliest*, and these can never be used as adverbs.

iii	ADJECTIVE TO NOUN	*She's very professional*_{ADJ}.

iii ADJECTIVE TO NOUN   *She's very professional*_ADJ_.   *She's a professional*_N_.
iv ADJECTIVE TO VERB   *The bottle is empty*_ADJ_.   *Please empty*_V_ *the bottle.*
v VERB TO ADJECTIVE   *The film was boring*_V_ *us.*   *It's a boring*_ADJ_ *film.*

Type [v] differs from the others in that it is not the plain form, or lexical base, of the verb that undergoes conversion, but an inflected form. In this example it is a gerund-participle, but it can also be a past participle as in *It had bored*_V_ *them*, which gives, by conversion, *They were very bored*_ADJ_.

There is nothing in the base created by conversion to mark it as such. The direction of conversion reflects the distinction between primary and extended SENSES:

* the primary sense of *bottle* is to denote a narrow-necked container for liquids, and the verb *bottle* incorporates that sense: it means "put into a bottle";
* the primary sense of *water* is that it denotes the physical substance H_2O, and the verb *water* incorporates this sense: it means "provide with water".

(d) Derivation by base modification

There are also cases where the extension of a base from one category to another is accompanied merely by a **phonological modification** of the base, not the addition of any affix. Usually the modification is a change in the vowel or final consonant, or a shift in the stress from one syllable to another. With minor exceptions, such modifications are not reflected in the spelling. We illustrate here with noun–verb pairs, marking stressed syllables where relevant by putting them in SMALL CAPITALS, but without attempting to indicate which form is the primary one:

[35] NOUN   VERB
   i a. *This is the document you need.*   b. *We will document its development.*
  ii a. *I want to stay in this house.*   b. *We must house them locally.*
 iii a. *The interview was sheer TORment.*   b. *They want to torMENT me.*

* In [i] the noun and verb usually differ in the vowel of the last syllable. The last syllable of the noun has a reduced vowel, so it sounds the same as the last syllable of *informant*. The verb, however, has a full vowel, so it rhymes with *bent*.
* In [ii] there is a difference in the final consonant: the noun rhymes with *mouse*, whereas the verb rhymes with *rouse*.
* In [iii] the noun has the stress on the first syllable, while the verb has it on the second.

(e) Back-formation

A kind of opposite of affixation is found in some cases where the history of a word is that a word with an affix is taken to have a related form without that affix. We get a derived word that is formed by SUBTRACTING an affix from a base rather than adding one. This book is mostly not concerned with facts about the history of English, but this is one historical process that is worth noting.

- The verb *self-destruct* is a clear example. It was formed from the noun *self-destruction* by dropping the ·*ion* suffix. Notice that the verb related to *destruction* is *destroy*, not *destruct. The verb *self-destruct* came into the language after the noun, not the other way round. This backwards derivation by removing an affix is known as **back-formation**.
- The classic example is the verb *edit*, which is known to have arisen through back-formation from the noun *editor*: again, the noun preceded the verb historically.

There is nothing in the forms themselves that enables one to distinguish between affixation and back-formation: it's a matter of historical formation of words rather than of their structure. In fact, we have already listed two compound verbs that are back-formations: *baby-sit* and *sleepwalk* in [32iii]. These arose by back-formation from the nouns *baby-sitter* and *sleepwalking*. Structurally they are compounds, since they consist of two bases, but they did not arise historically by compounding.

(f) Clipping

Clipping is another minor process of word formation that removes part of a base (sometimes with a change in spelling for the part that remains), as in these examples:

[36]	FULL FORM	*delicatessen*	*microphone*	*helicopter*	*telephone*	*influenza*
	CLIPPING	*deli*	*mike*	*copter*	*phone*	*flu*

Deli and *mike* lose the last part of the original word; *copter* and *phone* lose the first part; and in *flu* both the beginning and the ending of the original base is lost, leaving a middle syllable (which in the original base is not even stressed).

Clipping should not be confused with back-formation. The two key differences are these:

- The clipped form does not differ in meaning from the original: it is merely a **variant** with the same meaning, usually a more informal one (though the degree of perceived informality changes over time: today *phone* is not particularly more informal than *telephone*).
- What is removed in a clipping is typically not any kind of morphological element: . . . *catessen*, . . . *rophone*, and . . . *enza*, for example, are certainly not bases or affixes or anything else (though *tele·* happens to be a bound base meaning "far away", seen also in *telepathy, telescope*).

(g) Blending

The process of **blending** is comparable to compounding, except that part of one (or both) of the source bases is dropped at the boundary between them. Examples are given in [37]:

[37]	SOURCE	*breath analyser*	*parachute troops*	*chocolate alcoholic*	*motor hotel*
	BLEND	*breathalyser*	*paratroops*	*chocoholic*	*motel*

In *breathalyser* the beginning of the second base (the *an* of *analyser*) is lost; in *paratroops* the end of the first base (the *chute* of *parachute*) is lost. In the others, both bases lose parts.

(h) Initialism

The final word-formation process we consider creates bases from the initial **letters** of a sequence of words (or, in a few cases, of parts of words). We call this process **initialism**. There are two subtypes (though people often confuse them): an **acronym** is formed by initialism in a way that picks initials that spell out a pronounceable word. An **abbreviation** is pronounced simply by uttering the names of the letters.

[38]   i ACRONYM   *NATO* (*North Atlantic Treaty Organisation*)

                                 AIDS (*acquired immune deficiency syndrome*)

      ii ABBREVIATION   *CIO* (*Chief Information Officer*) *UN* (*United Nations*)

                                 DNA (*deoxyribonucleic acid*)   *TV* (*television*)

- In acronyms the word spelled out by the letters is pronounced the way we would expect a word with that spelling to be pronounced: *NATO* rhymes with *Plato*, *AIDS* rhymes with *maids*.
- In abbreviations we just string together the letter names: *CIO* sounds like *sea eye owe*. (It would be possible to pronounce *CIO* as 'sigh-oh' or *UN* as 'un', but people don't. This means that when you first see an initialism in print, you may not always know whether it is an acronym or an abbreviation, and you might guess wrong. There is no way to tell until you hear someone say it.)

Initialisms are usually written with upper-case letters. The most common exceptions to this are abbreviations of Latin phrases: *e.g.* (*exempli gratia* "for example"), *i.e.* (*id est* "that is"), and others (dictionaries commonly contain lists of these).

Some words written in lower case originated as acronyms but are now not easily recognisable as such. They include *scuba* (*Self-Contained Underwater Breathing Apparatus*) and *radar* (from *RAdio Detecting And Ranging*). These have been in the language for decades, and many speakers will be unaware of their origin as acronyms.

7.3   Productivity and lexicalisation

A word-formation operation is said to be **productive** if it is still available for the creation of new words, and **non-productive** if it is not.

Affixation by means of such suffixes as *·able*, *·ness*, *·er* or such prefixes as *un·* and *pre·* is productive. You can generally put these affixes even on words that have only entered the language relatively recently: *emailable*, *nerdiness*, *rapper*, *ungoogled*, *prexeroxed*.

But there are other affixes which are no longer productive in Present-day English, like the ones underlined in *bond·age*, *duck·ling*, *drunk·ard*, *en·able*, *inform·ant*, or *young·ster*.

Productive affixes have different **degrees of productivity** – they have differing ranges of bases they can attach to. Among suffixes forming nouns, for example, ·*ness* is highly productive, ·*ity* somewhat less so, while ·*dom* is of very low productivity (though it is productive nevertheless, as evident from such a recent coinage as *yuppiedom*).

At the highest degree of productivity it is unnecessary, and indeed not feasible, to list in the dictionary all the words formed by the process in question. For example, ·*like* can be added very freely indeed to nouns to form such compound adjectives as *catlike, doglike, mouselike, wolflike, apple-like, banana-like, pear-like*, and it would be a mistake to try and include all words of this kind in the dictionary.

Words which couldn't be formed with their present meaning by means of operations still productive in the grammar today are said to be **lexicalised**: they absolutely have to be included in a dictionary. These include words formed through processes in the past that have not given rise to productive operations in the language as it is now, such as *drunkard, bondage*, and so on, because merely from having seen *drunk* and *bond* and ·*ard* and ·*age* we can't figure out what words can be made from them (**bondard, *drunkage?*) or what they would mean. But lexicalisation covers other cases too, notably:

- Words like *durable, knowledgeable, perishable*: although ·*able* suffixation is a highly productive operation, what's productive is its use on transitive verb bases, not bound bases (*dur·*), nouns (*knowledge*), or intransitive verbs (*perish*).
- Some words have meanings not predictable from the combination of their component parts. The meanings have to be specified individually. For example, the salient meaning of *considerable* doesn't match that of numerous words like *achievable* ("can be achieved") or *climbable* ("can be climbed"): it doesn't mean "can be considered", but "large, significant, or notable". Similarly, the compound *loudmouth* mentioned in §7.2 doesn't mean "mouth which is loud", but "person who talks a lot, typically one who gives offence". And *gentleman* doesn't mean "gentle man", but "man of chivalrous manner and good breeding or high social position" – or it may be just a courteous variant of *man*.

Information about words like this must appear in the dictionary, because no matter how well you are acquainted with the general principles of lexical morphology, you can't figure out what you need to know about them. In general, the grammar of a language can only cover the rule-governed aspects of its ways of structuring words or sentences. To complete the description we also need a dictionary, to list the unpredictable parts.

Exercises

1. Explain why *·ing* is an **inflectional** suffix in [i] but a **lexical** one in [ii]:
   i *They're building more town houses at the end of the street.*
   ii *We left the building by the back exit.*
2. Explain carefully why the suffix *·ish* (as in *greenish, sweetish, newish*) is NOT one of the inflectional suffixes of English.
3. Explain why there is **consonant doubling** in the first member of the following pairs, but not in the second:
   i *hopping   hoping*
   ii *referring   mothering*
   iii *stemming   steaming*
   iv *quizzing   boxing*
   v *starred   stars*
4. For each of the following verbs say whether the final *e* is deleted or retained when the **gerund-participle** is formed. Relate your answers to the rule of *e* deletion discussed in §3.2.
   i *age*   vi *judge*
   ii *be*   vii *plane*
   iii *centre* [BrE] viii *sortie*
   iv *impinge*   ix *tinge*
   v *implore*   x *wage*
5. For each of the following lexical bases give the **inflectional form** specified below, and show how the treatment of the final *y* follows the rule of final *y* replacement.
   i *dry*   gerund-participle
   ii *embody*   preterite
   iii *guy*   plural
   iv *silly*   superlative
   v *try* [V]   3rd sing present
6. Rewrite these examples with all noun phrases changed to their **plural** counterparts and all present-tense verbs changed to the correct **preterite** form.
   i *The other student sings in a rock band.*
   ii *The TV series made from that novel is as good as any film ever made.*
   iii *The bison roams the prairie and the wolf preys on the deer in the forest.*
   iv *The man drives the Mercedes into a garage and hopes no thief has a key to the building.*
   v *The chief focus of this task is investigating the larva and developing a criterion for distinguishing its response to an environmental stimulus from any similar phenomenon at a later stage.*
7. The following irregular verbs have **shape-sharing** between the **preterite** and the **past participle**. Assign them to one or other of Types A–H in [16] according to the relation between these forms and the lexical base, and note those which also have regular variants of the preterite and past participle.
   i *bind*   vi *hold*
   ii *burst*   vii *kneel*
   iii *dig*   viii *leave*
   iv *dream*   ix *lend*
   v *fight*   x *meet*
8. As in the previous exercise, these are irregular verbs with shape-sharing between the preterite and the past participle. Assign to a type, noting those which also have regular variants of the preterite and past participle: [i] *slide*; [ii] *spell*; [iii] *spread*; [iv] *strike*; [v] *weep*.
9. The following irregular verbs have distinct **preterite** and **past participle** forms. Assign them to Types A–H in [18] according to the way these forms are related to the lexical base.
   i *fall*   vi *get* [AmE]
   ii *give*   vii *grow*
   iii *shrink*   viii *slay*
   iv *sow*   ix *strive*
   v *swell*   x *wake*

10. For each word in the sentence *Our children said those earlier stories had been her worst*, say what **inflectional form** it is, and what **lexeme** it belongs to:

    i   *our*
    ii *children*
    iii *said*
    iv *those*
    v   *earlier*
    vi *stories*
    vii *had*
    viii *been*
    ix *her*
    x   *worst*

    (For example, if we had given the sentence *Pigs will fly*, then for the word *pigs* you would say that it is the plural form of the lexeme *pig*. For inflection of personal pronouns, recall the analysis given in Ch. 5, §8.)

11. Show for some plural-only words other than *scissors* that the **lexical base** sometimes occurs in compounds.

12. Discuss the choice between the *·es* and *·s* alternants of the plural suffix with the following nouns, after gathering evidence about how they are actually spelled in real texts:

    i   *cameo*
    ii   *echo*
    iii *eunuch*
    iv   *garage*
    v   *innuendo*
    vi   *lunch*
    vii *mango*
    viii *patio*
    ix   *photo*
    x   *piano*

13. Nouns with lexical bases ending in *f* or *fe* either have (a) **obligatory** modification of the base in plural formation; (b) **optional** modification; or (c) **no** modification. Give plurals of the following nouns, grouping them into these three types:

    i   *elf*
    ii   *handkerchief*
    iii *life*
    iv   *oaf*
    v   *self*
    vi   *sheaf*
    vii *shelf*
    viii *spoof*
    ix   *waif*
    x   *wharf*

14. Give plurals of the following nouns, grouping them into three types: (a) those with only **foreign** plurals; (b) those that have foreign and regular plurals as **variants**; or (c) those with only **regular** plurals.

    i   *alumnus*
    ii *amoeba*
    iii *appendix*
    iv *crucifix*
    v   *desideratum*
    vi   *foetus*
    vii *mausoleum*
    viii *millennium*
    ix   *phobia*
    x   *radius*

15. Give **genitives** of the following nouns, grouping them into three types: (a) those with only **bare genitives**; (b) those that have *'s* and **bare genitives** as variants; or (c) those with only *'s* **genitives**: [i] *children*; [ii] *Jones*; [iii] *kids*; [iv] *species*; [v] *Xerxes*.

16. Construct examples (grammatical and ungrammatical as the case may be) to show clearly that the adjective *kindly* can inflect for grade despite being formed with the *·ly* suffix, but the adverb *kindly* cannot be inflected for grade at all.

17. List all the **bases** that occur in the following words, bearing in mind that one base can be contained within another.

    i   *clothes-drier*
    ii   *handwriting*
    iii *disinterestedness*
    iv   *self-righteously*
    v   *taxpayer-funded*
    vi   *injustice*
    vii *upbringing*
    viii *babysitting*
    ix   *unavoidability*
    x   *underachiever*

18. Discuss the form of the underlined **lexical bases** in the following examples: identify the **morphological operations** and the bases and affixes involved in their formation.

    i   *I got it from a CNN <u>newscast</u>.*
    ii   *It was formed by a process of <u>adjectivalisation</u>.*
    iii *She works for <u>UNESCO</u>.*
    iv   *We didn't have <u>lead-free</u> fuel in those days.*
    v   *They are involved in some <u>illegal</u> operation.*
    vi   *They have decided to <u>euthanase</u> the whale.*
    vii *<u>Calm</u> down.*
    viii *He's always <u>mouthing</u> off about his boss.*
    ix   *I'll meet you in the <u>lab</u>.*
    x   *I was working as a <u>window-cleaner</u>.*

Further reading

In this short book we do not even try to incorporate all the bibliographical references that would be appropriate; to even sketch the vast array of scholarship on English grammar from 1580 to the present would take a separate book. We will just give some pointers to a few useful works for the student who wants to read further, and signal a few of our most important intellectual debts in linguistics.[1]

For the general reader

This book is based on our much larger work *The Cambridge Grammar of the English Language* (Rodney Huddleston & Geoffrey K. Pullum et al., CUP, 2002; henceforth *CGEL*). That is the first place to turn to for further details of the analysis we adopt.

An influential earlier work that inclines more to the older tradition in English grammar is Randolph Quirk et al., *A Comprehensive Grammar of the English Language* (London: Longman, 1985); this was of great value to us in preparing *CGEL*, but see Rodney Huddleston's critical review (*Language* **64** (1988): 345–54) for a number of reasons for disagreeing with its analyses.

A still earlier grammar is Otto Jespersen's classic *Modern English Grammar on Historical Principles* (7 vols.; London: Allen & Unwin, 1909–49). Jespersen was a radical rather than a traditionalist, and made many important innovative proposals, too many of which were overlooked.

An example of a nineteenth-century grammar worth looking at is Henry Sweet, *New English Grammar* (2 vols.; OUP, 1891). His statement that 'the rules of grammar have no value except as statements of facts: whatever is in general use in a language is for that very reason grammatically correct' (§12) expresses forthrightly the point of view we state in Ch. 1 of this book. The prescriptive grammars of the twentieth century might have been more useful if they had paid more attention to Sweet instead of simply trying to transmute personal prejudice into authority.

The best usage manual we know is *Merriam-Webster's Dictionary of English Usage* (Merriam-Webster, 1994), which contains a wealth of examples from print sources and always draws its advice from scholarly study of the actual facts of

---

[1] In our citations, 'CUP' means Cambridge University Press, 'OUP' means Oxford University Press, 'et al.' means 'and other authors'. Publication details are shortened or omitted for extremely well-known works that are easy to find.

usage. But usage manuals should in general be treated with caution, because many of the best-known ones are dogmatic, uninformed, and much more out of date than you might think. For example, much of the content of *The Elements of Style* by William Strunk & E. B. White (4th edn; Allyn & Bacon, 2000) is about a hundred years old (Strunk was born in 1869 and had published the first version of this slim book by 1918); its advice is often ludicrously old-fashioned, rooted in claims about 'correctness' that cannot be taken seriously.

Practical matters like punctuation and spelling are not systematically covered in the present book. Our concern has been rather to provide the grammatical basis on which a better understanding of punctuation could be based (there is no profit in being told that it is unacceptable to put a comma between subject and predicate if you cannot identify the subject and the predicate). But there are many good practical guides to punctuation in various works for writers, e.g., the *MLA Handbook for Writers of Research Papers* (6th edn, ed. Joseph Gibaldi; New York: Modern Language Association, 2003), and particularly *The Chicago Manual of Style* (15th edn; University of Chicago Press, 2003). There is a thorough and more theoretical treatment of punctuation in Ch. 20 of *CGEL*.

One of the best practical investments a student of English can make is to purchase a good dictionary or to become well acquainted with one that is regularly accessible in a library. Most university libraries will have the greatest of all dictionaries of English: the *Oxford English Dictionary* (2nd edn, 20 vols., 1989), a crucial scholarly resource for the study of English and its history, generally known as the *OED*. For American English specifically, the staunchly descriptive *Webster's Third New International Dictionary* is deservedly a classic, and *The American Heritage Dictionary* is also very useful. For purchase and everyday use by students, a number of publishers including CUP, OUP, HarperCollins, and Macmillan offer excellent, compact, affordable, up-to-date, descriptively oriented dictionaries.

For linguistics students

The review article by Peter Culicover (*Language* **80** (2004): 127–41) relates *CGEL*, and thus indirectly this book, to current issues in linguistics. James McCawley's encyclopaedic work *The Syntactic Phenomena of English* (2nd edn; University of Chicago Press, 1998) is an excellent introduction to the analysis of a wide range of syntactic facts in transformational-generative terms. Our discussion of the important distinction between general (universal) and language-particular definitions (Ch. 1) draws on ideas of John Lyons (see 'Towards a "notional" theory of the "parts of speech"', *Journal of Linguistics* **2** (1966): 209–36; expanded reprinting in his *Natural Language and Universal Grammar*, CUP, 1991).

Our analysis of the verb (Ch. 3), the clause (Ch. 4) and the noun (Ch. 5) rests on a vast literature. One indication of this is that whole books have been written on most of the individual classificational features relevant to the grammar of verb phrases and noun phrases; CUP has published *Aspect* (Bernard Comrie, 1976), *Case*

(Barry J. Blake, 2001), *Definiteness* (Chris Lyons, 1999), *Gender* (Greville Corbett, 1991), *Mood and Modality* (F. R. Palmer, 2001), *Number* (Greville Corbett, 2000), *Person* (Anna Siewierska, 2001), and *Tense* (Bernard Comrie, 1985), all of which will be of interest in comparing the grammar of English with that of other languages.

This book treats auxiliaries as heads, not dependents, rejecting the dependent-auxiliary analysis implicit in the work of both most traditional grammarians and also most generative grammarians (with some dissenters, such as J. R. Ross and J. D. McCawley). *CGEL*, pp. 1209–20, offers detailed justification. The generative literature is reviewed by Gerald Gazdar et al., 'Auxiliaries and related phenomena in a restrictive theory of grammar' (*Language* **58** (1982): 591–638).

With regard to adjective and adverb phrase structure (Ch. 6), as well as various other topics, we drew on Ray Jackendoff's monograph $\overline{X}$ *Syntax* (MIT Press, 1977), though we discovered he was wrong about whether adverbs take complements (quite a few do); and our analysis of prepositions (Ch. 7) was much influenced by Joseph E. Emonds, 'Evidence that indirect object movement is a structure-preserving rule' (*Foundations of Language* **8** (1972): 546–61) and Ray S. Jackendoff, 'The base rules for prepositional phrases' (in S. R. Anderson & P. Kiparsky (eds.), *A Festschrift for Morris Halle*, 345–56; New York: Holt Rinehart & Winston, 1973). Both were interestingly foreshadowed by Jespersen (*The Philosophy of Grammar*, 87–90; London: Allen & Unwin, 1924).

Our description of negation (Ch. 8) owes a great deal to three works: Edward Klima ('Negation in English', in J. A. Fodor & J. J. Katz (eds.), *The Structure of Language*, 246–323; Englewood Cliffs, NJ: Prentice-Hall, 1964); Laurence Horn (*A Natural History of Negation*; University of Chicago Press, 1989); and William A. Ladusaw (*Polarity Sensitivity as Inherent Scope Relations*; New York: Garland, 1980). The relation between clause type and illocutionary force (Ch. 9) connects grammar to the classification of speech acts begun by the philosopher of language J. L. Austin in *How to Do Things with Words* (OUP, 1962). The importance of semantics in the interpretation of subjectless non-finites (Ch. 13) is demonstrated by Ivan A. Sag & Carl J. Pollard, 'An integrated theory of complement control' (*Language* **67** (1991): 63–113).

The rich technical literature on subordination, coordination, and unbounded dependencies raises many intertwined issues. Important generative works include John Robert Ross, *Infinite Syntax!* (New York: Ablex, 1986; originally a 1967 MIT doctoral dissertation called 'Constraints on Variables in Syntax'); Joan Bresnan & Jane Grimshaw, 'The syntax of free relatives in English' (*Linguistic Inquiry* **9** (1978): 331–91); Joan Bresnan, 'Syntax of the comparative clause construction in English' (*Linguistic Inquiry* **4** (1973): 275–343); Gerald Gazdar, 'Unbounded dependencies and coordinate structure' (*Linguistic Inquiry* **12** (1981): 155–84); and Ivan A. Sag et al., 'Coordination and how to distinguish categories' (*Natural Language & Linguistic Theory* **3** (1985): 117–71). All of these are technical works giving various kinds of theoretical accounts of subsets of the facts dealt with here in Chs. 10–14. Many others that have influenced us could be cited.

Betty Birner & Gregory Ward discuss information packaging (Ch. 15) in their *Information Status and Noncanonical Word Order in English* (Amsterdam: John Benjamins, 1998), and many further references to the rest of the literature are cited there. Our treatment of inflection in Ch. 16 owes much to F. R. Palmer, *The English Verb* (2nd edn; London: Longman, 1987), and Peter Matthews, *Morphology* (2nd edn; CUP, 1991). A linguistic defence of this lexeme-based rather than morpheme-based view of morphology is given by Stephen R. Anderson, *A-Morphous Morphology* (CUP, 1992).

Glossary

The aim of the glossary is to provide brief reminders of the meaning of a subset of the technical terms used in the book: we do not include terms used only in the section where they are introduced and explained. Fuller explanations can be found by using the index.

Accusative. The inflectional **case** of the pronouns *me, him, her, us, them, whom*. Contrasts with **nominative**.

Active. Opposite of **passive**.

Adjective. A category of lexemes characteristically denoting properties of persons or objects (*old, big, round, blue, good*). The prototypical adjective can be used both **attributively** and **predicatively** (*hot soup, The soup is hot*), participates in the system of **grade** (occurs in the **comparative** and **superlative**), and takes **adverbs** as **modifier** (*extremely hot, very useful*).

Adjunct. A **modifier** in clause structure (*The meeting ended on Sunday*) or a **supplement** attached to a clause (*It was, on Sunday, already too late*).

Adverb. A category of lexemes whose prototypical members are derived from **adjectives** by adding ·*ly*: *audibly, cleverly, remarkably, softly*, etc. Generally function as modifiers of verbs (*speaks clearly*) and other categories other than nouns.

Affix. A **prefix** or **suffix**, added to a **base** to make up a word (or larger base): *unfriendly, befriended*.

Agreement. Change in **inflectional form** to match properties of another constituent: in *She loves you* the verb *loves* agrees with the subject (replacing *she* by *they* yields *They love you*).

Anaphora. The relation between a **personal pronoun** or similar form and an **antecedent** from which it gets its interpretation: *they* is anaphoric to *my colleagues* in *I thanked my colleagues for the support they had given me*.

Antecedent. Constituent whose meaning dictates the meaning of a pronoun or other such expression in cases of **anaphora**.

Ascriptive. The use of *be* illustrated in *Mike was a loyal party member*, where the **predicative complement** (underlined) expresses a property that is ascribed to Mike. Contrasts with **specifying**.

Aspect. A verbal category mainly indicating the speaker's view of the temporal structure of the situation the clause describes, such as whether it is habitual or complete. The English **progressive** (*He is working*) is an aspect conveying a view of the situation as being in progress.

Attributive. Applies to an adjective or other **pre-head internal modifier** in NP structure: *a hot day* illustrates attributive use of *hot*.

Auxiliary verb. A subclass of verb that prototypically marks **tense, aspect, mood** or **voice**. In English, auxiliaries can invert with the **subject** in **interrogatives** (*Can you swim?*), and have special **primary negation** forms (*She hasn't seen it*).

Backshift. Prototypically, a shift from present tense to preterite in reported speech: you ask *Has she seen it?* and I report your question by saying *You asked whether she had seen it*.

Bare coordinate. A **coordinate** not marked with a **coordinator**.

Bare infinitival clause. An **infinitival clause** lacking the marker *to*: *you must do your best*.

Bare role NP. Singular NP like *treasurer* with no determiner, denoting a role or office. Can be **predicative complement** (*She became treasurer*) but not subject (**Treasurer resigned*).

Base. One of the two main kinds of unit found in the structure of words; contrasts with **affix**. In *friendly* the *·ly* is an affix attached to the base *friend*, making another base, *friendly*.

Base plural. Plural noun identical with the **lexical base** for the **lexeme**: *sheep, cod, barracks*.

Canonical clause. **Declarative, positive**, non-**coordinate, main clause** not belonging to any of the special **information-packaging** constructions (**passive, it-cleft**, etc.). The syntactically most basic form of clause; e.g., *We must get some milk*.

Case. An inflectional system of the noun with the primary use of marking various syntactic functions, such as subject and object in clause structure or determiner in NP structure. In English the main distinction is between **genitive** and **plain** case (e.g. *Kim's* vs *Kim*). A few pronouns have distinct **nominative** and **accusative** cases (e.g. *I* vs *me*) instead of a plain case.

Catenative complement. A **non-finite clause** functioning as **internal complement** of a verb (with a few exclusions, e.g., those where the clause is complement to *be* in its **ascriptive** and **specifying** senses). Examples: *You seem to like her; I regret doing it; We arranged for them to meet; I believe it to be genuine*.

Catenative verb. Verb with **catenative complement**: *You seem to like her; I regret doing it*.

Clause type. A classification of clauses into syntactic types, associated in main clauses with different kinds of **speech act**. See: **declarative, exclamative, imperative, interrogative**.

Closed interrogative. A subtype of interrogative clause characteristically used, in **main clauses**, to ask a **closed question**. Marked in main clauses by **subject–auxiliary inversion** (*Is it raining?; Is he alive or dead?*), and in **subordinate clauses** by *whether* or *if* (*I wonder whether it's raining; I don't know if he's alive or dead*).

Closed question. Question with a closed set of answers: *Is it raining?* (answers: *Yes, No*); *Is he alive or dead?* (answers: *He's alive, He's dead*).

Collective noun. A noun denoting a collection of individuals. In BrE especially, can function as head of a singular NP taking plural verb agreement: *%The committee have not yet decided*.

Common noun. The default subclass of **noun**, lacking the distinctive properties of **pronouns** and **proper nouns**: *cat, boy, woman, window*, etc.

Comparative (grade, form). The term in the system of **grade** indicating "more than"; it is marked either inflectionally (as in *hotter*) or by the adverb *more* (*more useful*).

Comparative clause. A kind of **subordinate clause** (usually **finite**) functioning as complement to *than, as* or *like* and expressing one of the two terms in a comparison: *It is colder [than it was yesterday]*; *I went to the same school [as she did]*.

Complement. A kind of **dependent** that must be **licensed** by the head. In *It shakes the building*, *the building* is a complement because it's allowed only with a certain kind of head verb: *shake* licenses dependents of this kind, but *quake* doesn't (**It quakes the building*).

Complex catenative construction. A clause containing a **catenative complement** whose verb is separated from the verb of the **matrix clause** by an NP understood as subject of the non-finite clause: *I asked her to help me*; *I knew them to be friends*.

Complex-intransitive. A clause containing a predicative complement but no object (*I'm sorry*; *It looks promising*), or a verb used in such a clause (*be, look* – in the sense illustrated).

Complex-transitive. A clause containing a predicative complement and an object (*I find that incredible*), or verb used in such a clause (*find* – in the sense illustrated).

Composite symbol. A sequence of two or more letters representing a single sound: in *heat* the vowel (sound) is represented by the composite symbol *ea*.

Conditional (construction). Prototypically, one containing an **adjunct** introduced by *if*: *I'll do it if you pay me*.

Consonant, consonant symbol. A consonant is a sound produced by means of some audible constriction of the airflow; a consonant symbol is a letter or sequence of letters representing a consonant. In *quick* there are three consonant symbols: *q, u*, and *ck*.

Content clause. The default kind of **finite subordinate clause**, lacking the special properties of **relative** and **comparative clauses**: *I think you're right*; *I wonder whether it is*.

Continuative perfect. A use of the **perfect** indicating a situation lasting over a period starting before a certain time and continuing up to it: *She had been in bed for two hours when we arrived* means she was in bed two hours before we arrived and continued to be until we arrived (and possibly after that).

Coordinate. An element in a **coordination** construction. *Sue or her son* has two coordinates: *Sue* (a **bare coordinate**) and *or her son* (an **expanded coordinate**).

Coordination. A construction with two or more constituents of equal status, prototypically linked by a **coordinator** (*and, or, but*): *It rained and it snowed* (coordination of clauses); *Sue or her son* (coordination of NPs); *some rice and beans* (coordination of nouns).

Coordinator. A small lexeme category (part of speech) whose members serve to mark one element as **coordinate** with another: *Kim and Pat*; *today or tomorrow*; *poor but happy*.

Correlative coordination. Coordination with the first **coordinate** marked by a **determinative** (*both*, *either*, or *neither*): *Both Sue and her husband went*; *It's neither illegal nor unethical*.

Count noun. Noun denoting an entity that is countable; hence a noun that can combine with numerals: *two cats, a hundred times*.

Declarative clause. The default **clause type**; in **main clauses**, characteristically used to make a statement: *The dog is barking*; *She can swim*.

Default. What holds if nothing special is stated. The default position of the subject of a clause is before the verb, though where the verb is an **auxiliary**, it may, under restricted conditions, follow the verb.

Definite article. The determinative *the*. Prototypically functions as determiner in NP structure with the sole meaning of indicating that the head is sufficient in the context to identify the referent: when I ask, *Where's the car?*, I assume you know which car I'm referring to.

Definite NP. NP marked by the **definite article** *the* or by certain other **determiners** (e.g., *this*, *that*, *my*), or with no determiner but having a **proper noun** as head. Characteristically used when the content of the NP is sufficient in the context to identify the referent.

Deictic. Used in a way that allows the interpretation to be determined by features of the act of utterance like when and where it takes place, and who the speaker and addressee are; e.g. *I* (refers to the speaker), *now* (refers to a time that includes the time of utterance).

Deontic modality. Meaning relating prototypically to requirement or permission: *must* in *You must help* expresses deontic necessity; *may* in *You may come in* expresses deontic possibility.

Dependent. An element in the structure of a phrase or clause other than the **head**: *the new doctor*; *wrote a book*; *very old*. Covers **complements**, **modifiers** and **determiners**.

Dependent vs independent genitive. A few personal pronouns have two **genitive** forms, a dependent one used with a following head (*your house*) and an independent when it is **fused** with the head (*Her house is bigger than yours*) or is head by itself (*All this is yours*).

Determinative. A category of words (or lexemes) which can function as **determiner** in an NP, marking it as **definite** or **indefinite**: *the*, *a*, *this*, *that*, *some*, *any*, *few*, etc. Most can occur with other functions too: e.g., *that* is modifier of an adjective in *It wasn't that great*.

Determinative phrase (DP). A phrase with a **determinative** as **head**: *not many*, *almost every*.

Determiner. A kind of **dependent** occurring only in NP structure, and serving to mark the NP as definite or indefinite. Usually has the form of a **determinative** (*the dog*), a **determinative phrase** (*very few errors*), or a **genitive** NP (*this guy's attitude*).

Direct object. The default kind of object of a verb (not an **indirect object**). In a **canonical clause**, a single object is always a direct object: *Jill paid the bill*. In canonical clauses with two objects, the first is indirect, the second direct: *He gave me the key* (*me* is indirect object).

Directive. Cover term for requests, commands, orders, instructions and similar **speech acts** aimed at getting the addressee(s) to do something.

Ditransitive. Clause with two **objects** (*I lent her my bike*) or verb of such a clause (*lend*).

Dummy. A meaningless word required in some construction to satisfy a syntactic requirement; e.g. *do* in *Does she know him?*, where the construction requires an **auxiliary verb**.

Epistemic modality. Meaning relating to what's necessary or possible given our beliefs: *must* in *You must be exhausted* expresses epistemic necessity; *may* in *You may be right* expresses epistemic possibility.

Exclamative clause. A **clause type** characteristically used, in **main clauses**, to make an exclamatory statement: *What a mess they made!*; *How stupid I was!*

Existential clause. A clause which prototypically has the **dummy** pronoun *there* as subject and a complement corresponding to the subject of a more basic construction: *There was a key on the table*. Here *a key* corresponds to the subject of the more basic *A key was on the table*.

Expanded coordinate. **Coordinate** prototypically beginning with a **coordinator**.

External. Located outside the VP or the nominal: (*She* [*lost her key*]); (*this big a hole*).

Extraposed object. A postverbal element, normally a subordinate clause, in a clause with dummy *it* as object: *I consider it a scandal that we weren't paid*.

Extraposed subject. A postverbal element, normally a subordinate clause, in a clause with dummy *it* as subject: *It is fortunate that you could come*.

Extraposition. A clause construction which prototypically has **dummy** *it* as subject and a postverbal **subordinate clause**: *It is fortunate that you could come*.

Finite clause. Clause that is either headed by a **primary verb-form** (*Ed is careful*) or is **imperative** (*Be careful*) or is **subjunctive** (*I insist that he be careful*). **Main clauses** are always finite, **subordinate clauses** may be finite or **non-finite**.

Fossilised. Of a word combination, lacking the syntactic variation that would be expected. *Come across* (= "find by chance") is fossilised in that the preposition must immediately follow the verb: *the letters which I came across*, not **the letters across which I came*.

Fronted preposition. Preposition placed along with its complement at the front of the clause: [*To whom*] *are you referring?*

Fused relative construction. NP in which the relative word (*what* and *whoever*) functions simultaneously as head of the NP and as an element within a modifying relative clause, as in *What you say is true* or *Whoever told you that is mistaken*.

Fused-head construction. An NP where the **head** is fused with a dependent element, usually a **determiner** or **internal modifier**. In *We have three eggs but* [*two*] *are cracked*, *two* is both **determiner** and **head**. In *the poor* the adjective *poor* is simultaneously **modifier** and **head**.

Futurate. Prototypically, a use of the **present tense**, permitted in **main clauses**, to indicate future time: *The week ends tomorrow*; *Exams start next week*. Also corresponding uses of the **preterite**: *I thought that exams started next week*.

Gender. A grammatical classification which in English applies primarily to the 3rd person singular **personal pronouns**. It correlates largely (not perfectly) with sex: *he* (masculine) usually refers to males, *she* (feminine) to females, and *it* (neuter) to inanimates.

Genitive. An inflectional **case** of the noun whose primary use is to mark an NP as determiner within the structure of a larger NP: *Kim's book*. Some pronouns have two genitive forms: **dependent genitive** (*my*) and **independent genitive** (*mine*).

Gerund-participial. Clause with a **gerund-participle** as head verb: *I recall her being there*.

Gerund-participle. The form of the verb marked by the suffix *·ing*: *They are sleeping*.

Goal. Clause constituent prototypically indicating where something moves to: *I went home*.

Gradable. Denoting a property that can apply in varying degrees. Gradable adjectives take degree modifiers: *very hot*, *rather good*, *slightly dubious*, etc.

Grade. The system of contrasts between **plain**, **comparative**, and **superlative**.

Head. The function of the most important element in a phrase. Often stands alone without any **dependents**, as in *Dogs were barking*: the subject NP contains just the head noun *dogs*.

Hollow clause. Non-finite clause with missing non-subject element such as an object deriving its interpretation from an **antecedent**: *He's easy to get on with*; *It's a difficult thing to do*.

Idiom. Combination of words with meaning not systematically derivable from the meanings of those words: *kick the bucket* (= "die"); *tie the knot* (= "get married").

Imperative clause. **Clause type** characteristically used to express a **directive**: *Don't move*; *Please sit down*. Verb in **plain form**; **subject** usually omitted but understood as "you".

Imperfective interpretation. An interpretation of a clause making reference to the internal temporal structure of a situation rather than taking it as a whole: *Kim was writing a letter*.

Indefinite article. The **determinative** *a* (or *an*), prototypically used as **determiner** in **count singular** NPs indicating that the content is not sufficient to identify a specific referent: *a bus*.

Indefinite NP. An NP that is not **definite**: *a book*, *some dogs*, *several students*.

Independent genitive. See **dependent vs independent genitive**.

Indirect complement. Complement **licensed** not by the head but by a dependent. In *a longer delay than we expected* the *than* phrase is in the NP but licensed by a modifier (*longer*).

Indirect object. Object of a verb prototypically (but not invariably) having the semantic role of recipient. Precedes the **direct object** in **canonical clauses**: *I gave Max the key*.

Infinitival clause. **Subordinate** clause containing a **plain form** of the verb (subject marked by *for* if there is one). Covers *to*-**infinitivals** (*To err is human*) and **bare infinitivals** (*I will go*).

Inflection, inflectional form. Inflection is variation in the form of a lexeme determined by syntactic properties like singular or plural **number** in nouns, **preterite** or **present tense** in verbs. *Cat* (singular) and *cats* (plural) are the two non-genitive inflectional forms of the lexeme *cat*.

Information-packaging construction. Construction presenting information differently from the way a **canonical clause** would, prototypically having the same **truth conditions** as a syntactically more basic counterpart. Examples: **passive**, **existential**, **extraposition**, *it*-**cleft**, etc. Compare *It was Kim who broke the vase* (*it*-**cleft**) with *Kim broke the vase* (**canonical**).

Integrated vs supplementary. Relative clauses are **integrated** if spoken as an integral part of the containing construction and normally not marked off by commas, their meaning being presented as an integral part of the message. They are **supplementary** if spoken as a separate intonation unit and generally marked off by commas, dashes, or parentheses. *Politicians who make extravagant promises aren't trusted* has an integrated relative clause (underlined); *Politicians, who make extravagant promises, aren't trusted* has a supplementary one.

Internal. Within the VP, like the underlined complement in *I [lost my key]*, or in NP structure, within the head nominal, like the underlined constituents in *that [new biography of Stalin]*.

Interrogative clause. A **clause type** characteristically used, in **main clauses**, to ask a question: *Are you ready?* (**closed interrogative**); *What have you done?* (**open interrogative**).

Interrogative tag. Truncated interrogative clause added to the end of another clause, generally requesting some kind of confirmation: *He hasn't seen her, has he?*

Interrogative word. Word such as *who, whom, what, which, when*, etc., appearing in an **open interrogative clause**: *What do you want?*

Intransitive. Having no object, as with a verb like *faint* or a clause like *I fainted*.

Irrealis (mood). The special mood form instanced solely by *were* with 1st or 3rd person singular subject: *I wish she were here*. Often replaced by the less formal preterite form *was*.

Irregular lexeme. Lexeme whose inflectional forms are not all predictable by general rule: *build* is irregular because the **preterite** and **past participle** form is *built* (not *builded).

It-**cleft**. A clause like *It was Sue who had the key*, which corresponds to the more basic *Sue had the key*, but divides it in two: *Sue* is foregrounded as complement of *be* in a main clause with dummy *it* subject; *had the key* is backgrounded and expressed in a **relative clause**.

Lexeme. Unit corresponding to a word seen abstractly enough to include all of its **inflectional forms**: *take*, *takes*, *took*, *taken*, and *taking* are the forms of the lexeme *take*.

Lexical base. Starting point for describing **inflectional forms** of a **lexeme**. Usually one form is identical with the lexical base; the others are formed from it by suffixes or modifications.

Lexical verb. A verb belonging to the vast majority that are not **auxiliary** verbs.

Licensing. A head licenses a dependent when only a subset of expressions filling the head position allow a dependent of that kind. In *I broke a cup*, for example, the object *a cup* is licensed by **break** since it can occur with only some verbs – not, for example, with **sneeze**.

Main clause. Normally, a clause that is not embedded as a **dependent** within some larger clause. A prototypical main clause can stand alone as a sentence: *It is raining*.

Matrix clause. Clause within which a subordinate clause is embedded. In *I think she said he was ill*, the underlined clause is the matrix clause in which *he was ill* is embedded.

Modal auxiliary. **Auxiliary verb** that marks **mood**: *can*, *may*, *must*, *will*, etc. Modals lack **secondary forms** and prototypically **license** a **bare infinitival complement**.

Modal preterite. Use of the **preterite** where the meaning has to do with **modality** rather than past time: in *He'd be upset if you knew* the preterite suggests that you may not know (not that you knew).

Modality. A kind of meaning involving non-factuality or non-assertion: *He may know her* presents his knowing her as a possibility; *You must go* presents your going as an obligation.

Modifier. Optional **dependent** that does not have to be **licensed** by the **head**: *ripe* tomatoes; met him *in the morning*; *extremely* rich; girl *that everyone likes*.

Mood. Verbal category expressing various kinds of **modality**. Mostly marked in English by **modal auxiliaries**. The *were* of *I wish that were true* is an isolated **irrealis** mood form.

Mute *e*. The letter *e* when it occurs at the end of a base in written English following a **consonant symbol**, and does not itself represent any sound: the *e* of *hope*, *size*, *please*.

Negative clause. The simplest negative clauses are marked by *not* modifying the verb (*She is not here*) or by a verb containing the suffix ·*n't* (*She isn't here*); the verb in such cases must be an **auxiliary**. A negative declarative clause prototypically has the opposite **truth conditions** to its **positive** counterpart: in a context where *She is here* is true, *She is not here* will be false, and vice versa.

Negative word. Word such as *not*, *isn't*, *can't*, *nothing*, or *never* that can mark a **negative clause**, or a word containing an affix like *un·* or *dis·* with meaning similar to *not*.

New information. The information in a sentence which is not **old information**.

Nominal. Unit intermediate between the NP and the noun, head of the NP. The nominal in *the guy who fainted* is underlined. It has the noun *guy* as its own head.

Nominative. The inflectional **case** of *I, he, she, we, they, who*. Contrasts with **accusative**.

Non-affirmative contexts. **Negative**, **interrogative** and certain related constructions where we can get expressions like *at all* which do not occur in positive assertions. Notice: *He didn't complain at all*; *Did he complain at all?*; **He complained at all*.

Non-affirmative items. Words or expressions such as *at all, ever*, and modal ***need***, normally found in **non-affirmative contexts**: *You needn't go*, but not **You need go*.

Non-count noun. Noun denoting an entity that is uncountable; hence a noun unable to combine with cardinal numerals: **one furniture*, **two remains*.

Non-finite clause. **Subordinate** clause headed by **gerund-participle** (*his writing it*), **past participle** (*having written it*), or **plain form** in the **infinitival** construction (*to write it*).

Non-personal. The gender of *what* as contrasted with *who*. See **personal vs non-personal**.

Noun. A category of lexemes that includes those denoting all kinds of physical objects, such as persons, animals and inanimate objects. They prototypically inflect for **number** (*dog* vs *dogs*), and head phrases functioning as **subject** or as **object** of a verb or preposition (*The dog barked, I found a dog, Give it to the dog*).

Number. The grammatical contrast of singular vs plural, as with most nouns (*cat* vs *cats*).

Object. **Internal complement** in VP or PP with the form of an NP: *Jill paid the bill*. Distinguished from **predicative complement** (*Jill is a genius*). Prototypically corresponds to subject of the corresponding **passive**: *The bill was paid by Max*.

Old information. Information assumed to be familiar to the addressee(s) via earlier mention in discourse, features of the utterance situation, or (in some cases) background knowledge.

Open conditional. Conditional characteristically neutral as to whether the condition is or will be met: *If he loves her he'll change* leaves it open whether he loves her or not.

Open interrogative clause. Interrogative clause characteristically used, in main clauses, to ask an **open question**: *Who said that?* Contains at least one **interrogative word**.

Open question. A question with an open-ended set of answers: *Who broke it?* (with an open-ended set of answers of the form *X broke it*, where *X* stands for some person or persons).

Paradigm. The set of **inflectional forms** of a **lexeme** together with their grammatical labels (in the paradigm of verbs, **preterite**, **3rd person singular present tense**, etc.).

Partitive fused-head construction. NP construction with an explicit or understood *of* phrase, denoting part of larger set or quantity: [*Some* of the photos] *are great*; [*some*] *are not*.

Passive clause. Prototypically, a clause with auxiliary *be* followed by a **past participle** followed optionally by *by* + NP, and having an **active** counterpart: *The record was broken by Lance* (compare active *Lance broke the record*).

Past participial. A clause with a **past participle** as head verb: *a letter <u>written by my aunt</u>*; *Elvis has <u>left the building</u>*.

Past participle. Verb form used in the **perfect** (*She has <u>gone</u>*) and **passive** (*It was <u>cancelled</u>*).

Past tense. **Tense** primarily indicating past time: *wrote* (**preterite**); *have written* (**perfect**).

Perfect (tense). A past tense formed by means of the **auxiliary** *have*, normally followed by a **past participle**: *She <u>has gone</u> home*; *They may <u>have seen</u> you*.

Perfective interpretation. An interpretation of a clause describing a situation considered as a whole without reference to its temporal structure: *Kim wrote a letter*.

Person. The grammatical system classifying primarily a subset of **pronouns** (and then derivatively NPs) in terms of the roles of **speaker** and **addressee**. **1st person** *I* and *we* normally indicate reference to (a group containing) the speaker; **2nd person** *you* normally indicates reference to (a group containing) the addressee but not the speaker. **3rd person** is the default category with no indication of reference to either.

Personal pronoun. The subclass of **pronoun** to which the system of **person** applies: *I* and *we* are **1st person**, *you* is **2nd person**, *he*, *she*, *it*, etc. are **3rd person**.

Personal vs non-personal. A **gender** system applying primarily to **interrogative** and **relative** pronouns, contrasting e.g. personal *who* (for persons and sometimes certain animals) vs non-personal *what*. *<u>Who</u> is that?* asks about a person; *<u>What</u> is that?* asks about something else.

Plain case. A non-genitive case that is neither **accusative** nor **nominative**: *you, cat, cats*, etc.

Plain form. Verb-form identical with the **lexical base** that is not a present tense; used in **imperatives** (*Stop*), **subjunctives** (*It's vital that he <u>stop</u>*), and **infinitivals** (*I tried to <u>stop</u>*; *You must <u>stop</u>*).

Plain present. Present tense form of the verb identical with its **lexical base** and normally used with subjects that are either plural or 1st or 2nd **person**: *I <u>like</u> it; you <u>do</u> too*.

Polarity. The system contrasting **positive** and **negative**: *I'm ready* has positive polarity, while *I'm not ready* has negative polarity.

Positive clause. Non-**negative** clause: *She is here* (contrasts with negative *She isn't here*).

Predicand. What a **predicative** complement or adjunct relates to (usually an NP): *<u>Sue</u> seems capable*; *I consider <u>Sue</u> capable* (Sue is the one who is thought capable).

Predicate. The **head** of a clause, a function filled by a **verb phrase**: *We <u>washed the car</u>*.

Predicative adjunct. Phrase functioning as adjunct in clause structure, related to an overt or understood **predicand**. *Unwilling to lie, Max confessed* (Max is the one who was unwilling to lie).

Predicative complement. Complement of V or P related to a **predicand**: *Sue seems capable*; *I regard Sue [as capable]* (the property of being capable is assigned to Sue).

Predicative use. Use of an adjective or other expression as **predicative complement** or **adjunct** (as opposed to **modifier**): *I'm hot* illustrates the predicative use of *hot*.

Predicator. **Head** of a VP, the function of the **verb**: in *I [saw you]* the predicator is *saw*.

Prefix. An **affix** that attaches to the beginning of a **base**.

Preposing. Placement before the subject of an element whose position in a more basic clause construction would be after the verb: *Most of them he hadn't even read*.

Preposition. A category of words whose most prototypical members denote relations in space or time (*in*, *on*, *under*, *before*, etc.) and take NPs as complement (*in the car*, *on the chair*).

Prepositional verb. A verb taking a complement consisting of a PP with a particular preposition as head: ***ask*** in *I asked for help*; ***come*** in *I came across some old letters*.

Present tense. An **inflectional** category of verbs whose primary use is to indicate present time.

Preterite. A **past tense** marked by **inflection**: *took* is the preterite form of the lexeme ***take***.

Primary tense. The **tense** system marked by verb inflection, contrasting **preterite tense** (*I knew her*) with **present tense** (*I know her*).

Primary verb-form. For verbs other than ***be*** the primary forms are those marked for **tense** (**present** or **preterite**). For ***be*** they also include **irrealis mood** *were* (as in *if I were you*).

Progressive (aspect). Construction marked by auxiliary ***be*** taking a **gerund-participle** complement: *She was writing a novel*; usually represents a situation as being in progress.

Pronoun. A small subclass of **noun** not taking **determiners**. Includes **personal pronouns** (*he*, *us*, etc.), **interrogative** and **relative** pronouns (*who*, *what*, etc.), **reciprocals** (*each other*).

Proper noun. A large subclass of **noun** characteristically functioning as head of proper names – names individually assigned to particular people, places, etc.: *Bach, Paris, Islam, July*.

Pseudo-cleft. Construction like *What we need is a knife*, splitting the basic counterpart *We need a knife* into two parts: *a knife* is foregrounded in an extra clause as complement of ***be***, and the residue is backgrounded in a **fused relative construction** (*what we need*).

Reciprocal pronoun. One of the pronouns *each other* and *one another*.

Reflexive pronoun. One of the **personal pronouns** ending in *·self* (or, in the plural, *·selves*).

Regular lexeme. **Lexeme** with **inflectional forms** all predictable by general rule.

Relative clause. **Subordinate clause** of which the most central type functions as modifier to a noun: *I've met the woman who wrote it*. The noun serves as **antecedent** for an element within the relative clause which may be overt (like *who* in the above example) or merely understood (as in *I've met the woman you are referring to*).

Relative pronoun. One of the pronouns *who*, *which*, *what*, etc. as used in a **relative clause** or **fused relative construction**: *He's the one [who caused the trouble]*; *[What she said] is true*.

Relativised element. What is **anaphorically** linked to an **antecedent** in a **relative clause**; e.g., *which* in *the book [which she reviewed]*, where the relativised element is object.

Remote conditional. Conditional where the condition is not fulfilled (*I wouldn't do that if I were you*) or presented as a relatively remote possibility (*If he loved her he'd change*).

Reversed polarity tag. An **interrogative tag** with the opposite **polarity** to that of the clause it's attached to: *You told them, didn't you?*; *You didn't tell them, did you?*

Scope of negation. The part of the sentence that the negative applies to semantically. In *I didn't log out purposely* (with no pause), *purposely* is IN the scope of the negative: it means "I logged out, but not purposely". But *I purposely didn't log out* has *purposely* OUTSIDE the scope of negation: it means "I chose not to log out".

Secondary form. A non-**primary** inflectional form of the verb: **plain form**, **gerund-participle**, or **past participle**.

Secondary tense. The **tense** system contrasting **perfect tense** (*I have lived in Paris*) and absence of perfect tense (*I live in Paris*).

Shape. Spelling or pronunciation; different from **inflectional form** in that different inflectional forms may share a shape (the **preterite** and **past participle** of *tie* share the shape *tied*).

Simple fused head. Construction where fused head can be replaced by dependent plus an understood head: in *Should I wear the red shirt or [the blue]?* (*blue* means "blue shirt").

Situation. What is described in a clause, such as an action (*She raised her hand*), a process (*The snow melted*), or a state (*He is asleep*).

Special fused head. Construction where the interpretation is not derivable from anything in the context: *Many would disagree* (*many* has the special interpretation "many people").

Specified preposition. Preposition whose presence in a PP is determined by the head verb, noun or adjective of which the PP is complement: *rely on it*; *gifts to charity*; *afraid of her*.

Specifying. The use of *be* illustrated in *The last one to leave was Jane*, where the **predicative complement** specifies (i.e., identifies) the last one to leave. Contrasts with **ascriptive**.

Speech act. An act like making a statement, asking a question, or issuing a directive.

Stranded preposition. Preposition which is not followed by the NP that is understood as its complement: *Who did you give it to?*; *This is the book [I was talking about]*.

Subject. The function in clause structure (usually filled by an NP; before the predicate in canonical clauses) that in **active** clauses describing action normally denotes the actor: *Ed ran away*.

Subject–auxiliary inversion. Placement of the subject after (instead of before) the auxiliary: *Is he ill?*

Subject-determiner. A **genitive** NP combining the functions of determiner and complement in NP structure: *Kim's house*.

Subjunctive clause. One of the three major constructions headed by a **plain form** verb (the others are **imperatives** and **infinitivals**): *It is vital that I be kept informed*.

Subordinate clause. Normally, a clause embedded as a **dependent** in a larger clause, often differing in form from a **main clause**; e.g., *This is the book she reviewed*.

Subordinator. A small class of words generally serving to mark a clause as **subordinate**: *I know [that it's possible]*; *I wonder [whether she's ill]*; *[For her to be late] is quite unusual*.

Suffix. An **affix** that attaches to the end of a **base**.

Superlative (grade, form). The term in the **grade** system indicating "most"; marked either inflectionally (as in *hottest*) or by the adverb *most* (*most useful*).

Supplement. Loosely attached expression set off by intonation (and usually punctuation) presenting supplementary, non-integrated content. Usually an **adjunct** (*Luckily, we don't have to do that*) or a **supplementary relative clause** (*I saw her son, who's quite worried*).

Symbol. A letter or sequence of letters representing a single sound. In *heat* there are three symbols: *h*, *ea* (a **composite symbol**), and *t*.

Tag. Truncated interrogative clause added to the end of another clause, requesting some kind of confirmation: *He hasn't seen her, has he?*

Tense. A system marked by verb **inflection** or **auxiliaries** whose basic use is to locate the situation in time: *I liked it* (past tense, past time), *I like it* (present tense, present time).

To-infinitival clause. **Infinitival clause** containing the marker *to*: *I want to see them*; *We arranged for them to meet*.

Transitive. A clause containing at least one object (*I broke the vase*), or verb used in such a clause (*break*).

Truth conditions. The conditions that must be satisfied for the statement made by uttering a declarative main clause in a given context to be true: *Oswald shot Kennedy* and *Kennedy was shot by Oswald* have the same truth conditions, because if one is true the other is.

Verb. A category of lexemes whose most distinctive property is that they normally inflect for **tense** (*She was ill* vs *She is ill*; *We liked it* vs *We like it*).

Verbal idiom. Idiom with a verb as the main element: ***kick*** *the bucket* ("die"), ***fall out*** ("quarrel").

Verbal negation. Negation of the verb, marked either by *not* (*You <u>need not</u> answer*) or by a verb-form containing the suffix ·*n't* (*You <u>needn't</u> answer*).

Voice. The grammatical system contrasting **active** and **passive** clauses: *Ed broke it* is in the active voice, *It was broken by Ed* is in the passive voice.

Vowel. Speech sound produced with unimpeded smooth airflow through the mouth.

Vowel symbol. Letter or sequence of letters representing a vowel: *u* is a vowel symbol in *hut*, but not in *quick*.

Index

abbreviation, 287
absolute negator, 153–4
accusative, 5, 67–8, 105–7, 165–6, 190, 210, 295
acronym, 287
across the board, 229–30
active clause/voice, 26, 239–43, 295
addressee, 101–3, 171
adjectival passive, 246
adjective, adjective phrase, 16, 18–20, 96, 100, 112–24, 133–5, 195, 280–1, 295
adjunct, 65–7, 71, 78–80, 179–80, 195, 295
adverb, adverb phrase, 16, 19–20, 122–5, 130–3, 140, 280–1, 295
affix, affixation, 27, 150–1, 282, 284, 295
affixal negation, 150–1
agreement, 39, 68, 88–90, 108, 229n, 242, 295
alternation, 266–7
alternative question, 163–4
American English vs British English, 2, 40n, 49n, 57n, 89–90, 128, 153n, 177, 200, 202, 267, 269, 271, 276n
anaphora, 101–2, 183–4, 259, 295
answer, 162, 166–7
antecedent, 101–2, 106, 183–4, 189, 191, 206–7, 211, 259, 295
appositive, 96
approximate negator, 153–4
ascriptive use of *be*, 76–7, 295
aspect, 41–2, 51–2, 295
asymmetric coordination, 230–1
attributive (adjective, etc.), 18, 112, 296
attributive genitive, 110
attributive-only adjective, 120
auxiliary verb, 18, 37–42, 152, 219–20, 260, 296

back-formation, 285–6
backgrounded element, 251, 253–4

backshift, 47–8, 50, 57, 296
bare coordinate, 226–7, 296
bare existential, 249–50
bare genitive, 279
bare infinitival, 31–2, 213, 296
bare passive, 245–6
bare relative, 184–5
bare role NP, 74, 88, 140, 296
base, 27, 282, 296
base plural, 278–9, 296
be-passive, 245
blending, 286–7
bound element, 282
British English: *see* American English vs British English

canonical clause, 24–7, 63, 77–8, 296
cardinal numeral, 86
case, 67–8, 82, 106–7, 165–6, 190, 210, 296
category, 14–15, 93n, 228–9
category-changing/preserving affix, 284
catenative, 214–22, 245–6, 260, 296
clausal negation, 151–4
clausal sentence, 12
clause, 12–14
clause reduction, 260
clause structure, 63–80
clause type, 24–5, 159–72, 175, 296
clipping, 286
closed interrogative/question, 159–63, 167, 175, 178–80, 296
collective noun, 89–90, 297
command, 8
common noun, 17, 84–5, 297
comparative (grade, etc.), 100, 112, 115, 123, 195–9, 280–1, 297
comparative clause, 174–5, 201–2, 297
comparison, 195–202
comparison of equality, 199–200
complement, 22–3, 65–7, 93–5, 118–19, 125, 139–42, 175–6, 178, 180, 256, 297

complex catenative, 220–2, 297
complex preposition, 146–7
complex word, 281–2
complex-intransitive/transitive, 78, 119, 246, 248–9, 297
composite symbol, 268, 297
compound, compounding, 100, 283–4
compound sentence, 12
compound tense, 48
conditional, 47, 171, 231, 297
conjunction, 21
consonant, 268, 297
consonant doubling, 269–71
constant polarity tag, 150
constituent, 64, 145, 221, 234–6, 252
content clause, 174–81, 184, 192, 202, 247, 297
continuative perfect, 51, 297
conversion, 284–5
coordinate, coordination, 12, 16, 25, 88, 104, 107, 147, 161, 163, 210n, 225–37, 297
coordinator, 16, 21, 225–6, 230–3, 298
core meaning, 217, 222, 238–41
correlative coordination, 232, 298
count noun, 85–8, 169, 259, 298
current relevance, 49

dangling modifier, 207–9
declarative, 8–9, 24, 159–61, 164, 172, 175–7, 298
default, 13, 26, 50, 53, 83, 85, 102, 120, 130, 149, 159, 161, 174, 197, 226, 234, 243, 248, 250, 256–7, 272–3, 277, 279, 298
definite, definiteness, 19, 91–3, 250–1, 298
definite article, 91–2, 117, 298
definitions, 5–9
deictic, deixis, 101–2, 242, 261, 298
delayed right constituent coordination, 236
denotation, 187